India

*Five Years of Stabilization and Reform
and the Challenges Ahead*

*The World Bank
Washington, D.C.*

World Bank Country Studies are among the many reports originally prepared for internal use as part of the continuing analysis by the Bank of the economic and related conditions of its developing member countries and of its dialogues with the governments. Some of the reports are published in this series with the least possible delay for the use of governments and the academic, business and financial, and development communities. The typescript of this paper therefore has not been prepared in accordance with the procedures appropriate to formal printed texts, and the World Bank accepts no responsibility for errors. Some sources cited in this paper may be informal documents that are not readily available.

The World Bank does not guarantee the accuracy of the data included in this publication and accepts no responsibility whatsoever for any consequence of their use. The boundaries, colors, denominations, and other information shown on any map in this volume do not imply on the part of the World Bank Group any judgment on the legal status of any territory or the endorsement or acceptance of such boundaries.

The material in this publication is copyrighted. Requests for permission to reproduce portions of it should be sent to the Office of the Publisher at the address shown in the copyright notice above. The World Bank encourages dissemination of its work and will normally give permission promptly and, when the reproduction is for noncommercial purposes, without asking a fee. Permission to copy portions for classroom use is granted through the Copyright Clearance Center, Inc., Suite 910, 222 Rosewood Drive, Danvers, Massachusetts 01923, U.S.A.

For a copy of *Update* describing new publications, contact the Distribution Unit, Office of the Publisher, The World Bank, 1818 H Street, N.W., Washington, D.C. 20433, U.S.A., or Publications, The World Bank, 66, avenue d'Iéna, 75116 Paris, France. A catalog and ordering information are also available on the Internet at http://www.worldbank.org.

ISSN: 0253-2123

Library of Congress Cataloging-in-Publication Data

India : five years of stabilization and reform and the challenges
    ahead.
        p.   cm. — (A World Bank country study)
    "Prepared by a team led by Zoubida Allaoua"— P. vii.
    Includes bibliographical references.
    ISBN 0-8213-3838-2
    1. India—Economic policy—1980.   2. India—Economic
conditions—1947–   I. Allaoua, Zoubida.   II. World Bank.
III. Series.
HC435.2.I532   1996
338.954—dc21
                                                    96-48266
                                                        CIP

TABLE OF CONTENTS

LIST OF TABLES

LIST OF BOXES

LIST OF FIGURES

ABSTRACT

The stabilization and reform measures introduced over the past five years have considerably improved India's growth prospects. Growth accelerated to over 6 percent in 1995-96 from less than one percent in 1991-92. The progressive integration of the Indian economy into the global economy with the liberalization of the investment, trade and foreign exchange regimes has improved productivity, particularly in the industrial sector, which has been growing at rates exceeding 10 percent in the last two years. In addition, the exchange rate devaluation and the reduction in the level of protection of the industrial sector have been beneficial to agriculture. Growth is now driven by exports and private investment, and is being accompanied by an increase in domestic savings. At US$2 billion in 1995-96, foreign direct investment is 15 times higher than it was before the economy was liberalized and portfolio investment has stabilized at around US$2-3 billion--that is 10 percent of world portfolio investment in emerging markets. Inflation has declined and the external accounts have strengthened.

Notwithstanding these remarkable achievements, this report, like the Government's June 1996 Common Minimum Program and the Ministry of Finance 1995-96 Economic Survey, re-emphasizes the importance of urgently addressing the remaining structural constraints to higher growth. Chief among them are: reducing the country's chronically high fiscal deficits; removing the remaining investment and trade restrictions, particularly in agriculture; averting a crisis in infrastructure; and strengthening the country's human capital base.

ACKNOWLEDGMENTS

This Memorandum was prepared by a team led by Zoubida Allaoua. It draws on contributions from Paul Beckerman (monetary and financial sector developments and policies); Uri Dadush, T.G. Srinivasan, Milan Brahmbhatt and Kim Murrell (India in the global economy); Xinghai Fang, IFC, (private infrastructure financing); Mona Haddad (balance of payments); Dinanath Khatkhate and Lystra Antoine (public savings); Sanjay Kathuria (recent macroeconomic developments); Valerie Kozel (beneficiary assessments); Norman Loayza (savings); William McCarten (recent fiscal developments and tax reform); Luis Serven (fiscal deficit and public sector solvency); Donald McIsaac (insurance sector and other contractual savings institutions); Djamal Mostefai and Mohinder Gulati (impact of power subsidies on states finances); Dan Mozes (mutual funds); Martin Ravallion and Gaurav Datt (poverty); Clemencia Torres (contribution of central public enterprises to public savings), with guidance from Ahmad Galal; David Wilton (money and bond markets); Fahrettin Yagci (industrial sector performance); and Dimitri Tzanninis, IMF (current expenditure reform). The primary author of chapter 4 was Benoit Blarel drawing on contributions from Dina Umali-Deininger, Garry Pursell, Jaime Quizon and Manoj Panda. Hans Binswanger (Senior Adviser) was the lead advisor for this chapter. The primary author of Chapter 5 was Colin Bruce drawing on contributions from Joelle Chassard (legal regulatory and administrative issues in the power sector); Mohan Gopal (legal framework); Harald Hansen and Ernst-August Huning (financial, institutional, legal and regulatory issues in the transportation sector); and Hugh Lantzke (legal, regulatory and administrative issues in the telecommunications sector). Robert Burns advised on urban and general infrastructure issues. Primary statistical and computational assistance was received from Maria Almero-Siochi, Rajni Khanna and Bhaskar Naidu.

Background studies for the CEM were also prepared by NCAER (impact of economic reforms on large, medium and small scale enterprises in the organized and unorganized sectors), Pullapre Balakhrishnan (savings rate in India since 1991, and economic reforms and productivity growth in India), Tata Energy Research Institute (impact of power subsidies on states finances), and Ajit Ranade and Mahendra Dev of IGIDR (public expenditure in agriculture). Beneficiary assessment surveys were carried out by Ravi Srivastava, Nisha Srivastava, Madhavi Kuckreja, N. Thangaraj, Sarthi Acharya and S.S. Gill. Financial support for these surveys was provided through a Trust fund set up by the Netherlands Government.

Arrangements for missions to India were made by Padma Gopalan and Sheni Rana. Production assistance was provided by Lin Chin who was aided by Zelena Jagdeo and Naomi Dass. Uri Dadush (Division Chief) and Roberto Zagha (Lead Economist) were initial reviewers before becoming direct contributors to the report. Robert J. Anderson (Lead Economist) was reviewer for the whole report and Amarendra Bhattacharya (Economic Adviser) for chapters 2 and 3. Rui Manuel Coutinho (Acting Chief Economist for the South Asia Region) reviewed the report and provided general guidance. The document was prepared under the supervision of Luis Ernesto Derbez (Division Chief) and Roberto Zagha (Lead Economist).

We gratefully acknowledge the cooperation of government officials, in particular the staff of the Department of Economic Affairs and the RBI as well as members of the private business community. The document was discussed with the Indian authorities during July 25-29, 1996.

ABBREVIATIONS AND ACRONYMS

AAI	Airports Industry of India
ADB	Asian Development Bank
AMT	Alternative Minimum Tax
APEC	Asia Pacific Economic Cooperation
BE	Budget Estimates
BEL	Bharat Electronics Limited
BHEL	Bharat Heavy Electricals Limited
BIFR	Board for Industrial and Financial Reconstruction
BKU	Bhartiya Kisan Union
BO	Butter Oil
BOLT	Build-Operate-Lease-Transfer
BOP	Balance of Payments
BOT	Build-Operate-Transfer
BSE	Bombay Stock Exchange
CEA	Central Electricity Authority
CEM	Country Economic Memorandum
CES	Constant Elasticity of Substitution
CFS	Container Freight Station
CGE	Computable General Equilibrium
CIA	Central Information Agency
CIF	Cost Insurance and Freight
CMP	Common Minimum Program
CONCOR	Container Corporation of India
CPE	Central Public Enterprises
CPI	Consumer Price Index
CPIAL	Consumer Price Index for Agricultural Laborers
CRR	Cash Reserve Requirement
CSI	Contractual Savings Institutions
CSO	Central Statistical Organization
DAP	Di-Ammonium Phosphate
DDP	Desert Development Program
DFHI	Discount Finance House of India
DGCA	Directorate General of Civil Aviation
DGCIS	Directorate General of Commercial Intelligence and Statistics
DM	Deutsche Mark
DOT	Department of Telecommunications
DPAP	Drought Prone Areas Program
DRS	Debt Reporting System
EAS	Employment Assurance Scheme
EC	Essential Commodities Act
ECA	Europe and Central Asia
ECB	Euro-Convertible Bond
ED	Electricity Duty
EDI	Electronic Data Information
EGF	Employment Generation Fund
EGS	Employment Guarantee Scheme
EP	Export Promotion Strategy
EPF	Employees Provident Fund
EPTD	Environment and Production Technology Division
EU	European Union (formerly the EC)
FCBOD	Foreign Currency (Banks & Others) Deposits
FCCB	Foreign Currency Convertible Bonds
FCI	Food Corporation of India

FCNRA	Foreign Currency (Non-Resident) Accounts
FCNRB	Foreign Currency (Non-Resident) Accounts Bank Scheme
FCON	Foreign Currency (Ordinary) Non-Repatriable Deposit Scheme
FDI	Foreign Direct Investment
FII	Foreign Institutional Investor
FOB	Freight On Board
FRN	Foreign Rate Notes
FSU	Former Soviet Union
GATT	General Agreement on Tariffs and Trade
GDP	Gross Domestic Product
GDR	Global Depository Receipts
GIC	General Insurance Company
GNFS	Goods and Non-factor Services
GNP	Gross National Product
GOI	Government of India
HMT	Hindustan Machine Tools
HSEB	Haryana State Electricity Board
HYV	High Yielding Varieties
ICAR	Indian Council of Agricultural Research
ICC	International Chamber of Commerce
ICD	Inland Container Depot
ICDS	Integrated Child Development Scheme
ICICI	Industrial Credit and Investment Corporation of India
ID	Irrigation Departments
IDBI	Industrial Development Bank of India
IDF	Indian Development Forum
IDFC	Infrastructure Development Finance Company
IFCI	Industrial Financial Corporation of India
IFPRI	International Food Policy Research Institute
IIP	Index of Industrial Production
IMF	International Monetary Fund
INS	Information Notice System
IPP	Independent Power Producers
IRBI	Industrial Reconstruction Bank of India
IRDP	Integrated Rural Development Program
IS	Import Substitution Strategy
ISIEC	Indian Sugar and General Industries Import and Export Corporation
ISO	International Standards Organization
IT	Information Technology
JRY	Jawahar Rozgar Yojana
KSA	Kurt Salmon Associates
Kwh	Kilowatt-hour
LAC	Latin America and the Caribbean
LES	Linear Expenditure System
LIBOR	London Inter-Bank Offer Rate
LIC	Life Insurance Company
M&A	Mergers and Acquisitions
MAT	Minimum Alternate Tax
MFA	Multifiber Agreement
MMF	Man Made Fibers
MMMF	Money Market Mutual Fund
MMPO	Milk and Milk Products Order

MNA	Middle East & North Africa	RFC	Resident Foreign Currency Account
MNC	Multinational Corporation	RFI	Regional Financial Institutions
MNE	Multinational Enterprises	RFP	Request for Proposals
MODVAT	Modified Value Added Tax	RLDC	Regional Load Dispatch Center
MOF	Ministry of Finance	RLEGP	Rural Landless Employment Guarantee
MoP	Muriate of Potash		Program
MOP	Ministry of Power	RPDS	Revamped Public Distribution System
MOST	Ministry of Surface Transport	RRB	Rural Regional Bank
MOU	Memorandum of Understanding	SAIL	Steel Authority of India Ltd.
MPBF	Maximum Permissible Bank Finance	SAM	Social Accounting Matrix
MRTP	Monopolies and Restrictive Trade	SAP	State Advised Price
	Practices Act	SBI	State Bank of India
MTM	Mark to Market	SC	Scheduled Castes
MTO	Multimodal Transport services	SCICI	Shipping Credit and Investment
MUL	Maruti Udyog Limited		Corporation of India
MUV	Manufactures Unit Value	SDF	Sugar Development Fund
MW	Megawatt	SDP	State Domestic Product
NABARD	National Bank for Rural Development	SDR	Special Drawing Rights
NCAER	National Council of Applied Economic	SDS	Special Deposit Scheme
	Research	SEB	State Electricity Board
NEP	New Economic Policy	SEBI	Security and Exchange Board of India
NFA	Net Financial Assets	SEEPZ	Santacruz Electronics Export Processing
NGO	Non-Governmental Organization		Zone
NHAI	National Highways Authority of India	SFC	State Financial Corporations
NHB	National Housing Bank	SICA	Sick Industrial Companies Act
NPK	Nitrogen, Phosphate & Potash	SIDBI	Small Industries Development Bank of
NPV	Net Present Value		India
NR(NR)D	Non-Resident (Non-Repatriable) Deposit	SIL	Special Import License
	Scheme	SITC	Standard International Trade
NRER(A)	Non-Resident External Rupee Account		Classification
NRF	National Renewal Fund	SLR	Statutory Liquidity Requirements
NRI	Non-Resident Indians	SMP	Skim Milk Powder
NRY	Nehru Rozgar Yojana	SPE	State Public Enterprise
NSE	National Stock Exchange	SSA	Sub-Saharan Africa
NSS	National Sample Survey	SSI	Small Scale Industry
NSSO	National Sample Survey Organization	ST	Scheduled Tribes
NTB	Non-Tariff Barriers	STCI	Securities Trading Corporation of India
NTPC	National Thermal Power Corporation	TEU	Twenty-feet Equivalent Unit
O&M	Overhaul and Maintenance	TFC	Tenth Finance Commission
OECD	Organization for Economic Cooperation	TFP	Total Factor Productivity
	and Development	TLC	Total Literacy Campaign
OTCEI	Over-the-Counter Exchange	TOT	Terms of Trade
P and K	Phosphate and Potash	TRAI	Telecom Regulatory Authority of India
PD	Primary Dealers	TRIPS	Traded Intellectual Property Rights
PDS	Public Distribution System	TRYSEM	Training of Rural Youth for Self-
PE/ PSE	Public Enterprise/ Public Sector		Employment
	Enterprise	UNCITRAL	United Nations Commission on
PLF	Plant Load Factor		International Trade Law
POL	Petroleum, Oil and Lubricants	UNESCO	United Nations Educational, Scientific
PPP	Purchasing Power Parity		and Cultural Organization
PRI	Panchayati Raj Institutions	UP	Uttar Pradesh
PSU	Public Sector Units	UST	United States Treasury
PWD	Public Works Department	UT	Union Territory
QR	Quantitative Restrictions	UTI	Unit Trust of India
R&M	Renovation and Modernization	VAT	Value Added Tax
RBI	Reserve Bank of India	VSAT	Very Small Aperture Terminal
RBNZ	Reserve Bank of New Zealand	WPI	Wholesale Price Index
RE	Revised Estimates	WTO	World Tourism Organization
REB	Regional Electricity Board	WUA	Water Users' Association
REER	Real Effective Exchange Rate		

CURRENCY

Currency		Rs/ US$		
		Official	Unified	Market [a]
Prior to June 1966		4.76		
June 6, 1966 to mid-December 1971		7.50		
Mid-December 1971 to end-June 1972		7.28		
	1971-72	7.44		
	1972-73	7.71		
	1973-74	7.79		
	1974-75	7.98		
	1975-76	8.65		
	1976-77	8.94		
	1977-78	8.56		
	1978-79	8.21		
	1979-80	8.08		
	1980-81	7.89		
	1981-82	8.93		
	1982-83	9.63		
	1983-84	10.31		
	1984-85	11.89		
	1985-86	12.24		
	1986-87	12.79		
	1987-88	12.97		
	1988-89	14.48		
	1989-90	16.66		
	1990-91	17.95		
	1991-92	24.52		
	1992-93	26.41		30.65
	1993-94		31.36	
	1994-95		31.40	
	1995-96		33.46	
April	1996		34.24	
May	1996		34.99	
June	1996		34.99	
July	1996		35.52	
Aug	1996		35.69	

Note: The Indian fiscal year runs from April 1 through March 31.

Source: IMF, International Finance Statistics (IFS), line "rf"; Reserve Bank of India.

---

[a] A dual exchange rate system was created in March 1992, with a free market for about 60 percent of foreign exchange transactions. The exchange rate was reunified at the beginning of March 1993 at the free market rate.

ECONOMIC DEVELOPMENT DATA

GNP Per Capita (US$, 1994-95): 330 [a]

Gross Domestic Product (1994-95)

	US$ Bln	% of GDP	Annual Growth Rate (% p.a., constant prices)					
			70-71- 75-76	75-76- 80-81	80-81- 85-86	85-86- 90-91	92-93- 93-94	93-94- 94-95
GDP at Factor Cost	272.0	90.3	3.4	4.2	5.4	5.9	5.0	6.3
GDP at Market Prices	301.2	100.0	3.3	4.2	5.6	6.2	3.9	6.3
Gross Domestic Investment	69.7	23.2	5.3	3.7	5.7	9.5	-5.8	19.8
Gross National Saving	67.0	22.3	4.4	2.6	3.5	8.7	-1.1	17.2
Current Account Balance	-2.7	-0.9	--	--	--	--	--	--

Output, Employment and Productivity (1990-91)

	Value Added		Labor Force [b]		V. A. per Worker	
	US$ Bln.	% of Tot	Mill.	% of Tot.	US$	% of Avg.
Agriculture	82.5	31.0	186.2	66.8	443	46.4
Industry	78.0	29.3	35.5	12.7	2195	230.0
Services	105.7	39.7	57.2	20.5	1849	193.7
Total/ Average	266.2	100.0	278.9	100.0	954	100.0

Government Finance

	General Government [c]			Central Government		
	Rs. Bln.	% of GDP		Rs. Bln.	% of GDP	
	1994-95	1994-95	90-91-94-95	1994-95	1994-95	90-91-94-95
Revenue Receipts	1809.0	19.1	19.5	910.8	9.6	10.1
Revenue Expenditures	2219.0	23.5	23.5	1221.1	12.9	13.3
Revenue Surplus/ Deficit (-)	-409.9	-4.3	-4.0	-310.3	-3.3	-3.2
Capital Expenditures [d]	337.9	3.6	4.3	266.8	2.8	3.5
External Assistance (net) [e]	51.5	0.5	0.7	51.5	0.5	0.7

Money, Credit, and Prices

	89-90	90-91	91-92	92-93	93-94	94-95	95-96p
	(Rs. billion outstanding, end of period)						
Money and Quasi Money	2309.5	2658.3	3170.5	3668.3	4344.1	5308.0	6005.0
Bank Credit to Government (net)	1171.5	1401.9	1582.6	1762.4	2039.2	2224.2	2626.7
Bank Credit to Commercial Sector	1517.0	1717.7	1879.9	2201.4	2377.7	2896.6	3386.4
	(percentage or index numbers)						
Money and Quasi Money as % of GDP	50.6	49.6	51.4	52.0	54.2	56.1	54.7
Wholesale Price Index (1981-82 = 100)	165.7	182.7	207.8	228.7	247.8	274.7	295.8
Annual Percentage Changes in:							
Wholesale Price Index	7.4	10.3	13.7	10.1	8.4	10.9	7.7
Bank Credit to Government (net)	20.3	19.7	12.9	11.4	15.7	9.1	18.1
Bank Credit to Commercial Sector	14.4	13.2	9.4	17.1	8.0	21.8	16.9

a. The per capita GNP estimate is at market prices, using World Bank Atlas methodology. Other conversions to dollars in this table are at the prevailing average exchange rate for the period covered.

b. Total Labor Force from 1991 Census. Excludes data for Assam and Jammu & Kashmir.

c. Transfers between Centre and States have been netted out.

d. All loans and advances to third parties have been netted out.

e. As recorded in the government budget.

Balance of Payments (US$ Millions)

	1992-93	1993-94	1994-95p
Exports of Goods & NFS	23,585	28,925	34,141
Merchandise, fob	18,869	22,700	26,857
Imports of Goods & NFS	26,825	29,433	39,450
Merchandise, cif	23,237	23,985	31,672
of which Crude Petroleum	3,711	3,468	3,428
of which Petroleum Products	2,208	2,285	2,500
Trade Balance	-4,368	-1,285	-4,815
Non Factor Service (net)	1,128	777	-494
Resource Balance	-3,240	-508	-5,309
Net factor Income[a]	-3,422	-4,002	-3,905
Net Transfers[b]	2,773	3,825	6,200
Balance on Current Account	-3,889	-685	-3,014
Foreign Investment	587	4,110	4,895
Official Grants and Aid	363	370	390
Net Medium & Long Term Capital	1,636	1,716	278
Gross Disbursements	4,586	5,884	5,091
Principal Repayments	2,949	4,169	4,814
Other Capital Flows[c]	-961	2,086	3,462
Non-Resident Deposits	2,001	940	847
Net Transactions with IMF	1,290	190	-1,174
Overall Balance	-263	8,537	6,858
Change in Net Reserves	263	-8,537	-6,858
Gross Reserves (end of year)[d]	6,749	15,476	21,160

Rate of Exchange

End-March 1996[e]	US$ 1.00 = Rs. 34.45

Merchandise Exports (Average 1990-91-1994-95)

	US$ Mill	% of Tot.
Tea	415	2.0
Iron Ore	480	2.3
Chemicals	1,679	8.1
Leather & Leather products	1,382	6.7
Textiles	2,483	12.0
Garments	2,542	12.3
Gems and Jewelry	3,449	16.7
Engineering Goods	2,674	13.0
Others	5,536	26.8
Total [f]	20,641	100.0

External Debt, March 31, 1995

	US$ Mill.
Public & Publicly Guaranteed	87,880
Private Non-Guaranteed	1,709
Total (Including IMF and Short Ter	98,990

Debt Service Ratio for 1994-95

	% curr receipts
Public & Publicly Guaranteed	19.6
Private Non-Guaranteed	1.2
Total (Including IMF and Short Ter	25.3

IBRD/ IDA Lending, March 31, 1995 (US$ Mill)

	IBRD	IDA
Outstanding and Disbursed	11,120	17,666
Undisbursed	4,227	4,663
Outstanding incl. Undisb.	15,347	22,329

-- Not available.

a. Figures given cover all investment income (net). Major payments are interest on foreign loans and charges paid to IMF, and major receipts is interest earned on foreign assets.

b. Figures given include workers' remittances but exclude official grant assistance which is included within official loans and grants, and non-resident deposits which are shown separately.

c. Includes short-term net capital inflow, changes in reserve valuation and other items.

d. Excluding gold.

e. The exchange rate was reunified at the market rate in March 1993.

f. Total exports (commerce); net of crude petroleum exports.

India

Indicator	Unit of measure	Latest single year 1970-75	Latest single year 1980-85	Most recent estimate 1989-94	Same region/income group South Asia	Same region/income group Low-income	Next higher income group
Resources and Expenditures							
HUMAN RESOURCES							
Population (mre=1994)	thousands	613,459	765,147	913,600	1,220,285	3,182,221	1,096,881
Age dependency ratio	ratio	0.77	0.72	0.66	0.71	0.66	0.63
Urban	% of pop.	21.3	24.3	26.5	26.0	28.3	55.9
Population growth rate	annual %	2.3	2.0	1.7	1.8	1.7	1.3
Urban	"	3.7	3.0	2.7	3.1	3.2	2.7
Labor force	thousands	260,515	329,608	394,330	528,108	1,590,533	488,647
Agriculture	% of labor force	70	67	64	63	67	36
Industry	"	13	14	16	16	14	26
Female	"	31	32	32	32	39	40
Labor participation rates							
Total	% of pop.	42	43	43	43	50	45
Female	"	13	14	14	29	41	36
NATURAL RESOURCES							
Area	thou. sq. km	3,287.59	3,287.59	3,287.59	5,133.49	40,391.42	40,594.43
Density	pop. per sq. km	186.60	232.74	273.21	233.41	77.44	26.66
Agricultural land	% of land area	60.83	60.86	60.89	59.11	52.42	41.05
Change in agricultural land	annual %	0.47	-0.07	-0.05	-0.02	0.16	-1.38
Agricultural land under irrigation	%	18.65	23.09	25.96	29.63	17.84	11.40
Forests and woodland	thou. sq. km	..	551.19	517.29	658.32	7,632.00	5,969.25
Deforestation (net)	% change. 1980-90	..	..	0.63	..	..	..
INCOME							
Household income							
Share of top 20% of households	% of income	49	41	43	..	..	..
Share of bottom 40% of households	"	16	20	21	..	..	..
Share of bottom 20% of households	"	6	8	8	..	..	..
EXPENDITURE							
Food	% of GDP	43.6	35.3	..	..	..	..
Staples	"	20.6	12.4	..	..	..	..
Meat, fish, milk, cheese, eggs	"	6.5	7.4	..	..	..	..
Cereal imports	thou. metric tonnes	7,669	205	694	6,211	36,922	68,936
Food aid in cereals	"	1,582	304	276	1,624	8,516	5,771
Food production per capita	1987 = 100	94	104	115	113	115	102
Fertilizer consumption	kg/ha	19.3	47.0	67.5	69.7	58.5	46.3
Share of agriculture in GDP	% of GDP	36.6	29.5	26.9	26.6	27.6	14.0
Housing	% of GDP	4.4	7.1	..	..	..	..
Average household size	persons per household	5.2	5.6	..	..	..	..
Urban	"	4.8	5.5	..	..	..	..
Fixed investment: housing	% of GDP	2.3	2.8	..	..	..	..
Fuel and power	% of GDP	2.4	2.3	..	..	..	..
Energy consumption per capita	kg of oil equiv.	124	170	243	219	373	1,602
Households with electricity							
Urban	% of households	..	..	..	..	..	..
Rural	"	..	..	..	..	..	..
Transport and communication	% of GDP	4.7	5.1	..	..	..	..
Fixed investment: transport equipment	"	1.4	2.3	..	..	..	..
Total road length	thou. km	1,375	1,546	2,962	..	..	..
INVESTMENT IN HUMAN CAPITAL							
Health							
Population per physician	persons	4,900	2,522	..	..	..	3,064
Population per nurse	"	3,710	1,701	..	..	..	..
Population per hospital bed	"	1,700	1,300	1,371	1,675	1,034	592
Oral rehydration therapy (under-5)	% of cases	..	..	37	37	38	..
Education							
Gross enrollment ratios							
Secondary	% of school age pop.	26	37	49	45	48	63
Female	"	16	26	38	35	42	62
Pupil-teacher ratio: primary	pupils per teacher	42	58	63	61	39	..
Pupil-teacher ratio: secondary	"	21	21	26	26	20	..
Pupils reaching grade 4	% of cohort	51	58	..	..	..	..
Repeater rate: primary	% of total enroll	17	..	..	..	..	..
Illiteracy	% of pop. (age 15+)	66	56	48	51	35	..
Female	% of fem. (age 15+)	..	71	62	64	46	..
Newspaper circulation	per thou. pop.	15	26	31	26	..	236

World Bank International Economics Department, April 1996

India

Indicator	Unit of measure	Latest single year 1970-75	Latest single year 1980-85	Most recent estimate 1989-94	Same region/income group South Asia	Same region/income group 'Low-income	Next higher income group
Priority Poverty Indicators							
POVERTY							
Upper poverty line	local curr.	..	..	..	..	..	..
Headcount index	% of pop.	..	..	..	..	..	..
Lower poverty line	local curr.	..	..	..	..	..	..
Headcount index	% of pop.	..	..	..	..	..	..
GNP per capita	US$	180	280	310	320	390	1,670
SHORT TERM INCOME INDICATORS							
Unskilled urban wages	local curr.	..	..	..	..	..	..
Unskilled rural wages	"	..	..	..	..	..	..
Rural terms of trade	"	..	84	94	..	..	..
Consumer price index	1987=100	45	85	189	..	..	..
Lower income	"	..	..	..	..	..	..
Food[a]	"	27	..	..	..	..	..
Urban	"	..	83	176	..	..	..
Rural	"	..	..	..	..	..	..
SOCIAL INDICATORS							
Public expenditure on basic social services	% of GDP	..	..	..	..	..	..
Gross enrollment ratios							
Primary	% school age pop.	79	96	102	98	105	104
Male	"	94	110	113	110	112	105
Female	"	62	80	91	87	98	101
Mortality							
Infant mortality	per thou. live births	132	108	70	73	58	36
Under 5 mortality	"	..	..	97	106	101	47
Immunization							
Measles	% age group	..	..	85.8	84.2	86.2	77.4
DPT	"	..	41.0	90.2	88.6	89.1	82.0
Child malnutrition (under-5)	"	..	..	63.0	61.5	38.2	..
Life expectancy							
Total	years	50	55	62	61	63	67
Female advantage	"	-1.9	-0.4	1.3	1.2	2.4	6.4
Total fertility rate	births per woman	5.6	4.8	3.3	3.6	3.3	2.7
Maternal mortality rate	per 100,000 live births	..	460	437	..	..	..
Supplementary Poverty Indicators							
Expenditures on social security	% of total gov't exp.	..	..	..	..	..	..
Social security coverage	% econ. active pop.	..	..	..	..	..	..
Access to safe water: total	% of pop.	31.0	56.3	..	..	..	..
Urban	"	80.0	76.0	..	..	..	..
Rural	"	18.0	50.0	..	..	..	..
Access to health care	"	..	75.0	..	..	..	..

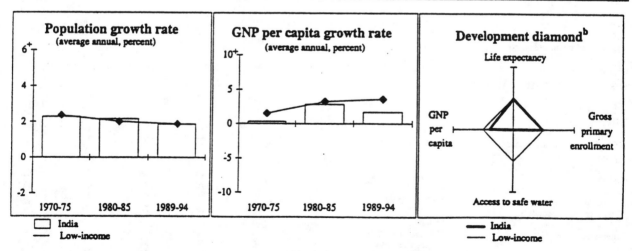

Population growth rate (average annual, percent) — 1970-75, 1980-85, 1989-94 — India / Low-income

GNP per capita growth rate (average annual, percent) — 1970-75, 1980-85, 1989-94

Development diamond[b] — Life expectancy, GNP per capita, Gross primary enrollment, Access to safe water — India / Low-income

a. See the technical notes, p.387. b. The development diamond, based on four key indicators, shows the average level of development in the country compared with its income group. See the introduction.

EXECUTIVE SUMMARY

The Ministry's of Finance's 1995-96 Economic Survey and its July 1996 update analyze candidly and insightfully the accomplishments of five years of stabilization and reform. The new government's Common Minimum Program of June 1996 identifies the key challenges ahead: reducing the country's chronically high fiscal deficits, further liberalizing the economy, agriculture in particular, meeting the infrastructure challenge, and ensuring social justice. These documents are the point of departure of this Country Economic Memorandum (CEM). Part I sums up the achievements and shortcomings of five years of stabilization and reform. Part II outlines the challenges ahead.

A Summing Up

India has Fundamentally Altered Its Development Strategy

India's pre-1991 planned approach to development helped the country escape from the massive illiteracy, recurrent famines, fertility rates of about 7 children per woman, and secular stagnation prevailing before Independence. However, it also led to an over-extended public sector, responsible for half of the country's gross investment, and created severe financial imbalances which are yet to be corrected. It isolated the country from the rest of the world with the result that from 2 percent in the 1950s, India's share of world trade had declined to less than half of one percent in the late 1980s. It forced Indian consumers to pay higher prices for goods of lower quality and deprived the country of the benefits of foreign direct investment and modern technology. It discouraged production for exports, created recurrent shortages of foreign exchange, and made the balance of payments extremely vulnerable to external circumstances. Most important of all, it held back the country's growth and thus the pace at which poverty could have been reduced.

In June 1991, in the midst of severe fiscal and external imbalances, which had generated double-digit inflation and put the country on the verge of defaulting on its external debt obligations, a new government undertook the major task of stabilizing and liberalizing the economy. Over the past five years, reform of the investment, exchange-rate and trade regimes, of the financial sector, and of the tax system have ended four decades of planning and have initiated a quiet economic revolution. With these reforms, India has joined the growing group of countries which, starting in the 1970s and 1980s, have gradually but persistently taken measures to deregulate their domestic markets, increase their integration with the global economy, and reduce the role of government.

India did not have the inflation, external debt, and social inequities so severe in Latin America--and was thus able to stabilize the economy more rapidly and at a lower social cost. Unlike former centrally planned economies in Eastern Europe and elsewhere, and while extremely regulated, India already had an ubiquitous private sector, all the institutions of a free market economy, and a relatively well-developed financial sector. India was thus able to avoid the costly industrial and financial closures and restructuring, so frequent and so painful in most of the former socialist economies of Eastern Europe and Central Asia, and which have considerably delayed the supply response to reforms.

On the other hand, the fact that India's macroeconomic problems were considerably less traumatic than in Latin America also meant that they were less palpable. Consequently, it has been much harder to reach political consensus on the need to reduce fiscal imbalances. India has adjusted its fiscal accounts much less than Latin American, East Asian and Western European countries--and fiscal imbalances remain the most important threat to India's long term growth. Similarly, India's pre-1991 trade regime yielded levels of protection considerably higher than Latin American and East Asian countries'. Even after five rounds of significant trade reforms, India's tariff and non-tariff barriers still remain among the world's highest. Likewise, before 1991, India's private sector probably was the most controlled in the non-socialist world. Thus, and in spite of five years of liberalization measures, regulation still remains a problem in important segments of the economy--the financial sector, agriculture and agro-industry in particular. In addition, in the financial sector, the public sector continues to be the major shareholder of India's largest banks, insurance companies, and contractual savings institutions-- raising questions on how truly autonomous these financial institutions can be. Finally, the development of India's human resources has been slow in comparison with countries in East Asia or Eastern Europe.

Highlights of Five Years of Stabilization

The economic recovery has been unexpectedly rapid and robust. Initially, growth declined sharply in response to the devaluation and contractionary fiscal and monetary policies adopted in June 1991 to address the foreign exchange crisis India was facing then. From over 5 percent in 1990-91, GDP growth declined to less than one percent in 1991-92. Then, helped by an unprecedented sequence of good monsoons, a relaxation in fiscal policies, and a strong supply-response to the reforms, growth accelerated to 5 percent in 1992-94, 6 percent in 1994-95 and 7 percent in 1995-96. With growth rates exceeding 10 percent in the last two years, the industrial recovery has been particularly strong. Because it is being driven by exports and private investment, and is being accompanied by an increase in domestic savings, the recovery has thus far not put pressure on inflation or the external accounts. However, unless pressing stabilization and reform issues are expeditiously addressed, the country may not be able to sustain this performance.

Inflation has declined from the high 14-15 percent levels prevailing in 1991-92. This was achieved by generally strict monetary policies which were maintained in spite of persistently high public sector deficits, and liberalization of interest rates. Unexpectedly large capital inflows starting in late 1993 complicated monetary management in 1993-95 and caused money supply temporarily to increase at rates exceeding 20 percent and inflation to rise above 10 percent (after it had declined to below 8 percent). By early 1994, concern with the repercussions of higher inflation and loss of real exchange-rate competitiveness led the authorities to implement a pragmatic mixture of measures to slow down certain categories of capital inflows--particularly those that are easily reversible, or imply a high debt service burden. Helped by increases in US interest rates and adverse developments in emerging markets in the wake of the Mexican crisis, these measures worked well and allowed the RBI to tighten its monetary stance and inflation to decline to below 5 percent in 1996. However, in the absence of a sufficiently strong fiscal correction, this has come at the cost of high real interest rates which are a threat to the sustainability of the recovery and to the soundness of the banking system. In addition, the current rate may not be indicative of the true underlying inflation since, recent increases notwithstanding, the administered prices of some petroleum products and some food items need adjustment.

The external accounts, both current and capital, have improved significantly. In response to a sharp depreciation of the real exchange rate and reduction of import tariffs, and therefore of the anti-export bias implicit in the previous trade regime, exports grew at rates in excess of 20 percent for the past three years, and prospects for 1996-97 are equally encouraging. Consequently, and in spite of the rapid growth of imports (mostly of intermediates and capital goods) of the last two years resulting from the industrial recovery, the current account deficit has remained below 2 percent of GDP--an amount well within prudential levels. Improvements in the capital account have been equally significant. At US$2 billion in 1995-96, while well below China's US$31 billion, foreign direct investment is 15 times higher than it was before the economy was liberalized and portfolio investment has stabilized at around US$2-3 billion--that is 10 percent of world portfolio investment in emerging markets, a share in line with that of China and Indonesia. These developments in the current and capital accounts led foreign exchange reserves to increase to US$17 billion, that is 5 months of imports and the debt service ratio to decline--from 30 percent of current account receipts in 1990-91 to 24 percent in 1995-96.

However, meaningful fiscal adjustment has yet to take place. With the exception of the first year of the stabilization and reform program, when its deficit was reduced from 8.3 percent of GDP in 1990-91 (with a primary deficit of 4.3 percent of GDP) to 6 percent in 1991-92, the Central Government has persistently relaxed its fiscal deficit targets. In 1995-96, at 5.9 percent of GDP (with a primary deficit of 1.1 percent of GDP), the fiscal deficit was one half percent of GDP above the 1995-96 target--and well over the 3 percent of GDP the Government set as a target at the beginning of the stabilization and reform program. There are several reasons.

First, several of the structural reforms have had a relatively high fiscal cost. For example, the reduction of import tariffs and the rationalization of excises (to make the excise system more closely resemble a value added tax) came at a cost, which in some years exceeded one percent of GDP in foregone revenues. The liberalization of financial markets meant higher interest costs on Central Government debt--interest payments on the Central Government debt are close to 1 percent of GDP higher than they were five years ago.

Second, political and social considerations led the Government to retain some important subsidies such as the fertilizer subsidy. While this may have reduced the social cost of the stabilization and reform program for the poor, it has cost the budget over half of a percent of GDP per year.

Third, progress in reforming public enterprises has been much slower than expected. Contrary to the experience of other countries, India's fiscal adjustment did not benefit from the proceeds of privatization nor from the dividends that better managed public enterprises could have generated. The Central Government is the majority shareholder, and in some cases the sole shareholder, of 240 enterprises, about 27 large banks, and two large insurance companies. While some of these enterprises are highly profitable, most generate profits and dividends insufficient to compensate the Government for the cost of funds invested in them. Over the past five years, losses of loss-making enterprises have not declined, while profits of profit making enterprises have increased only marginally.

Fourth, fiscal adjustment by the Central Government has been limited by the absence of corresponding adjustment by India's 25 states. One-fourth (about 4 percent of GDP excluding states' share of taxes collected by the Central Government) of Central Government spending is in the form of grants and loans to the states which the Central Government has found difficult to curtail. As a result, over the last five years, the states' consolidated fiscal deficit has not declined--it has hovered around 3 percent of GDP. As discussed in last year's World Bank Economic Memorandum on India, there is evidence that the current system of transfers discourages fiscal discipline because: (a) "grants-in-aid" to the states at least partly are meant to cover their current deficits and thus create incentives for increasing them; (b) transfers in the form of loans and grants authorized by the Planning Commission (set up soon after Independence with a mandate rooted in India's pursuit of a centrally planned development strategy, it has become a de-facto development bank without the prudential financial standards that typically guide such banks) are not used for their intended productive purposes and thus increase the states' debt without increasing their capacity to service it; and (c) periodic Central Government loan forgiveness and refinancing, without conditionality, have created an expectation of future debt relief. In addition, the deterioration in the states' finances is being compounded by a decline in the quality of their spending. There is growing evidence of a crisis of expenditure composition at the state level whereby resources for the provision of operations and maintenance of key infrastructure (roads, irrigation, primary education and health facilities) for which the states have responsibility are being cut to sustain less productive expenditure and subsidy programs.

Highlights of Five Years of Structural Reforms

The liberalization of the investment regime is nearly complete. Five years ago, investment in the most important areas of the economy was a public sector monopoly and foreign investment was discouraged--at US$150 million in the early 1990s, foreign direct investment in 900 million India was as high as in 17 million neighboring Sri Lanka. Currently, there are few areas where private investors, domestic or foreign, cannot invest and India's foreign investment regime is as investor friendly as that of the East Asian countries. In telecommunications, power and mining, it is significantly more open than that of its East Asian neighbors. With the recent liberalization of pharmaceuticals and, in part, coal, the main areas still reserved for the public sector are insurance and railways. This progress notwithstanding, the remaining licensing restrictions mainly to protect small scale industry, including agro-industry, have considerable negative repercussions. For example, continuing regulation of the sugar industry is extremely costly while the reservation of about 800 products for small scale enterprises discourages economies of scale and adoption of modern technology. In addition, in many instances, investing in India remains difficult because of mostly state-level regulations and administrative burdens that are far from transparent and differ from state to state--and affect domestic and foreign investors alike.

The trade and foreign exchange regimes have been substantially liberalized, but protection levels are still high. In June 1991, India had the most restrictive trade regime of the non-socialist world. Virtually all goods could only be imported if authorized by the Government and, with maximum tariffs over 300 percent and average (import-weighted) tariffs of 87 percent, India had the world's highest tariffs. Several rounds of trade reforms have lifted all licensing restrictions on imports of intermediate and capital goods, liberalized marginally imports of consumer goods, and reduced maximum tariffs for non-consumer goods to 40 percent and the import weighted average tariff to 22.7 percent. Tariffs for imports of capital goods have been reduced more rapidly than for other items. In parallel, the exchange-rate regime has been liberalized, and full convertibility has been established for current account transactions. This progress notwithstanding, India will need to liberalize its trade regime even further if the country is to reach the openness of its East Asian and Latin American competitors where import weighted tariffs are in the 10-15 percent range.

A skillful and significant liberalization of the financial sector--but the public sector remains dominant. With a financial savings rate of 9 percent of GDP in 1990-91 (11 percent of GDP at present), India's pre-1991 policies had been successful at developing a solid deposit base, and a diversified stock of financial instruments. However, until very recently, the financial sector had been dominated by public banks which had limited discretion in allocating their lending (in 1991 as much as 63.5 percent of increases in bank deposits had to be held in cash reserve requirements and government securities, and 40 percent of the remaining had to be allocated to priority sectors designated by government) and publicly-owned insurance companies still have to hold more than half of their portfolio in government-designated securities. Prudential regulations had no real role to play in the deployment of capital and in any case were inadequate making it difficult to assess the true quality of bank portfolios or bank profits. Interest rates and financial instruments were tightly regulated, and competition was limited by restrictions on entry of new banks, insurance companies, or mutual funds. Pricing and terms of new equity issues were regulated.

Because of persistently large public sector borrowing requirements and weak public banks balance sheets, the government has chosen a phased approach to liberalizing the financial sector--but this approach has been excessively gradual in the case of privatization of the public banks and deregulation of insurance companies and contractual savings institutions. Much of the reform effort has focused on establishing the institutional base required for deregulated financial markets to operate efficiently, and in deregulating the markets themselves. In particular, prudential regulations that meet international standards have been introduced, and to improve its capacity to enforce the new prudential guidelines, the RBI created a Board of Financial Supervision which began functioning in December 1994. Several steps have been taken to develop markets in government securities, including the creation by RBI of a dealer network to operate in and provide liquidity to government security markets, followed by the approval of the first six private primary dealers in 1996. In parallel, measures have been taken to develop the Securities and Exchange Board of India's (SEBI) capacity to provide oversight regulation in India's stock markets and to increase the transparency of stock market transactions. In particular, legislation has been enacted to improve title transfers and a code for takeovers has been formulated. A new modern electronic securities exchange system, the National Stock Exchange (NSE), which allows scripless transactions, began operating in 1995. In November 1995, the government established an insurance regulatory body, to prepare the basis for eliminating the public monopoly in this sector--although a decision on this has yet to be taken.

Interest rates are now market determined for most transactions and the government is committed to eliminate by 1997 its automatic access to RBI credit. However, while progress has been achieved in relaxing controls, reducing government's pre-emption of financial savings, and reestablishing the soundness of the financial system, much remains to be done. In particular, forced holdings of government debt by banks, while reduced, remain at a high 37 percent of deposits and 40 percent of banks' loan portfolios still must be allocated to designated "priority sector lending". While barriers against the entry of private banks (domestic and foreign) have been relaxed, public sector banks continue to hold around 90 percent of the sector's assets and little progress has been achieved in reducing government equity holdings in the public banks or in improving their autonomy in key areas such as staffing and pay. As a result, financial intermediation costs remain excessive and the increased autonomy of financial sector institutions also remains in doubt.

The tax regime has been simplified and strengthened. Prior to 1991, India's tax base was excessively dependent on custom revenues, and was characterized by taxes with a multiplicity of high rates falling on a narrow base. Several steps have been taken to address this problem. In the 1994-95 Budget, taxes on corporate income were unified at 46 percent for widely held companies and 55 percent for branches of foreign banks. A major reform of excises was implemented to make it more closely resemble a value-added tax and address its major problems. Meanwhile, the Government extended the coverage of MODVAT (a modified value-added tax) to include manufacturing sectors thus far excluded, and, for the first time, some services. Of particular importance also were the decisions to: (a) shift most excise rates from specific to ad-valorem to increase buoyancy; (b) reduce the number of rates; and (c) simplify the system by relying on invoices for value determination. These reforms considerably simplified and modernized India's tax system and made it possible for the Central Government to focus its efforts on improving tax administration. The 1995-96 Budget further reduced peak excises and continued the emphasis on simplification, strengthened compliance, lower rates, and greater buoyancy. Further and significant tax reforms were introduced in the 1996-97 budget including the full incorporation of the textile sector into the VAT.

The effects of five years of stabilization and reform on the poor. A key objective of India's liberalization program has been employment creation and poverty alleviation through accelerated growth. Many of the measures introduced over the past five years have brought India's development policies closer to those of East Asian countries such as Indonesia and China which have been successful in reducing the incidence of poverty in a relatively short period of time. In particular, the sharp devaluation of the rupee and the decline in the protection of manufacturing have improved the agricultural terms of trade. Also, the reduction in the anti-export bias implicit in the pre-1991 trade regime has led to a rapid expansion of labor-intensive exports--which in other countries have been a key factor in employment generation and poverty reduction.

However, at the same time, there has been considerable concern on the effects that some of the stabilization and structural reform measures introduced over the past five years might have had on the living standards of the poor. In particular, there have been significant increases in the prices of key commodities such as fertilizer, rice, sugar, cotton, and gasoline. Further, increases in inflation due to rapid monetary growth in 1993-94 and 1994-95 (because of the monetization of capital inflows), and increases in the prices of key agricultural commodities (the result of higher issue prices and the delayed effect of the sharp devaluation) accentuated fears that the program of stabilization and reform might be putting an excessively high burden on the poor.

The 1993-94 National Sample Survey (NSS) released in July 1996 indicates that the incidence of poverty has declined. The publication of this survey is too recent, however, for a careful analysis of its findings to be included in this CEM. It is also not possible to provide definitive answers about how poverty has evolved over the past two years since no NSS data are available as yet. For the purposes of this report, and as a very first approximation, case studies were carried out by Indian economists and social scientists, between January and March 1996, in Maharashtra, Tamil Nadu, Punjab, and Uttar Pradesh.

The results of this exercise suggest that poverty is unlikely to have increased in the recent past. In addition, variables that are good predictors of poverty (such as wages for unskilled agricultural labor, agricultural production, overall growth and inflation) have evolved in a direction that suggests that the incidence of poverty might in fact have declined. This view is reinforced by the case studies results which document no noticeable decline in food consumption. However, in the absence of firm data for the last two years these results cannot be generalized. More interestingly perhaps, a strong result that also emerges from the case studies is that the existing welfare and safety net programs seem to be barely noticed by those who were being interviewed. In spite of the significant resources that the country allocates to such programs, there is little evidence that they have a palpable effect on the living standards of the poor. This may be because the newer programs (i.e., RPDS, EAS schemes, benefits for widows) have not yet reached intended beneficiaries on any significant scale. This also can be, however, an indication that the older programs have failed to reach their targeted population. Again in this case, only with the household survey results will it be possible to clarify the underlying reasons and reach definitive conclusions regarding the impact of the reforms on the poor and the cost effectiveness of the various anti-poverty programs.

Highlights of the 1996-97 Budget

On July 22, the Minister of Finance presented to Parliament the 1996-97 budget, the first of the 13-parties United Front (UF) government. The budget takes several steps to implement the Common Minimum Program (CMP) and makes it clear that this government intends to continue the reforms started in 1991.

On *stabilization*, the budget proposes a welcome fiscal correction of 0.9 percent of GDP. However, the measures envisaged in the budget may not be sufficient to attain this target. The 0.9 percentage point reduction is to be achieved through a 0.7 percentage points of GDP increase in revenue, and a 0.2 percentage point reduction in expenditure. Some of the assumptions underlying both the revenue and the expenditure forecasts may be overoptimistic. *On the revenue side*, it is assumed that sales of government equity in public enterprises will reach US$1.5 billion and that tax revenues will increase by 20 percent on account of a 14 percent increase in nominal GDP (half real growth and half inflation) and of several tax measures introduced in the budget. *On the expenditure side*, a 9 percent increase in provision for wages is deemed to be sufficient to accommodate wage increases stemming from the Pay Commission recommendations. Finally, defense expenditure has continued to decline relative to GDP (from 2.9 percent of GDP five years ago to 2.2 percent of GDP at present) and there may be some pressure to restore it at higher levels. At the same time, new claims have been put on the budget to increase the fertilizer subsidy (0.2 percent of GDP) and support for public enterprises (0.1 percent of GDP), expand an already existing rural infrastructure fund, strengthen the capital base of the national agricultural bank (0.1 percent of GDP), and, for a relatively small amount, recapitalize several small public banks.

The budget also announces a cautious, but clear commitment to permit *greater decentralization* within India's federal structure by: (a) gradually transferring most centrally sponsored schemes to the control of the states; (b) proposing constitutional change to include all central taxes in the federal transfer division pool as recommended by the Tenth Finance Commission; (c) designing a Ninth Five-Year Plan which will put emphasis on decentralization of responsibility; and (d) convening a conference of Chief Ministers on center-states relations and federalism. In addition, the budget also announces the government intention to *target the Public Distribution System* and, potentially, other social safety nets programs, to families below the poverty line. Finally, the Minister of Finance proposed to appoint a *high level Expenditure Management and Reforms Commission* to submit within four months recommendations on how to improve public expenditure control and management, and proposed to place before Parliament a *discussion paper on subsidies* and their appropriate targeting. These are welcome initiatives that will permit a public discussion of the structural reasons for India's chronically high fiscal deficits.

On the *structural front,* except for taxation, and in spite of progress in modestly further liberalizing the trade and foreign investment regimes, the budget refrains from bold structural reform initiatives at this time while stimulating the public debate on these issues. In particular, several much discussed and awaited reforms have not taken place: (a) the end of the public sector monopoly on insurance has been postponed; (b) imports of consumer goods have not been liberalized; and (c) deregulation of agriculture has not started.

Reform of the tax regime has continued. Several tax measures have been taken to continue the broadening the tax base, reduce rates and improve tax administration. This has been particularly important in the case of excises and corporate taxation. Corporate taxation has been reduced from 46 percent to 43 percent, and a new Minimum Alternate Tax has been introduced to bring into the tax net corporations that avoid paying taxes on corporate income or benefit from excessive exemptions. The long-term capital gains tax for domestic companies has been reduced to 20 percent in line with that for foreign companies. The *foreign investment regime has been further liberalized* by allowing portfolio investors to invest in non-listed securities, and by raising the limit of the maximum of equity they can hold in any given company. Regarding the *trade regime,* import tariffs have been reduced on a number of items with the result that the maximum tariff for non-consumer goods is now 40 percent.

On social issues, the new government has used its first budget to *signal strong commitment to poverty reduction and rural development.* Besides the support to the national agricultural bank and rural infrastructure, the budget introduced several initiatives to improve the living standards of the rural poor. In particular, it provides Rs 24 billion (0.2 percent of GDP) for state-level social programs aimed at increasing the provision of safe drinking water, primary education, primary health, housing, mid-day meals for primary school children, rural roads and a strengthened public distribution system covering all below the poverty line. It also reiterates commitment to achieving 100 percent coverage of provision of safe drinking water, universalisation of primary education and basic health care, and extension of the mid-day meal program.

A new initiative to mobilize additional capital for the development of infrastructure. The budget also announced that an Infrastructure Development Finance Company (IDFC) will be established, involving a budgetary outlay of Rs 5 billion for equity. This is to be matched by an equal contribution from the Reserve Bank of India. The IDFC is intended to play the role of direct lender, refinance institution as well as the provider of financial guarantees, that will induce private financiers to advance "long-term funds at the lowest possible market rates".

The Challenges Ahead

The stabilization and reform measures introduced over the past five years have considerably improved India's growth prospects. The growth performance of the last two years and preliminary indications for 1996-97 confirm this view and may suggest that the reforms have created the preconditions for India to grow at a stable 6-7 percent annual growth. This inevitably raises the question of whether India will be able to grow at high, East Asian rates. The answer is that strong corrective measures are necessary for this to happen. Not only is the country facing serious fiscal imbalances that the 1996-97 budget corrects only partially, but there also remains a challenging agenda of structural reforms that needs urgently to be addressed even to sustain the current growth rate, let alone exceed it.

Addressing Fiscal Constraints

India's persistently large fiscal imbalances have led to an increasing volume of public debt, which has been accompanied by a rising trend in real interest rates in recent years. At present, the marginal real interest rate that the Government pays on its domestic debt is close to the economy's growth rate itself. Therefore, unless fiscal imbalances and thus real interest rates are significantly reduced, India will be in a debt trap and will not be able to maintain the current mix of low inflation and relatively high growth. It is therefore not surprising that, as recognized in the Common Minimum Program, and highlighted in the last few Economic Surveys of the Ministry of Finance, and Annual Reports of the RBI, excessively large financial imbalances at the level of the Central Government, State Governments, and public enterprises are the single most important economic management issue facing the authorities.

The consolidated deficit of the central government, state and public enterprises amounts to about 10 percent of GDP. This is only 2 percent of GDP below the level prevailing at the beginning of the liberalization process because the Central Government is the only part of the public sector that has adjusted its finances. Fiscal imbalances have remained basically unchanged for states and public enterprises--and their savings have in fact deteriorated. These trends are not sustainable. To stabilize public sector debt in relation to GDP, maintain inflation at below 6 percent and growth at 6-7 percent would require the consolidated public sector *primary deficit* to be reduced immediately by 1.5 percentage points from its 1995-96 level of 3.1 percent. If the central government were the only part of the public sector to adjust, this would mean a central government *fiscal deficit* of about 4.5 percent of GDP, that is a fiscal correction of 0.5 percent of GDP beyond what is envisaged in the 1996-97 budget. To the extent that states and public enterprises increase their financial performance and reduce their claims on the country's savings, the required fiscal adjustment is correspondingly less. However, as the financial sector is liberalized and banks have more discretion on portfolio composition, there will inevitably be pressure on real interest rates to increase--implying an increase in central government interest payments. Higher real interest rates would reduce private investment and thus growth while, if monetized, the increase in the central government interest payments would increase inflation. To avoid these two negative consequences, a further fiscal adjustment of about 1 percent of GDP is needed--making it necessary to increase the fiscal correction to 2.5 percent of GDP, implying a reduction in the central government *fiscal deficit* to around 3.5 percent of GDP. A more ambitious fiscal scenario is warranted and feasible, however--in which the consolidated public sector savings increase by 6 percent of GDP over the next four to five years. This would allow fiscal imbalances to be brought to sustainable levels while generating resources for critically needed public investment, and could enable growth to be sustained at 7 percent per year until the end of the decade before increasing possibly to over 8 percent thereafter.

The essential elements of a medium-term fiscal adjustment strategy. Any significant structural fiscal consolidation will need to rely on both raising the public sector's revenue effort as well as reducing expenditure and improving its quality. Consolidation of the central government finances is likely to include the following elements: (a) a reduction-cum-retargeting of subsidies, in particular the fertilizer and food subsidy--the latter may require an overhaul of the current PDS and Food Corporation of India; (b) gradual contraction of central government employment, mainly through attrition and associated operating expenditures; (c) commercialization-cum-privatization of public enterprises, including banks and other financial institutions; and (d) improvement in public expenditure management. Improvement of State finances will likely require actions to: (a) increase recovery of expenditure on O&M for irrigation and water supply; (b) reduce power subsidies through an increase in tariffs for agricultural users and households; (c) reduce power theft and improve tariff collections; (d) reduce overstaffing; and (e) broaden the base of taxation, in particular to include agriculture--according to the Constitution only the states can tax income generated in agriculture and, with few exceptions, most states chose not to tax it. A reduction of central government financial assistance to the states--particularly of those items on which fiscal discipline is the most difficult to enforce, such as the on-lending of deposits in the postal small-savings accounts and the different centrally sponsored expenditure schemes should also be considered, although it is not discussed here. These measures can be implemented only gradually, however, and their full effect will not begin to materialize before the end of the decade. Therefore, *correcting fiscal imbalances requires further tax efforts* of the kind recommended by the Chelliah Committee on tax reform--in particular, it is estimated that further reform of corporate taxation could increase tax revenue by at least one percent of GDP.

Full fiscal consolidation will be difficult, however, without a *restructuring of center-states fiscal relations*. Expenditure responsibility assigned to state governments by the Constitution accounts for about one half of total general government expenditure. At the same time, states are assigned taxation powers that result in their collecting only one-third of total tax revenues. The difference is covered by transfers in the form of shared central revenue, grants and loans. Since a part of these transfers is determined by the states' gap, and there have been periodic write-offs; states have in practice been faced with a relatively soft budget constraint--even though in theory state deficits are constrained by limits on borrowing imposed by the central government. More importantly perhaps, states do not face the discipline of financial markets, as the annual program of state security issues is still allocated administratively among commercial banks by the RBI. Thus, all the states borrow on the same terms, regardless of their creditworthiness. It is clear that center-state fiscal relations will need to be restructured if the states are to be encouraged to address their major problems of weak tax collections, growing wage bills, uneconomic enterprises and poor cost recovery. Similar considerations apply to the financial relationships between state and local governments.

Addressing Structural Constraints

Besides *completing the reforms initiated in 1991*, there also is an urgent need to extend reforms to other areas of the economy. As highlighted in the Common Minimum Program, a comprehensive *reform of agricultural policies* is essential to broaden the base of growth, increase agricultural productivity, and improve the living standards of India's poor--the vast majority of which live and work in the rural areas. As amply recognized in India, and reiterated in the Common Minimum Program, *the inadequacy of existing infrastructure* is emerging as one of India's most serious constraints to faster growth--and even a constraint to the maintenance of the current levels of growth. There is no simple response to the country's infrastructure problems--and any sensible response will have to be based on a variety of initiatives and innovations involving the financial sector, state and local governments, and the private sector. Similarly, *urban reform*--whereby India's cities and towns are endowed with the financial capacity to overcome chronic underinvestment in urban areas and supply critically needed urban services--is also emerging as an area for priority action. Finally, as discussed in the last two CEMs, it is urgent to *accelerate the development of India's human resources* by intensifying recent initiatives in the areas of primary health and primary education.

Completing the reforms started in 1991. Significant measures have been taken over the last five years to liberalize the investment and trade regimes and much has been accomplished. That said, a number of steps remain to be taken in these areas. Regarding the investment regime, regulations continue to restrict investment in small scale industries because the Government has been concerned with the employment consequences of a full liberalization of the sector. While this concern is legitimate, studies in India and elsewhere suggest that small scale industries benefit more from adequate access to infrastructure, finance, and imported inputs, than protection from competition. There is also evidence that the economic costs of size limitation in agro-industry are considerable and this is likely to be the case in other industrial areas. Other restrictions such as those applying to the expansion of private banks need also to be eliminated.

Regarding the *trade regime*, it will be important for India to continue to lower tariffs to be able to compete with the more open economies of East Asia, Latin America, and the emerging European former socialist economies, and also to provide a stronger foundation to India's growth process. At present, Indian producers continue to pay higher costs for capital goods and intermediate inputs than their competitors. In addition, important anomalies persist in the tariff structure that can only be corrected by a significant reduction of tariffs. Similarly, the elimination of import licensing restrictions on consumer goods is extremely important to protect the interests of the Indian consumers. In addition, several empirical studies show that the growth impact of foreign direct investment under high protection is smaller than that expected under more competitive conditions. In particular, because of the large size of India's markets, unless they are subject to international competition, domestic producers will have little incentive to be export-oriented and this may delay India's *integration into the world market*.

It will be critically important to complete rapidly the *financial sector reforms* started in 1991. This is necessary not only to promote the efficient allocation of investments needed to achieve higher growth, but also to strengthen the implementation of both fiscal and monetary policies and preserve macroeconomic stability. However, some of the most important remaining aspects of financial sector reform can only be implemented if fiscal consolidation is achieved because further liberalization in the presence of large public sector borrowings and consequently high interest rates could weaken the financial system--as company balance sheets deteriorate and non-performing assets of banks rise.

Assuming that fiscal consolidation is achieved, four financial sector reforms are of priority. *First*, the restructuring of the public banks needs to be brought to its logical conclusion. This means granting these banks increased managerial autonomy over branch networks, employment and compensation issues, as well as portfolio decisions. In this context, reducing the Government's equity share in these banks below 50 percent would create strong incentives for improved bank management and profitability. This would have to go hand in hand with strengthening the Government's oversight capacity. *Second*, remaining controls on banks' and insurance companies' portfolios need to be phased out and forced holdings of government debt should be reduced pari-pasu with the development of markets for government debt. *Third*, as the fiscal deficit is reduced, it should be possible to accelerate the development of money markets by reducing the intervention of the RBI in the placement of government debt and by reducing restrictions on insurance and pensions funds investment decisions. This should make it possible to establish liquid and deep money markets which can provide the basis for benchmark interest rates, help develop financial market linkages, and support development of a corporate debt market. *Fourth*, the Government will need to continue strengthening prudential regulations, supervision, capital market infrastructure, and legal and regulatory framework. A delivery-versus-payment system was recently established for government securities, but further efforts are needed to create modern settlement and registration systems for corporate bond markets, while regulatory oversight needs to be made more effective. In addition, improvements in India's payments system are essential to the integration of the country's regional financial and non-financial markets, and also for better management of the country's scarce financial resources.

The Chelliah Committee on *tax reform* produced a well conceived program of reforms for the Central Government taxes aimed at broadening the tax base, lowering rates, and streamlining the rate structure--thus providing a basis for improvements in tax administration. A part of the agenda set by this Committee has already been implemented and some of the most severe distortions of the tax system have been corrected. It should now be possible to concentrate on further enhancing the contribution of each tax and on strengthening institutional capacity in this area. In particular, it will be important to *extend the base of the excise system*. Exemptions have increased in recent years, and long-standing exemptions above reasonable thresholds for the small-scale industry encourage tax evasion and the inefficient fragmentation of production. Correcting this, and reducing the rates to no more than two or three could bring the excise system closer to a value added tax, and facilitate its integration with the critically needed establishment of VATs at the state level.

There also is considerable scope to increase the efficiency of *corporate income taxation*, as well as revenues, by reducing both the rates and exemptions associated with this *tax and introducing an alternative minimum tax on gross corporate assets*. The exclusion of profits arising from export sales, accelerated depreciation, fringe benefits and other tax preferences imply that a nominal rate of 46 percent (including a 15 percent surcharge) translates into an effective rate of less than 20 percent--with the result that the surge in corporate profits of the last few years has not been accompanied by corresponding increases in tax revenue. While the Minimum Alternate Tax introduced in the last budget will correct some of this, it will be unable to address under-reporting problems associated with transfer pricing and other methods of under-reporting profits. Similar considerations apply to *the personal income tax*. Particularly important in this regard is the exemption of agricultural income by the states--to whom the Constitution delegates its taxation. To facilitate its political acceptability, effective taxation of this income would require improved delivery of economic services and infrastructure in rural areas by local governments in the context of the on-going decentralization. Last but not least, critically important to the improvement of India's taxation system is the implementation of the recommendation of the *Tenth Finance Commission to shift the base for revenue sharing from a high share of two taxes at present* (personal income taxes and excises) to a lower share of total tax receipts--which would provide states more stable revenue streams while no longer influencing how the central government raises revenue.

Reforming Agriculture. The performance of agriculture is central to the welfare of the over 300 million poor who live and work in rural areas. Increasing agricultural productivity has been a central objective of India's development strategy--essential to the elimination of famines, reduction of poverty, and successful industrialization. Before 1991, the two conflicting objectives of ensuring food supplies to consumers at low prices, and making production remunerative to farmers led to a complex set of policies. Farmers were penalized by: (a) the high protection granted to manufacturing which meant that they had to pay for essential machinery and inputs higher than international prices; (b) overvalued exchange rates that affected negatively the domestic terms of trade for agriculture; (c) restrictions on exports of agricultural commodities which meant that producer prices were generally below their international equivalent; and (d) an extremely complex set of domestic regulations on the trade of agricultural and agro-industrial products aimed at reducing the ability of large traders to influence domestic prices, which penalized farmers by increasing the wedge between farm gate and consumer prices. The price distortions created by these policies resulted in misallocation of resources and production patterns that did not fully correspond to the country's comparative advantage.

On the other hand, farmers benefited from large public spending for infrastructure (irrigation schemes, rural roads), support services (research and extension) and subsidies (for fertilizer, credit, water and power for irrigation pumping). No country in the world spends as much on agriculture as India--over one-fourth of agricultural GDP. These policies helped agricultural growth and contributed to the eradication of once chronic famines. The results were particularly noticeable in the 1980s when, for the first time in India's history, agriculture grew at a significantly higher rate than the population. Since 1980 agricultural growth has increased and spread across regions (to the East), crops and agricultural activities. Because it was scale neutral, and it increased real rural wages, it contributed to an important reduction in poverty. The driving force behind this trend was the massive subsidization of agricultural inputs, including rural credit, and the protection afforded to oilseeds at least until 1991. The exchange rate policy and the protection of the manufacturing sector prevailing until then on the other hand actually lowered agricultural prices by 25 percent in relation to the industrial and service sectors.

Accelerating a trend started in the mid-1980s, the 1991 economy-wide reforms virtually eliminated the anti-agricultural bias implicit in the trade and foreign exchange regime. This, the large amount of public resources spent on agriculture (8 percent of GDP), and an unprecedented sequence of good monsoons explain the rapid growth of agriculture since 1991. However, the much needed fiscal adjustment makes it important to device a "quality" agricultural reform program to support agricultural growth that is not so demanding in terms of fiscal resources.

Such a program would consist of four essential components. The *first* would consist of fiscal measures reducing unsustainable subsidies pari-pasu with measures increasing productive public expenditure (on research, extension, roads, irrigation, and other infrastructure important for agricultural productivity). The *second* would consist of a comprehensive deregulation of domestic agricultural trade and agro-processing. Such deregulation would significantly reduce marketing and processing margins to the benefit of both farmers and consumers. It would increase rural incomes and accelerate productivity growth. The gains of deregulation are particularly important in the case of rice, sugar, oilseeds, cotton, and livestock. The ratification of the Trade Related Aspects of Intellectual Property Rights (TRIPs) agreement should be an essential element of a deregulation strategy because it would improve farmers' access to productivity enhancing technologies. The *third* would consist of fundamental reform of the rural credit system--now decapitalized and inefficient.

It should be recognized, however, that the elimination of subsidies and the deregulation of external and domestic agricultural trade could have negative distributive implications, at least during a transitional period. Therefore, the necessary *fourth* prong of an agriculture reform strategy consists of measures to improve the targeting of the existing subsidy programs while reducing their overall fiscal cost. The reform of agriculture is a complex and time consuming undertaking which will need *careful coordination*. Responsibilities for reform are spread almost equally across the central and state governments, as well as multiple agencies at both the central and state levels. Overcoming the coordination problem would require a strong, shared commitment and consensus about the objectives of the reform program.

The reform of expenditure programs for agriculture will need to be underpinned by structural reforms. For, example, rehabilitation and modernization of medium and large irrigation schemes are needed to restore reliability of water delivery without which farmers will be reluctant to pay higher charges. It would also permit volumetric pricing of water and improved water management practices as recommended by the 1992 Report of the Committee on Pricing of Irrigation Water. Institutional reforms are also needed to provide the basis and necessary financial incentives for improved cost recovery as well as improved accountability in the delivery of water farmers. Tamil Nadu and Orissa have recently initiated reforms that would lead to improved cost recovery, quality of service delivery to farmers, and systems turnover to beneficiaries. Karnataka, in its 1995 Agricultural Policy Resolution, is proposing radically to transform institutional incentives in the irrigation sector by turning the Irrigation Departments into financially and managerially autonomous entities responsible and accountable to water users.

India is facing an imminent crisis in infrastructure. An unprecedented power supply deficit, and growing freight transport congestion problems (in roads, ports, and railways), threaten to undermine the supply response to the country's stabilization and reform efforts. To address the major infrastructure needs, the 1991-96 reforms ended decades of public sector monopolies (with the exception of railways), and the government has invited the private sector to play a significant role in raising the level of infrastructure investment and the efficiency of infrastructure services. The response of the shipping industry and air transport has been strong and positive--with dramatic improvements in the quantity and quality of services. In telecommunications, private operators have been inducted in cellular services and other private services are expected to be licensed shortly. In July 1996, a bill for the creation of the independent Telecom Regulatory Authority of India (TRAI) was presented to Parliament and is awaiting approval. Significant private investments would be encouraged by the timely establishment of TRAI. However, in other critical areas such as power (except for captive capacity), roads, and ports, few private investments have been brought to closure under the new national policies.

The fundamental obstacle to private sector investment in the power sector is the weak financial position of the State Electricity Boards (SEBs) which operate virtually all the country's distribution networks through which the power supplied by potential private investors would have to be sold. At this time, the SEBs are not financially viable clients for potential private power producers. The SEBs generally are prevented by their respective state government from charging commercially viable tariffs; they are not allowed to cut power from non-paying customers, and many of them are institutionally too weak to contain power theft in rural and urban areas. As a result, the SEBs' financial condition is one of the country's most serious structural constraints to the reduction of the public sector deficit. To alleviate the power supply crisis in the short-run, the government has encouraged captive plants (based on liquid hydrocarbons) where the purchaser is one or more selected industrial consumers. While this approach alleviates the short-term supply constraints, it exacerbates the financial problems of the SEBs by making them loose their best paying customers. Some states (Orissa) are beginning to address these problems through cautious tariff adjustments and through the phased privatization of distribution. But most have yet to begin meaningful power sector reform. In this context, and given growing power shortages in most states, the central government has been concerned to bring to closure at least some of the more viable independent power producers (IPPs) proposals. To that effect, it has committed itself to provide counterguarantees to selected power purchasing agreements between SEBs and IPPs, thereby adding its creditworthiness to the insufficient creditworthiness of the respective state and SEB. Since 1995 the Government has refrained from adding to its pending contracts to extend counterguarantees to IPPs because of the considerable contingent liability which these guarantees create for the Central Government.

In the case of highways, the international experience suggests that private investment can only be a solution in a few, albeit important, high density corridors, bridges and by-passes. Cost-effective public investment is therefore needed to improve India's road network. *The National Highway Authority of India (NHAI) has been mandated to manage the expansion of the highway sector.* Although it lacks the skills and finances to develop a modern capacity for highway construction and up-grading, there is considerable scope for private participation in road design, construction, and maintenance. The traditional reliance on state-level Public Work Departments (PWDs) and small labor-intensive road contractors does not provide the capacity to carry out the urgently needed construction program. Without major reforms in the way in which highway construction is designed, procured and managed, India will be unable to overcome the emerging road transport crisis and utilize the substantial funding potentially available for this purpose from multilateral and bilateral development agencies.

MOST is just beginning to take steps to induct private investment into the ports-sub-sector. To date, concrete actions in support of private investment in ports have largely come from state governments. For instance, the Government of Maharashtra has sponsored techno-economic feasibility studies for developing about 30 intermediate and minor ports in the state. Similarly, the Gujarat Maritime Board has initiated such studies for the development of new ports. Thus, the private sector has preferred to deal with the minor ports under the various state governments rather than to deal with the big ports under MOST. In addition, the private sector has taken advantage of the recent deregulation of coastal shipping to set up bulk domestic shipping operations in coal, fertilizer and cement to shift cargo off the congested road and rail systems onto previously underutilized coastal shipping lines. As in the case of power, however, this is not a fully effective way of addressing the sector's problems.

Several lessons have emerged from India's experience with the involvement of the private sector in infrastructure. In particular: (a) processes for selection of developers need to be predictable and based on rules that are transparent; (b) projects proposed by government to the private sector need to be preceded by high quality preparatory work covering their technical, social and environmental aspects; (c) the existence of a transparent regulatory framework is critical for the efficient induction of private operators and for the commercial operation of the projects they undertake; and (d) guarantees, counterguarantees, escrow accounts and other financial arrangements are no substitute for an adequate policy and institutional framework providing the basis for predictable revenue streams and financially viable buyers.

Urban Reform. There is growing evidence that India's cities and towns are facing a crisis of serious proportions stemming from chronic underinvestment in urban areas and consequent shortages of key urban services. At the heart of the problem are the cities' weak fiscal base--eroded by state legislation imposing rent controls, limits on the amount of land an individual can hold, restrictions on land markets, and unrealistically low water charges. In some of the main cities, revenues are excessively dependent on extremely inefficient taxes which need to be eliminated--such as octroi. Thus, any program of urban reform would need to include measures to: (a) improve urban areas' use of the existing resource base (such as a better cost recovery and enforcement of existing taxes); (b) strengthen the resource base and make it more efficient (such as lifting rent controls in the major cities, eliminating octroi, establishing efficient land markets with an effective system of land titling); and (c) establish a rule-based, efficient system of capital transfers to replace the present system. Such measures would provide the basis for the restoration of the finances of the country's cities and towns--and thus restore their capacity to invest in critically needed infrastructure. Over time, they would help municipalities become creditworthy borrowers, able to access capital markets and mobilize financing for critically needed investments.

External Financing Requirements

As of March 1995, India's US$99 billion external debt is, in net present value terms, more than twice the value of the country's exports. Based on this, the World Bank debt tables classify India, together with Indonesia and Chile as "moderately indebted". Of the world's two major credit rating agencies, only one has rated India's sovereign foreign currency debt above investment grade. In response to this, the authorities have adopted a prudent approach to the management of the capital account. Since the 1990-91 crisis, they have placed considerable emphasis on achieving a strong balance of payments position with a lower indebtedness and debt service ratio.

Consistent with these objectives, and an indirect way of influencing the size of the current account deficit, the authorities have brought different degrees of liberalization to different types of capital inflows--depending on their contribution to the country's development, their potential volatility, interest cost, maturity profile, and risk sharing features. Thus, while there are virtually no restrictions on foreign direct investment, there are some on portfolio investment. In particular, although there are no limits on the total amount of investment by foreign institutional investors, there are restrictions related to the type of financial assets they can hold (for example, they cannot invest in government papers, nor can they hold more than 30 percent of their portfolio in debt papers) and to their equity holdings (they cannot hold equity positions which exceed 24 percent of a firm's total equity). Equivalent restrictions apply to Indian firms issuing equity or debt abroad. The rationale for these limitations is that while portfolio investment is attractive for the country because its servicing is not fixed and the foreign investors share the risks associated with fluctuations in domestic income and exchange rates, it does create long-term claims on the country' s foreign exchange resources. Thus, its growth needs to remain in line with the growth in India's capacity to service it--that is in line with export growth. In the case of commercial borrowing, an indicative ceiling is set annually (US$5 billion in 1995-96) and, based on published guidelines and criteria, discretionary authority is used to direct borrowing to priority areas, and to limit short-term borrowing.

The authorities see full capital account liberalization as a medium-term objective, to be reached after a sustainable fiscal framework is firmly in place, and financial sector reforms are completed. They have wisely resisted the temptation to relax restrictions on external commercial borrowing over the past year as a means of relieving pressure on domestic interest rates. This would have not only diminished pressure for the urgently needed fiscal correction, but could have also stimulated a destabilizing consumption boom.

One consequence of this self-imposed discipline is that, for the foreseeable future, India will mostly need to rely on foreign direct investment and assistance from external development agencies to meet its substantial needs for infrastructure and human resource development. Therefore, this report continues to make a case for India's sustained access to long-term development assistance, including a substantial concessional component. With a modest current account deficit of 2 percent of GDP over the next few years, India would still require total gross financing of about US$8 billion in 1995-96, and an average of about US$13 billion in each of the following four years. Over the last two years, bilateral and multilateral participants in the India Development Forum have pledged about US$6.5 billion in official assistance as a recognition of India's strong commitment to reform and poverty reduction.

Over the last few years, the Government has taken several specific measures to improve the utilization of ODA: (a) advance release of funds are being made to state governments; (b) procedures for awarding contracts and procurement have been streamlined; and (c) a central Project Management Unit has been established in the Department of Economic Affairs, Ministry of Finance, for better portfolio management and project implementation. While these measures have accelerated aid disbursments, there remains scope for further improvements.

In conclusion, the Bank would advise the participants of the IDF to support India's ongoing fiscal adjustment and structural reforms through long-term official development assistance for high priority public investments in physical infrastructure and human capital development. With sustained improvements in the utilization of such aid commitments and gradual recourse to debt and non-debt commercial sources, India's remaining external financing needs would be met.

PART I

FIVE YEARS OF STABILIZATION AND REFORM

A SUMMING UP

FROM CRISIS TO GROWTH

INTRODUCTION

India Has Fundamentally Altered Its Development Paradigm

Over the four decades after Independence, India followed a planned development strategy based on extensive public ownership of commercial assets; a complex industrial licensing system; substantial protection against imports (including some of the world's highest tariffs on imports of capital goods, and a ban on imports of consumer goods); restrictions on exports; virtual prohibition of foreign investment; and extensive regulation of financial intermediation. At some point in the 1970s and early 1980s, these policies enabled the government to control the most basic business decision down to the firm level. Thus, while India's private sector has always been important and produced at least two-thirds of GDP, its activities were restricted and used for the goals of a planned development process.

This development strategy helped the country escape from the massive illiteracy, recurrent famines, fertility rates of about 7 children per woman, and secular stagnation prevailing before Independence. However, it also was the source of severe financial imbalances which are yet to be corrected. It isolated the country from the rest of the world with the result that from 2 percent in the 1950s, India's share of world trade had declined to less than half of one percent in the late 1980s. It forced Indian consumers to pay higher prices for goods of lower quality and deprived the country from the benefits of foreign direct investment and modern technology. It discouraged production for exports, created recurrent shortages of foreign exchange, and made the balance of payments extremely vulnerable to external circumstances. Most important of all, it held back the country's growth and thus the pace at which poverty could have been reduced. As argued by India's own eminent economists, among them Bhagwati (1993), *low productivity rather than inadequate savings explains the weak growth performance of the past decades.*

Throughout most of this period, macroeconomic policies were conservative and, except for a few episodes associated with unfavorable harvests or external shocks, inflation was contained to single digits. External current account deficits were modest and financed primarily by concessional aid flows. During the 1980s however, and driven by an unprecedented surge in

---

Box 1.1: India's Social Profile

The People. India is a country of striking contrasts and enormous ethnic, linguistic and cultural diversity. There are more than 1600 languages, nearly 400 of which are spoken by more than 200,000 people. The dominant religion is Hinduism (83 percent of the population), which, through its caste system, has profoundly affected the nation's social structure. Muslims account for a sizable 11 percent of the population, while Christians, Sikhs, Buddhists, Jains and Parsis account for the balance. India ranks first in the world in terms of the number added to its population each year, currently about 16 million. The total population, estimated in mid-1996 at 931 million, is second only to China. Since independence, successive governments have taken steps to improve the socio-economic status of the nation's tribal peoples and the lowest subcastes. Designated officially as *scheduled castes* (SCs) and *scheduled tribes* (STs), these groups number over 206 million (1991). STs are scattered throughout the country, but tend to live in relatively inaccessible areas, including forests, hills and deserts. SCs are a dispersed group, varying from predominantly rural to exclusively urban. Both groups, despite constitutional protection, fare proportionately worse than the population as a whole in areas of health, nutrition, education and employment.

Poverty and tradition have also produced severe gender inequalities. Despite some improvement, India's female population continues to face higher malnourishment and lower levels of education than men. The sex ratio is disturbingly male-biased, at 929 females per 1,000 males. Unlike most countries, in India more women than men die before the age of 35. Female illiteracy, a national problem, is particularly acute in rural areas, within certain state districts, and among SC/STs. Generally lacking land, women remain locked out of the formal financial system and are constrained in their ability to acquire capital assets or working capital. These and other inequalities continue to constrain attempts to improve labor productivity, reduce fertility, alleviate poverty and promote accelerated economic growth.

Urban patterns vary widely, although Maharashtra, West Bengal, Tamil Nadu and Karnataka have comparatively higher urban ratios than the other states. Bombay (12.6 million) and Calcutta (11.0 million) rank among the 30 largest cities in the world. Nonetheless, the country has not experienced the rapid rural-urban migration typical of other developing nations in Asia. In fact, about 60 percent of all Indians still live in villages with fewer than 5,000 people.

Education. India possesses a large pool of highly qualified manpower, including business professionals, engineers and scientists of international caliber. However, these groups represent only a tiny fraction of the population. As a whole, the country faces unacceptably high levels of illiteracy and low learning achievement. More than half the overall population over 15 and two-thirds of all women over 15 are illiterate. In addition, the average educational attainment of the adult labor force is only 2.4 years. While most children enroll at the beginning of primary school, more than half of rural students drop out before completing the cycle, while only a third of females make it to the secondary level. Overall, about 33 percent of children who should be in school are non-enrolled, with a disproportionate number nationwide coming from the poorest households, girls, and SC/STs.

Health. There have been substantial gains in health over the past 40 years. Much remains to be done. Infant mortality rates vary widely by state, from 13 per thousand in Kerala to 110 per thousand in Orissa. The average for low income countries (excluding China and India) is 91 per thousand. The risk of death for children under 5 years of age remains high, at 12.4 percent, about 30 percent higher than the average risk faced by the world's population and higher than in all regions of the world except Sub-Saharan Africa. The frequency and severity of maternal morbidity--400 deaths per 100,000 live births--is distressing, and compares unfavorably with all but a small number of countries. Largely preventable communicable diseases account for a high share of deaths in the country, currently around 470 per 100,000. This is in contrast to 117 per 100,000 in China and 187 per 100,000 for the world as a whole.

Nutrition. India has made significant improvements in food availability and distribution, rendering famines, even in drought, a thing of the past. However, much remains to be done in improving nutrition within regions and among various groups. By state, severe malnutrition is prevalent in Bihar, Uttar Pradesh, Madhya Pradesh, Kerala, West Bengal, Orissa and Rajasthan. SCs and STs record lower levels of nutrient intake than the average for other groups, and below recommended levels in all states and locations - rural as well as urban. Gender discrimination in food intake occurs, and is most discernible among young girls in the northern states. Overall, nearly two-thirds of children under five are malnourished, and about a third of newborns are of low birthweight.

---

public investment, fiscal policies became more expansionary. The overall public sector deficit widened from about 9 percent of GDP at the beginning of the 1980s to 12 percent of GDP by the end of the decade. Expansionary aggregate demand policies combined with some improvement in productivity in response to the gradual liberalization, produced annual growth of almost 6 percent. This was unsustainable, however. By 1990-91, inflation increased to 10.3 percent, and the external current account deficit reached 3 percent of GDP (US$10 billion), with increasing reliance on short-term capital inflows to finance it.

The fragility of the economic situation was exposed when India was faced with the consequences of the Middle East crisis and a period of frequent changes in government which created political uncertainty and delayed the correction of the serious internal and external imbalances. As India's credit standing in international capital markets fell sharply, access to external capital borrowing dried up and substantial amounts of private capital left the country. The result was that India had to face one of its most serious foreign exchange crisis. In June 1991, in spite of a severe squeeze on imports and emergency financing from the IMF, the World Bank, and other bilaterals, particularly Japan, with reserves at less than US$1 billion, the country was on the verge of defaulting on its external debt obligations.

The new government that came to power in June 1991 responded to the crisis by stabilization and reform measures intended not only to correct the unsustainable macroeconomic policies of the 1980s, but also to address long-standing constraints to higher economic growth. Over the last five years, changes of the investment, exchange-rate and trade regimes, the financial sector, and the tax system have ended four decades of development policies based on planning and have initiated a quiet economic revolution. With these reforms, India is now closer to the growing group of countries which, starting in the 1970s and 1980s, have gradually but persistently liberalized their economic policies, increased their integration with the global economy, and reduced the role of government.

India did not have the inflation, external debt, and social inequities so severe as in Latin America--and was thus able to stabilize the economy more rapidly and at a lower social cost. Unlike former centrally planned economies in Eastern Europe and elsewhere in Asia, India already had an important private sector and all the institutions of a free market economy. India was thus able to avoid the costly industrial and financial closures and restructurings, so frequent and so painful in most of the former socialist economies of Europe and Central Asia, and which have considerably delayed the supply response to reforms. On the other hand, because India's macroeconomic crisis was considerably less traumatic than in Latin America, it has been much harder to reach political consensus on the need to reduce fiscal imbalances to the levels achieved for instance by Latin American, East Asian and Western European countries. And fiscal imbalances remain the single most important threat to India's long term growth. Similarly, notwithstanding five rounds of trade reforms, India's trade protection remains among the world's highest. Likewise and in spite of five years of liberalization, excessive regulation remains a problem particularly in the financial sector, agriculture and agroindustry. In addition, in the financial sector, the public sector continues to be the major shareholder of India's largest banks, insurance companies, and contractual savings institutions raising questions on how truly autonomous these institutions can be. Finally, the development of India's human resources has been slow in comparison with countries in East Asia or Eastern Europe.

MACROECONOMIC DEVELOPMENTS

An Unexpectedly Strong Recovery

The economic recovery has been unexpectedly rapid and robust. Initially, growth declined sharply in response to the devaluation and contractionary fiscal and monetary policies adopted in June 1991 to address the foreign exchange crisis India was then facing. From over 5 percent in 1990-91, GDP growth declined to less than one percent in 1991-92. The recession was particularly severe and prolonged in manufacturing where negative growth rates persisted in the main sectors until 1993-94 (Table 1.1).

Table 1.1: Growth Performance, 1981-96 (percent)								
	1981-90	1990-91	1991-92	1992-93	1993-94	1994-95	1995-96[a]	1996-97[b]
GDP at Factor Cost	5.5	5.4	0.8	5.1	5.0	6.3	7.0	6.6
Agriculture	3.4	3.8	-2.3	6.1	3.3	4.9	2.4	2.3
Industry	6.9	7.2	-1.3	4.1	4.2	8.3	11.7	8.5
Mining & Quarrying	7.4	10.7	3.7	1.1	4.1	4.3	5.0	--
Manufacturing	7.2	6.1	-3.7	4.1	4.3	9.0	12.2	--
Registered	8.0	5.0	-2.3	3.0	4.3	8.1	--	--
Unregistered	6.1	7.9	-6.0	6.0	4.3	10.4	--	--
Electricity, Gas, & Water	8.9	6.5	9.6	8.3	7.3	8.0	--	--
Construction	4.4	11.6	2.2	3.3	2.3	7.1	--	--
Services	6.6	5.2	4.9	5.1	6.8	6.0	7.0	8.1
-- Not available.								
a. Quick estimates.								
b. Advanced estimates.								
Source: CSO, National Accounts Statistics, 1996.								

Helped by reforms, a relaxation in fiscal policies and an unprecedented sequence of good monsoons, growth accelerated to 5 percent in 1992-94, 6 percent in 1994-95 and 7 percent in 1995-96. The industrial recovery has been especially strong, particularly for capital goods (Table 1.2) which had experienced negative growth for three successive years. India has a capital goods industry which is unusually large for a country with a US$350 per capita income, and the severe recession it faced was an important motivation for the less stringent fiscal policies adopted in 1993-94 and 1994-95.

Table 1.2: Index of Industrial Production, 1981-95 (annual percent increase)								
	Weight	1981-91	1990-91	1991-92	1992-93	1993-94	1994-95	1995-96[a]
Overall Index	100.0	7.8	8.2	0.6	2.3	6.0	9.3	12.4
Basic Goods	39.4	7.5	3.8	6.2	2.6	9.4	5.3	9.0
Capital Goods	16.4	11.5	17.4	-12.8	-0.1	-4.1	24.9	20.4
Intermediates	20.5	6.2	6.1	-0.7	5.3	11.7	3.7	10.3
Consumer Goods	23.6	6.7	10.4	-1.8	1.9	4.0	8.7	12.9
Durables	2.6	13.0	14.8	-12.5	-0.7	16.1	10.2	38.0
Non-Durables	21.0	5.7	9.4	1.2	2.5	1.3	8.4	6.6
a. April-February.								
Source: CSO.								

Because it has been driven by exports, domestic and foreign private investment, and domestic savings are increasing, the economic recovery is not putting pressure on inflation or the external accounts. India's growth performance over 1991-96 is much better than that of other countries, which underwent stabilization and structural transformation. A time-series analysis (IMF, 1995) of potential GDP and output gaps further indicates that the 1991-93 recession was considerably milder than previous recessions.

Growth is being accompanied with productivity improvements. One of the main objectives of India's reform program was to make the industrial sector more efficient and increase its export orientation by dismantling bureaucratic controls over investment and production decisions, giving a greater role to entrepreneurial decision-making, and increasing competition. The available evidence suggests that these objectives are being reached. Industrial growth is being driven by positive structural changes and improvements in productivity, particularly in the industrial sector where there is a sense of a "mini-industrial revolution".

In particular, in response to the increase in competition both from domestic firms and from multinationals, *corporations are restructuring.* Corporate attitudes and cultures are changing, domestic companies are remodeling their operations to become niche players, manufacturing partners, or strategic allies--with a view to strengthening their competitiveness. Reports on individual companies in the organized sector and surveys of firms in the organized and unorganized sectors carried out for this report indicate that restructuring is taking place along several lines. *First,* some firms are consolidating around core competencies and selling off units unrelated to their core activities. *Second,* mergers and acquisitions continue to increase in an effort to expand capacity quickly and consolidate market share. *Third,* a number of companies have entered into strategic partnerships, mostly with foreign companies, to acquire new technologies, management techniques, and access to outside markets. *Fourth,* taking advantage of the liberalization of financial markets and increased access to international capital markets, firms are reducing interest costs by retiring high-cost domestic debt. *Fifth,* family-owned and managed companies are changing their organizational structure and professionalizing their management. *Finally,* some companies are strengthening management and reducing excess labor through training programs and voluntary retirement schemes.

As a result, there are clear indications of important *efficiency gains. First,* in response to the reduction in the anti-export bias implicit in India's pre-1991 trade and exchange rate regime, *export and import intensity have increased since 1991 in most sectors* (Table 1.3). Easier access to imported capital and intermediate goods has been particularly important for this evolution, especially for newly emerging agro-based industries such as floriculture, aquaculture, and horticulture.

Table 1.3: Change in Trade Orientation, Profitability, and Productivity since 1991 Compared to the pre-1991 Period				
	Return to Fixed Capital	Return to Risk Capital	Productivity	Export Intensity	Import Intensity
Basic Materials	↓	↓	↔	↑	↑
Capital Goods	↔	↓	↑	↑	↑
Consumer Cyclicals	↔	↓	↔	↔	↑
Consumer Staples	↑	↔	↔	↑	↔
Technology	↔	↔	↓	↑	↑

Note: ↑ increase; ↓ decrease; ↔ no change
Source: NCAER, "Impact of Economic Reforms on Large, Medium and Small Scale Industries in the Organized and Unorganized Sector". These results are based on a survey of over 1,000 large

Second, declining mark-ups in most sectors (Table 1.4) suggests that productivity has increased--even after taking into account the influence of cyclical factors on mark-ups. One exception is transport equipment, a sector where import restrictions (particularly on automobiles) remain severe and domestic demand has grown rapidly in the recent past. However, the many new recent entries in this sector are expected to bring new technologies, increase productivity, expand capacity, strengthen competition--and thus offset the impact of cyclical factors on markups. *Third,* for the past two years, *corporate profits have been at record levels.* Results for

Table 1.4: Change in Profitability and Productivity since 1991 Compared to the pre-1991 Period		
	Price-Cost Ratio	Productivity
Electrical Machinery	↓*	↑
Non-Electrical Machinery	↓	↑
Electronics	↓*	↑*
Transport equipment	↑*	↑*
Textiles	↓*	↓*
Chemicals	↓*	↓*

Note: The sign (↓) indicates a decline and (↑) an increase. (*) indicates that the estimated change is statistically significant at 5% level. *Source:* P. Balakrishnan, "Economic Reforms, Competition and Productivity Growth in India: A Panel Study of Manufacturing Firms", April 1996. The study covers over 1,000 large companies.

1569 non-financial companies for the financial year 1995-96 indicate that gross margins increased to 16.3 percent, up from 15.8 percent for 1994-95 (CMIE, June 1996). The largest improvements in gross profit margins have been experienced in such industries as cement and allied products, alunimum, glass and mineral products, hotel and transport services. There also is some evidence, however, that the increase in profits cannot be attributed to productivity gains alone. Access to finance may have played some role. In particular, firms with no access to international finance seem to report lower profits than those that could avoid high domestic interest costs. **Fourth**, there also is some evidence of *improvements in quality*. Quality improvements are obviously hard to measure. However, the cumulative number of Indian companies seeking and receiving ISO 9000 certification in recent years has risen from 8 in January 1993 to around 1,200 by May 1996 and survey results indicate that large firms are more concerned about the quality of their products now than they were prior to 1991.

The results of surveys of large, medium and small enterprises in the organized and unorganized sectors conducted for this report indicate that the business community is generally supportive of the reforms implemented thus far. In particular, the surveys suggest that: (a) businesses favor the new liberalized environment despite the stiffer competition, only few are skeptical of the benefits; (b) export-oriented businesses are upbeat, they see greater potential for business expansion provided the government adopts a more consistent hands-off policy and concentrates on relieving infrastructure bottlenecks; (c) business complains of still cumbersome administrative procedures for tax returns, duty drawbacks, and other transactions with the public administration; (d) except for import-competing industries, there is a strong desire for faster trade liberalization and tariff reductions especially on raw materials, intermediates and capital goods; and (e) a large number of respondents indicated that the current power charges are too high in view of the quality of service, and expressed their willingness to pay higher rates in return for more reliable power. In general, businessmen were impatient at the slow pace at which administrative and legal reforms are proceeding.

Although the reform program did not contain initially an explicit agricultural component, it created a number of favorable conditions for the sector. The stabilization and economy-wide reforms provided an environment favorable to agricultural growth as early as 1992-93 through two channels: (a) the rapid and broad-based economic recovery led to rising domestic incomes which, combined with the improved international competitiveness of primary and processed agricultural commodities (e.g., cotton textiles, oilseed meals, horticultural crops, fish products, leather goods), provided most of the needed impetus to sustain demand for a rapidly increasing supply; and (b) the virtual elimination of the bias against agriculture caused by economy-wide policies. By 1994-95, the devaluation of the rupee and the more open trade regime in manufacturing eliminated the economy-wide discrimination against agriculture which along with the successive years of good monsoons translated into an acceleration of growth from negative 2.3 percent in 1991-92 to 4.9 percent in 1994-95. The performance of the agricultural sector is discussed in detail in Chapter 4.

The recovery of private investment is being financed mostly by foreign direct investors and domestic savings. As indicated in Table 1.5, foreign direct investment (FDI) has doubled every year since 1991-92. In addition, FDI approvals in 1995-96 increased to US$10 billion. Assuming an average 3-4 years project implementation period, this suggests that actual flows of FDI could reach US$10 billion by the end of the decade. This would still be much less than the about US$30-40 billion of FDI seen in China in recent years. That said, the response of FDI to India's liberalization is similar to what was seen in China five years into the latter's liberalization process.

Table 1.5: Foreign Direct and Portfolio Investment (US$ million)						
	1990-91	1991-92	1992-93	1993-94	1994-95	1995-96 [p]
Direct Investment						
Foreign Direct Investment	165	150	341	620	1314	1981
Portfolio Investment	0	8	92	3493	3581	2096
Foreign Institutional Investment	0	0	1	1665	1503	1892
Euro-issues/ GDR	0	0	86	1463	1839	204
Others [a]	0	8	5	365	239	--
Total Direct and Portfolio Investment	165	158	433	4113	4895	4077
Memorandum item:						
Foreign Currency Convertible Bonds FCCB) [b]	0	0	0	914	34	--
Floating Rate Notes (FRN)	0	0	0	0	167	--

Note: p = provisional.
a. Includes NRI portfolio investments, offshore funds, and others.
b. FCCBs are treated as commercial borrowing before conversion into equity.
Source: Reserve Bank of India; Ministry of Finance, Economic Survey 1995-96.

Domestic savings are recovering in spite of the weak performance of public savings. After declining to 21 percent of GDP in 1992-93 and 1993-94, domestic savings increased to 24 percent of GDP in 1994-95 (CSO's quick estimates). Helped by the liberalization of the financial sector which increased the availability and attractiveness of financial instruments, households' financial savings increased from 8.7 percent of GDP in 1990-91 to 11.1 percent in 1994-95. Similarly, the rise in corporate profitability led corporate savings to rise from 2.8 percent of GDP in 1990-91 to 3.8 percent in 1994-95. However, as a result of the slow progress in fiscal adjustment, the public sector savings performance (the excess of central and state government revenues over current expenditure plus gross profits of public enterprises) continued its 1980s deteriorating trend before recovering marginally for the first time in 1994-95. After falling to a half of one-percent of GDP in 1993-94, public saving recovered to 1.7 percent of GDP in 1994-95, but is still well below levels reached in the 1970s and 1980s (Table 1.6).

The recovery in private savings laid to rest an intense debate in India on the significance and reasons for the fall in the rate of households savings, physical savings in particular, seen after 1991-92. Three reasons were offered. Some blamed it on the financial liberalization which prompted an increase in the availability of consumer credit, allowing formerly credit-constrained individuals to borrow against future income and therefore consume more and save less. Others attributed it to a contraction of household-based manufacturing investment as a result of the stabilization-cum-adjustment program. Finally, others attributed it to measurement errors because the methodology to measure saving and investment in India is generally regarded as unsatisfactory.

Table 1.6: Domestic Demand, 1981-95 (percent of GDP at market prices)											
	1981-91[a]		1990-91		1991-92		1992-93		1993-94		1994-95	
Total Consumption Expenditure	78.3	(4.8)	73.6	(3.7)	73.7	(1.4)	72.9	(3.9)	72.8	(4.5)	70.7	(4.2)
Government final consumption	11.1	(7.2)	11.5	(3.3)	11.3	(-0.5)	11.1	(3.3)	11.2	(6.1)	10.7	(3.0)
Private final consumption	67.2	(4.5)	62.1	(3.8)	62.4	(1.8)	61.7	(4.0)	61.6	(4.2)	60.0	(4.3)
Gross Capital Formation	23.2	(5.9)	25.2	(12.2)	22.7	(-11.0)	24.0	(12.3)	21.3	(-5.8)	23.2	(19.8)
Gross Fixed Capital Formation	21.1	(6.8)	23.2	(9.9)	22.1	(-4.0)	22.5	(6.9)	21.5	(3.4)	22.5	(14.8)
Public Sector	10.0	(4.3)	9.4	(4.8)	9.5	(2.0)	8.5	(-7.2)	8.4	(6.5)	8.7	(14.0)
Private Corporate Sector	3.8	(7.7)	3.9	(24.2)	5.7	(47.3)	6.0	(9.4)	6.9	(27.7)	6.9	(7.3)
Household Sector	7.2	(9.3)	9.9	(9.1)	6.9	(-35.2)	8.0	(26.5)	6.2	(-23.8)	7.0	(28.3)
Change in Stocks	2.1		2.1		0.6		1.5		-0.2		0.6	
Domestic Demand	101.5	(5.1)	98.8	(5.7)	96.4	(-1.5)	96.9	(5.7)	94.2	(2.1)	93.9	(7.5)
Memo Items:												
Gross Domestic Savings	20.5		23.6		22.8		21.2		21.4		24.4	
Public Savings	2.7		1.0		1.9		1.5		0.5		1.7	
Household Financial	7.6		8.7		10.1		8.4		10.8		11.1	
Private Corporate Sector	2.1		2.8		3.2		2.8		3.5		3.8	

Note: Real growth rate in parentheses.
a. Average of 1981-82 through 1991-92.
Source: Central Statistical Organization, National Accounts Statistics 1996.

Two other explanations are however more plausible. First, increases in savings in gold could have led to the decline in measured household savings because accumulation of gold is counted as consumption in the National Accounts. Demand for gold increased sharply from 260 tons in 1991 to 454 tons in 1992, the year in which gold imports were liberalized, amounting to about 0.8 percentage points of GDP. Given that the biggest jump in the demand for gold occurred in the first quarter of 1992, an asset portfolio shift in favor of gold may explain in part the decline in household savings in 1991-92 and to a large extent the further decline in 1992-93. This decrease and the subsequent rise in savings in 1993-94 and 1994-95 may thus be linked to the temporary character of portfolio stock adjustment following liberalization. *Second,* the slowdown of economic growth in 1991-92 and ensuing households' attempts at stabilizing consumption likely explain most of the decline in the domestic savings rates. In cases when a large share of the population does not have access to credit facilities, as in India, this reduction would be reflected in total household savings.

In addition, the fall in household physical saving can have positive effects on resource allocation. While the shift from physical towards financial savings experienced after 1991 has been another subject of concern, this is in fact a positive development. It suggests that households' financial savings were previously constrained by the absence of financial instruments suited to their needs. And, because the range of investment opportunities offered by financial intermediation is so much greater than that offered by physical assets, the increase in the share of savings kept in the form of financial instruments is likely to lead to better allocation of investment and thus improved growth performance. But the consistent fall in the public saving rate over the last decade continues to be a major concern.

Inflation Declined but Monetary Management Became More Complex

Prior to 1993-94, monetary policy, while not entirely subservient to fiscal policy, was nevertheless closely tied to it. There was no limit on government borrowing through the RBI and the interest rate on its borrowing was significantly lower than market rates. With a closed capital account, the RBI counteracted the effect of government borrowing on broad money growth through relatively high cash reserve requirements (CRR) and extremely high Statutory Liquidity Ratios (SLR).

This situation changed in 1993-94. *First*, the financial sector reforms reduced the Central Government pre-emption of bank assets and allowed banks greater, albeit still limited, freedom in their portfolio management and interest rate policies. *Second*, foreign investment was liberalized, both direct and portfolio through several measures taken over 1991-93. As a result, foreign investment increased from US$0.6 billion in 1992-93 to US$4.1 billion in 1993-94--with a sharp acceleration towards the end of 1993--and contributed to a large surplus in the capital account. While these inflows were a significant "vote of confidence" in India's macroeconomic policies and growth prospects, they posed complex macroeconomic management issues to the RBI at a time when the fiscal deficit was still high. Initially, RBI chose not to sterilize the capital inflows, and reserve and broad money grew in excess of 20 percent in 1993-94 and 1994-95 (Table 1.7) in spite of some corrective measures taken in early 1994. This led to an increase in inflation to 11-12 percent (after it had declined to below 8 percent), and a real effective exchange rate appreciation of close to 4 percent (Table 1.8).

The steps taken in early 1994 consisted of a pragmatic mixture of measures aimed at discouraging certain categories of inflows (particularly those that are easily reversible, or more expensive to service) and relieving supply pressures. *First*, following a procedure established at the time of the last IMF Stand-By (November 1992-May 1994), the authorities continued to set annual limits for *external commercial borrowing*. *Second*, because a large part of the inflows originated from Indian firms raising funds abroad, new guidelines in May and October 1994, established (i) a maximum of one (two) issue(s) per year per company (group of companies); (ii) required that money raised abroad be for already identified physical investment projects; and (iii) stipulated that these funds not be brought into the country until a clear use for them existed. *Third*, Non-Resident Indian (NRI) deposits were discouraged both to contain growth in commercial banks' liquidity base and reduce a volatile component of India's external debt. The measures included: imposition of CRR on NRI accounts, a reduction in the maximum interest rates payable on such accounts, and a phasing out of new flows into the Foreign Currency Non-Resident (FCNRA) Scheme under which the RBI bears the exchange rate risk.

Table 1.7: Selected Monetary Indicators, 1990-96
(Rupees billion)

Money aggregate	Stocks (End-March of each year)											
	1990-91		1991-92		1992-93		1993-94		1994-95		1995-96p	
Sources of Reserve Money	878	(100)	995	(100)	1108	(100)	1387	(100)	1693	(100)	1943	(100)
Net RBI credit to Government	888	(149)	940	(44)	984	(39)	993	(3)	1015	(7)	1270	(102)
Net foreign exchange assets (RBI)	80	(19)	188	(93)	226	(34)	514	(103)	747	(76)	741	(-3)
Other assets (net)	-91	(-68)	-133	(-37)	-103	(27)	-121	(-6)	-69	(17)	-67	(1)
Sources of Broad Money	2658	(100)	3170	(100)	3668	(100)	4344	(100)	5308	(100)	6005	(100)
Net bank credit to Government	1402	(66)	1583	(35)	1762	(36)	2039	(41)	2224	(19)	2627	(55)
Credit to commercial sector	1718	(58)	1880	(32)	2201	(65)	2378	(26)	2897	(54)	3386	(67)
Net foreign exchange assets	106	(11)	212	(21)	244	(6)	526	(42)	759	(24)	754	(-1)
Other assets (net)	-567	(-35)	-504	(12)	-540	(-7)	-599	(-9)	-572	(3)	-728	(-21)
Memo Items:												
M3/ Base Money	3.0		3.2		3.3		3.1		3.1		3.1	
M3/ GDP	0.6		0.6		0.6		0.6		0.6		0.6	
Growth rates												
Reserve money	13.1		13.4		11.3		25.2		22.1		14.8	
M3	15.1		19.3		15.7		18.4		22.2		13.8	
Nominal GDP (factor cost)	17.8		15.7		14.0		14.7		18.1		15.6	

-- Not available.
Note: The flow as a percentage of the change in base money or the change in broad money stock is in parentheses. Increases in foreign assets following a devaluation are offset by declines in other assets.
Source: RBI.

Table 1.8: Real Exchange Rate of India's Main Trading Partners and Competitors 1981-96 [a]
(end of period)

	Export Share	1981	1989	1990	1991	1992	1993	1994	1995	1995 I	1996 I
India											
in US$		0.93	1.05	1.00	1.26	1.17	1.28	1.17	1.21	1.14	1.19
in SDR		0.76	0.98	1.00	1.27	1.13	1.24	1.20	1.28	1.25	1.22
REER [b]		0.56	0.91	1.00	1.28	1.29	1.29	1.28	1.40	1.35	1.36
India's Main Market											
USA	20.0	1.20	1.05	1.00	1.02	1.01	1.00	0.97	0.95	0.96	0.94
Japan	12.2	1.47	1.10	1.00	0.98	0.97	0.88	0.82	0.83	0.74	0.86
Germany	8.0	1.69	1.18	1.00	1.03	1.03	1.12	1.01	0.91	0.90	0.95
United Kingdom	7.2	1.56	1.29	1.00	1.02	1.16	1.16	1.07	1.04	1.03	1.04
Belgium [c]	5.4	1.75	1.23	1.00	1.02	1.00	1.07	0.95	0.86	0.85	0.87
France [c]	2.8	1.75	1.21	1.00	1.03	1.01	1.08	0.98	0.88	0.90	0.89
Netherlands	2.4	1.64	1.18	1.00	1.01	1.00	1.08	0.99	0.90	0.88	0.91
India's Main Competitors											
Indonesia		0.81	1.11	1.00	1.06	1.06	1.06	1.00	0.95	0.97	0.94
Malaysia [c]		1.03	1.03	1.00	0.97	0.87	0.84	0.80	0.76	0.78	0.76
Philippines [c]		0.99	0.93	1.00	0.84	0.74	0.75	0.61	0.59	0.64	0.58
Thailand		1.16	1.10	1.00	0.99	1.00	0.98	0.92	0.85	0.88	--
Korea		1.12	1.01	1.00	1.04	1.06	1.07	1.01	0.95	0.97	0.95
Singapore		1.06	1.15	1.00	1.08	1.10	1.10	1.00	0.96	0.97	1.03
Hong Kong [c]		1.39	1.11	1.00	0.91	0.82	0.76	0.69	0.64	0.68	0.63

-- Not available.
Note: Increase = depreciation.
a. Index of a country's nominal exchange rate vis-a-vis the US$ divided by this country's wholesale price index or, if not available, the consumer price index.
b. Real Effective Exchange Rate, based on the IMF's Information Notice System (INS) methodology Trade weights are based on trade flows averaged over 1980-82.
c. Uses CPI.
Source: IMF, International Finance Statistics; World Bank Staff estimates.

In addition, the authorities increased the CRR and postponed the planned reduction of SLR. Steps were also taken to develop the government securities market to allow it to use open market operations to manage monetary policy more effectively. Finally, in September 1994, the RBI and the Treasury signed an agreement to limit and then phase out by 1997 the automatic monetization of the Treasury's cash deficits. The agreement established a ceiling on the Treasury's credit line at the RBI of not more than Rs. 90 billion for any ten consecutive days and Rs. 60 million for the year as a whole. The government was to meet the balance of its borrowing requirements by issuing securities directly in the market. These measures aimed at monetary tightening and insulating monetary policy from deficit financing were complemented with measures to reduce supply pressures. These included: (i) relaxation of import restrictions on goods that were in short supply (sugar, pulses, cotton and all major edible oils); (ii) continuation of FCI's open market sales of rice and wheat to dampen prices; and (iii) relaxation of import restrictions on some manufactured consumer goods and reduction in customs and excise duties.

These measures, helped by increases in US interest rates and the pull back of private flows from most emerging markets following the Mexican crisis, allowed the RBI to tighten its monetary stance, and hold broad money supply growth (M3) within the 15.5 percent target announced in its April 1995 Credit Policy, and inflation to decline in recent months to below 5 percent. *In the absence of a strong fiscal correction this has been, however, at the cost of extremely high real interest rates, which are a threat to the sustainability of current growth and the soundness of the banking system.* Further, the lower inflation rate is also due to the maintenance of unrealistically low administered prices for some food items and some petroleum products such as kerosene and diesel.

The industrial recovery started in 1994-95 was helped by a monetary policy which reduced interest rates, easy access to domestic and foreign capital markets and a stable rupee which did not require importers and banks to cover their positions. Banks also increased their lending and invested voluntarily in government securities to meet their prudential requirements and also because returns on these "risk" free securities were high in comparison with returns on other assets. However, since the last quarter of 1994-95, firms' sources of funds have been reduced to bank credit and retained earnings because of the depressed domestic stock market and the reduced access to foreign markets (itself partly the result of the measures to curb capital inflows). As a result, demand for commercial-bank credit surged sharply making macroeconomic management more difficult.

The tight monetary stance and investment recovery led to some problems in exchange rate management. The surge in imports led by the industrial recovery put strong pressures on the rupee and, after 30 months of a quasi-fixed exchange rate, triggered some nervousness in the foreign exchange market and speculation. Importers advanced their purchases, hence increasing their demand for foreign exchange and for credit. Exporters began delaying surrender of foreign exchange, and maintained their outstanding financing positions in order to do so. Pressures on domestic liquidity caused call money rates to reach at times highs of 38 percent during November 1995. These developments were further complicated as companies and commercial banks with foreign-exchange exposures arising from their NRI deposits used the forward market to cover exchange-rate exposure. The forward premium rose, and soon exceeded bank deposit rates. For enterprises able to do so, it became profitable to withdraw deposits, purchase spot foreign exchange and sell foreign exchange forward. While this may have reduced some of the pressure on the forward premium, it diminished deposit growth and intensified the pressure on the spot dollar rate. In addition, RBI's attempt to defend the rupee by withdrawing liquidity out of the system helped reinforce an already acute credit rationing situation.

The absence of a secondary market for government securities meant that it was difficult for banks to sell their excess holdings of government securities. The banks limited their purchases of new government securities forcing the RBI to increasingly substitute for the market to fund the government. In 1995-96, central bank financing in the form of ad hoc T-bills, rose to 1.7 percent of GDP up from 0.2 percent of GDP the previous year, often exceeding the allowed ceiling of Rs. 90 billion over ten consecutive days under the September 1994 RBI-Treasury Agreement.

The authorities took several steps toward the end of 1995 to restore equilibrium in the call and foreign exchange markets. The RBI injected funds into the call market through reserve and refinance facilities to banks against their holdings of government and other approved securities. The ceiling interest rate on new NRI rupee accounts was raised, and the CRR applicable to various classes of NRI deposits were progressively reduced or removed. A particularly important step was a tightening of the foreign-exchange surrender requirements for exporters, with a sharp increase in the interest rate on export financing past 90 days. Equally important was the dramatic increase in foreign inflows during the last quarter of 1995-96, on account of portfolio flows as well as the normal bunching of aid inflows in the last quarter of the fiscal year. The partly unexpected foreign inflows as well as the strict RBI action stabilized the rupee-dollar exchange rate at a level that corrected for the previous appreciation, and brought down the call money rate to 12.6 percent at end March 1996.

With inflation under control, the RBI announced in its April 1996 Credit Policy a set of measures to ease the "liquidity crunch" and also to deepen the money and foreign exchange markets. The main measures are: (i) a further reduction in the CRR from 14 to 13 percent (and more recently 12 percent); (ii) further reductions of CRR applicable to selected NRI deposits, together with increases in the maximum allowable interest rates; (iii) a reduction of SLR on NRI deposits from 30 percent to 25 percent; (iv) a change in the formula for export credit refinance intended to reduce commercial banks' standing entitlement to this facility; and (vi) a reduction in the share of new bank credit business could receive under the "cash credit" modality, from the current 60 percent of "maximum permissible bank finance" to 40 percent; the remainder would have to come in the form of term lending. In addition, in July 1996, the RBI allowed mutual funds and corporates to operate in money markets.

On the whole, the RBI's tight monetary stance offset the impact of the monetization of the deficit on inflation. It has nuanced its policy, however. Its intervention has prevented interest rates from rising further in the short-run and seriously affecting the recovery of investment and growth of the last two years. However, developments over 1995-96 show the effects of an unbalanced mix between monetary and fiscal policy that cannot be sustained over the long-term. The danger of excessively relying on monetary policy to control inflation in the

Table 1.9: Balance of Payments, 1991-96 (US$ billion)						
	Actuals					Estim.
	90-91	91-92	92-93	93-94	94-95	95-96[a]
Total exports of GNFS	23.0	23.3	23.6	28.9	34.1	40.9
Merchandise (FOB)	18.5	18.3	18.9	22.7	26.9	32.4
Non-factor services	4.6	5.0	4.7	6.2	7.3	8.4
Total imports of GNFS	31.5	24.9	26.8	29.4	39.5	47.9
Merchandise (CIF)	27.9	21.1	23.2	24.0	31.7	39.4
Non-factor services	3.6	3.8	3.6	5.4	7.8	8.5
Resource balance	-8.5	-1.6	-3.2	-0.5	-5.3	-7.1
Net factor income	-3.8	-3.8	-3.4	-4.0	-3.9	-4.5
Factor receipts	1.1	0.8	0.7	0.3	1.3	1.3
Factor payments	4.9	4.6	4.2	4.3	5.2	5.8
Interest (scheduled)[b]	4.8	4.5	4.0	4.1	4.5	4.7
of which interest payments on NRI	1.3	1.0	0.9	0.9	1.0	1.4
Other factor payments[c]	0.1	0.1	0.1	0.1	0.6	1.1
Net private current transfers	2.1	3.8	2.8	3.8	6.2	6.2
Current receipts	2.1	3.8	2.8	3.9	6.2	6.2
of which workers remittances	1.9	3.4	2.5	3.1	5.0	4.9
Current payments	0.0	0.0	0.0	0.0	0.0	0.0
Current account balance	-10.1	-1.6	-3.9	-0.7	-3.0	-5.4
Official capital grants	0.5	0.5	0.4	0.4	0.4	0.3
Foreign investments	0.2	0.2	0.6	4.1	4.9	4.1
Direct foreign investments	0.2	0.2	0.3	0.6	1.3	2.0
Portfolio investments	0.0	0.0	0.2	3.5	3.6	2.1
Net long-term borrowing	2.7	4.3	1.6	1.7	0.3	0.2
Disbursements (net of NRI)	5.1	6.9	4.6	5.9	5.1	5.2
Repayments (scheduled)[b]	2.4	2.6	2.9	4.2	4.8	5.0
Other long-term inflows (net)[d]	1.5	0.3	2.0	0.9	0.8	1.4
Other capital flows	2.5	-1.0	-1.0	2.1	3.5	-2.5
Net short-term capital	1.0	-1.5	-0.7	-2.7	1.5	0.5
Capital flows n.e.i.[e]	-1.2	-1.2	-0.9	-0.7	-1.1	-1.0
Errors and omissions	2.7	1.7	0.6	5.5	3.0	-2.0
Changes in net international reserves[f]	2.8	-2.6	0.3	-8.5	-6.9	1.9
IMF (net)	1.0	0.8	1.3	0.2	-1.2	-1.8
Change in Gross Reserves	1.8	-3.4	-1.0	-8.7	-5.7	3.7
Memorandum items:						
Current Account Balance / GDP	-3.4	-0.7	-1.6	-0.3	-1.0	-1.7
Gross Foreign Exchange Reserves	2.3	5.7	6.7	15.5	21.2	17.4
in months of imports (goods)	1.0	3.3	3.5	7.7	8.0	5.3
External Debt (percent of GDP)	27.5	33.4	36.9	36.1	32.9	30.2
Debt Service (% of total current receipts)	30.1	27.0	27.0	25.6	25.3	23.8

a. Preliminary estimate based on Economic Survey, 1995-96 update.
b. Although World Bank and Government of India sources show similar historic total debt service data, discrepancies exist in the sahre of interest and amortization. These discrepancies are under review.
c. Includes interest on military debt to the FSU and returns on foreign investments.
d. Net flows in NRI deposit schemes, except the non-repatriable NR(NR)D Scheme.
e. Servicing of the Russia debt.
f. (-) = indicates increase in assets.
Source: Government of India; RBI; Ministry of Commerce; World Bank Staff estimates.

face of a lax fiscal policy was clearly demonstrated by the events since August 1995: real interest rates will increase, negatively affecting private investment and with it the foundations for sustainable medium-term growth. *Again, unless there is serious fiscal adjustment, developments over 1995-96 could be the early signs of underlying short-run demand management tensions, which could threaten the gains achieved over the past 5 years in stabilizing the economy.*

The External Accounts Improved Significantly

In response to a sharp depreciation of the real exchange rate and reduction of import tariffs, and thus of the anti-export bias implicit in the previous trade regime, exports grew at rates in excess of 20 percent for the past three years, and prospects for 1996-97 are equally encouraging. Agricultural exports grew at almost the same rate as manufactured exports following the relaxation of restrictions on exports of agricultural commodities and favorable external markets conditions. After falling dramatically in 1991-92 (a year when strict rationing was imposed to cope with the foreign exchange crisis), and as the domestic recovery and corporate restructuring gained momentum, imports grew by 8 percent in 1992-93, 10 percent in 1993-94, and slightly over 20 percent in 1995-96, a rate that is expected to decline slightly in 1996-97. Regarding the invisibles accounts, software exports continued to grow at 25 percent a year and workers' remittances surged following the liberalization of the exchange rate and payments regime (which reduced the parallel market premium to 2 percent in 1994). Accordingly, the current account deficit declined from 3.5 percent of GDP in 1990-91 to less than 1 percent of GDP in 1994-95 and 1.6 percent of GDP for 1995-96--a very manageable level.

Improvements in the capital account have been significant. At US$2-3 billion in 1994-96, foreign direct investment is about 15 times higher than it was before the economy was liberalized and portfolio investment has stabilized at around US$2-3 billion. The liberalization measures, well-known corporate names with established track records; reasonably well developed stock markets; familiar accounting and legal systems; and the potential for growth in a large market with inexpensive labor have made India a destination favored by foreign investors. India now absorbs 10 percent of the world portfolio investment in emerging markets, a share in line with that of China and Indonesia. These positive developments in the external accounts translated into comfortable levels of foreign exchange reserves--US$17 billion at present, that is five months of imports. They also led the debt service ratio to decline from 30 percent of current account receipts in 1990-91 to 24 percent in 1995-96 (Table 1.9).

Fiscal Adjustment is One Area of Serious Concern

With the exception of the first year of the stabilization and reform program, when its deficit was reduced from 8.3 percent of GDP (with a primary deficit of 4.3 percent of GDP) in 1990-91 to 6.1 percent in 1991-92, the Central Government has relaxed its fiscal deficit targets. In 1995-96, at 5.9 percent of GDP (with a primary deficit of 1.1 percent of GDP), the fiscal deficit was barely 2 percent of GDP below the fiscal deficit in 1991-92. Several factors explain these developments.

First, some of the structural reforms have had a relatively high fiscal cost. For example, the reduction of tariffs on imports and the rationalization of excises came at a cost which in some years exceeded 1 percent of GDP in foregone tax revenues. The liberalization of financial markets meant higher interest costs on public debt--interest payments on the Central Government debt are close to 1 percent of GDP higher than they were five years ago even though its total debt remained relatively constant in relation to GDP. For instance, real interest rates on 91-day T-Bills rose from negative 8 percent in 1991-92 to over 6 percent in 1995-96 (Table 1.11).

Table 1.10: Evolution of the Public Deficit, 1990-96 (percent of GDP)						
	1990-91	1991-92	1992-93	1993-94	1994-95	1995-96 [a]
1 Central Government						
Gross Deficit	8.3	6.1	5.7	7.5	6.3	5.9
Gross Primary Deficit [b]	4.3	1.8	1.3	2.9	1.7	1.1
Net Primary Deficit [c]	5.9	3.6	3.1	4.8	3.4	2.8
2 General Government						
Gross Deficit	10.4	8.0	7.2	8.8	7.9	8.1
Gross Primary Deficit [b]	5.7	2.9	2.0	3.4	2.3	2.4
Net Primary Deficit [c]	6.8	4.4	3.2	4.6	3.3	3.3
3 Consolidated Non-financial Public Sector						
Gross Deficit	12.3	9.7	8.8	11.0	9.6	9.6
Primary Deficit	6.6	3.6	2.4	4.5	3.1	3.1
Memo Item:						
RBI Financing to General Government (net)	2.8	0.8	0.6	0.1	0.2	1.7

a. 1995-96 is projected.
b. Gross deficit excluding gross interest payments.
c. Gross deficit excluding net interest payments
Source: Budget documents; RBI; IMF; and staff estimates.

Second, concern over the potential political and social repercussions led the government to keep costly subsidies and in some cases increase expenditure on anti-poverty programs (whose effectiveness in reaching the poor is in doubt). For instance, the fertilizer subsidy alone cost the budget over half of a percent of GDP per year.

Third, reform of public enterprises has stalled. Contrary to the fiscal adjustment experience of other countries, India's fiscal adjustment process did not benefit from the proceeds of privatization nor from the dividends that a better public enterprise sector could have generated. The Central Government remains majority shareholder, and in some cases the sole shareholder, of 240 enterprises, about 27 banks, and two large insurance companies. While some of these enterprises are highly profitable, most generate profits and dividends insufficient to compensate the government for the cost of funds invested in them. In general, losses of poor performing enterprises have not declined, while profits of profit making enterprises have increased only marginally. Initially, the government planned to eliminate public enterprise budget support, protection and monopoly privileges--so that public enterprises would operate on a commercial basis as well as reduce gradually its equity holdings through sales of shares. This plan, however, has been only very partially implemented. At less than US$3 billion, proceeds from privatization have been well below what would have been potentially possible--and would have permitted the government to retire an important share of its public debt.

Fourth, fiscal adjustment by the Central Government has been limited by the absence of corresponding adjustments by India's 25 states. One-fourth of Central Government spending (about 4 percent of GDP excluding about 3 percent of GDP of states' share of taxes collected by the center) is in the form of grants and loans to the states which the center has found it difficult to

Table 1.11: Key Interest Rates, 1990-96[a]							
	Call Money Rate (Mumbai)[b]	Treasury Bills[c]			Minimum[d] Lending Rate	Maximum[e] Deposit Rate	Certificates of Deposit[f]	Inflation[g]
		364-day	182-day	91-day				
1991-92								
June	24.8	--	10.0	4.6	17.0	12.0	12.0 - 16.8	12.2
September	12.8	--	10.0	4.6	18.5	13.0	11.5 - 16.0	15.9
December	12.7	--	10.0	4.6	20.0	13.0	12.5 - 17.6	14.3
March	14.3	--	9.3	4.6	19.0	13.0	12.0 - 17.0	13.6
1992-93								
June	15.8	11.4	--	4.6	19.0	13.0	12.3 - 25.0	12.3
September	11.4	11.3	--	4.6	19.0	13.0	13.0 - 20.0	10.2
December	11.2	11.2	--	4.6	18.0	12.0	12.3 - 17.5	8.4
March	13.9	11.1	--	11.0	17.0	11.0	12.5 - 16.5	7.0
1993-94								
June	8.0	11.4	--	10.1	16.0	11.0	11.0 - 16.5	7.1
September	5.0	11.2	--	8.4	15.0	10.0	8.0 - 15.0	8.8
December	5.3	11.0	--	7.8	15.0	10.0	7.0 - 15.0	8.8
March	4.3	10.0	--	7.5	14.0 - 15.0	10.0	7.0 - 12.2	10.5
1994-95								
June	6.7	10.0	--	8.8	14.0 - 15.0	10.0	7.5 - 12.0	11.8
September	15.3	9.4	--	9.1	14.0 - 15.0	10.0	7.5 - 12.0	8.9
December	9.7	9.8	--	10.3	Free[d]	10.0	8.0 - 12.0	11.2
March	13.7	11.9	--	12.0	Free[d]	11.0	10.0 - 15.0	10.2
1995-96								
June	14.4	12.6	--	12.6	Free[d]	12.0	11.0 - 14.5	9.2
September	12.1	12.9	--	12.7	Free[d]	12.0	10.0 - 14.8	8.9
December	16.8	13.0	--	13.0	Free[d]	12.0[e]	--	6.4
March	28.8	13.1	--	13.0	Free[d]	12.0[e]	--	5.1
1996-97								
June	11.1	13.0	--	12.4	Free[d]	12.0[e]	--	5.4
July	--	--	--	--	Free[d]	11.0[e]	--	--

-- Not available.

Note: March 1996 is preliminary.

a. Unless otherwise specified, interest rates/yields are those prevailing at the end of the month.

b. Call money rate of major commercial banks, average for the month.

c. Implicit yield at cut-off price (for the last auction in the month). 364-day Treasury Bills were introduced in April 1992, and are sold through periodic auctions. No fresh 182-day Treasury Bills were issued after April 16, 1992. Since January 1993, 91-day Treasury Bills are being periodically auctioned. Earlier they were sold on tap at 4.6%.

d. Since October 18, 1994, lending rates of scheduled commercial banks were freed for credit limits of over Rs 200,000; at 13.5 percent per annum for credit limits over Rs 25,000 and upto Rs 200,000; and at 12 percent per annum for credit limits upto and inclusive of Rs 25,000.

e. Refers to rate on term deposit. Up to April 1992 rates were fixed for different maturities. Since April 1992 only a maximum deposit rate is specified. Beginning October 1, 1995, the maximum rate of 12 percent refers only to deposits of less than two years. On July 1, 1996 the maximum deposit rate for deposits upto one year has been cut to 11 percent. The rate was freed for deposits above one year.

f. Effective interest rate (range) of CDs of all maturities, issued during the last fortnight of the month.

g. Wholesale price index, annual increase, point-to-point.

Source: RBI Monthly Bulletin, various issues; Report on Currency and Finance; Center for Monitoring Indian Economy (CMIE), Monthly Review of the Indian Economy, various issues.

curtail. As a result, over the last five years, the states' consolidated fiscal deficit has not declined--it has hovered around 3 percent of GDP. As discussed in last year's World Bank Economic Memorandum on India, there is evidence that the current system of transfers may be discouraging fiscal discipline because: (a) at least partly, "grants-in-aid" to the states are meant to cover their current deficits and thus create incentives for increasing them; (b) transfers in the form of loans and grants authorized by the Planning Commission (set up soon after Independence with a mandate rooted in India's pursuit of a centrally planned development strategy, it has

Table 1.12: Central Government Finances, 1990-97 (percentage of GDP)								
	90-91	91-92	92-93	93-94	94-95	95-96 BE	95-96 RE	96-97 BE
A. Revenue	10.3	10.7	10.5	9.6	9.6	9.7	10.1	10.5
Tax revenue	8.1	8.1	7.7	6.8	7.1	7.1	7.4	7.8
Corporation tax	1.0	1.3	1.3	1.3	1.5	1.5	1.5	1.6
Income tax	1.0	1.1	1.1	1.2	1.3	1.3	1.4	1.4
Excise duties	4.6	4.6	4.4	4.0	3.9	4.1	3.8	3.8
Customs	3.9	3.6	3.4	2.8	2.8	2.8	3.2	3.6
Other	0.3	0.4	0.5	0.3	0.2	0.2	0.2	0.3
Less: States' share	2.7	2.8	2.9	2.8	2.6	2.8	2.7	2.8
Non-tax Revenue	2.2	2.6	2.9	2.8	2.5	2.5	2.7	2.7
(Interest receipts)	1.6	1.8	1.8	1.9	1.7	1.8	1.7	1.7
B. Revenue expenditure[a]	13.8	13.4	13.2	13.8	12.9	13.1	13.1	13.0
Interest payments	4.0	4.3	4.4	4.7	4.7	5.0	4.8	4.8
Subsidies	2.3	2.0	1.7	1.6	1.4	1.2	1.3	1.3
Food	0.5	0.5	0.4	0.7	0.5	0.5	0.5	0.5
Fertilizer	0.8	0.8	0.9	0.6	0.6	0.5	0.6	0.7
Others	1.0	0.7	0.4	0.4	0.3	0.2	0.2	0.2
Defense	2.0	1.9	1.7	1.9	1.7	1.7	1.7	1.5
Grants to states	2.5	2.6	2.5	2.7	2.1	2.1	2.0	1.9
Wages and salaries[b]	2.0	1.9	1.8	1.9	1.8	1.6	1.7	1.6
Other	1.0	0.8	1.0	1.0	1.3	1.5	1.7	1.9
C. Capital expenditure	2.3	1.9	1.8	1.7	1.6	1.4	1.3	1.2
Defense	0.9	0.8	0.8	0.9	0.7	0.7	0.7	0.7
Economic Services	1.3	0.9	0.9	0.7	0.7	0.5	0.4	0.3
Others	0.2	0.1	0.1	0.1	0.1	0.2	0.2	0.2
D. Gross Loans	3.7	2.9	2.4	2.6	2.5	2.0	2.3	2.2
to states and UTs	2.6	2.0	1.7	1.8	2.0	1.6	1.8	1.8
to PEs[c]	0.7	0.6	0.4	0.6	0.5	0.4	0.4	0.4
Others	0.5	0.3	0.2	0.2	0.0	0.1	0.1	0.1
E. Repayment of loans	1.1	1.0	0.9	0.8	0.7	0.6	0.7	0.6
F. Net lending (D-E)	2.6	1.9	1.4	1.8	1.8	1.4	1.6	1.7
G. Disinvestment in PEs	0.0	0.5	0.3	0.0	0.6	0.7	0.1	0.4
Fiscal Deficit (A-B-C+F+G)	8.4	5.9	5.7	7.7	6.1	5.5	5.9	5.0
Memo Items					0.0			
Total Expenditure (B+C+D)	19.7	18.1	17.4	18.0	17.0	16.5	16.8	16.4
Total Expenditure (B+C+F)	18.7	17.1	16.4	17.3	16.3	15.8	16.1	15.9
Total Revenue (A+G)	10.3	11.2	10.8	9.6	10.2	10.3	10.2	10.9
Primary Deficit [d]	4.4	1.6	1.3	3.0	1.4	0.5	1.1	0.2
Non-interest spending[e]	15.7	13.8	13.0	13.4	12.3	11.5	12.0	11.6

Note: BE= budget estimates; RE=revised estimates.
a. Revenue expenditure is the budget terminology for current expenditure.
b. Revised Estimates (1990-91 to 1993-94).
c. Revised Estimates unless otherwise mentioned.
d. Fiscal deficit minus interest payments.
e. B+C+D-interest.
Source: Government of India, Budget documents.

become a de-facto development bank without the prudential financial standards that typically guide such banks) are not used for the intended productive purposes and thus increase the states' debt without increasing their capacity to service it; and (c) periodic Central Government loan forgiveness and refinancing, without conditionality, have created the expectation of future debt relief. In addition, the deterioration in the states' finances is being compounded by a decline in the quality of their spending. There is evidence of a *crisis of expenditure composition* whereby resources for the provision of key infrastructure and social services (roads, irrigation, primary education, health) for which the states have responsibility is being shrank to make room for less productive expenditure programs. In particular, there is evidence of growing budgetary support for loss-making state enterprises and massive subsidies for water, irrigation, and transport undertakings. Losses of the State Electricity Boards (SEBs) alone have amounted to about 1.5 percent of GDP in 1994-95.

Although several states are contemplating ambitious plans for fiscal and regulatory reform, implementation has been slow and inadequate. *On the revenue side*, the reform measures have concentrated on partial cost recovery programs in health and education; sales tax policy and administration simplification to enhance revenue; enhanced availability of central loan financing by stimulating growth in small savings (Punjab); and planned irrigation cost recovery projects (Orissa, Karnataka). *On the expenditure side*, reforms have been initiated in the areas of PSU restructuring with provisions for privatization (partial and complete), liquidation and reorganization under public control; state level "renewal funds" to facilitate privatization and liquidation; some zero based budgeting or expenditure program review mechanisms; formal policy statements on reform of SEB's including provision for private participation in power generation. Orissa is leading the way in this last area. Some states are also determined to liberalize their economy to improve their finances through growth. It is clear that unless the states improve their financial condition, the center will find it difficult to continue reducing its transfers to the states, which might compromise the center's efforts to reduce its

> **Box 1.2: Four Stylized Facts Seem to Emerge From the States as a Result of the Central Government Stabilization and Adjustment Program.**
>
> *First*, there are significant regional disparities. Western states seem to be in a better fiscal position and are growing faster while the eastern states are lagging behind on both counts; Maharashtra's growth and fiscal performance is short of outstanding.
>
> *Second*, these fast growing states are also those which seem to have benefited most from the Central Government industrial and trade liberalization since they have reasonably adequate infrastructure and for some, adequate human capital stock (Kerala) which attracted new investments to the states.
>
> *Third*, these states did streamline their investment approvals procedures considerably. But infrastructural bottlenecks such as short power supply are reducing states potential to attract new investment. Indeed, for investment to take place, investors must first receive clearance for power use. This procedure remains cumbersome and prone to rent-seeking since power rationing and clearance are based on non-price decisions.
>
> *Fourth*, investors are working with states to circumvent infrastructural bottlenecks especially regarding ports. Since the Central Government has been slow in restructuring its inefficient and highly unionized central ports, investors are seeking to build small ports within the states.

deficit. As a result of these developments, after a decline in 1991-92, the consolidated deficit of the public sector has remained relatively stable at a high 10 percent of GDP. As discussed in more detail in Chapter 3, this is an excessively high deficit which threatens the achievements of the last five years, constitutes a major destabilizing force to the financial sector, and may deprive the country from the high growth that the reforms of the past five years could generate.

Fiscal Adjustment in the 1996-97 Budget

On July 22, the Minister of Finance presented to Parliament the 1996-97 budget, the first of the 13-parties United Front (UF) government. The budget takes several steps to implement the Common Minimum Program (CMP, Box 1.3) and makes it clear that this government intends to continue the reforms started in 1991.

On *stabilization*, the budget proposes a welcome fiscal correction of 0.9 percent of GDP. However, this correction is less than half of what would be necessary for the long run sustainability of the current mix of low inflation and relatively high growth. More seriously perhaps, the measures envisaged in the budget may not be sufficient to attain this target. The 0.9 percentage points of GDP fiscal deficit reduction is to be achieved through a 0.7 percentage points of GDP increase in revenue, and a 0.2 percentage points reduction in expenditure. Some of the assumptions underlying both the revenue and the expenditure forecasts may be overoptimistic. On the revenue side, it is assumed that sales of government equity in public enterprises will reach US$1.5 billion, and that tax revenues will increase by 20 percent on account of a 14 percent increase in nominal GDP (half real growth and half inflation) and of several tax measures introduced in the budget. On the expenditure side, a 9 percent increase in provision for wages is deemed to be sufficient to accommodate wage increases stemming from the Pay Commission recommendations. Finally, defense expenditure has continued to decline relative to GDP (from 2.9 percent of GDP five years ago to 2.2 percent of GDP at present) and there may be some pressure to restore it at higher levels. At the same time, new claims have been put on the budget to increase the fertilizer subsidy (0.2 percent of GDP), support public enterprises (0.1 percent of GDP), expand an already existing rural infrastructructure fund, strengthen the capital base of the national agricultural bank (0.1 percent of GDP), and, for a relatively small amount, recapitalize several small public banks.

The budget also announces a cautious, but clear commitment to permit *greater decentralization* within India's federal structure by: (a) gradually transferring most centrally sponsored schemes to the control of the states; (b) proposing constitutional change to include all central taxes in the federal transfer division pool as recommended by the tenth Finance Commission; (c) designing a Ninth Five-Year Plan which will put emphasis on decentralization of responsibility; and (d) convening a conference of Chief Ministers on center-states relations and federalism. In addition, the budget also announces the government intention to *target the Public Distribution System* and, potentially, other social safety nets programs, to families below the poverty line. Finally, the Minister of Finance proposed to appoint a *high level Expenditure Management and Reforms Commission* to submit within four months recommendations on how to improve public expenditure control and management, and proposed to place before Parliament a *discussion paper on subsidies* and their appropriate targeting. These are welcome initiatives that will permit a public discussion of the structural reasons for India's chronically high fiscal deficits.

Box 1.3: The Common Minimum Program of the United Front Government

India's general elections concluded in May 1996. None of the major national parties won a ruling majority in Parliament. Following the short-lived government of the Bharatiya Janata Party (BJP), a United Front (UF) government--a coalition of thirteen regional and leftist parties with divergent ideological orientations--came to power in June 1996. Shortly thereafter, on June 5, 1996, the UF unveiled its "Common Approach to Major Policy Matters and a Minimum Program".

On Fiscal Management. "Highest priority" is to be given to the management of the fiscal deficit, to bring it to below 4 percent of GDP. Both revenue enhancing and expenditure reducing strategies to be followed. Public debt is to be retired in a phased manner. None of these will however "...be followed at the cost of development or investment."

On Federalism. The UF Government plans to "...advance the principles of political, administrative and economic federalism". States will be given greater freedom in determining their own priorities in development programs, in drawing up their state plans, and most centrally sponsored schemes will be transferred to State governments. A high-level committee will be appointed to review and update the recommendations of the Sarkaria Commission (set up ten years ago to advise on center-state relations) and examine the question of devolution of financial powers to the states.

On the Investment and Trade Regime. Foreign direct investment of at least $10 billion per year will be needed and can be absorbed. To achieve this, the Foreign Investment Promotion Board will be revamped, and rules and regulations will be made more transparent to attract foreign investment. A new law will be made to deal with industrial sickness and the Board for Industrial and Financial Reconstruction will be revamped. The consumer courts network will be expanded. On **foreign trade**, the "...progress towards the goal of bringing India's tariffs in accord with world levels will be measured and calibrated". An independent Tariff Commission will be established within three months to decide on tariff disputes and to recommend appropriate tariffs for different products and industries.

On Infrastructure. Investment in infrastructure will be increased from the present 3.5-4 percent of GDP to at least 6 percent in the next few years. The cumulative investment requirements of infrastructure investment over the next five years are estimated to be at least US$200 billion, implying ample room for public, private, domestic and foreign players. Both domestic and foreign companies will be encouraged to invest in the core and infrastructure sectors.

On Public Enterprises. Public enterprises should show a "healthy" return on capital. Public enterprises will be strengthened and their managements professionalized. Sick companies will be rehabilitated by measures which may include handing over management to professional groups or workers' cooperatives. A Disinvestment Commission will be established to examine the question of withdrawing the public sector from "non-core" and "non-strategic" areas, subject to assuring job security or alternative employment to employees. Disinvestment will be done in a transparent manner.

On Financial Markets. Further reforms will be carried out in the financial sector to ensure a greater flow of domestic and foreign funds into infrastructure. The experience gained in the banking sector (where private banks have been allowed) will be "...applied to the restructuring of the insurance industry but at the same time public sector companies like LIC, GIC etc. will be strengthened."

On Agriculture. The agriculture sector "...cries out for reforms". Investment in agriculture and rural infrastructure will be increased. All controls and regulations in the way of increasing farm incomes will be reviewed immediately and abolished where found unnecessary, such as the controls on movement as well as processing of agricultural products. Fair and remunerative prices will be ensured for farm produce. Rural credit will be restructured and the flow of credit to agriculture and agro-industries will be doubled within five years. Input supplying agencies will be professionalized and if feasible be converted into farmer-owned cooperatives. Research and extension will be strengthened.

Social Sectors and Poverty Alleviation. Six percent of GDP will be earmarked for education, of which half for primary education. Full literacy will be achieved by 2005. The right to free and compulsory education will be made a fundamental right and be suitably enforced. Special programs will be launched to take care of children and the disabled and to eradicate child labor. The mid-day meal scheme will be implemented in all states. One primary health center will be established for every 5000 people. Anti-poverty programs will be redesigned for greater employment and asset creation, and to raise the incomes of the very poor. A program for guaranteeing 100 days of employment for every unemployed person will be implemented through Panchayati Raj institutions. Access to the Public Distribution System (PDS) will be barred for the affluent. Special cards will be given to families below the poverty line, and essential articles under PDS sold to them at half the normal issue price. PDS shops will be handed over to the elected Panchayats. One-third of the elected membership of Parliament and state legislatures will be reserved for women and so will one-third of government posts. Suitable legislation will be enacted for this purpose, including, if necessary, an amendment to the Constitution.

Box 1.4: Reforms in the 1996-97 Budget

The budget has continued the process of reform started in 1991. In particular, it introduced several measures to open further the foreign investment regime, reform the tax system, continue the liberalization of trade, and modestly liberalize some segments of the financial sector.

Foreign investment regime has been further liberalized by allowing portfolio investors to invest in non-listed companies' securities and by raising the limit of the maximum equity any Foreign Institutional Investor (FII) can hold from 5 percent to 10 percent of share capital subject to the overall limit of 24 percent for equity held by FIIs..

Several *tax measures* have been taken to continue to broaden the tax base, reduce rates, and improve tax administration. This has been particularly important in the case of excise and corporate taxation. Regarding *excise taxes*, the Finance Minister emphasized the need to move to a more transparent and simpler four-rate excise tax structure--zero, a lower rate of excise duty on goods of mass consumption, a single normal rate on all other goods, and a higher rate on luxury items in a year or two. In the meantime, the MODVAT has been extended to the textile fabrics sector with a special tax incentive package (excise and customs duties have been reduced on important inputs) to boost the sector. And excise duties were raised on several items, including all petroleum products except on LPG and kerosene.

The noteworthy development for *company income tax* was the reduction of the surcharge on corporate tax from 15 percent to 7.5 percent and the introduction of a "Minimum Alternate Tax" (MAT) on companies' book profits to bring into the tax net some 1,000 companies currently under the zero-tax bracket or benefiting from excessive exemptions. Finally, the tax on long-term capital gains for domestic companies has been reduced from 30 percent to 20 percent to bring it in line with that for foreign companies.

Regarding *personal income tax*, the budget has reduced the income-tax rate for the first bracket from 20 percent to 15 percent. Allowances were also granted for various deductions (interest payments on owner-occupier mortgages, health insurance, fiscal incentives for savings schemes).

The budget has continued the process of *trade reform* by reducing further the maximum duty rate to 40 percent for non-consumer goods imports. The latter continue to be restricted and when allowed are at the maximum rate of 50 percent. A two percentage points surcharge is imposed on all imports to finance the starting capital of an infrastructure fund.

In the *financial sector*, the budget announced that amendments to the RBI Act will be proposed to strengthen the regulatory powers of the RBI over all types of non-financial companies. New legislation was enacted to ensure transparent and secure clearing settlements while minimum capital adequacy requirements were reduced to encourage small local banks to incorporate the modern financial sector.

The budget has also introduced several new initiatives to improve the living standards of the rural poor and respond to the growing infrastructure crisis. These include funding for state-level social programs for the provision of safe drinking water, primary education, primary health, housing, mid-day meals for primary school children, rural roads and a strengthened public distribution system covering all below the poverty line. These are first steps towards the government goal of ensuring safe drinking water to 100 percent of the population and universal primary education. A 0.2 percent of GDP increase in transfers to states is envisaged in the budget to finance these initiatives. In addition, the budget provides also resources for new social programs such as the establishment of old-age homes, residential primary schools for the poor, training and production facilities for destitute women, and a public medical insurance fund to be financed through tax exempt donations--the aggregate value of all the new welfare measures proposed add up to less than Rs 1 billion.

A new initiative to mobilize additional capital for the development of infrastructure. An Infrastructure Development Finance Company (IDFC) will be established, involving a budgetary outlay of Rs 5 billion for equity. This is to be matched by an equal contribution from the Reserve Bank of India. The IDFC is intended to play the role of direct lender, refinance institution as well as the provider of financial guarantees, that will induce private financiers to advance "long-term funds at the lowest possible market rates". It will also rely on the funds generated by the 2 percent surcharge on imports.

PROGRESS IN STRUCTURAL REFORM

The program of structural reforms has been carefully prepared. Since June 1991, the government has appointed several committees of experts to formulate reform proposals in the different reform areas--the investment regime, trade policies, the financial sector, taxation and public enterprises. These committees' work was amply discussed with academics, industrialists, and unions, which helped build consensus (except for public enterprises where the political resistance has been considerable) around the economic reform program thus reducing the possibility of future reversals--which have plagued and some times derailed adjustment programs elsewhere in the world. It also enabled the government to assess the extent of political resistance to sensitive reforms (e.g. consumer goods imports and privatization) and thus leave them out of the initial phases to avoid derailing the whole process. *This said, and while the government has been successful at changing India's economy, major challenges remain, particularly regarding the reform of the financial, agricultural, and infrastructure sectors and public enterprises.* In addition, India needs to correct the effects of decades of chronic underspending in health and education, and articulate a strategy to address serious urban problems.

The liberalization of the investment regime is nearly complete. Five years ago, investment in the most important areas of the economy was a public sector monopoly and foreign investment was discouraged. Even in the areas which were not a public sector monopoly, severe licensing restrictions regulated the amount of investment that private firms could undertake. Now there are few areas where private investors, domestic or foreign, cannot invest and India's foreign investment regime now compares favorably with East Asian countries. In telecommunications, power and mining it is significantly more open than that of its East Asian neighbors. With the recent liberalization of pharmaceuticals and parts of coal mining, the main areas still reserved for the public sector are insurance and railways. However, a number of costly licensing restrictions remain for selected industrial sectors, mostly agroindustry. For instance, regulations governing the sugar industry are estimated to cost the country about US$2 billion per year by 2005. The reservation of about 800 products that can only be produced by small scale enterprises has equally serious negative effects because it discourages economies of scale and adoption of modern technology. In addition, in many instances investing in India remains difficult because of numerous regulations and administrative burdens that are far from transparent and differ from state to state which affect domestic and foreign investors alike. *The 1996-97 budget of July 1996* introduced further reforms (Box 1.4) to expand the set of enterprises in which foreign institutional investors can invest and, shortly after the budget was presented to Parliament, the Ministry of Industry removed licensing restrictions for 10 industries still subject to prior--approvals. While this measure may not have considerable effects--since essentially all approvals have been granted on request--it does provide a further simplification of the investment regime and sends a positive signal to domestic and foreign investors.

The trade and foreign exchange regimes have been substantially liberalized, but protection levels are still high. India's pre-1991 trade regime was very restrictive. Virtually all goods could only be imported if authorized by the government and, with maximum tariffs of over 300 percent and average (import-weighted) tariffs of 87 percent, India had the world's highest tariffs. Since June 1991, several rounds of trade reforms have lifted all licensing restrictions on imports of intermediate and capital goods, liberalized partially imports of consumer goods, and reduced maximum tariffs to 50 percent, and the import weighted average tariff to 25.2 percent. In parallel, the exchange-rate regime has been liberalized, and full convertibility has been established for current account transactions. The most recent round of tariff reform introduced in the *1996-97 budget* reduced maximum tariffs for non-consumer goods to 40 percent (see Box 1.4) and the import weighted average tariff to 22.7 percent. This progress notwithstanding, India will need to liberalize its trade regime even further if the country is to reach the openness of its East Asian and Latin American competitors (where import weighted tariffs are in the 10-15 percent range) and some anomalies of the trade regime are to be eliminated (Chapter 2). Also, current licensing restrictions on consumer goods imports are significantlty more severe than in most other countries.

A skillful and significant liberalization of the financial sector--but the public sector remains dominant. With a financial savings rate of 9 percent of GDP in 1990-91 (11 percent of GDP at present), India's pre-1991 policies had been successful at developing a solid deposit base, and a diversified stock of financial instruments. However, until very recently, the financial sector had been dominated by public banks which had limited discretion in allocating their lending (in 1991 as much as 63.5 percent of increases in bank deposits had to be held in cash reserve requirements and government securities, and 40 percent of the remaining had to be allocated to priority sectors designated by government) and publicly-owned insurance companies still have to hold more than half of their portfolio in government-designated securities. Prudential regulations had no real role to play in the deployment of capital and in any case were inadequate making it difficult to assess the true quality of bank portfolios or bank profits. Interest rates and financial instruments were tightly regulated, and competition was limited by restrictions on entry of new banks, insurance companies, or mutual funds. Pricing and terms of new equity issues were regulated.

Because of persistently large public sector borrowing requirements and weak public banks balance sheets, the government has chosen a phased approach to liberalizing the financial sector--but this approach has been excessively gradual in the case of privatization of the public banks and deregulation of insurance companies and contractual savings institutions. Much of the reform effort has focused on establishing the institutional base required for deregulated financial markets to operate efficiently, and in deregulating the markets themselves. In particular, prudential regulations that meet international standards have been introduced, and to improve its capacity to enforce the new prudential guidelines, the RBI created a Board of Financial Supervision which began functioning in December 1994. Several steps have been taken to develop markets in government securities, including the creation by RBI of a dealer network to operate in and provide liquidity to government security markets, followed by the approval of the first six private primary dealers in 1996. In parallel, measures have been taken to develop the Securities and Exchange Board of India's (SEBI) capacity to provide oversight regulation in India's stock markets and to increase the transparency of stock market transactions. In particular, legislation has been enacted to improve title transfers and a code for takeovers has been formulated (Box 1.5). A new modern electronic securities exchange system, the National Stock Exchange (NSE), which allows scripless transactions, began operating in 1995. In November

---

Box 1.5: Capital Market Reforms Led to Improvement in Transparency, Reliability and Fairness of Transactions

Since 1992, when SEBI became a statutory body, a number of reforms have strengthened SEBI, reinforced its autonomy, increased the transparency of stock market transactions and increased investors' protection. The roles and responsibilities of various market participants have been clarified, disclosure requirements in offer documents strengthened and the extant guidelines for bonus shares have been relaxed.

Regarding *primary public issues*,. following the recommendations of the Malegam Committee on existing disclosure requirements and issue procedures, SEBI has strengthened further disclosure standards to protect investors, introduced prudential norms and simplified issue procedures The new guidelines cover inter-alia unlisted companies, finance companies, enhanced transparency in the draft prospectus filed with SEBI (and simultenously with the stock exchanges) and requirements for prospectus submitted to SEBI for vetting (within 21 days). The due diligence certificate by lead managers, regarding disclosures made in the offer document, has been made a part of the offer document itself for better accountability. Companies also are required to disclose all material facts and specific risk factors associated with their projects while making public issues. Stock exchanges required to ensure that companies concerned have a valid acknowledgment card issued by SEBI. SEBI vets the offer document, to ensure that all disclosures have been made by the company in the offer document, at the time the company applies for listing of its securities in the stock exchange.

The mandatory period between the date of approval of the prospectus by the Registrar of companies and the opening of the issue has been reduced to 14 days. The stock exchanges now are advised to amend the listing agreement to ensure that a listed company furnishes annual statement to stock exchanges, showing variations between financial projections and projected utilisation of funds made in the offer documents and actuals. To reduce the cost of issue, underwriting by issuer was made optional, subject to the condition that if an issue was not underwritten and was not able to collect 90 per cent of the amount offered to the public, the entire amount collected would be refunded to investors. The practice of making preferential allotment of shares at prices unrelated to the prevailing market prices was stopped and new guidelines were issued by SEBI. Finally, SEBI reconstituted governing boards of the stock exchanges, introduced capital adequacy norms for brokers and established clear rules for making the client/broker relationship more transparent, in particular, segregating client and broker accounts..

To improve *secondary market trading* and protect investors, a recently promulgated Presidential ordinance provides the legal underpinnings for the setting up of central depositories to record ownership transfer for securities. This would remedy previous problem impeding secondary trading due to poor title transfer infrastructure. The depository system would also enable trading to take place without stamp duties, another impediment to primary issue and trading of securities. Further, a code for takeovers has been formulated. The procedure for lodgment of securities for transfer was considerably eased for institutions through the introduction of 'jumbo' transfer deed and consolidated payment of stamp duty.

Following the recommendations of the Patel Committee on the *carry forward* system, SEBI introduced a revised carry forward system subject to the following prudential conditions: (i) stock exchanges would be allowed to introduce carry forward system only with the prior permission of SEBI and subject to effective monitoring and surveillance system, and infrastructure; (ii) the financiers funding the carry forward transactions will not be permitted to square up their positions till repayment of the loan; (iii) a cap of Rs. 100 million applies to carry forward transactions; (iv) the carry forward position shall be disclosed to the market, scrip-wise and broker-wise by the stock exchanges at the beginning of the carry forward session; and (v) individuals brokers and corporates should conform to capital adequacy norms of 3 percent and 6 percent respectively.

Regarding *mutual funds*, the noteworthy reform was the inclusion of UTI under the regulatory jurisdiction of SEBI to level the playing field with other mutual funds. In addition, new guidelines governing rules for advertising by mutual funds were issued and the requirement of pre-vetting of advertisements was removed. To improve the scope of investments by mutual funds, mutual funds were permitted to underwrite public issues and guidelines for investment in money market instruments were relaxed.

Finally, SEBI is setting up an institutional infrastructure to discourage insider trading and unfair trade practices. To achieve effective coordination between the exchanges especially on matters of general interest, and market monitoring, an Inter-Exchange Co-ordination Group would be set up. In addition, the major stock exchanges are to set up Investor Information Centers to provide information about investors' rights and obligations and about their listed companies.

1995, the government established an insurance regulatory body, to prepare the basis for eliminating the public monopoly in this sector--although a decision on this has yet to be taken.

However, while progress has been achieved in relaxing controls, reducing government's pre-emption of financial savings, and reestablishing the soundness of the financial system, much remains to be done. Interest rates are now market determined for most transactions. The exceptions are for small loans (below Rs 200,000, that is about US$6,000 at 13.5 percent) and for the maximum rate that remains on deposits of less than 30 days (see Table 1.11). Forced holdings of government debt by banks, while reduced, remain at a high 37 percent of deposits and 40 percent of banks' loan portfolios still must be allocated to designated "priority sector lending". While barriers against the entry of private banks (domestic and foreign) have been relaxed, restrictions on the expansion of their branch network remain. And public sector banks continue to hold around 90 percent of the sector's assets and little progress has been achieved in reducing government equity holdings in the public banks or in improving their autonomy in key areas such as staffing and pay. As a result, financial intermediation costs remain excessive and the autonomy of financial sector institutions is very much in doubt.

The tax regime has been simplified and strengthened considerably. In the 1994-95 Budget, taxes on corporate income were unified at 46 percent for widely held companies and 55 percent for branches of foreign banks. A major reform of excises was implemented to make it more closely resemble a value-added tax and address its major problems. Meanwhile, the government extended the coverage of MODVAT (a modified value-added tax) to include manufacturing sectors thus far excluded, and, for the first time, some services. Of particular importance also were the decisions to: (i) shift most excise rates from specific to ad-valorem to increase buoyancy; (ii) reduce the number of rates; and (iii) simplify the system by relying on invoices for value determination. These reforms considerably simplified and modernized India's tax system and made it possible for the Central Government to begin to focus its efforts on improving tax administration. The 1995-96 Budget further reduced peak excises. It did not reduce corporate tax rates further but it continued the emphasis on simplification, lower rates and greater buoyancy. To strengthen compliance, the authorities proposed tax deduction at source for fees for professionals, technical services and service contracts, and interest income on time deposits. Further and significant tax reforms were introduced in the ***1996-97 budget*** (see Box 1.4) maintaining the overall direction and goals of the tax reforms initiated in the last few years.

PERSPECTIVES FROM THE POOR

The pillars of the government's poverty reduction strategy are accelerated and sustained labor-intensive growth, and investment in human capital development. Anti-poverty programs have a supplementary role. Although growth has accelerated over the past few years, there has been concern that some of the stabilization and structural reform measures started in 1991 might have had a negative impact on the living standards of the poor. In particular, the sharp devaluation and the fiscal stabilization measures taken in the first few years of the program led to significant increases in the prices of key commodities such as fertilizer, rice, sugar, cotton, and gasoline. This was compounded by a poor monsoon in the first year of the program which caused agricultural production to fall, while the industrial sector started a two-year relatively serious recession. Finally, results of the 1991-92 National Sample Survey suggested a sharp increase in the incidence of poverty. Although this increase is difficult to explain (Box 1.6) on the basis of variables that are good predictors of poverty (such as wages for unskilled agricultural laborers, agricultural production, and inflation), and may be associated with methodological sampling weaknesses, it nonetheless generated considerable public debate on the social consequences of stabilization and reform.

This debate has faded in the recent past as evidence gathered that the economic program is producing positive results, that many of the reforms introduced over the last five years (particularly the devaluation of the rupee and the decline in the protection of manufacturing) have improved the agricultural terms of trade and thus real wages for unskilled agricultural labor (such wages, after declining by 6 percent in 1991-92, have increased during 1992-95 for the country as a whole) and that the reduction in the anti-export bias implicit in the trade regime has led to a rapid expansion of labor-intensive exports--which in other countries have been a key factor in employment generation and poverty reduction. In addition, in spite of the relatively high fiscal cost of these decisions, the government has postponed reductions in subsidies, notably for fertilizer which have even increased in the 1996-97 budget, and expanded some nation-wide safety net programs--essentially a revamped PDS, and employment and nutrition programs. Finally, the recent publication of the 1993-94 National Sample Survey suggests that poverty has actually declined in relation to the pre-1991 period.

There have been questions, however, on what has been the evolution of poverty in the last two years. The acceleration of growth in the last two years, the sustained agricultural

---

Box 1.6: Did India's Macroeconomic Stabilization Increase Poverty in 1992?

The National Sample Surveys of 1990-91 and 1991-92 indicates that the incidence of poverty increased from 36 percent of the population to 41 percent. To isolate the effects on the poor of the various economy-wide factors, research for this report examined how India's rural poverty measures have responded in the past to changes in key economic variables such as real agricultural state domestic product (SDP) per hectare of sown area in the state, real non-agricultural SDP per capita, rural rate of inflation, per capita real state development expenditure, and real male agricultural wage. Time-series measures of the incidence, depth and severity of rural poverty were estimated using state-level data from 19 rounds of the National Sample Survey spanning 1960-61 to 1992. These variables accounted for 90 percent of the variance in measured poverty. The model were then used to assess what role those same variables may have played in the increase in poverty in 1992. A sub-set of these variables can be identified as likely channels through which stabilization would affect living standards of the poor. Those are real non-agricultural product per person, real state development expenditure, the inflation rate, and the real male agricultural wage. Of course these variables are changing for other reasons, including the effects of the crisis preceding the reforms and current exogenous shocks (such as the effects of the bad agricultural year on real wages in agriculture).

The results indicate that the joint effect of the crisis and stabilization accounted for at most 36 percent of the increase in the poverty rate in 1992, and a smaller share of the increase in the depth and severity of poverty. The rest do not appear to be attributable to the direct or indirect short-run impacts of policy changes, at least as they affected the key economic variables which matter to the poor. However, the study was less successful in explaining what did in fact account for the increase in poverty in 1992. That remains, in large part, a mystery. One possible explanation could be the small size of the 1991-1992 NSS survey.

Source: Gaurav Datt and Martin Ravallion, "Why did poverty increase sharply after India's macroeconomic stabilization?", mimeo, Poverty and Human Resources Division, Policy Research Department, World Bank.)

---

performance, the positive evolution of real wages for unskilled agricultural labor, and the decline in inflation would all suggest that the incidence of poverty has declined further in the last two years. But in the absence of more recent comprehensive data of the kind provided by the quinquennial surveys, it is impossible to conclude with any degree of certainty the effects on poverty of the developments of the last two years. For the purposes of this report, however, and as very first approximations case studies were carried out by Indian economists and social scientists, between January and March 1996 in four states (Maharashtra, Tamil Nadu, Punjab, and Uttar Pradesh). While they still need to be validated by actual data, this exercise suggests that the incidence of poverty is unlikely to have increased. More interestingly perhaps, a strong result which emerged from these case studies is that the welfare and safety net programs seem to be barely noticed by those who were being interviewed. In spite of the significant resources that the country allocates to such programs, there is little evidence that they have a palpable impact on the living standards of the poor. This may be because the newer programs (i.e., RPDS, EAS schemes, benefits for widows) have not yet reached intended beneficiaries on a significant scale. This also can be, however, an indication that these programs fail to reach their targeted population. Below is a more detailed discussion of how the beneficiary assessments were conducted, and of their results (see Annex III for studies' executive summaries).

The case studies (Box 1.7) were carried out in four states--Maharashtra, Tamil Nadu, Punjab, and Uttar Pradesh. One of the primary benefits of the work is that it provides very timely information on how poor people view their opportunities and living conditions at the time of inquiry. This timeliness and responsiveness comes at a cost, however: regions (and villages and individuals within villages) were chosen to be broadly representative of, e.g. certain cropping patterns, agro-climatic zones, social or ethnic groupings, and are not formally or statistically representative of the country as a whole. The case studies were designed to address two questions: *first*, how have the poor in India fared since 1991 and what has been the likely impact of reform and stabilization measures on their incomes and living standards; and *second*, how well have safety net programs--both government and non-government--worked to protect living standards of the poor.

A number of general findings emerged. *First*, across all regions respondents in both rural and urban areas reported no dramatic changes in their standards of living following the advent of the 1991 stabilization and reform program. In fact, few respondents knew of the economic crisis in 1991 or were aware of the shift in economic policies started in 1991. Although respondents are typically aware of changes in local prices and government programs in rural areas--PDS prices and availability of goods, changes in fertilizer and other input prices, and public works programs--they seldom saw these changes as dramatic or related to a country-wide shift in economic policy. The changes mentioned were typically due to idiosyncratic or localized effects: for example, death or illness in the family, late or scant rainfall, loss of employment for a particular household member. A slightly higher share (although still few) of people in urban areas are aware of economy-wide changes, but their knowledge tends to be fragmentary and there was no sense that they had been affected by such changes.

Second, there were marked regional disparities. In richer areas with better infrastructure, natural endowments and commercially oriented agriculture (such as in Punjab or Maharashtra), cultivators were generally positive. Many people witnessed a general improvement in standards of living both in rural areas (due to the impact of high agricultural growth on real wages) and urban areas. *In the rural areas, increases in producer prices were appreciated*. In many regions, farmers have responded to changing market incentives by shifting

**Box 1.7: Selected Case Studies:
The Impact of Economic Reforms on the Poor**

As an alternative to more conventional approaches, and in recognition of the importance and timeliness of the issues, a series of case studies were commissioned to seek tentative answers designed to address two key questions:

• What has been the impact of recent reforms (in particular, trade, domestic, and expenditure reforms) on the poor?
• What safety net programs are available to protect the poor from adverse impacts and how well do they appear to be working?

The case studies were carried out between January and March 1996 by Indian researchers working in four states -- Maharashtra, Tamil Nadu, Punjab, and UP. The researchers used a mix of field techniques -- individual interviews, focus groups, interviews with community leaders -- as well as secondary sources of data, all designed to yield rapid results and to reflect how the poor themselves feel that they have been impacted by recent policy changes.

In *Maharashtra*, case studies were based primarily on focus group interviews carried out in rural villages in four districts (Osmanabad, Parbhani, Pune, and Thane) and additional interviews carried out in Mumbai, India's largest commercial-cum-industrial city. The urban work focused on the living conditions of semi and unskilled workers in small-scale manufacturing, transport, construction, and personal services. In contrast, case studies for *Tamil Nadu* were based primarily on individual interviews (augmented by group discussions) with farmers and other rural workers living in Thanjavur District and Dharmapuri District. Interviews were also conducted with persons living in two small towns, one for each district (Papanasam in Thanjavur and Pennagaram in Dharmapuri). Work was also undertaken in *Punjab*, one of India's more prosperous agricultural states. Individual interviews were conducted with farmers, agriculture laborers, and artisans in 10 villages in 10 blocks in Patiala and Fatehgarh Sahib districts. In addition, group and individual interviews were carried out with farmers and agriculture laborers in *Uttar Pradesh*, including rural villages in Allahabad District and Gorakhpur District. The rural sample was augmented by individual interviews with persons living in two medium-sized cities: Allahabad and Gorakhpur. The urban work focused on poor people working in one of four occupational groups -- the handloom and power loom sector (Gorakhpur) and construction workers, rickshaw pullers, and domestic workers (Allahabad). Finally, a field study of the various impacts of reform measures on very poor women living in Banda District, UP, was undertaken.

cropping patterns to more profitable or less input-intensive crops (for example, sunflower seeds require less water and are more resistant to disease and insects than more traditional crops like sorghum). In addition, some farmers are producing for relatively new export markets (i.e. grapes in Maharashtra). A number of farmers expressed concern about a potential squeeze on profits due to input price increases and deteriorating water supplies. However, a substantial number of the more commercially oriented farmers in the case studies said that the higher input prices were more than offset by the increase in producer prices. As evidence of increasing profits, many farmers are actually applying more fertilizer rather than less post-1991, despite significant increases in fertilizer prices.

But small and marginal farmers in the case studies reported less favorable outcomes. In general, small and marginal farmers (Table 1.13) are slower to diversify or change cropping patterns and few report sufficient additional earnings (cash or in-kind) to compensate for the rise in input prices. Interestingly, little evidence was found of small and marginal cultivators being forced off their land or pushed out of the market for rented or share-cropped land. One exception was Punjab, where the case study described an active land-lease market, and cited several cases of marginal farmers who had sold their land or relinquished leases in order to enter different occupations (e.g. dairying and agriculture laborers)--but there was no evidence that this was different from what was already happening before 1991, and could be expected in a region where commercial agriculture predominates. There were reports of stagnated or even

Table 1.13: State-Wise Shares of Marginal and Small Farmer Holdings (percent of total holdings)	
Maharashtra	57
Punjab	43
Tamil Nadu	88
UP	88
Source: Agriculture Statistic at a Glance (1993).	

deteriorating living standards in some of the poorer regions, in particular, very isolated areas (i.e. a tribal region in Thane district, Maharashtra, parts of Bundelkhand in Southern UP).

Third, case study findings on rural wages and employment are mixed. Contrary to what is suggested by wage statistics, in many regions covered in the case studies agriculture wages seem to have just kept pace with cost of living increases since 1991 and most individuals report working the same number of days post-1991 as pre-1991. There are some exceptions. For example, in several of the surveyed districts in Maharashtra, both real wages and employment are reported to have increased since 1991. A number of respondents in Tamil Nadu likewise claim that wages have risen, and, in one of the arid districts, off-farm employment levels appear to have increased as well. Contract or permanent laborers in Punjab also report rising wages as compared to 1991. In contrast, the wages of casual farm laborers in Punjab seem to have fallen in recent years.

The limited work done in urban areas -- medium-to-large cities in Maharashtra and UP-- seem to reinforce the view that wages and employment movements after 1991 depend to a large extent on the relative wealth of the region and type of occupation. Secure employment is rare among the poor, with the exception of certain sectors (i.e. domestic employment) where it appears that lower monetary wages (domestic workers surveyed in UP earn on average half of other low-skill occupations) are traded for more stable employment. In prosperous Mumbai, unskilled workers in the construction sector report more competition for jobs (due to higher influx of rural workers), falling wages, and a drop in average annual days of employment. In contrast, drivers and maintenance staff in the transport sector--which has doubled in size since 1991--report a moderate increase in wages but good employment prospects. In UP, however, the most populous among the poorer states, many urban workers complained of greater job competition with stagnant or sometimes falling wages. In contrast with the ambiguous results on wages, and in contradiction to other information sources, there was little evidence of a decline in cereals consumption since 1991.

Fourth, the case study findings regarding India's extensive system of social safety nets suggest the following:

- The PDS is almost universally viewed as an ineffective food safety net. In most states, the price of food grains available through the PDS is on a par with prices in the market, and PDS quality is generally lower. One exception was Tamil Nadu. In addition, poor people often do not have enough cash to make the bulk (monthly) purchases required by most PDS shops. Although the RPDS has been operational for several years, none of the respondents in RPDS case study blocks reported purchasing food grains or other commodities from RPDS supply depots.

- Few villages have operating ICDS centers, another food safety net program for pre-school children. By contrast, the mid-day meals program in certain districts of UP is seen as an effective inducement to attend school, as were SC/ST scholarship programs.

- With the exception of Maharashtra, Employment Assurance Schemes (EAS) and other public works programs (including the JRY) are not effective at providing employment for the poor. Those employed under the schemes typically work many fewer days than stated targets. Rural Maharashtra is an exception: casual laborers worked an average of 30 EGS days annually and 30 days on other public works programs, while farmers worked an average of 30 EGS days annually. Neither are public works initiated under the JRY, a dependable source of employment for the rural poor. Respondents in several states complained that JRY projects are given to subcontractors who hire work teams from outside the village rather than local workers and adjust their books in order to pay higher wages.

- Credit schemes have an uneven history of success in rural India. Many respondents received loans through the IRDP. But these loans often did not serve their stated purpose--to increase assets and thereby raise incomes in some sustainable way--and many are not repaid. For example, in the case study for rural UP, out of 40 respondents who received IRDP assistance, only 10 report a sustained increase in income levels, 5 diverted the resources to other uses, and 25 report no income improvement. When asked what kinds of services or programs might help to make them better off, few of the respondents cite cheaper or more available credit: deeper indebtedness is not desirable.

Taken in total, India's safety net programs while entailing significant fiscal costs seem not to reach their target population as suggested by these case studies. While many recipients of benefits from safety net programs are poor, many of the poorest people do not use the programs. However, these findings cannot be generalized and further study is necessary. This said, however, participants mentioned numerous examples of misuse of funds by local elites and ineffective local institutions in indentifying the poor and monitoring their access to these programs. The new programs are also problematic, for example, while many respondents are aware of the 1995-96 new social security initiatives (e.g. pensions to elderly widows, a state-level life insurance scheme for rickshaw pullers in UP), few have tried to access the programs, and of those who did, even fewer received the promised benefits--suggesting that it may be warranted to rethink of how these programs are being delivered.

MACROECONOMIC VULNERABILITIES AND STRUCTURAL WEAKNESSES

INTRODUCTION

The stabilization and reform measures introduced over the last five years have considerably improved India's growth prospects. The growth performance of the last two years and preliminary indications for 1996-97 reinforce this view and may suggest that India is on a trajectory of a stable 6-7 percent real annual growth. This inevitably raises the question of whether India will be able to repeat the experience of its successful East Asian neighbors.

The answer is that strong corrective measures are necessary to make this happen. Not only is the country facing serious fiscal imbalances that have yet to be corrected, but there also remain a number of macroeconomic vulnerabilities and structural weaknesses that need to be addressed even to sustain the current 7 percent growth rate, let alone exceed it. *First*, because of the public sector poor savings performance, India's savings rate is considerably lower than that of its East Asian competitors. *Second*, agriculture which accounts for 30 percent of GDP and 70 percent of employment is still being penalized by numerous restrictions inhibiting the trade and processing of agricultural commodities and inadequate composition of public spending for agricultural development. *Third,* relative to the East Asian high performing economies, India has invested relatively little in the development of the country's human resources and social indicators are thus considerably lower. *Fourth*, India's infrastructure bottlenecks are considerably more severe than in East Asian countries. More importantly perhaps, the resolution of India's infrastructure bottlenecks is not just a problem of resources but requires extensive institutional and regulatory reform at all levels of government. *Fifth*, there is growing evidence that India's cities and towns are facing a crisis of serious dimension and that urban policies and institutions are in urgent need of reform. None of these constraints can alone threaten the acceleration of private investment and growth but, taken together, they constitute a serious obstacle. *Finally*, as highlighted in the previous chapter, there remains an important unfinished reform agenda that needs to be brought to its logical conclusion, particularly regarding the trade regime, the tax system, and the financial sector.

The central message of this report, however, is that India is in a unique position to strengthen its macroeconomy and address structural weaknesses over the next four to five years. This would not only ensure the sustainability of the current growth trends but also enable India to start to grow at rates possibly exceeding 8 percent per year by the beginning of the next decade. This chapter examines the nature and extent of India's remaining macroeconomic vulnerabilities and structural weaknesses and leads into the second part of this report which articulates possible strategies to address them.

MACROECONOMIC VULNERABILITIES

Fiscal Vulnerabilities

An important source of fiscal pressure is expected from the Pay Commission which will give its recommendations on civil service pay before the end of this calendar year (the last Pay Commission recommended a 20 percent increase five years ago). While the Central Government's expenditure on wages is relatively small (less than 2 percent of GDP), states' expenditure on wages has been around 4-5 percent of GDP and significant wage increases would considerably further erode their finances. In addition, salaries in public enterprises are based on pay levels in the civil service. While essential to restore the competitiveness of pay in the civil service, in the absence of offsetting measures, a significant pay increase would also weaken the finances of public enterprises.

Another source of pressure is related to the repercussions of states' indebtedness on the Central Government. While in theory the states have no discretion to increase their own fiscal deficits beyond the financing authorized by the Central Government, they can do so indirectly by delaying payments to creditworthy public enterprises which in turn access financial markets. They also can delay payments to service their debt to the Central Government. States' interest payments on their debt to the Central Government alone account for 13 percent of the Central Government revenue. Thus far public enterprises and the Central Government have made no financial concessions. However, for the first time since Independence, net transfers from the Central Government to the states are on the verge of being negative. This may weaken the states' ability to comply with their financial obligations vis-à-vis the Central Government and could become one avenue whereby states' fiscal imbalances spill over to the Central Government's finances.

Finally the new government has announced its intention to increase significantly public spending on primary education. This is a welcome decision. Over the last four decades the public sector emphasis to building up the country's productive potential was achieved at the cost of some neglect of human resource development. In addition, even before 1991, the states responded to their financial difficulties by reducing spending on the social sectors and on infrastructure. As discussed later in this chapter, for India to successfully compete in world markets it will be essential to accelerate the development of its human resources, an objective that will necessarily entail additional claims on public resources. In addition, there has been considerable underspending in recent years on the maintenance of existing infrastructure and on building critically needed new one. While the government is taking important steps to involve the private sector to fill India's infrastructure gaps, it is evident that the public sector will continue to have a major role in the provision of infrastructure. Therefore, unless considerable efforts are made to reduce unproductive public spending and mobilize additional resources, responding to India's urgent infrastructure and human resource development needs will exacerbate fiscal imbalances.

It will be difficult to achieve these goals, however, without a ***restructuring of center-states fiscal relations***. Expenditure responsibility assigned to state governments by the Constitution accounts for about one half of total expenditure. At the same time, states are assigned taxation powers that result in their collecting only one-third of total tax revenues. The difference is covered by transfers in the form of shared central revenue, grants and loans. Since a part of these transfers is determined by the states' gap, and there have been periodic write-offs; states have in practice been faced with a relatively soft budget constraint--even though in theory state deficits are constrained by limits on borrowing imposed by the Central Government. More importantly perhaps, states do not face the discipline of financial markets, as the annual program of state security issues is still allocated administratively among commercial banks by the RBI. Thus, all the states borrow on the same terms, regardless of their creditworthiness. It is clear that center-state fiscal relations will need to be restructured if the states are to be encouraged to address their major problems of weak tax collections, growing wage bills, uneconomic enterprises and poor cost recovery. Similar considerations apply to the financial relationships between state and local governments.

India needs to emulate the experience of other countries that have succeeded in reducing their fiscal deficits and raise their public savings considerably (Table 2.1). For instance, while public expenditure was reduced in Chile and the East Asian countries between 1980 and 1990, that of India actually increased (Table 2.2). A central element of fiscal restructuring in Malaysia, Singapore, Thailand, Indonesia and Korea was the reduction of public expenditure through better management of nonfinancial public enterprises and reduction of subsidies and transfers. India will need to make similar efforts. This will be important to accelerate the country's growth rates even further and needs to be given the highest priority. It is encouraging that the new government has made the correction of fiscal imbalances one of its economic management highest priorities, but it is too early to assess how this statement of priorities will be translated into concrete actions.

Table 2.1: Gross National Savings for Selected East Asian Countries and India, 1992; 1994 (in percent of GDP, current price)		
	1992	1994
India		
Private	19.6	22.7
Public	1.5	1.7
Total	21.1	24.4
Hongkong		
Private	30.3	29.4
Public	3.5	4.5
Total	33.8	33.9
Indonesia		
Private	22.9	25.2
Public	7.6	6.8
Total	30.5	32.0
Korea		
Private	27.3	25.6
Public	7.8	9.2
Total	35.1	34.8
Malaysia		
Private	18.0	17.9
Public	11.7	14.0
Total	29.7	32.8
Philippines		
Private	16.5	16.6
Public	3.0	3.0
Total	19.5	19.6
Singapore		
Private	36.5	38.6
Public	12.3	10.9
Total	48.8	49.5
Thailand		
Private	22.6	22.1
Public	11.4	12.9
Total	34.0	35.0
Sources: Various IMF and government statistics.		

Table 2.2: Total Public Expenditure, Regional Comparison (percent of GDP)			
Country	1980	1985	1990
India	19.4	21.9	25.6
Malaysia	32.3	32.3	29.3
Chile	29.0	27.3	21.3
Indonesia	23.7	19.6	19.0
Korea	21.5	18.5	16.8
Thailand	19.8	19.6	15.5
Source: World Bank.			

Other countries' experience suggests that strong fiscal adjustment has been central to a successful liberalization of their economy. Table 2.3 shows that India has adjusted its fiscal imbalances much less than other countries which often started from situations much more serious than India's.

Table 2.3: Fiscal Balances Consolidated Government Fiscal Deficits (as % of GDP)			
	1986-90	1991-94	Change
India	-11.4	-9.7	1.7
East Asia (5)	-1.3	-0.1	1.1
Latin America (4)	-6.8	0.2	7.0
Other South Asia (3)	-9.2	-7.5	1.7
MNA (3)	-6.5	-1.9	4.7
SSA (4)	-6.8	-8.8	-2.0

Note: Regional Values are simple averages. East Asia: China, Indonesia, Korea, Philippines, Thailand. Latin America: Argentina, Brazil, Chile, Mexico. Other South Asia: Bangladesh, Pakistan, Sri Lanka. MNA: Algeria, Egypt, Iran. SSA: Cote d'Ivoire, Kenya, Nigeria, South Africa. *Source*: IMF Government Finance Statistics, World Bank Staff estimates.

External Account Vulnerabilities

Notwithstanding favorable external prospects and the remarkable improvements in India's current and capital accounts, *India's external accounts and debt position continue to be vulnerable in several important respects*. *First*, while growing agricultural production is reducing the country's vulnerability to fluctuations in world food prices, its dependency on oil imports is increasing. Domestic production is leveling off and, current trends persisting, India's oil imports will double to US$12 billion in the next five years. Several reasons are behind these developments.

On the demand side, subsidies on petroleum products have been substantial and reached nearly US$3 billion in 1994-95 (about 1 percent of GDP). This is stimulating a growth in demand at a considerably faster pace than GDP--a trend that will continue unless subsidies are reduced. In addition, reflecting unresolved policy issues, the expansion in power supply is taking the form of imported oil- rather than domestic coal-based thermal plants. On the supply side, potential production is thought to be significantly higher than current levels. However, private domestic and foreign investment--which is critical to achieve major increases in production--has not been forthcoming because of uncompetitive terms vis-à-vis other countries in the world.

Second, fiscal adjustment in the OECD countries and consequent reduction of multilateral and bilateral concessional development aid will increase the country's borrowing costs and make it more vulnerable to foreign interest rate shocks. Such vulnerability can only partially be offset by increased recourse to non-debt capital flows.

Third, of India's US$99 billion external debt (which includes US$5 billion of short-term debt), about US$25 billion is due to be repaid in the next four years with a peak of US$8 billion in 1996-97. This is in addition to the rollover of the short-term debt and the roll-over of NRI accounts. Added to the financing requirements of the current account deficit, this means that over the next four years, India will need to mobilize about US$46 billion of external finance, excluding the rollover of short-term debt and NRI accounts. These vulnerabilities are, however, tempered by India's sustained good export performance, the fact that portfolio investment in India has taken place in instruments that are costly to reverse, and by India's strong liquid position--US$17 billion in reserves versus short-term liabilities (including NRI deposits with remaining maturities of less than one year) roughly about half that size.

STRUCTURAL WEAKNESSES

Consolidating the success of the last few years is of fundamental importance if India is to emulate the performance of the East Asian countries and draw on the benefits of economic integration to achieve faster and sustainable economic growth. A comparison between India and other high performing economies, and an examination of what mattered in the success of these economies, suggest that a broad-based growth driven by labor-intensive production for exports is the best instrument for India to significantly reduce the "scourge" of poverty. This is reinforced by the 1996 World Bank "Global Economic Prospects" report which found that many of the countries that are insufficiently integrated with the world economy are among the poorest. The government has recognized this crucial link between integration and economic growth by fundamentally changing its development strategy in 1991 and made accelerating export growth a central objective of its reform program. This year's Economic Survey reinforced this view by further emphasizing the role of foreign direct investment in promoting higher growth, exports and employment.

Export growth in East Asia has served two key functions. At a *macroeconomic level,* it allowed rapid growth in capital goods and technology imports required by high domestic investment rates without the emergence of unsustainable external sector deficits and liabilities. It also circumvented limitations imposed by the small size of domestic markets. At a *microeconomic level,* the need to succeed in highly competitive world markets forced local firms to raise the efficiency with which they used capital and other scarce resources. Competition in global markets exposes exporters to new products and management techniques and allows them to be efficient since it provides access to imports which were previously unavailable or which embody new technologies that can contribute to productivity gains and higher allocative efficiency. Such spillovers may account for most of the rise in developing country total factor productivity in 1971-90 (Box 2.1). To consolidate the success of the last few years, and draw on some of India's unique strengths to accelerate exports growth, important structural weaknesses need, however, to be addressed. These are discussed in the rest of this section.

Protection levels are still excessively high. Inter-alia, this may not only reduce foreign direct investment, but also its benefits. The progress of the last five years notwithstanding, India's tariffs still are among the highest in the world. It will be important for India to continue to lower tariff levels to be able to compete with the more open economies of East Asia, Latin America, and the emerging European former socialist economies, and also to provide a stronger foundation to India's growth process. Though precise international comparisons of quantitative trade restrictions are difficult to make, it is nonetheless the case that quantitative trade restrictions had been largely eliminated in most major Latin American countries by the early 1990s while QRs in East Asian countries such as Korea, Thailand and Malaysia covered less than 5 percent of tariff lines--whereas they remain extremely important in India because virtually all imports of consumer goods are under license, and so are most agricultural imports. China was an exception to the East Asian rule with around 70 percent of imports subject to a variety of quantitative trade restrictions. Average unweighted tariffs were also high (around 40 percent) though, due to an extensive system of exemptions and rebates aimed at export promotion, actual duty collection was low, around 5 percent of import value.

Box 2.1: Spillover Effects of FDI

There are good *a priori* reasons to expect MNCs to have a positive effect in host countries whose economies are not subject to major domestic policy distortions. Recent thinking on the nature of MNCs stresses their ownership of proprietary largely intangible value-creating assets such as technological knowledge, capacity for innovation, or design, production, marketing, management or other skills as a key necessary condition for their existence. In the absence of artificial inducements such as high trade protection of domestic markets in a foreign country it is mainly these proprietary assets which provide an incentive for the MNC to enter that country and allow it to offset the natural advantages possessed by local firms such as better knowledge of domestic resources and conditions. And it is just these assets which are the basis for the "spillover" technology transfer and productivity gains developing countries seek to obtain through FDI.

The research evidence, though not unequivocally, supports the idea that FDI generates significant productivity gains in host countries. There is, first, a large body of cross country evidence for *direct* positive effects. These occur through MNC subsidiaries having a higher level of labor and total factor productivity than local firms, through transfers of technology or of management and quality control standards to local suppliers (the effect of the Maruti joint venture in developing a high quality components industry in India is a good case in point, see Box 2.4), or through supply of previously unavailable products to customers.

There is also considerable though not uniform evidence for a variety of *indirect* or spillover benefits. These include more rapid spread of knowledge about new technologies, products, management techniques or foreign markets to unrelated local businesses. They can include spillover benefits of training of local labor and management, and the effect of increased competition in forcing efficiency improvements among local firms. Of particular interest for India is evidence that export activity by MNCs, which are a natural conduit for information about foreign markets, can have large spillovers on exports by local firms, acting as a catalyst for a domestic export industry. Aitken, Hanson and Harrison (1994) demonstrate this effect in the wake of trade liberalization in Mexico and cite the example of Bangladesh where the entry of a single Korean multinational in garment exports led to the establishment of hundreds of locally owned export firms and the creation of what is now the country's largest export industry.

In one set of regressions a study by Balasubramaniam et al (1996) investigates evidence for hypothesis that the growth enhancing effects of FDI are larger in export oriented countries (EP) than in import-substituting counties (IS). The study looked at 34 developing countries in 1970-85, classifying them into countries pursuing EP or IS strategy using the World Bank's World Development Report's 1991 classification of countries as having outward or inward oriented trade regimes. The study found that, after accounting for the impact of domestic investment, labor force growth and export growth, the latter as another global integration variable that is expected to promote technological innovation and dynamic learning gains from abroad, the impact of FDI on GDP growth was substantial and statistically significant in EP countries while it was negligible and statistically insignificant in IS countries. A secondary result was that the output impact of FDI was substantially higher than that of domestic investment in EP countries but not in IS countries.

Other studies consider factors influencing technology royalties and fees paid by MNCs affiliates to their parent companies. In the case of US MNCs affiliates operating in Mexican manufacturing, a variety of measures of *competitive pressure from local companies* were found to be highly significant. (Blomstrom, Kokko and Zejan, 1992). The impact of local rivalry in inducing technology transfer was found to be particularly strong in consumer goods industries, leading to the hypothesis that "foreign multinationals are especially sensitive to the local market environment when barriers to entry in the form of complex technology or high capital requirements are low". A related study (Kokko and Blomstrom, 1995) found that technology transfers to affiliates of US MNCs in 33 host countries were more affected by the intensity of domestic market competition than by technology transfer laws or regulations, which in fact had an insignificant impact. Thus apart from trade liberalization, policies that expand the scope of domestic competition may well increase technology spillover gains from the presence of MNCs.

Another way to maximize benefits from MNC presence is to increase the capacity of the economy to absorb spillover gains. The previously cited analysis by Borenzstein et al (1995) finds the impact of FDI on aggregate growth to increase with the level of human capital. In the context of the study it took a male secondary school attainment level of 0.45 years for FDI to start having a positive effect. Since India's 1985 attainment level was 1.2 years (Barro and Lee, 1994), it can be concluded that FDI in India has had a positive effect on productivity growth. However, it must have been less pronounced than in several East Asian comparators where secondary school attainment levels were higher such as Korea (3.4), Taiwan (2.8) or Malaysia (1.8), though higher than in Indonesia or Thailand (both 0.8 years).

At present, Indian producers continue to pay higher costs for capital goods and intermediate inputs than their competitors and, because of their still high levels, important anomalies such as potential negative effective protection exist in the tariff structure that can only be corrected by a reduction of tariffs. Similarly, the elimination of import licensing restrictions on consumer goods is extremely important to protect the interests of the Indian consumers. In Argentina and Brazil the elimination of restrictions on imports of automobiles was motivated by the outdated automobile technology to which local consumers were subjected after three decades of protection granted on infant industry argument grounds--an infant that never grew. In addition, liberalizing imports of consumer goods would reduce the excess rents that are likely to be realized in a non-competitive market. High protective barriers will attract "tariff hopping" foreign direct investment, which empirical studies suggest has a smaller growth impact than that under more competitive conditions (see Box 2.1). In particular, because of the large size of India's markets, unless they are subject to international competition, domestic producers will have little incentive to improve their efficiency and produce for exports, which may delay India's *integration into the world market and the associated welfare improvements.*

Because foreign investors, notably multinational enterprises, increasingly operate complex global production and supply networks, protection and its associated red tape reduces a country's attractiveness in these networks. This is further confirmed by the recent experience of the transition economies in Central and Eastern Europe which have undertaken major trade liberalization in recent years. The improvement in export performance of these economies is strongly associated with growth in vertical intra-industry trade with European Union firms and the latter with FDI inflows into these countries. Vertical intra-industry trade and associated FDI inflows have also been important in the experience of China and the South-East Asian Newly Industrializing Economies like Malaysia and Thailand over the past decade. In China the share of exports from enterprises with foreign investment rose from 0.3 percent of exports in 1984 to 20.4 percent in 1992. Similarly in Europe, following the accession of Portugal and Spain to the EU in the mid-1980s, FDI as a share of GDP increased from 1 percent to 3 percent of GDP for Portugal and from slightly more than 1 percent to 2.5 percent of GDP for Spain.

However, liberalization of FDI--particularly in consumer goods industries--is also among the most controversial post-1991 reforms, generating debate about its potential advantages and ills. There is concern among the public that multinational enterprises (MNCs), through which most FDI is undertaken, dump obsolete technology in India, invest in "low-tech" consumer product markets with no benefit to the country, focus on "unproductive" areas like marketing or trading rather than manufacturing, are interested in short term "quick profit" investments, and exploit India's large domestic market without contributing to exports.

Concerns about FDI concentrating in consumer goods or in trade and service sectors reveal significant underestimation of the contribution of these sectors to raising productivity and growth. Low productivity (particularly of public enterprises in infrastructure, financial and other services) was the main cause of India's disappointing growth performance in previous decades. Regardless of the level of technology needed for consumer goods (which in fact is rising dramatically with advances in electronics, biotechnology etc.) what matters is how far MNCs contribute (through more competition, better management, superior technology) to raising

---

Box 2.2: Are Potato Chips more Important than Computer Chips?

India has hopes of becoming a food superpower. It may get the boost it needs from Ruffles potato chips and McDonald's ketchup.

American food giants recognize that Indian agrobusiness has lots of room to grow, especially in food processing. India processes a minuscule 1 percent of the food it grows, compared with 70 percent for the U.S., Brazil and the Philippines. A third of all Indian produce is wasted due to poor distribution and storage facilities. But improvements don't come cheap. Raising India's capacity to process fruit and vegetables to just 15 percent of output will require investment of US$3 to US$6 billion, according to McKinsey & Co. Much of this money will have to come from abroad. And as in other industries, India will have to compete for resources with other developing markets such as China. India notched up a small victory last year when Franklin Farms Inc., a Connecticut mushroom producer, chose it over China as a base for growing and processing mushrooms. Franklin Farms opted for a partnership with India's Weikfield Agro Products Ltd., a family-run company in the western city of Pune that was eager to tap new technology and markets. Franklin is building 48 hothouses and a US$9 million canning plant. This year the facility will produce several thousand tons of mushrooms for Franklin to sell in the US. To continue attracting foreign companies, India's food industry must overcome several high hurdles, including poor roads and a retail network dominated by mom-and pop shops. It also must solve an image problem: Food doesn't command as much attention from economic planners as high-tech industries do. And nationalists protest that the country doesn't need foreign expertise in food. Kito de Boer, a principal at McKinsey, turning a common argument in favor of high tech on its head, counters that "potato chips are more important than computer chips." India's agricultural output is US$65 billion a year and accounts for a third of the country's gross domestic product. So Mr. de Boer and other experts say food processing will create many more jobs, especially in rural areas, home to 70 percent of Indians. They also note that food processing is a technology-based industry, a fact they say Indian policy makers overlook. PepsiCo unit Pepsi Foods Ltd. offers a case in point. Five years ago, it set up a research farm in the northern state of Punjab to develop high-yield tomato plants. It contracted farmers to grow the tomatoes, helping 1,200 growers more than triple their output to 32 metric tons an acre. Partly thanks to Pepsi's improvements, Punjab's tomato production in 1994 reached 130,000 metric tons, up from 25,000 tons in 1990.

---

productivity, reducing costs, increasing employment, and improving the quality and range of products available to the population (Boxes 2.2 and 2.3). Similarly, domestic trade and other sectors that provide productive services for the rest of the economy are of increasing importance in economic development, and are of key importance in defining international competitiveness in the world economy. Low efficiency levels in many of these sectors generate an enormous drag on the productivity of the Indian economy as a whole and on the international competitiveness of its exports so that much more rather than less FDI in services appears to be appropriate.

The possible ill-effects of FDI may in fact arise in response to prevailing policy induced distortions and can best be treated by addressing the underlying distortions themselves. A more open trade regime, un-inhibited domestic market competition and high levels of literacy are the channels through which India could benefit most from FDI (see Box 2.1). The most important policy issue is therefore not whether FDI has significant spillover or other benefits for India--it does--but rather under what circumstances it does and how such gains can be maximized.

The Chelliah Committee on *tax reform* produced a well conceived program of reforms for the Central Government taxes aimed at broadening the tax base, lowering rates, and streamlining the rate structure--thus providing the basis for improvements in tax administration. A large part of the agenda set by this Committee has already been implemented. It should be possible now to concentrate on completing this agenda while improving tax administration, and strengthening institutional capacity in

Box 2.3: The Success Story of India's Maruti Udyog

The 1982 establishment of Maruti Udyog Limited (MUL), a joint venture between the Government of India and Suzuki Motor Company of Japan, was a watershed in the development of the Indian automobile industry. Since then, car sales have soared 16 percent a year, with MUL selling more units in its first five years of operation than all other domestic manufacturers combined in the previous forty years. Productivity levels have reached nearly fifty-three cars per employee per year, compared with five for the next big Indian producer and twenty-three cars or trucks for General Motors, the biggest producer in North America, and are still rising. The company produces nearly three-quarters of the passenger cars in India and has entered foreign markets, with about 10 percent of production exported.

MUL's presence also has generated significant spillover benefits for Indian industry, particularly the auto components sector. A recent study of Asian auto markets found that the company's strict quality and close collaboration with vendors have "changed the market's perception of design and quality and revolutionized the components industry through its philosophy of vendor upgradation" (Maxton 1994). MUL actively nurtured some critical component industries by establishing eleven joint venture companies to help push quality and productivity concerns upstream. As a result about 75 percent of components are now sourced from domestic suppliers, with the rest manufactured in-house or imported. The local content of MUL's most popular model is now 95 percent.

The improvements spawned by MUL have supported 22 percent annual growth in the components industry since 1986 and led to the industry achieving US$2 billion in output and US$300 million in exports in 1995. Though most exports are replacement parts for older models in industrial countries, supplies to original equipment manufacturers are on the rise. For instance, Sundram Fasteners, a company in Madras, supplies 85 percent of General Motor's need for radiator caps in the US market.

However, the opening of the automobile market to new entry has created an immense challenge to Maruti, which requires quick action. The current ownership structure (50% Suzuki, 50% GOI), has, however, led to different assessment of management and investment requirements.

this area. In particular, it will be important to *extend the base of the excise system*. Exemptions have increased in recent years, and long-standing exemptions for the small-scale industry encourage tax evasion and the inefficient fragmentation of production. Correcting this, and reducing the rates to no more than two or three should make it possible to make the excise system close to a value added tax, and facilitate its integration with the critically needed establishment of VATs at the state level.

There also is considerable scope to increase the efficiency of *corporate income taxation*, as well as revenues, by reducing both the rates and exemptions associated with this tax. The exclusion of profits arising from export sales, accelerated depreciation, fringe benefits and other tax preferences imply that a nominal rate of 46 percent (including a 15 percent surcharge) translates into an effective rate of less than 20 percent-- with the result that the surge in corporate profits of the last few years has not been accompanied by corresponding increases in tax revenue. Similar considerations apply to *the personal income tax*. Particularly important in this regard is the exemption of agricultural income by the states--to whom the Constitution delegates its taxation. Last but not least, critically important to the improvement of India's taxation system is the implementation of the recommendation of the *Tenth Finance Commission to shift the base for revenue sharing from a high share of two taxes at present* (personal income taxes and excises) to a lower share of total tax receipts--which would provide states with a more stable source of revenue while no longer influencing how the Central Government raises revenue.

Other policy and structural weaknesses erode the competitiveness of India's exports. While India's low wages are likely to attract significant export-oriented FDI, their effect may be considerably diminished or even negated by other characteristics such as rigid labor legislation, low literacy rates and labor productivity and other factors boosting unit costs such as the inadequacies in transport and communications infrastructure noted below.

Labor Costs. Indian hourly labor costs for production workers in manufacturing are among the lowest in the world for the 31 countries for which the United States Bureau of Labor Statistics calculates comparable data. In the clothing industry, 1993 Indian hourly wage costs of US$0.27 compared with US$4.61 in Taiwan, US$2.71 in Korea, US$1.62 in Hungary, US$0.71 in Thailand. They are, however, in line with those in China (US$0.25 per hour) whose labor force exceeds all these countries combined. However, a recent study (Majumdar, 1996) found that the actual labor cost in India's clothing industry is

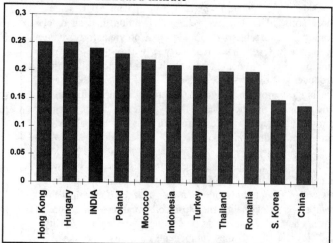

Figure 2.1: Comparative Clothing Production Costs, 1995, Deutsche Mark/ standard minute

Source: KSA, 1995, cited in Majumdar, 1996.

substantially higher than in many competitor countries after taking into account factors such as productivity and absenteeism. On this basis, Indian unit labor costs in clothing manufacture are on a par with those in Eastern Europe, around 25 percent higher than in Thailand and around two-thirds higher than in Korea or China (Figure 2.1).

*Indian **labor markets** in the industrial sector are characterized, especially in relation to East Asian countries, by exceptional inflexibility (World Bank, 1993).* A complex legal regime--some 50 major pieces of legislation covering labor welfare and dispute settlement--govern industrial relations in the organized sector where most FDI would be directed. Rules governing termination of employment and closing of an industrial establishment (exit policy) render it virtually impossible to restructure ailing public and private sector firms. Fractious industrial relations add to this inflexibility. Industrial relations have shown an improvement following the reforms compared to the late 1980s when India is estimated to have lost 20 to over 100 times more days per worker to strikes than several other East Asian countries. In 1994-95, 19.2 million mandays were lost due to strikes compared with 34.57 million in 1991-92. However, the available number of working days is still estimated to be lower than that in East Asian countries when these lost days are combined with the important level of absenteeism, a large number of holidays and customary leave entitlements.

Labor market rigidities will become more costly as India integrates further in the world economy. The labor market inflexibility may limit India's ability to attract significant FDI in labor intensive manufacturing exports, a pre-requisite for growth and poverty reduction. Evidence from India and other countries indicates that restrictions affecting hiring and firing decisions increase the sunk costs associated with new investment and lead to postponement of investment or high capital intensity. The government recognizes the inadequacy of its outward development strategy with the existing labor legislation. It is in the process of reviewing existing laws such as the Industrial Disputes Act and the Trade Unions Act, with the objective of establishing an efficient system of labor dispute settlement.

Literacy. *High levels of enrollment in primary and secondary education have been shown to be a key factor in sustained high levels of growth in eight East Asian export-led economies.* Greater investments in human resources--especially by providing adequate nutritional levels and basic education--are essential for both generating higher rates of economic growth and reducing poverty. The average 3-4 years of schooling of India's population in the mid 1980s was comparable to the more slowly integrating developing countries (3.4 average years) and was about 3 years less than the median for the fast integrating countries (6.7 average years). In India, while primary enrollments have risen rapidly, literacy rates have not kept pace because of the high drop-out rates, particularly in rural areas and among females. While literacy has risen from 18 percent in 1951 to 52 percent in 1991, it is still much below that in the East Asian countries when they began to integrate their economies with the world market. For Korea and Thailand, literacy rates were 71 percent and 68 percent respectively in 1960. Last year's CEM discussed in detail the actions required for a significant improvement in education performance in India.

But India's high number of scientists and engineers is likely to provide a comparative advantage in trade and attract FDI to certain high-skill intensive industries. While the broad educational standard of the population as a whole was low, the absolute numbers of scientists and engineers in India--around 2.5 million in 1990--was among the largest in the world (see Table 2.4). This number comprised around 0.8 percent of the labor force, higher than in Korea in 1981 (in the midst of its takeoff phase). This advantage is thus expected to provide comparative advantage in trade and an attraction to FDI in certain high-skill intensive industries such as software. Anecdotal evidence (including several interviews with business executives) suggests

Table 2.4: Scientific and Technical Workers									
Country	Scientists and Engineers ('000)	% of Labor Force	Tech-nicians ('000)	% of Labor Force	Total ('000)	% of Labor Force	Scient. & Engin. as % of Total	Year	Type of Data*
India	2,471	0.77	639	0.20	3,111	0.96	79.4	1990	EA
China	...		...		9,661	1.48		1988	EA
Indonesia	193	0.34	1,664	2.96	1,858	3.30	10.4	1980	ST
Korea	94	0.62	1,931	12.77	2,026	13.40	4.6	1981	EA
Pakistan	287	0.85	210	0.62	498	1.48	57.6	1990	EA
Iran	295	2.49	171	1.45	468	3.96	63.0	1982	ST
Turkey	708	3.71	163	0.85	875	4.58	80.9	1980	ST
Argentina	695	6.09	245	2.15	946	8.29	73.5	1988	EA
Brazil	1,362	3.08	...					1980	ST
Nigeria	22	0.07	80	0.25	102	0.32	21.7	1980	ST
Japan	8,672	14.28	4,955	8.16	13,641	22.46	63.6	1987	EA
*EA = Economically active qualified labor. *ST = Stock of qualified labor.									
Sources: UNESCO Statistical Yearbook, 1992, Statistics on Science and Technology and World Bank.									

that India has a unique advantage in this stock of low-cost English speaking professionals. However, this pool of high-skill professionals may not be so great an advantage for labor intensive export-oriented manufactures, the dramatic expansion of which has been so essential in the improvement of living standards in East Asia and where basic labor force skills may be of more importance. For instance, a 1993 survey of workers in textile mills targeted for restructuring found that less than 30 percent had completed primary education and 25 percent had 5-7 years of education. The Bank's 'East Asia Miracle' study notes that East Asian countries have allocated considerably more educational spending to broad-based primary and secondary level education than countries in Latin America or South Asia. The shift in Central Government resources from higher and technical education towards primary education over the period 1989-94 is a step towards redressing the imbalance.

Besides addressing the above reform agenda, there are a number of other structural weaknesses that would need to be removed for India to reach a path of rapid and sustainable growth, and translate this growth to improvements in the educational and living standards of the population at large. In particular, infrastructure constraints are emerging as one of India's most serious constraint to faster growth--and even a constraint to the maintenance of the current level of growth. Resolving India's serious infrastructure bottlenecks is not going to be easy since it involves the complex issues of domestic capital market development and the establishment of an enabling framework for private investment. The former will depend on the government's ability to reduce its fiscal deficit to release resources, including those of the contractual savings institutions, for investment in high returns infrastructure projects. Contractual savings institutions are the driving force behind the mobilization of long term financial savings and the development of a long-term debt market. Besides the financing issue, encouraging private investment in infrastructure will depend to a large extent on an enabling legal, administrative and regulatory framework at the state level. This is the subject of Chapter 5 of this report.

Deficiencies in transport, ports, power and telecommunications, are a major handicap for India's growth and export competitiveness. At an aggregate level, India had an infrastructure stock of a little over US$500 per capita in 1993 (Figure 2.2), lower than most Asian comparators. Two of the countries which had lower infrastructure stocks--China and Indonesia--had significantly higher per-capita incomes, suggesting that inefficiencies in delivery of infrastructure services are also a significant problem in India. Growth in demand for all transport services, substantial under-investment, slow pace of technological and skills upgrading, non-commercial pricing policies, poor maintenance, low operating efficiencies, low labor productivity and restrictive trade union practices have contributed to significant physical

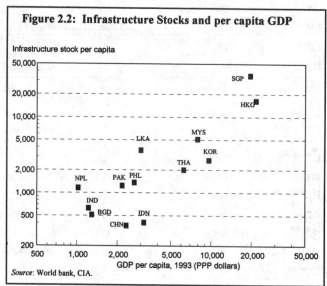

Figure 2.2: Infrastructure Stocks and per capita GDP

constraints in ports, inland transport links and international aircargo capabilities. In today's highly competitive international markets, such constraints affect the ability of India to participate in the "just-in-time" global production structures established by multinational companies, to respond promptly to rapidly changing market conditions in world markets, and to participate in new export markets for long-distance services such as data processing, software programming, back-office services and customer support. Availability and quality of infrastructure services are among the most important determinants of export-oriented FDI flows because of their impact on cost competitiveness. *Deficiencies in transport and telecommunications infrastructure*, which are discussed in the rest of this sub-section, are an issue arising repeatedly in the evaluation of individual export sectors (see Chapter 6).

*India's major **ports** are over-crowded, poorly equipped and inefficiently laid out.* Eleven ports account for over 90 percent of the country's total ports throughout. They are used beyond their capacity, with average utilization rates currently ranging from 118 to 135 percent compared with international norms of between 55 and 65 percent. This degree of congestion leads to extraordinary turnaround delays; vessels entering Bombay and Calcutta, for example, currently take five to six days to turn around. This contrasts with six to twelve hours in most other ports in the region. Lengthy delays and inadequate port services have induced carriers to charge higher freight rates from Indian ports than from other Asian ports.

Demand forecasts suggest India will need additional port capacity of roughly 200 million tons by the end of the century (ADB, 1996). Current estimates place capacity at 174 million tons. However, capacity addition during the Eighth Five-Year Plan 1992-97 is expected to fall below target by 45 percent. In addition to the basic structural problems, such as insufficiently wide shipside aprons, berths with insufficient draughts, and a general lack of dockyard real estate for warehousing and expansion, inefficiencies are attributable, according to the Federation of Indian Exporter Organizations, to obsolete equipment, burdensome bureaucracy, poor management and extremely low labor productivity. The 11 major ports and 139 minor ports are all managed by the government controlled port trusts. The number of Twenty Feet Equivalent Units (TEUs) handled per crane hour in Indian ports is significantly lower than in many competitors--7 in Bombay compared to 32 in Singapore. These factors combine to increase container handling costs. A World Bank study (1994) compared Indian port handling costs to those in selected other countries, and, not counting the loss of potential exports, estimated the comparative cost disadvantage at US$80 per container for exporters and US$190 for importers.

Roads. Nowhere is the contrast between high stock and low efficiency as marked as with roads. The length of paved roads per-capita is high relative to most East Asian comparators (around 1000 kilometers per million people versus around 150 in China and 550 in Thailand). But only 20 percent of paved roads are estimated to be in good condition, compared with 70 percent in Korea and 50 percent in Thailand. *Road usage is growing rapidly however.* Road freight grew at nearly 9 percent a year over the past 20 years, currently accounting for about 60 percent of all freight. Road travel also accounts for approximately 80 percent of India's passenger traffic. By the year 2000 these shares are expected to rise to 65 percent and 87 percent, respectively. A large proportion of the total road system is used at well over 100 percent of its intended economic capacity. The National Highway network, with 2 percent of the total road system, carries close to 40 percent of the country's total traffic. Excessively heavy traffic directly contributes to worsening road conditions and takes a further economic toll in terms of vehicle operating costs and delays.

The **air transport sector** *is where India has made the most progress over the past five years.* Reforms in the air cargo market have led to increased competition and investment and lowering of airfreight rates. Airborne import/export traffic in 1992-95 grew some 49 percent and is expected to continue to grow at an annual rate of 15-20 percent. The entry of private airlines contributed to a more than doubling in the rate of growth of passenger air traffic, 12 percent per year in 1992-95 compared with 5 percent in the 1980s, and growth is expected to continue at similar or higher rates in the medium term. Measures taken to support development of adequate airport infrastructure include merging of the domestic and international airport authorities and the opening to the private sector of airport construction. Nevertheless, with the exception of China, airport capacity remains low relative to East Asia (Table 2.5). However, concerns about the ability of the public airline industry to compete have restricted the expansion of private activity in this area.

Table 2.5: International Comparison of Airport Capacity		
	Airports per 1 million pop.	Airports per 1000 km^2
India	0.38	0.11
Malaysia	5.83	0.35
Philippines	3.67	0.52
Singapore	3.46	15.81
South Korea	2.50	1.16
Indonesia	2.21	0.23
Thailand	1.74	0.20
China	0.17	0.02

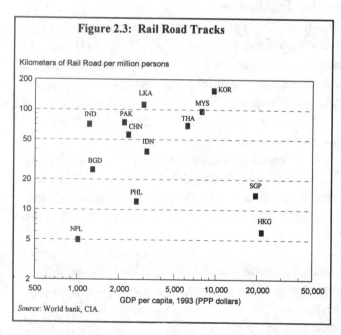

Figure 2.3: Rail Road Tracks

Kilometers of Rail Road per million persons

Source: World bank, CIA.

Indian railways *have been losing freight market share to road transport* despite a relatively high length of railways per capita (Figure 2.3) and per square kilometer, and despite the problems associated with the road system. One reason has been the low priority on container cargo leading to slow and widely variable delivery times. *A recent World Bank study indicates it takes about a quarter of the time to send a container from Madras to Northern India by truck as by rail.* There is also a shortage of rolling stock and equipment which has also contributed to bottlenecks in the movement of cargo. Nevertheless freight transport demand is expected to grow between eight to ten percent per annum in the medium term. *Massive investment is needed to keep pace with these demand forecasts.*

Telecommunications. Table 2.6 shows India underperforming to comparable countries on a range of telecommunications sectors indicators in particular for telephone density and line faults. India has already recognized the importance of this sector in enhancing its ability to compete by inviting private sector participation. The main objectives include making a wide range of quality telecommunications services more widely available including village access to basic telephone services, at reasonable prices. The policy permits private companies in India to supplement the services provided by DOT, but requires them to maintain a balanced service coverage. This policy is expected to promote labor-intensive exports by removing a large obstacle to companies relocating to rural areas where labor costs are lower.

Table 2.6: Telecommunications Sector Indicators, 1993			
	Telephone Density per 100 pop	Waiting Period (years)	Faults per 100 lines per year
India	0.89	2.5	218.0
EUROPE	30.85	2.9	NA
Argentina	12.29	1.3	12.5
Mexico	8.79	1.0	NA
Brazil	7.51	0.7	43.2
ASIA	4.27	1.4	NA
Egypt	4.26	5.8	NA
Thailand	3.71	6.5	32.2
AFRICA	1.6	4.9	NA
China	1.47	0.8	NA
Philippines	1.31	9.9	10.0
Pakistan	1.31	4.9	120.0
Indonesia	0.92	0.5	49.0
Sri Lanka	0.9	>10	15.0

Source: ITUs World Telecommunications Development Report. World Telecommunications Indicators - 1994-96.

The power deficit is chronic and the situation is rapidly deteriorating. The power supply gap has continued to increase during the Eighth Five-Year Plan. The overall energy deficit has risen from 9 to about 14 percent with the peak deficit getting close to 30 percent today. This power shortage is estimated to cost India US$2-3 billion a year at least. *The factors underlying this deficit are well known.* Chief among them is the inability of the sector to expand the country's power supply capacity at a pace commensurate with a rapidly growing demand. The latter is fueled by economic liberalization and industrial development as well as the low subsidized tariffs to agriculture and households. The additional capacity created during the Eighth Plan fell well short of the targets. Out of the 48,000 MW initially envisaged, approximately 18,000-19,000 MW are expected to be commissioned by end-1997. Despite government's efforts to encourage private investment in the sector, the addition of private generating capacity is unlikely to exceed few hundred megawatts by the end of the Eighth Plan period, most of it coming from distribution licensees.

For the Ninth Five-Year Plan period, the government has estimated that the additional capacity required to eliminate the power deficit would be around 57,000 MW, which means investments in generation, transmission and distribution of more than US$100 billion. Given the disastrous financial situation of most, if not all, SEBs (Box 2.4), it will not be possible to mobilize the resources needed to eliminate the power shortage. The problems of the sector are too deep and far-reaching: insufficient generation, poorly maintained equipment (generation, transmission, and distribution), inadequate tariffs and revenue shortfalls, deep cross-subsidies, and widespread government interference. It is not surprising that the deep revenue shortfalls that stem from inadequate tariffs and exacerbate the sector's operational problems, also render it incapable of meeting the supply needs of its consumers. But the problems transcend the revenue shortfall; long-term improvement requires more than an increase in tariffs and a phased reduction of internal cross-subsidies. *Significant, comprehensive, reform is necessary.* This means restructuring the power sector at the state level, along the lines, for example, of what has been undertaken in Orissa; reconstituting the system at both the state and central levels; and reallocating responsibilities between them. There is a key or core set of changes that are required at the state level; short of them, attempts at reform are not likely to yield long-term success. Other types of measures will only be second-best initiatives with marginal and short-lived impacts (e.g., encouragement of captive generation--see Chapter 5).

Box 2.4: Haryana's Power Crisis

The very poor power supply situation in Haryana threatens to severely undermine the growth potential of the state. System losses are reported at 33%, but are probably closer to 40%, with non-technical losses - i.e., unbilled supply, theft and pilferage of power--running probably at some 20%. The plant load factor (PLF) on thermal plants averages 44%, well below India's average. Large voltage fluctuations commonly deteriorate electrical equipment. Every year, about 27% of distribution transformers fail because of overloading. Farmers have to rewind irrigation pumpsets two or three times a year because of the poor quality of power supply. Unserved demand has increased from 9% to 25% between 1993 and 1996, representing a cost to the economy of at least Rs. 1,740 crores (US$530 million).

The financial losses of Haryana State Electricity Board (HSEB) have now reached close to half its annual sales revenue. HSEB's accumulated losses (about Rs.2,800 crores) exceed the total net investment (equity and loan) from the state government (Rs.2,300 crores) since the formation of the Board. Beside operational inefficiencies, revenue loss and theft of power, the main factor underlying these losses is the unremunerative tariff of power supplied to agriculture, and to a lesser extent, domestic consumers. Agricultural sales generate only 17 % of HSEB's revenue while representing, according to HSEB's accounts, 45 % of the overall consumption. Power supplied to agriculture is officially priced at the equivalent of 50 paise/kWh, which is less than one-fourth of the average cost of supply. By contrast, industrial power tariffs (2.5 Rs./kWh) are among the highest in India. But this heavy cross-subsidization is insufficient to compensate for the losses incurred on sales to agriculture and domestic consumers.

To cover the deficit, the state government has been heavily subsidizing HSEB's operations through cash support, conversion of debt into equity, and forgiveness of debt service obligations. *Over the last 5 years, the total net transfers from the state to HSEB can be conservatively estimated at about Rs.2,044 crores (US$680 million),* which is equivalent to the cost of constructing a 500-MW plant, about four times Haryana's total revenue expenditure on medical, public health and family welfare (Rs.544 crores), more than the total expenditure on irrigation and flood control (Rs.1,530 crores), and of the same order of magnitude as expenditure on education, sports, arts and culture (Rs.2,337 crores) over the same period. [This is also to compare to subsidies accounted for in HSEB's financial accounts and the State's budget (Rs.487 crores).] State support has been increasingly diverted to cover cash operating expenses and debt service obligations on institutional debt, leaving little, if anything, for capital expenditure. In 1997, HSEB will face a cash deficit of Rs.350-450 crores, and will not be able to cover its cash obligations in the absence of significant tariff increases.

Under normal circumstances, demand for power would likely grow at about 8% annually, requiring new investments in generation, transmission and distribution of about Rs.12,000 crores (US$3 billion). Given the present financial distress of the sector, there is no way these resources can be mobilized. If nothing were done, Haryana's power sector would continue to deteriorate further, drain public resources and stall the economic growth of the state altogether. By contrast, when Haryana reforms its power sector, as already decided, the state is expected to reap enormous economic benefits. *A rough estimate puts the net present value of these benefits at least Rs.7,200 crores (more than about US$2 billion) over the next 20 years, one-third of Haryana's 1994 gross domestic product!*

In addition to the under-investment and inefficiencies in the use of existing infrastructure stock, the engineering, administrative and construction constraints are just as binding --as the World Bank's 25 year experience with relaxing financial constraint through infrastructure lending indicates. For instance, State Public Work Departments (PWDs) and small labor-intensive road constructors, who have monopolized *road* planning, design and construction in India for decades, do not have the capacity to build the expressway now needed for the high density corridors. Thus, *unless there is dramatic improvements in the efficiency of service delivery, infrastructure constraints are likely to remain a significant constraint on achieving progress in global integration,* and sustained rapid export growth.

Finally, there is growing evidence that India's cities and towns are facing a crisis of serious proportions stemming from chronic underinvestment in urban areas and consequent shortages of key urban services. At the heart of the problem are the cities' weak fiscal base-- eroded by state legislation imposing rent controls, limits on the amount of land an individual can hold, restrictions on land markets, and unrealistically low water charges. In some of the main cities, fiscal revenues are excessively dependent on extremely inefficient taxes which need to be eliminated--such as octroi. Thus, any program of **urban reform** would need to include measures to: (a) improve urban areas' use of the existing resource base (such as a better cost recovery and enforcement of existing taxes); (b) strengthen the resource base and make it more efficient (such as lifting rent controls, eliminating octroi, and establishing efficient land markets); and (c) establish a rule-based, efficient system of capital transfers to replace the present system which is discretionary and unpredictable. Such measures would provide the basis for the restoration of the finances of the country's cities and towns--and thus restore their capacity to invest in critically needed infrastructure. They also would help municipalities become creditworthy borrowers, able to access capital markets and mobilize financing for critically needed investments.

It will be critically important to complete the financial sector reforms started in 1991. This is necessary not only to promote the efficient allocation of the investment needed to achieve higher growth, but also to strengthen the implementation of both fiscal and monetary policies and preserve macroeconomic stability. However, some of the remaining financial sector reforms can only be implemented if fiscal consolidation is achieved because further liberalization in the presence of large public sector borrowing requirements needs and consequently high interest rates could weaken the financial system--as companies balance sheets deteriorate and banks' non-performing assets rise.

Assuming that fiscal consolidation is achieved, the priority financial sector reforms are essentially four. **First,** the comprehensive restructuring of the public banks which started with their recapitalization needs to be brought to its logical conclusion. This means granting banks increased managerial autonomy over branch networks, employment and compensation issues, and portfolio decisions. At the same time, the government's equity share in these banks needs to be reduced below 50 percent--which would create incentives for improved bank management and profitability. It is clear that the phase in which the development of India's financial sector could benefit from direct government ownership is long over and that in this new phase the government's most important and challenging role is in fulfilling its oversight responsibilities and in strengthening the institutional base of India's financial markets. **Second**, remaining controls on banks and insurance companies forced holdings of government debt need to be phased out pari-pasu with the development of markets for government debt. **Third,** as the fiscal deficit is reduced, it should be possible to accelerate the development of money markets by reducing the intervention of the RBI in the placement of government debt. This should make it possible to establish liquid and deep money markets which can provide the basis for benchmark interest rates, help develop financial market linkages, and support the development of a corporate debt market. ***Fourth***, the government will need to continue strengthening prudential regulations, supervision, and the capital market infrastructure and legal and regulatory framework. A delivery-versus-payment system was recently established for government securities, but further efforts are needed to create modern settlement and registration systems for corporate bond markets, while regulatory oversight needs to be made more effective. In addition, improvements in India's payments system are key to the integration of the country's regional financial markets, and also to the better management of the country's public debt.

As noted in the government's CMP, "No strategy of economic reforms and regeneration in India can succeed without sustained and broad-based agricultural development". Agriculture accounts for 30 percent of India's GDP and 70 percent of total employment. Its performance is therefore central to the welfare of over 300 million poor who live and work in rural areas. Since Independence, increasing agricultural productivity has been a central objective of India's development strategy--essential to the elimination of famines, reduction of poverty, and successful industrialization. However, the two conflicting objectives of ensuring food products to consumers at low prices, and making production remunerative to farmers, led to an unsustainable agricultural growth pattern during the 1980s and mid-1990s which, if not corrected could erode the gains of the past decade and a half. There is therefore an urgent need to promote sustainable and rapid agricultural growth, based on a four-pronged strategy which is discussed in detail in Chapter 4.

Conclusion

As indicated earlier, none of these constraints can, in principle, alone threaten the acceleration of private investment, exports and growth. However, when combined together they can seriously stifle private sector investment intentions and thus hamper India's ability to draw on the benefits of global integration in improving its economic performance and welfare. India's past disappointing growth performance and poverty reduction are clear evidence of the importance of these constraints to growth. In addition, India's success in integrating global world markets will depend not only on how far macroeconomic performance and the enabling environment for private investment improve relative to its own past but will also be conditioned by the performance of other countries, an increasing number of whom are also embarked on the path of domestic reform and international integration for growth and welfare improvements. If a significant proportion of these constraints is addressed, then 8-9 percent growth rate is within reach.

PART II

THE CHALLENGES AHEAD

3 THE CENTRALITY OF FISCAL ADJUSTMENT

INTRODUCTION

At no point in India's recent history have circumstances been better to bring fiscal imbalances to levels consistent with sustainable higher growth. The strength of the economic recovery provides an ideal opportunity for the much needed fiscal correction. The latter combined with the expectation of a favorable external environment makes it much easier to complete the liberalization of the trade regime and that of the financial sector. More importantly, perhaps, the last five years have provided ample evidence on the extent to which India stands to gain from further stabilizing and reforming its economy and from a better integration with the world economy. There is now a broader consensus in favor of reforms. Indicative of this, the new United Front Government's first policy statement ("A Common Approach to Major Policy Matters and a Minimum Programme") proposes to continue the economic program with a focus on the areas where reforms are most urgently needed: fiscal consolidation, improvement of Center-States fiscal relations, and liberalization of agriculture.

This chapter first reviews the severity of India's fiscal imbalances. Next, it articulates a strategy to reduce them. Finally, the chapter concludes by examining the importance of fiscal adjustment for the continuation of critically needed financial sector reforms. The following two chapters discuss in detail the policy and structural reforms needed for productivity growth in agriculture and greater participation of the private sector in investment and provision of infrastructure services.

EXTENT AND NATURE OF INDIA'S FISCAL IMBALANCES

India's persistently large fiscal imbalances raise three concerns. *First*, the upward trend in the interest burden on public debt threatens the sustainability of the current macroeconomic stance. In particular, it threatens the current mix of growth and inflation. Assuming that real interest rates are equal to the GDP growth rate, solvency requires that in the long-run the primary (non-interest) public sector surplus be sufficient to finance the interest service on net outstanding public sector liabilities--that is be no larger than seignorage revenues. This would avoid an explosive situation in which new debt is issued to cover the interest payments on the mounting stock of old debt. Because a large share of the public debt has been contracted at interest rates well below current ones, and this debt will take time to mature and be rolled over at the higher current rate, India is far from such a situation. However, in the absence of a serious adjustment in India's tax or spending patterns, this situation will eventually materialize forcing either inflation to increase or growth to decline.

Second,
from a public finance angle, servicing the country's public debt puts large claims on public resources, which reduce the government's capacity to spend on key development activities. In addition, it also creates a need for higher taxation, which undermines efficiency. In 1994-95, the interest burden of public debt absorbed 37 percent of the general government's tax revenues (Tables 3.1 and 3.2).

Table 3.1: Evolution of the Public Debt Stock, 1990-96 (percent of GDP at end of period)						
	90-91	91-92	92-93	93-94 [a]	94-95 [a]	95-96 [ab]
I. Domestic debt [c]	70.1	69.5	68.5	--	--	--
General Government	59.4	58.2	57.7	60.7	58.4	56.5
Center [d]	52.7	51.2	50.7	53.5	51.2	--
States [e]	6.8	7.0	7.1	7.3	7.2	--
Non-financial Public Enterprises	10.6	11.3	10.7	--	--	--
II. External debt	23.3	27.5	30.6	25.5	23.2	23.4
General Government	16.0	19.6	22.2	20.6	20.6	20.3
RBI (net) [f]	2.9	1.9	2.1	-0.9	-2.8	-1.6
Non-financial Public Enterprises	4.4	6.0	6.3	5.8	5.4	4.7
III. Total debt (I + II)	93.4	97.0	99.1	--	--	--
General Government	75.5	77.8	80.0	81.4	79.0	76.7
Center	68.7	70.8	72.9	74.1	71.8	--
States	6.8	7.0	7.1	7.3	7.2	--
RBI	2.9	1.9	2.1	-0.9	-2.8	-1.6
Non-financial Public Enterprises	15.0	17.3	17.0	--	--	--
Memo items:						
General government debt held by RBI (net)	16.7	15.3	14.0	12.4	10.7	11.6
Center	16.3	15.0	13.7	12.1	10.5	10.9
States	0.4	0.3	0.3	0.3	0.3	0.8

Note: -- Not available.
a. Projected.
b. Includes debt held by RBI.
c. Excludes State's holding of Center debt.
d. Excluding States' debt to Center.
e. Excluding debt to general government.
f. RBI external debt minus foreign currency assets
Source: Union budget documents, RBI, and staff estimates.

Table 3.2: Interest Rates and Payments on Public Debt (percent per annum)						
	1990-91	1991-92	1992-93	1993-94	1994-95	1995-96 [a]
Central Government:						
1. Implicit Interest Rate on:						
Market Borrowings	10.2	10.4	10.4	11.3	10.7	11.3
Small Savings	9.6	9.9	9.4	12.2	13.4	13.2
External Debt	3.5	4.1	3.2	3.1	2.9	2.9
2. Interest Rate on New Issues of Dated Securities [bc]	11.0	11.5	12.5	13.1	12.0	13.8
3. Memo item: RBI Subscription of Dated Securities	44.3	48.2	22.1	4.3	1.6	17.5
General Government:						
Interest payments (percent of GDP)	4.7	5.1	5.3	5.4	5.6	5.7
Interest payments (percent of total tax revenue)	28.8	30.2	32.5	35.7	36.8	36.2
Non-financial Public Sector:						
Interest payments (percent of GDP)	5.6	6.1	6.4	6.5	6.5	6.5
Inflation rate (WPI)	10.3	13.7	10.1	8.4	10.9	7.7

a. Projected.
b. For 1990-91 - 1991-92, average of maximum and minimum rate on new placements. For the remaining years, weighted average of cutoff yields at auction, excluding funding operations.
c. For 1995-96, April-August actuals.
Source: Economic Survey; RBI; and staff estimates.

Third, the large fiscal imbalances pose a risk to macroeconomic stability as the financial sector is further liberalized. Since a large portion of the outstanding public debt stock carries interest rates well below current market rates, the overall interest bill will increase as these obligations mature and have to be rolled over at the higher current market rates. This convergence of the average rate to the marginal rate will have a sizable impact on public finances. For instance, if during 1995-96, the general government's *entire* domestic debt stock had earned the marginal interest rate, the interest payments additional to those actually made would have amounted to roughly another 1.8 percent of GDP or, equivalently, another 10 percentage points of total tax revenues. Moreover, as restrictions on financial intermediaries' portfolios--including in particular banks' SLR ratios--are eased, the captive demand for government securities will shrink. As the momentum for growth accelerates, and competition for the available pool of savings intensifies, higher rates of return will be required for investors to hold willingly the public sector liabilities. At the current public indebtedness levels, each one-percentage point increase in the average interest rate on domestic public debt would add around 0.6 percent of GDP to the general government's interest bill.

The upward trend in the interest bill on public debt places India among the top countries in terms of interest burden, both relative to GDP and to total tax revenues (Table 3.3). India's public debt burden indicators exceed those of virtually all developing countries, and particularly those of the successful East Asian countries. Only a few South Asian countries with highly indebted public sectors come closer to India in this regard.

Table 3.3: International Comparison of Public Debt Stocks and Interest Payments [a]			
(percentage)			
	Total Public Debt/ GDP	Interest payments/ Total tax revenue	Interest payments/ GDP
India [b]	68.2	36.8	5.6
Industrial Countries [c]			
Median	68.7	13.1	3.7
South Asia [d]			
Median	74.9	33.1	5.8
East Asia [e]			
Median	43.1	7.7	1.4
Baker-15 [f]			
Median	63.1	--	--
Latin America and the Caribbean [g]			
Average	--	12.0	2.0
Sub-Saharan Africa [h]			
Median	--	15.0	2.1

-- Not available.
a. Interest payment ratios pertain to 1993.
b. Debt stock and interest payment ratios refer to the general government, data for Indian fiscal year 1994-95.
c. Debt stock to GDP ratio is for the year 1994.
d. Debt stock to GDP ratio is average of 1988-93, includes: Bangladesh, Nepal, Pakistan and Sri Lanka; Interest payment ratios include: Bhutan, Pakistan and Sri Lanka.
e. Debt stock to GDP ratio is average of 1988-93, includes: Indonesia, Korea, Malaysia, Philippines and Thailand; interest payment ratios include: Indonesia, Rep. of Korea, Malaysia, Singapore and Thailand.
f. Pertains to the year 1988; Baker-15 = fifteen heavily indebted countries: Argentina, Bolivia, Brazil, Chile, Colombia, Cote d'Ivoire, Ecuador, Mexico, Morocco, Nigeria, Peru, the Philippines, Uruguay and Venezuela.
g. Bahamas, Bolivia, Chile, Colombia, Costa Rica, Dominican Republic, Nicaragua, Panama, Paraguay, Peru, St. Kitts and Nevis, Uruguay, and Venezuela.
h. Cameroon, Madagascar, Mauritius, Namibia, South Africa, and Zambia.
Source: Guidotti and Kumar (1991), Tanzi and Fanizza (1995), and Hinh Dinh (1995); World Bank data.

What is the extent of fiscal adjustment required to ensure sustainability? The analysis summarized in this report followed the conventional approach of computing the *sustainable* primary surplus/GDP ratio--i.e., the surplus consistent with stabilizing the public debt to GDP ratio permanently at its present level. The arithmetics of sustainability show that shifting from a potentially insolvent to a solvent fiscal path implies raising permanently either the public sector primary surplus or the collection of seignorage (money printing) or both. However, the empirical analysis carried out for this report shows the maximum revenue that the government could extract from seignorage is 2.5 percent of GDP but at the cost of inflation rates of around 28 percent. By contrast, the seignorage raised at moderate inflation level of around 4-5 percent (consistent with current Government inflation targets) is around 1.5 percent of GDP. Table 3.4 presents the level of *sustainable* public sector's primary deficit under alternative configurations of the economy's

Table 3.4: The Primary Deficit Consistent with Solvency (percent of GDP)			
Real GDP Growth Rate	Real Interest Rate (%)		
	5	5.5	6
4	0.7	0.4	-0.01
5	1.5	1.1	0.7
6	2.2	1.9	1.5

Note: Seignorage collection is assumed to equal 1.5% of GDP. The calculation are based on the following assumptions: External debt/GDP, net of RBI assets = 23.2% (World bank data); Domestic debt/GDP, net of debt to RBI = 55.1%; Foreign real interest rate = 5.5%.
Source: Staff calculations.

long-run real interest rate and growth rates. For instance, if the long-run real interest rate and real growth rate coincide (at 6 percent), then the sustainable public sector's primary deficit consistent with low inflation is just equal to long-run seignorage revenues--1.5 percent--therefore requiring the public sector primary deficit to be reduced by at least 1.6 percentage points of GDP from its current level of 3.1 percent of GDP (see Table 1.10).

However, this fiscal retrenchment is insufficient to stabilize the public debt/GDP ratio if financial reforms are undertaken. Fiscal sustainability would then require that either revenues are raised or expenditures are cut to match the implicit revenue loss from a lower "financial repression tax". A quantitative framework was used to assess the extent of fiscal adjustment needed under different scenarios for financial sector liberalization. The results are summarized in Table 3.5. As a starting point, column 1 of Table 3.5 shows the deficit that would be consistent with an inflation of 4 percent and a long-run economic growth and real interest rates on public debt of 5.5. It is further assumed that the status quo prevails in the financial sector (i.e the SLR and CRR are maintained at their current levels).

Table 3.5: Fiscal Consequences of Financial Reform						
	(1) Fiscal Adjustment Without Financial Reform	Reduction in SLR [a]		Reduction in CRR [b]		Reduction in Both CRR and SLR [c]
		(2) Without Fiscal Adjustment	(3) With Fiscal Adjustment	(4) Without Fiscal Adjustment	(5) With Fiscal Adjustment	(6) With Fiscal Adjustment
Primary Deficit/GDP	1.5	1.5	0.6	1.5	1.2	0.6
Inflation (percent)	4.0	13.0	4.0	9.6	4.0	4.0
Real Interest Rate on:						
Domestic Debt	5.5	7.0	7.3	6.0	5.6	7.0
Credit	9.1	8.5	8.2	8.5	8.4	7.8
Time Deposits	4.6	3.80	4.7	4.8	5.0	5.1
Overall Deficit/GDP	7.6	12.3	7.6	10.3	7.4	7.3

a. Decline in the average SLR to 25%.
b. Reduction in the CRR to 8%.
c. Both of the above measures, with additional fiscal correction.
Source: Staff calculations.

The result of this exercise confirms that the urgently needed financial reform will reduce considerably the extent to which the government can finance its deficit through monetization or financial repression. Setting the target inflation rate at 4 percent implies that the maximum amount of deficit financing through seignorage revenue cannot exceed 1.5 percent. As a result, the other columns of Table 3.5 illustrate the effects of financial liberalization on fiscal deficits, inflation, and real interests. In particular, the model shows that a reduction in the SLR to 25 percent will shrink captive demand for public debt and therefore require a higher real interest rate to clear the debt market. In this case, the long-run primary deficit has to decline to 0.6 percent of GDP in order to maintain 4 percent inflation--i.e. an additional reduction of one percentage point of GDP from the benchmark primary deficit of 1.5 percent in the absence of financial reforms (column 3). In turn, column 5 in Table 3.5 indicates that to maintain low inflation, the public sector primary deficit has to decline to 1.2 percent of GDP (0.3 percent of extra adjustment with respect to the benchmark in column 1) when the CRR is reduced to 8 percent of deposits (from 13 percent). Finally, the last column in Table 3.5 illustrates the case where the SLR and CRR are both reduced at the same time. In this case, the primary deficit of 1.5 percent of GDP becomes inconsistent with a stable debt to GDP ratio at any inflation rate. Therefore, the scenario considered in the table investigates the extra fiscal adjustment needed to maintain low long-run inflation (at 4 percent) in the face of the deeper financial reform. This requires a primary deficit of 0.6 percent of GDP.

In all cases, as shown in columns (3), (5), and (6) of Table 3.5, the reduction in SLR or CRR (or both) reduces intermediation margins, thus increasing the financial sector efficiency, but increases interest on public debt. The combined reduction in SLR and CRR (column 6, Table 3.5) leads to the largest decline in the financial intermediation margin (by close to two percentage points relative to the pre-financial reform scenario, column 1). However, the reduced captive demand for public debt and the increased real interest rates on deposits lead to a rise in public debt interest rates relative to the pre-financial reform situation.

These simulations illustrate the macroeconomic policy dilemmas now confronting India. Relying on financial repression to finance the public sector imbalance and postponing the remaining financial sector reforms would come at the cost of crowding out private investment and growth through its adverse effects on lending rates and credit availability. Proceeding with financial reforms but increasing the resort to deficit monetization to reduce the impact of higher interest rates on public debt--a strategy not very different from that followed in 1995-96--would, as Table 3.5 suggests, eventually lead to much higher inflation or even to outright insolvency in the long-run. Pursuing financial reforms and tightening monetary policy to counteract the effect of a lax fiscal stance on inflation would exacerbate the pressure on interest rates, increase the debt pileup, eventually demanding an even bigger fiscal correction to guarantee sustainability. Obviously, the only alternative if GDP growth is to be sustained at over 6 percent annual rate and poverty reduced is to implement a swift fiscal correction that will allow financial reform to proceed with little macroeconomic risk, raise investors' confidence in the reform process, reduce the excessively large public debt stock to lower real interest rates and free up financial resources for the rapid expansion of private investment. *In this context, the extent of fiscal retrenchment should aim to reach a position of primary surplus by the year 2000-2001.*

At a minimum to stabilize public sector debt in relation to GDP, maintain inflation at below 6 percent and growth at 6-7 percent would require the consolidated public sector *primary deficit* to be reduced immediately by 1.5 percentage points from its 1995-96 level of 3.1 percent (the 1995-96 Economic Survey actually proposes a slightly more ambitious target to be achieved, however, more gradually). If the central government were the only part of the public sector to adjust, this would mean a central government *fiscal deficit* of about 4.5 percent of GDP, that is a fiscal correction of 0.5 percent of GDP beyond what is envisaged in the 1996-97 budget. To the extent that states and public enterprises increase their financial performance and reduce their claims on the country's savings, the required fiscal adjustment is correspondingly less. However, as the financial sector is liberalized and banks have more discretion on portfolio composition, there will inevitably be pressure on real interest rates to increase--implying an increase in central government interest payments. Higher real interest rates would reduce private investment and thus growth while, if monetized, the increase in the central government interest payments would increase inflation. To avoid these two negative consequences, a further fiscal adjustment of about 1 percent of GDP is needed--making it necessary to increase the fiscal correction to 2.5 percent of GDP, implying a reduction in the central government *fiscal deficit* to around 3.5 percent of GDP. A more ambitious fiscal scenario is warranted and feasible, however--in which the consolidated public sector savings increase by 6 percent of GDP over the next four to five years. This would allow fiscal imbalances to be brought to sustainable levels while generating resources for critically needed public investment, and could enable growth to be sustained at 7 percent per year until the end of the decade before increasing possibly to over 8 percent thereafter.

ESSENTIAL ELEMENTS OF A FISCAL ADJUSTMENT STRATEGY

This section focuses on quantifying the increases over the short-to-medium-run (1996-97 to 2001) in gross public savings that would be consistent with reaching a primary surplus by the year 2001 and giving enough discretion to the government to share these gross savings between deficit reduction and increase in public investment. For the Central Government, the main potential areas for fiscal adjustment are on the expenditure side: (i) reducing the size of the Central Government; (ii) removing fertilizer subsidy from the central budget and re-targeting the food subsidy; and (iii) privatizing and commercializing Central Government's PEs. Another option that could be considered but is not discussed here, because it would require a review of center-state relations is to reduce non-statutory central government transfers to the states (in the form of grants and loans) and to subject them to greater scrutiny. For the states, the areas for fiscal adjustment are: (i) improving considerably the recovery of O&M for irrigation and water; (ii) reducing power subsidies through an increase in tariffs and collection rates; and (iii) adjusting public employment. Evidently, most of these measures can only be implemented gradually (it took about 10 years for Ms. Thatcher's government to reduce by half the size of the British civil service, mostly through attrition). In addition, the state fiscal adjustment will require progress in structural reforms and change in the public sector role and modus-operandi. For example, the reduction in power subsidies is dependent on the reforms of the State Electricity Boards (SEBs) while the increase in cost recovery in irrigation requires revamping the states' irrigation departments. *Therefore, in the short-run, any significant fiscal adjustment will also have to rely on revenue raising measures--such as the readjustment of oil prices (particularly for diesel and kerosene) beyond the increases of July 1996, and the full implementation of the Chelliah Committee recommendations on tax reforms (see below).*

Expenditure Reform

Reducing Central Government Size. A feasible strategy to control the growth of the government wage bill over the medium term could rely primarily on a temporary ban on new recruitment, which would allow natural attrition to erode the size of the civil service. About 3 percent of government (similar considerations apply to the state governments) employees are removed from the payroll each year due to retirement, resignation or death. This medium-term strategy could be implemented in two phases. During the first phase (about three years), no new recruitment would be allowed to take place to replace departing employees. Instead, vacancies would be filled only by surplus labor from elsewhere in the Central Government. New posts could still be created as long as they are filled by surplus labor in the Central Government. Unfilled vacancies for a period of, say, two years, would be abolished to bring the number of sanctioned posts closer to the true staffing needs of each department. Furthermore, the practice of hiring casual labor would have to be terminated since this could jeopardize government's efforts to control the size of its employment, given the legal requirement that casual labor be regularized after a certain period. In the second phase, which could last for the following two years, the government could adopt a simple rule of filling with new recruits only one in every two vacancies created during this period.

Close adherence to the above strategy could result in a reduction in Central Government employment by nearly 12 percent (close to half a million employees from the current 4 million), resulting in a reduction in the wage bill of about 0.2 percent of GDP over the medium term. The savings on government expenditure directly linked to the reduction in the civil service could reach as much as 0.2 percent of GDP (it is estimated that 44 percent of total departmental expenditure is on wages and salaries; a large portion of the remainder consists of operating expenses directly linked to the size of government employment) raising total savings from reducing the size of the government to about 0.4 percent of GDP by the beginning of the next decade.

Subsidies that do not benefit the poor could be reduced. Central Government subsidies have declined in recent years, from a total of 1.8 percent of GDP in 1990-91 to about 1.1 percent of GDP in 1995-96 (see Table 1.11). *Currently, fertilizer and food subsidies account for nearly the entire subsidy bill of the Central Government.* As will be discussed in more details in Chapter 4, these subsidies are costly and poorly targeted. Total direct savings from eliminating the fertilizer subsidy would amount to about 0.6 percent of GDP. Additional savings of close to 0.1 percent of GDP could be generated by reducing support to loss-making public fertilizer plants. And gross savings from reducing FCI's operating costs and re-targeting the PDS could reach 0.2 percent of GDP. However, savings from retargeting the food subsidy might not materialize if the geographic coverage of the RPDS is expanded. In this case, the gross savings from reducing subsidies is equal to the savings on removing the fertilizer subsidy (0.7 percent of GDP).

Gains from privatization of central public enterprises. The central government is the largest investment banker in the country. It holds equity positions in 240 enterprises in virtually all sectors of the economy. The problem is that the Central Government is not an efficient investment banker. With few exceptions, the dividends it earns on its investment in public enterprises are lower than the interest it pays on its debt. The reasons for this are well known and have to do with the fact that most managers of public enterprises do not have the mandate to function on profit making basis. The costs to the economy are considerable; they include the foregone returns that a better management of the assets would yield and the consequences of insufficient investment because of their financial constraints. Using a methodology developed to estimate the welfare gains and losses from divestiture (Box 3.1), the gains accruing to the government from privatizing 50 percent of Central Government equity in public enterprise portfolio have been estimated to amount to around 0.4 percent of GDP per year (see Annex I for detailed description of the methodology). These estimates are conservative and offer a lower

> **Box 3.1: Welfare Consequences of Selling Public Enterprises**
>
> *Does divestiture improve domestic welfare?* Who wins, who loses, and how much? One study evaluated these questions in a sample of twelve divestiture case studies in four countries (Chile, Malaysia, Mexico, and the United Kingdom). The cases cover nine monopolies (in telecommunications, energy, airlines, and ports) and three firms in competitive markets (in trucking, gambling, and electricity generation). They find that in eleven of the twelve cases divestiture made the world a better place by fostering more efficient operation and new investment. The gains in some cases were significant or unexpected. For example, productivity improved in nine of the twelve cases, most dramatically in Aeromexico, the Mexican airline, where it rose by 48 percent. In others, the gains did not necessarily follow from productivity improvement but from increased investment. This occurred in four of the twelve cases, doubling the number of telephone lines in the case of the Chilean phone company within four years following divestiture. Moreover, the gains were shared by most of the actors involved, including buyers, government, workers, consumers, and even competitors. This success did not follow from divestiture alone. Countries in the sample also did a host of other things right. These varied from case to case but included increasing competition in the product market where possible, regulating monopolies where required, and, in most cases, a competitive sale of enterprises. Moreover, divesting countries enjoyed sound macroeconomic policy at the time of divestiture.
>
> *Source*: Galal et. al. (1994), and Annex I.

bound of the potential benefits from reforming CPEs since they include neither the departmental CPEs nor the state-owned PEs (SPEs), nor the dynamic effects on savings from efficiency gains that such reforms will bring. They also do not include the gains from liquidating the sick enterprises (Box 3.2).

Gains from reducing subsidies to state public enterprises (SPEs). Two types of departmental enterprises: irrigation and power, are considered in this CEM, in view of their sizable impact on the states budgets.

Water charges and cost recovery of O&M on irrigation. In 1994-95, operation and maintenance (O&M) expenditure absorbed around 5.8 percent of states non-plan expenditure. Of this, approximately 6.8 percent is recovered through water charges. This deficit is the result of a failure to adjust water charges (in line with rising O&M costs) and also to achieve high collection rates of water charges. On the assumption that the ratio of O&M expenditures to the total non-plan expenditures of state governments remains at the same level in future years as in 1994-95 and that the uncovered gap in O&M expenditures is totally eliminated, public savings should rise by about 0.9 percent of GDP. It might go up even more if the state governments could recover a part of the capital charges.

Box 3.2: Liquidation of Manufacturing Sick Enterprises

The cost of delaying liquidation of these sick firms is very high (fiscal in addition to inefficient use of a large part of India's capital and labor force). In 1993-94 alone, the annual losses of 60 sick manufacturing PEs amounted to almost Rs.32 billion in 1994 prices (28.7 billion in current prices), that is, 1.7 times the value of their net fixed assets (NFA).

An estimate is provided of the increase in domestic savings that will occur if the government were to let these enterprises exit. The liquidation scenario is compared with a "no exit" one, where the same losses are assumed to continue. As in the previous exercise, the change in domestic savings is estimated as the difference between the stream of costs and benefits with and without the reforms. Here, the NPV without reforms is simply the discounted value of the losses, Rs.-280 billion. The NPV with liquidation is the discounted value of the net profits before taxes minus the cost of severance payments to laid off workers. Under the "reform" scenario, workers will have a severance payment equivalent to 20 months of wages each. The government takes over the liabilities and sells the assets at book value. The use of these fixed assets by the private sector yields a ratio of profits before taxes to sales of 0.085. The ratio of NFA to sales is 0.36. These numbers are based on the comparison between private and public firms in manufacturing made by O. Goswami (1995). Three possible cases are presented depending on the criteria the government will use to decide which firms to liquidate: An erosion factor greater than 1 (all 60 firms will be liquidated); equal or greater than 3 (44 firms only), equal or greater than 5 (15 firms only). In the last two cases, the firms that are not liquidated are assumed to continue to incur the same losses than in 1993/94. The most important conclusion from the results is that there is no justification for delaying the implementation of an exit policy. Even in the worst scenario, where the government simply closes down the firms, pays the severance payments and absorbs the liabilities of the firms, the country as a whole will benefit, and domestic savings will increase by 0.3 percent of GDP. This is because the losses will stop.

Improving State Electricity Boards (SEBs) financial performance. An extensive analysis of SEB's impact on states finances was carried out for 14 major states (Assam, Bihar, J&K and Meghalaya as well as the Union Territories were excluded for lack of data, but their impact on the overall subsidy is marginal). The impact of the SEBs' poor financial performance and their reliance on state governments' assistance can be seen from Table 3.6. The net transfer of resources from the states to the SEBs (revenue plus capital) is estimated to have reached Rs.59 billion in 1994-95, much higher than what is officially reported (Box 3.3). If the SEBs were financially autonomous (or if states withdrew from operating their utilities), then they would, on aggregate, release Rs. 59 billion, about 0.6 percent of GDP (ignoring investment in capacity

Table 3.6: Net Impact of SEB Performance on 14 State Budgets, 1991-95 (percent of GDP)					
	1991-92	1992-93	1993-94	1994-95	1995-96[a]
A. Revenue Accounts					
Revenue Receipts					
Interest from SEBs	0.2	0.4	0.1	0.4	0.2
Revenue Expenditures	0.7	0.7	0.6	0.7	0.5
Subsidy	0.4	0.4	0.3	0.4	0.2
Interest	0.3	0.3	0.3	0.3	0.2
Revenue Deficit	-0.5	-0.3	-0.5	-0.3	-0.3
B. Capital Account					
Capital Receipts					
Repayments by SEBs	0.2	0.4	0.2	0.2	0.2
Capital Expenditures	0.5	0.9	0.6	0.5	0.5
Capital Account Deficit	-0.4	-0.4	-0.4	-0.2	-0.2
C. Total State Deficits on Account of all SEBs	-0.9	-0.8	-0.8	-0.6	-0.5
a. Projected.					
Source: RBI Bulletin, State Finances; SEB Financial Statements.					

> **Box 3.3: Net Transfer of Resources from the States to the SEBs**
>
> The net flow of funds from a state government to a SEB is a more accurate measure of the degree to which the SEB's operations are actually "subsidized" by the state. The figures speak for themselves. Compared to a total revenue subsidy of Rs 17 billion in FY95 as reported in the latest economic survey, the net transfer of resources to the SEBs (revenue plus capital) is estimated to have reached Rs.59 billion, three and a half times as much as what is reported in the Economic Survey as the subsidy. The *revenue subsidy* is only a part of the funds flowing from the states to the SEBs. To it must be added the *capital transfers* from the government, which include loans and equity. Given the SEBs' current and expected financial situation, these capital transfers ought to be considered as subsidies: the loans provided by the states are rarely repaid although the state governments continue to bear the burden of servicing these loans; in most states, the losses accumulated by the SEBs have already wiped out whatever equity contributions have been made by the states. It is highly unlikely that the SEBs will be able to make up for their accumulated losses out of future earnings in any foreseeable future. A case in point is Andhra Pradesh which has "written off" its equity of Rs.9.4 billion in APSEB as subsidy payments. A similar situation exists in Haryana where HSEB's accumulated losses far exceed the state government loans and equity contributions. With the SEBs' losses mounting at a faster pace every year it is highly unlikely that the states will ever be able to recoup their investments in the SEBs; it is therefore logical to treat these too as subsidy.

to reduce losses and improve efficiency) of extra revenues which would reduce the states' deficit by an equivalent amount. In addition, the better performing SEBs would then be in a position to contribute positively to the states' budget through higher dividends. In all, the states could increase their revenue by around 1.5 percent of GDP.

Tax Reform

Achieving substantial progress towards fiscal consolidation through expenditure cuts is a medium-term solution since expenditures are dominated by wages, subsidies, and interest payments which will take time to adjust. Therefore in the short-run, any fiscal adjustment will have to rely mostly on revenue raising measures which puts the focus on taxation. A key objective of the fiscal adjustment pursued by the Center since 1991 has been to increase total tax to GDP ratio *as a means of achieving fiscal consolidation* and improving resource allocation. The Chelliah Tax Reform Committee proposed to: (i) decrease the share of trade taxes in total taxes; (ii) increase the share of domestic excises by transforming them into a VAT system, and (iii) increase the relative contribution of direct taxes. These objectives were to be achieved through base-broadening, rate reduction, and strengthening the capacity of the tax administration. As a result of growth and tax reforms, tax revenues of central and state governments recovered to almost 16 percent of GDP in 1995-96, after falling from 16.8 percent of GDP in 1990-91 to 15.8 percent in 1994-95. The main reasons behind the fall were due to structural reforms which had a relatively high fiscal cost (Chapter 1). Studies indicate that there is ample scope for raising the tax effort substantially. Specifically, strong revenue measures at both the center and states levels could raise the general government tax to GDP ratio by 2 percentage points of GDP by 2001-2002.

At the Central Government level, the scope for greater reliance on direct taxes (personal and corporate) has not yet been exhausted. Considerable potential exists for an increase in revenue from income tax through improvements in tax administration--as shown by the recent buoyancy of income tax revenue due to the expansion of withholding at source for fees for professionals, technical services and service contracts as well as interest on time deposits. To increase the revenue contribution of the company income tax, the government may broaden the corporate income base through: (i) repealing company tax incentives such as deductions for fringe benefits, the exclusion of profits from export sales, company tax holidays, and reducing the rate of depreciation on long-lived assets to more closely approximate the rate of economic depreciation; (ii) improving tax administration's capacity to deter abusive transfer pricing practices; (iii) abolishing the corporate income tax surcharge (which has been reduced in this year's budget from 15 percent to 7.5 percent) to align the top corporate income tax rate with that of the top personal income tax rate at 40 percent to discourage tax evasion and abusive transfer pricing practices; and (iv) adopting an alternative minimum tax (AMT) on gross corporate assets after depreciation or net worth similar to those in place in Mexico or Argentina. An asset-based tax is easier to administer than profit based-tax because physical assets are more difficult to under-report. The *Minimum Alternate Tax" (MAT) introduced in the 1996-97 budget* on book profits will achieve only some of the results of a tax on gross assets. However, it will not address issues related with under-reporting of profits due to manipulations in transfer pricing and the ability of the Indian corporate tax administration to detect sophisticated tax evasion.

In a recent study, Rajaraman and Koshy (1996) find that the first-round revenue impact of introducing an AMT would be between Rs. 100 billion and Rs. 150 billion in additional revenue based on realistic assumptions about coverage and a

> ### Box 3.4: Mexican Corporate Assets Tax
>
> Other countries, notably Mexico, faced with declining average effective company tax rates like in India, have adopted alternative minimum tax on gross corporate assets to capture more taxes from profitable corporations. Proponents of the alternative gross assets tax regard it as a necessary "backstop" for a business income tax in circumstances where a country's tax administration is not strong enough to properly enforce the regular tax by detecting sophisticated accounts-based tax evasion. In other words, part of the goal of the tax is to dissuade corporations from using tax evasion and tax avoidance practices to reduce their regular tax liability below the minimum tax liability. A minimum tax on gross assets can be designed as a proxy for a corporate income tax. Under this tax design, a business will pay either the regular corporate tax liability or the alternative assets tax liability, whichever is greatest.
>
> The Mexican AMT has been highly successful. While the direct revenue from the Mexican AMT was only 0.3 percent of GDP in 1994, the "backstop" effect is believed to have contributed substantially to the revenue performance of the basic corporate tax. A recent study indicates that, during its first year of implementation, for every Mexican Peso of assets tax generated directly, an additional 3.5 Mexican Pesos in revenue was generated under the regular corporate tax. Over time, the revenue generated directly from the assets tax fell as businesses cut back on their use of abusive transfer pricing practices. In other words, fewer and fewer foreign firms put themselves in a position where their regular corporate tax liability fell below their alternative minimum assets tax liability.
>
> The Mexican authorities also have adopted the AMT on gross assets to overcome the distortionary impact of the regular corporate tax and hence to improve economic efficiency. The tax discourages evasion and leads to economic efficiency by encouraging better use of assets. In addition, by raising the tax burden of sectors where there is a low tax presence, intersectoral tax differences are reduced, allowing the price system to become the main means of allocating resources without distortions arising from effective tax rates differentials.

rate of return of between 1.6 percent and 2 percent on the book value of assets. These incremental results are equivalent to between 1.0 and 1.5 percent of GDP. In 1994-95, the actual corporate tax yield was 1.3 percent of GDP. Hence, an AMT on gross assets could increase corporate tax revenues by 72 percent. However, if AMT payments are creditable or refundable in years when the regular corporate tax exceeds the AMT, then the long-run net revenue increase from the two taxes would be much less. Some combination of the measures discussed above should be capable of generating a 25 to 50 percent increase in corporate receipts.

In addition, studies of Indian income tax performance indicate that more rigorous auditing procedures, lower marginal tax rates, and less frequent or no tax amnesties would improve compliance.

At the state level, and assuming reforms in agriculture are carried through, broadening the tax base also should include taxing agricultural income (personal and corporate). According to the Constitution, only the states can tax income generated in agriculture, and with a few exceptions, most states chose not to tax agriculture. To facilitate its political acceptability, the taxation of agricultural incomes could be, at least partially, linked to the improved delivery of economic services and infrastructure in rural areas by local governments in the context of the on-going decentralization effort. This would require, however, a clear definition of the responsibilities to be delegated to the local government along with corresponding local resource mobilization power and strengthening of implementation capacity. Resource mobilization by local governments could assume a variety of forms, such as the systematic cost recovery of economic and social services, investment cost sharing arrangements with beneficiaries, and land betterment taxes.

Finally, there is scope to impose indirect taxation on a wider range of goods and services, *at the central level*, by removing special exemptions above a reasonable threshold for small scale industry, adopting special excise taxes for petroleum products, and extending the coverage of MODVAT to services. Further, *at the state level*, the proposed reforms of *states' sales tax* should be speeded up to replace the current states' sales taxes into a VAT to allow increased states control over their resource base. In the meantime, with a view to ensuring that a national VAT has comprehensive coverage, a wider range of services should be taxed either under MODVAT, the state VATs or independently as at present is the case for selected services (e.g., Maharashtra). Maharashtra and Rajasthan (Box 3.5) have allowed a more effective taxation of wholesale and retail margins (Maharashtra) and eliminated internal and border check posts (Rajasthan). Finally, there is a need to build up the administrative procedures similar to those adopted in countries with full-fledged VAT systems (Box 3.6).

> **Box 3.5: The States of Maharashtra and Rajasthan Lead the Way in Sales Tax Reforms**
>
> In 1995, the State of Maharashtra instituted a VAT for wholesale and retail margins of large dealers with turnover exceeding Rs 10 million with a full commodity coverage. This measure appears to have been very successful in overcoming the problem of underinvoicing in the case of sales by manufacturers to related or non-arm's length retailers. The authorities have been pleased with the results to date and plan to expand the scope of the tax by reducing the threshold. One of the strongest arguments in favor of this approach, particularly when implemented with few rates, is that it will not distort the relative prices faced by consumers from the underlying costs of production. A "large dealers" VAT will retain this characteristic for most wholesale and retail transactions in a state while a selected commodities approach, which has been adopted by some other states, will not.
>
> The State of Rajasthan abolished its internal and border check posts in mid-1995 and this has not resulted in lower sales tax revenues. This evidence could help to dispel fears of revenue losses associated with checkpost abolition.

Table 3.7 presents a summary of the additional gross public savings that could be generated by the beginning of the next decade from the strategy for fiscal consolidation outlined in the previous section. Gross savings of 6 percentage points of GDP could be generated. *This is a conservative estimate since second-order effects of the policy measures suggested here are not allowed for.* It is possible that, to the extent public savings is raised through withdrawal of subsidies or raising irrigation charges and power tariffs, which are analogous to tax increases, private savings might be adversely affected. In India's case, the offset factor is estimated to be 0.46, so overall domestic savings would still rise as a result of the measures proposed in this section.

Table 3.7: Estimated Additional Public Savings (percent of GDP)	
Elimination of Fertilizer Subsidy	0.7
50% Privatization of CPEs Portfolio	0.4
Recovery O&M on Water	0.9
Elimination of Power Subsidy	1.5
Reduced Central Government Employment	0.4
Broadened Tax Base	2.0
Total	5.9

Restructuring Center-States Fiscal Relations

Fiscal consolidation will be difficult without a restructuring of the complex system of intergovernmental transfers to encourage the states to address issues such as weak tax collection effort, unsustainable indebtedness of states, insufficient cost recovery, inadequate provisions for non-wage operations and maintenance, and uneconomic enterprises. While some states have recently taken initiatives on their own to overcome their problems, the fiscal impact of measures adopted to date has been inadequate relative to the size of the needed fiscal adjustment. A much broader and uniform reform effort within and among states is desirable. The Tenth Finance Commission's (TFC) recommendations are a step in the right direction for the reform of intergovernmental fiscal relations. The TFC has proposed a number of bold and innovative measures. The recommended move towards a mandated system of sharing the total tax revenue collected by the center (the proposed ratio is 71:29 between the center and the states), would contribute towards strengthening incentives for enhanced income tax collection by the center. The TFC also recommended that in fiscal year 1995-96, the share of MODVAT excise tax revenue going to states be increased from 45 to 47.5 percent while that of income tax revenues be reduced from 88 to 77.5 percent. So far, the government only has implemented the latter two temporary measures. The priority for reform should be to implement the TFC's recommendation of sharing 29 percent of total central tax collections with the states because the change would increase the center's interest in collecting income tax and would give the states greater transfer payment stability. In the short-run, the Central Government should continue to reduce discretionary grants and loans to states, which currently amount to 3.3 percent of GDP (net of repayments).

The TFC also has proposed two transparent, rule-based schemes of partial debt relief, one tied to using the proceeds of state privatization to retire debt owed to the center and the other tied to improvements in revenue account balance of a state, in a given year, relative to its performance in the three preceding years. These recommendations for "rule-based" debt relief are expected to encourage state fiscal consolidation and prepare the basis for a move towards market-based debt financing of states fiscal deficits as opposed to central control of states finances. While these "rule-based" schemes are not without their shortcoming, they deserve to be revisited by the center in its search for mechanisms which will encourage state fiscal consolidation.

Box 3.6: Reform of States' Sales Tax

At the end of 1995, State and Union Finance Ministers reached a broad consensus on a package of measures designed to harmonize state sales tax systems and to institute a dual value-added tax system over the medium term. Major components of the agreement are:

- Establishment of uniform set of 5 floor rate with commodities in all states to be assigned to the same 5 rate categories. The floor rates would be zero, 4, 8, and 12 percent with a special category of 20 for excise- type commodities. The rate harmonization scheme would take effect from April 1, 1997.
- Competition among states to give sales tax concessions as industrial incentives, which usually take the form of cumulative sales tax exemption or deferrals equal to some proportion of fixed capital investment, would also be phased out by April 1, 1997 with appropriate rules to honor existing commitments.
- A decision to move to a system of destination-based state VAT might be taken after due and careful preparation.
- Establishment of a Ministerial Committee of State Finance Ministers for monitoring the implementation of the agreement.

Establishment of floor rates and the phasing out of incentives would deter tax rate wars which currently impose a high and increasing cost in foregone state revenue. Sales tax revenue should become more buoyant if this agreement holds. But, interstate competition to attract foot loose industries has recently intensified with entry of major multinationals as direct foreign investors. Indian states have relatively little experience in assessing the optimality of incentives packages. Therefore states should maintain an ongoing dialogue among themselves and the Center to ensure that appropriate strategies and standards are set and that industrial attraction races do not become "races-to-the-bottom". Private Indian industrialists have indicated that in deciding where to site a unit, they are influenced more by the availability of adequate economic infrastructure, such as transport, power and skilled labor than by the promise of tax holiday. Moreover, an efficient, fair, and transparent sales tax regime is one of the best industrial incentive states could offer.

A true credit-invoice VAT, rather than the hybrid VATs, which some states have adopted, should be the medium-term goal for three reasons. First, a VAT will permit enterprises (units) to improve their operating efficiency. If the tax base is expanded to the final consumer and all input taxes are rebated, enterprises would no longer have an incentive to adopt inefficient forms of operation induced by tax minimization considerations. Second, a true VAT should reduce evasion since evasion at any point along the chain to final consumption would likely be recaptured later in the production chain. Third, the crediting of capital inputs by states would further improve growth and competitiveness.

Although a harmonized interstate VAT system appears to be three to five years away, states might use the lead time to implement fundamental reforms in their sales tax administrations. For the most part, states still rely on antiquated administration and enforcement system. The foundation of a VAT or even a reformed sales tax system should be self-assessment. Experience in Latin America indicates that a reform package with emphasis on administrative improvements can lead to a 10 to 15 percent improvement in revenue generation. A large part of this revenue enhancement can be achieved through adoption of transparent administrative procedures.

The Center-States agreement envisages all states moving toward the VAT system at the same time despite the varied degree of states' administrative capabilities. However, states with the most advanced administrative capabilities and/or taxpayer compliance ability should consider moving ahead with sales tax reforms to speed up the convergence of their systems to a VAT as Maharashtra has demonstrated.

At present, the precarious condition of most state finances indicates that the first priority should be to improve revenue performance and expenditure allocation. In the long run, however, an explicit objective of the system of intergovernmental transfers could be to encourage market-based fiscal discipline. Beyond seeking to improve their own revenue collection, cost recovery for economic services and expenditure efficiency, Indian states in the foreseeable future will have few other alternatives but to achieve better access to the maturing domestic capital market (they are constitutionally barred from borrowing abroad). To access the emerging domestic primary market, they will have to achieve substantial and sustained improvements in their finances. Last year's CEM discusses options to increase the states access to domestic capital markets.

Weaknesses in the planning process should also be addressed. Reform of the Planning Commission's budgetary guidelines and procedures would encourages states to undertake structural budgetary reforms to enhance their capacity to provide or supplement the provision of infrastructure effectively and efficiently. A quick way to cut the "Gordian Knot" of state budgetary design would be to abolish the distinction between "plan" and "non-plan" expenditure as it relates to current account expenditures; so that the vital budget distinction would become that between current and capital expenditure. Under the logic of existing arrangements states have incentives to propose plan projects greatly in excess of their absorptive capacity. Consequently, many of these schemes cannot be completed as proposed and transferred resources get diverted into current expenditures. Efforts should be aimed at ensuring that borrowed resources are utilized only for such expenditure that yield a return adequate to meet the cost of borrowing. Options for reform of central plan transfers could include: (i) delinking the grant and loan components of transfers from the center to the states, and replacing the loan component of state plan assistance with specific purpose loans that are best intermediated by banks, with generous provision of technical assistance, particularly for states with weak implementation capacity; and (ii) replacing the current system of thinly spread central resources across a multitude of central schemes (covering all states and monitored by different central ministries), with a more compact set of well targeted transfers focused on the most needy states, on the attainment of minimum national standards or on activities where interstate spillover effects are great. States should have more discretion over their expenditure program and should be encouraged to experiment with program design and delivery so that India can reap the benefits of "demonstration effects" which its federal structure potentially provides. Ultimately, reforming fiscal federalism in India will have an important impact on states finances and will shape their future, perhaps much more than reforms that can be undertaken solely at the states' level.

FINANCIAL SECTOR REFORMS AND CAPITAL MARKET DEVELOPMENT

Besides threatening macroeconomic stability, fiscal imbalances also are a major impediment to the full liberalization of the country's financial sector and the realization of the efficiency gains associated with such liberalization. One consequence is that an efficient money market has yet to emerge in India. In its absence, the long-term end of the market cannot fully develop thus impairing the availability of finance for private sector investment with long gestation periods--such as infrastructure investment. The remaining part of this section reviews the main priority reforms needed for the creation of long-term debt markets.

The first and central priority is a reduction of the fiscal imbalances. The government has chosen a very gradual approach--perhaps excessively in the areas of privatization of banks and deregulation of insurance and other contractual saving institutions--to liberalizing the financial sector. Its gradualism is based on a desire to avoid volatile and disruptive interest rates' movements which could accompany a rapid de-regulation of financial markets in the presence of large public sector borrowing requirements as has been the experience elsewhere. Accordingly, the twin pillars of government's strategy have been to: (i) maintain existing (but gradually relaxing) controls to repress the market's ability to price risk and; (ii) encourage during this transition the emergence of new institutions and development of skills required to manage at a later date a de-regulated financial market. However, this strategy has given rise to a number of issues. While the gradual reforms have encouraged a rapid increase in market skills and infrastructure, the remaining controls are inhibiting market participants from fully benefiting from the emerging gains of a more efficient allocation of capital based on greater sensitivity to and pricing of risk, and lower intermediation costs.

The continued success of this strategy (repressing risk pricing while developing institutional infrastructure) will depend vitally on the speed with which the government can reduce those risks that it is reluctant to have the market price them at their true level. *The most important of these risks are the market's perceptions of macro instability due to the size of the fiscal deficit and the quality of banks' balance sheets.* If the government can move rapidly to reduce these risks--to a level at which the government is comfortable with allowing the market to price them--it will be able to complete its deregulation of financial markets and achieve a relatively stable low-cost transition. Tardiness in reducing these risks will, however, prolong the transition; increase the cost of existing inefficiencies without necessarily reducing the potential for volatility when markets are finally de-controlled.

By any criteria, the financial sector continues to exhibit signs of

---

Box 3.7: Benefits of an Efficient Money Market

- *For banks*: An efficient money market improves liquidity management and so lowers costs. It allows banks to manage risks arising from interest rate fluctuations and to manage the maturity structure of their assets and liabilities. And it provides a stable source of funds in addition to deposits, allowing alternative funding structures and competition.

- *For savers*: An efficient money market encourages the development of non-bank intermediaries and thus increases competition for funds, leading to higher returns and new, more flexible savings instruments.

- *For borrowers*: A consistently liquid money market provides an effective source of long-term finance. This result is especially useful in countries where long-term debt is unavailable because of high inflation or because of some other form of uncertainty. In addition, direct access to the market for short-term capital allows larger borrowers to lower their cost of funds and manage their short-term funding or surpluses more efficiently.

- *For other financial markets*: An efficient money market supports the development of both primary and secondary securities markets. Participants can borrow in the money market to fund their security holdings. A liquid money market is necessary for the development of an efficient market in forward foreign exchange and for markets in derivative instruments.

- *For the government*: A liquid money market providing access to a wide range of buyers enables the government to achieve better pricing on its debt. An excessive government borrowing requirement, however, or a lack of coordination among fiscal, monetary, and exchange rate policies will disrupt the market.

- *For the central bank*: Monetary control through indirect methods (treasury bill auctions and open-market operations) is more effective if the money market is liquid. The market response to central bank policy actions will be both faster and less subject to distortion in a liquid market. The short-term yield curve that is a feature of liquid markets is a useful indicator for monetary policy.

Source: D. Wilton, "Money Markets Matter", *At a Glance, FPD note No. 27*, World Bank, Oct. 1994.

inefficiency. A well defined short term yield curve is missing; the money market is volatile; T-bills, government dated securities and private debt issues do not enjoy secondary liquidity; and the ability to manage portfolio risks is weak due to a lack of risk management expertise and illiquidity. In terms of further market development, two challenges stand out as priorities:

- *Developing a deep and stable money market capable of generating a term yield curve*. The overnight rate is currently very volatile and money market maturities do not extend beyond 14 days. This inhibits funding options for banks and the development of a forward foreign exchange market.

- *Developing a liquid secondary market in T-bills and Dated Securities*. There is little secondary trading in debt instruments, either government or private. This causes risk management problems for investors and inhibits the further development of a primary market in corporate debt.

The Indian government has already undertaken policy reforms over the recent years to increase the role of the money and bond markets in macroeconomic management and financing of private sector investments. The government has led the way by deciding to progressively move away from its previous practice of financing its fiscal deficit mainly through direct instruments (such as monetization, high reserve ratios and the obligatory placement of debt at below market interest rates) toward financing through market borrowing.

However, further progress in developing efficient money and debt markets is currently hindered by policy concerns about the financing of the fiscal deficit and retention of monetary control as well as the pervasiveness of publicly-owned banks with their non-commercial orientation. In making the transition to market-based financing and the development of financial markets, the authorities face many of the problems encountered by other countries engaged in the same process. In particular, financial sector reforms will increase--at least in the transition period--government funding costs. Therefore the proposed financial reforms should be coordinated with the government fiscal consolidation program to reduce the transitional costs and risk of backtracking.

The second priority is the development of the money market. Developing a stable money market and a liquid secondary debt market would require reforms in three broad areas. *First*, close coordination at the macroeconomic level between monetary, fiscal, and exchange rate policies. *Second*, better information management systems at RBI and MOF. This includes forecasting and managing government's short term cash flows and debt. *Third*, increased incentives for market participants to actively manage their portfolios and balance sheet risks--i.e. invest in the staff and information systems required for developing the skills to manage risk and allocate capital to market making.

The money market's most serious deficiencies are its volatility and the lack of a short-term yield curve. Call rates are also not fully unified around the country varying by about 50-75 basis points for reasons discussed further below. Volatility (Figure 3.1) is caused by: (i) excessive variations in liquidity due to fluctuations in the level of excess reserves (market participants particularly mentioned RBI's sales of debt during periods of low liquidity as a cause of volatility); and (ii) the 'Reporting Friday' effect. Every second Friday (Reporting Friday) the call rate falls to zero (Figure 3.2). The Reporting Friday effect is particularly toxic to the development of a short term

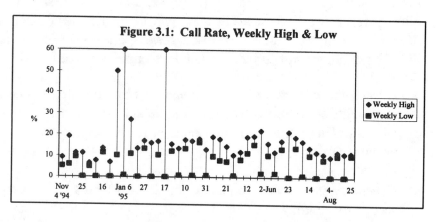

Figure 3.1: Call Rate, Weekly High & Low

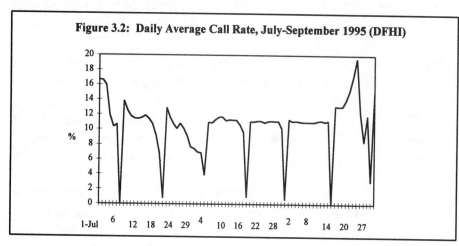

Figure 3.2: Daily Average Call Rate, July-September 1995 (DFHI)

yield curve. The disruption of liquidity every second Friday prevents the normal pattern of short term yield curve development, that is; stable call funding leading to stable 30-day funding, in turn leading to stable 90-day funding.

Reducing call market volatility and enabling a short-term yield curve to develop would require: (i) improving RBI's capacity to forecast the flows affecting the level of excess reserves; (ii) replacing the existing RBI refinance facilities with a single "passive" window better suited to controlling the reserve levels; (iii) changing the basis of calculation of the CRR either by using an average of demand and time liabilities over a fixed period rather than the position on a single day or by removing the interbank transactions from the calculation. Most countries now use averages; and there is no loss of monetary control from this; (iv) permitting two-way pricing of call money; (v) widening the range of participants allowed to both lend and borrow on the money market; and (vi) opening repurchase agreements (repos) to use by all parties subject to the requirement that no repurchase transaction be booked until source documents verifying title have been sighted and marked to indicate the lending party's interest in the scrip for the duration of the repo. Inability to use repos ads to the call market volatility by limiting financing options, and also reduces demand for debt securities by reducing their liquidity. In addition, public banks have not yet seized the profit opportunities associated with treasury and risk management operations--a situation that will likely change once these skills are built and they are privatized.

The RBI and the MOF also need to take steps to improve their ability to manage the government's accounts. Improvements are needed in two main areas. *First*, the day-to-day management of the Central Government's account with the RBI needs to be improved. This is a technical "payments-system" problem, which results in large measure from the sheer size and physical extension of India. Because there are so many centers in which revenue is collected and expenditure is made, the technical task of centralizing information about the standing of the government's account is unusually complex. The RBI's Committee on Technology Issues has made recommendations to improve the operations of this account, and these need to be implemented as soon as possible. *Second*, the Central Government needs to improve its intra-year programming and monitoring of revenue and expenditure. The MOF needs to be able to formulate a credible borrowing program over each year. This would enable other participants in the financial markets to plan their own portfolio positioning, and so help smooth the functioning of the financial markets.

Broadening participation in the call money market would improve the effectiveness of monetary policy, develop the debt market; and stimulate competition in intermediation. Participation is currently limited to banks and some financial institutions. Only banks can borrow in the market. A range of participants should have access to both sides of the market-- banks, blue chips firms, pension funds, mutual funds, finance and insurance companies. Such a range of participants contributes to both liquidity and the amount of information embedded in the market's pricing of instruments. Limiting borrowing by non bank financial institutions and mutual funds raises intermediation costs and limits their demand for T-bills, government dated securities and other term instruments since they cannot access money market funds to either fund portfolio positions or to cover short-term liquidity needs. Further, limits on participation in the market reduce competition for funds. The alternative balance sheet structures that competition for money market funds makes possible will not occur, and hence the efficiency gains in intermediation that markets permit will be stifled.

The third priority is the development of the Treasury Bills and long term debt market. Creating a deeper and more stable money market will contribute to the development of a secondary debt market by: (i) providing a more secure and stable funding source for debt portfolios; and (ii) by increasing the liquidity of debt instruments via use of repos. Developing greater liquidity in the T-bill market will assist the emergence of a short-term yield curve; reduce the cost to the government of the T-bill issue by improving the demand for T-bills; and allow the integration of foreign exchange, money and bond markets since the short-term yield curve directly affects the pricing of both forward foreign exchange and long-term bonds.

The main policy and institutional measures required to develop India's debt markets have been extensively discussed in the policy and financial circles and a fair degree of consensus has emerged around the unfinished agenda which the authorities need to address. *First*, in order for government securities to provide reliable "risk-free" benchmark rates, the RBI would need to auction all such securities, on a predictable timetable, and refrain from participating in the primary market. In addition, the changes in the basis of CRR calculation would also help achieve a relatively stable and deep interbank market, and thus an interbank rate resembling LIBOR, off of which floating rate issues could be priced. *Second*, the current stamp duty on primary issues of debt securities and secondary market trading are high and act as a discouragement to issuance and trading. It should be reduced--as in Maharashtra and Gujarat--and made uniform across states. Although these are state level issues, they could possibly be dealt with by the center if a booking center is set up in Delhi. Alternatively, one state could try to capture much of the business in trading of corporate debt securities by having a zero stamp duty and a highly reliable system for clearing and custody of bonds. *Third*, debt market regulations should be rationalized with only SEBI reviewing disclosure for such offerings to reduce transactions costs and time. *Finally*, trading is discouraged by poor title transfer. Smooth and secure delivery of securities and settlement of trades in an electronic environment is essential for sustained growth of the debt market. A recently promulgated Presidential ordinance provides the legal underpinning for the establishment of central depositories for securities. The depository mode of transaction in which securities would be dematerialized and transaction could be exempt from stamp duty, is a step in the right direction. However, credible and secure electronic clearing and settlement arrangements need to be implemented for corporate debt securities.

In addition, the authorities have recognized the urgent importance of upgrading the nation's payments systems. The RBI is acting on the recommendations of the Committee on Technology Issues to modernize check-clearing operations. The RBI plans to extend automated check processing to smaller, fast-growing banking centers, and to take additional steps to speed inter-cities check-clearing. The inefficiency of inter-city check clearing--which can take several weeks--is a standing source of inefficiency for commercial transactions, in particular, for transactions involving international trade. To provide more timely centralized reporting of transactions involving the Central Government's RBI account and commercial-bank branches with "currency chests," the Committee recommended modernization of electronic communications systems. The Committee recommended development and implementation of electronic funds transfer systems, both for crediting and debiting operations. To tighten prudential control of public-debt transactions, the RBI has followed the Committee's recommendation to set up a "delivery-vs-payment" system for the Public Debt Office in Mumbai.

The other elements of the reform agenda which are key to market development includes: (i) market making activity through the establishment of primary dealers; and (ii) deepening of the investors base through de-regulation of the investment guidelines affecting contractual savings institutions; particularly the insurance industry and pension funds.

The RBI has been active in promoting the establishment of private *Primary Dealers* as a means of improving the primary market in T-bills and developing a secondary market. The promotion of primary dealers may be a sound strategy for India, particularly if the government considers that it cannot improve its cash and debt management systems in the short-term, while the treasury management of market participants improves rapidly. In this case, creating a network of primary dealers to intermediate between a less efficient government and a more efficient market is a viable solution. However, in the long-term, primary dealers may not be the most efficient basis for market operation for two reasons. *First*, if a government has a very good cash management system (made possible by computing) and a debt management plan, then the government could be able to interact directly with the market. New Zealand provides such an example. Under such circumstances, the government will be able to manage its cash flows in such a way that a stable and reliable money market exists. Such a market will enable many firms to run books in government securities without undue liquidity or interest rate risk and without the need for recourse to RBI credit. Further, the government will be able to manage market liquidity such that there is always sufficient liquidity available to purchase its debt offerings. The government will not be selling into a market with insufficient liquidity, and so the risk of an issue failure in the absence of primary dealers with their access to RBI credit is very low. Finally, modern screen-based information systems allow sales announcements to, and bids from, geographically dispersed participants. Such a system of government debt sales exists in New Zealand. Figure 3.3 illustrates the symmetry on a daily basis between market liquidity and Reserve Bank of New Zealand (RBNZ) debt and repo operations.

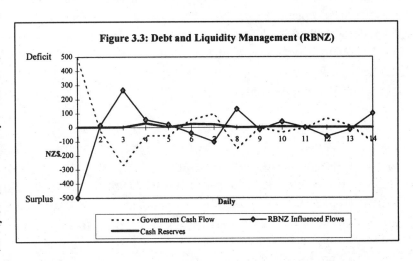

Second, in the short-term the controls and distortions in the market will impair the commercial viability of primary dealers. Over last year, it would have been difficult to profitably make a market in T-bills for two reasons. The first one concerns the discount (higher yield) T-bills generally sold at a discount in the secondary market compared to the primary market. This eliminates the possibility of profitable purchase and on-sale of T-bills by primary dealers, as shown in Figure 3.4. *The cut off rate in the primary market is thus not strictly market determined* especially since about 70 percent of 91 day T-bills is subscribed to by the RBI and non-competitive bidders (often government entities). The second reason is that call rates were higher than 91 day and 364 day T-bills, implying that the cost of financing the securities portfolio would have been higher than the yields (negative cost of carry). *Development of a government-securities market therefore implies that primary issues must be made at market-determined cutoff yields which would enable the primary dealers activities to be profitable.* Enabling market making to develop on a commercial basis will stimulate both the liquidity and transparency necessary for the development of benchmark rates.

Contractual savings institutions (insurance companies, pension funds, and mutual funds) play an increasingly important role in the financial systems of many countries. This trend reflects liberalization of insurance activities, privatization of pensions' provision, innovations in and growing popularity of mutual funds, and modernization of capital markets, among other things. Worldwide, contractual savings institutions dominate the securities markets. Institutional investment, particularly pension fund assets, is growing rapidly throughout the world. Chile's private pension system assets grew from a mere 1 percent of GDP following its introduction in 1981 to 26 percent in 1990. In Malaysia, the assets of the Employees Provident Fund (EPF) have grown from 18 percent of GDP in 1980 to 41 percent of GDP in 1987. In India, in 1994, the government-managed and various employer-run EPFs are estimated to have assets totaling 5.3 percent of GDP.

Although the quantitative effect of contractual savings institutions on total savings is unclear, there can be little doubt that they cause a shift in favor of long-term savings that can underpin money, equity and bond markets development. India has the institutions already and their assets are sizable, but major impediments to their development as a source of long-term savings and corporate finance have been the preemptive use of these funds by the government. At present, these institutions are required to invest mainly in government debt.

Contractual savings institutions in India include provident funds (both public and private), life and general insurance and mutual funds. Most are public sector institutions, operating in non-competitive sectors, and are heavily regulated and limited in their fund applications. The magnitude of their resources is significant. In 1994, combined assets of insurance companies, mutual funds, government-managed as well as private provident funds assets totaled 18.9 percent of GDP.

The fourth priority is therefore to liberalize the investment guidelines imposed on insurance and pension funds. The Insurance sector is the only remaining public Monopoly in the financial sector. The insurance industry, the Life Insurance Corporation of India (LIC) and the General Insurance Corporation (GIC) of India enjoy an absolute monopoly of India's vast insurance market. The industry suffers from lack of commercial incentives which prevent the adoption of efficiency enhancing procedures in line with technological developments elsewhere in the world. In addition, investment and pricing restrictions as well as lack of incentives to manage funds' actively to enhance returns, have limited their contribution to long-term savings and development of India's private capital market. Yet, successful innovative life insurance/personal investment products in use elsewhere in the world could increase household savings in India. As a result of the recommendations of the Malhotra Committee, GIC's investment guidelines were relaxed as of April, 1995. Unlike LIC which has still to invest 75 percent of its assets in government and government-guaranteed securities, GIC is required to invest only 45 percent of its assets in government and government-guaranteed securities.

Accordingly, and as recommended by the Malhotra Committee, the insurance industry should be further liberalized to help mobilize the large investment funds the industry is capable of generating, and allow these funds to be applied in and help develop the primary and secondary debt markets. This includes: (i) deregulating investment of insurance company assets to permit the development of new product types that offer better returns; (ii) apply the "prudent man" rule to insurance investment and eliminate rules requiring minimum investment in government securities; (iii) allow individual companies to price their policies; (iv) once regulatory supervision has been improved, open up the insurance market to greater competition, including foreign admission through joint venture with local firms. A first step in opening up the market would be the privatization of the four insurance companies that make up the GIC group. In a second step, they could be allowed to create life insurance subsidiaries that would create a new market for life insurance as is the case elsewhere in the world; and (v) define new role for LIC in a new competitive environment. LIC could be dedicated to delivery of insurance services in remote areas in view of its extensive rural network and experience. To be successful, however, such a reform agenda will also need to meet retraining needs of the large labor force in this sector and design appropriate safety nets for those displaced by the new technological developments that will take place as the industry is liberalized.

The regulations covering asset allocations of the Employee Provident Fund (EPF) Schemes are also very restrictive. The most striking feature of these regulations is the lack of exposure to equities and non-government debt and the use of the Special Deposit Scheme (SDS). The SDS is part of the Government Accounts. About 90 percent of the assets of the EPF are in the SDS. The SDS pays 12 percent interest on the daily balance. These asset allocation rules clearly inhibit active participation in the secondary market. While the asset allocations are very restrictive, active management of the provident schemes portfolios is *prevented* by investment policy guidelines established by the ministries in charge of administering the schemes. These guidelines forbid trading and stipulate the extent to which purchases can be made in the secondary market rather than the primary market. In most countries, contractual savings institutions (insurance and pension funds) have been the driving force behind the development of the long-term private bond market, since they have large needs for long-term assets with fixed returns. To stimulate such development in India, it will be necessary to allow the contractual savings institutions to invest in a broad range of private debt securities. For this, existing issuer-based guidelines would need to be phased out and replaced with guidelines based on prudential criteria allowing such institutions to invest their portfolios in securities with certain credit ratings as is common in other countries.

The fifth priority is to increase competition for the management of the Pension and Mutual Funds to develop a better retail distribution network for T-bills and dated securities. Contributions under the Employee Provident Funds (EPF) are currently viewed more as a tax on labor than as savings. This is because the returns to this investment are lower than what the funds could earn elsewhere. To enhance returns, management of EPF funds should be opened to competition, with performance-linked fees to increase incentives for managers to actively manage funds. This would increase the incentives for the EPF managers to invest in private debt securities on the primary and secondary markets in order to enhance their performance. In turn, this will improve debt market liquidity.

In general, contractual saving institutions are not competitively managed and have therefore no incentive to seek higher returns. In many countries, Money Market Mutual Funds (MMMF) have been very successful in increasing competition through widening access to the wholesale market for retail investors. There are no MMMFs in India. Recently, the RBI relaxed the guidelines on MMMFs to encourage their formation and allow competition to develop between providers of MMMFs. The move to permit competition is an important step. In many countries competition from MMMFs sponsored by insurance companies and other non-bank institutions has been a powerful incentive to banks to enter the MMMF market, so bringing the distribution power of their branch networks into action. The wider the group of people who have access to wholesale markets, the more wide-spread are the gains to borrowers and savers.

4 UNLEASHING AGRICULTURE'S GROWTH POTENTIAL

OVERVIEW

As the 1990s began, India was experiencing faster agricultural growth that was becoming more evenly spread across states, including rainfed regions. The poverty reduction potential from agriculture appears far from exhausted. Between 1980 and 1996, agricultural growth has accelerated and spread to the eastern regions and rainfed areas, and real rural wages improved. Together, this has contributed to an unprecedented decline in rural poverty, except during droughts and economic recession. Starting in 1985-86, the terms of trade--the price of crops relative to goods purchased from the non-agricultural sector--improved noticeably

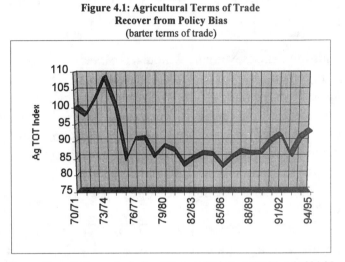

Figure 4.1: Agricultural Terms of Trade Recover from Policy Bias
(barter terms of trade)

Source: Commission on Agricultural Costs and Prices. 1993-94 and 1994-95 data are provisional.

(Figure 4.1). The contributing factors were the depreciation of the rupee and the reduction of manufacturing protection initiated during the 1980s (Table 4.1).

In addition, farmers benefited from large public spending for infrastructure, support services, and subsidies (for fertilizer, credit, water, and power for irrigation pumping), as well as the protection afforded to oilseeds at least until 1991. The objective of this chapter is to identify the conditions to sustain and accelerate further this process of more equitable agricultural growth.

Table 4.1: Economy-Wide Reforms are Removing the Anti-Agricultural Bias
(protection rate in percent)

Source of the Bias:	1970/1 to 1984/5	1985/6 to 1990/1	1991/2 to 1994/5
Economy-wide policies..........	-0.26	-0.25	-0.03
Ag policies.......	-0.04	+0.07	-0.07
Total................	**-0.30**	**-0.18**	**-0.09**

Source: Rosenblatt D., G. Pursell, A. Gupta, and B. Blarel, 1996: "Have Economy-Wide Reforms Helped Indian Agriculture?" World Bank, Washington.

The economy-wide reforms contributed to the acceleration of agricultural growth. Although the 1991 economic program did not contain an explicit agricultural component, it created a number of favorable conditions for the sector. Of particular importance were the further exchange rate devaluations and the reduction of protection of the manufacturing sector which virtually eliminated the already falling anti-agricultural bias (Table 4.1 and Box 4.1). Accordingly, the agricultural terms of trade improved further by around 4 percent after deteriorating temporarily in 1992-93. This

Box 4.1: Correcting for India's Large Size Reduces Significantly the Apparent Policy Bias Against Agriculture

The estimated mild protection of agriculture from agricultural price policies contrasts with earlier studies which indicated much higher levels of relative price discrimination, and deserves an explanation. The present estimates take into account the fact that India, because of its large size, cannot export infinite quantities of rice on the thin rice world market without affecting the world price. Ignoring this price-depressing (or large-country) effect of Indian rice exports would significantly over-estimate the extent of price discrimination imposed on rice by Indian food policies. The present estimates also treat wheat as non-traded, recognizing that under free trade its equilibrium domestic price would have remained within the import-export parity band for most years. Correcting for the large-country situation in rice, and the non-traded status of wheat, significantly lowers the price discrimination of Indian agriculture since rice and wheat alone account for about 30% of the Indian agricultural production basket.

additional improvement would have been greater but for three factors. *First*, a much needed realignment of prices within the agricultural sector began. In the closed trade regime for agriculture prior to 1994, changes in domestic supply and demand conditions combined with government price policies for rice, wheat, and sugarcane determined their price levels. However, as a result of changes in protection and as indicated by Table 4.2, the price of exportable and disprotected crops (rice, cotton) improved faster than the price of importables and protected crops (oilseeds, sugar, rubber). The domestic price of the non traded crops (wheat, coarse cereals) remained within the large export-import parity price band. As a result, price distortions within agriculture narrowed which meant that aggregate agricultural terms of trade did not improve significantly.

Second, the exchange rate devaluation and the trade liberalization after 1994-95 were not fully reflected in farmgate prices because of high marketing and processing margins.

Third, the world prices of agricultural commodities fell in

Table 4.2: Agricultural Price Movements, A Decomposition Analysis (percent change between 1990-91 and 1994-95)				
	Observed	Decomposition in terms of:		
	Change in real domestic price	Change in real world price	Change in real exchange rate	Agricultural policies
Exportables:	**20.9**	**-12.8**	**26.4**	**6.6**
Rice	19.4	-11.7	26.4	4.0
Cotton	37.5	-11.6	26.4	21.7
Importables:	**5.3**	**-4.8**	**26.4**	**-17.0**
Oilseeds	-21.7	11.8	26.4	-61.9
Sugarcane	17.4	5.8	26.4	-15.8
Rubber	16.7	25.7	26.4	-38.4
Pulses	12.9	-29.7	26.4	16.4
Non-traded:				
Wheat	11.9	-17.1	26.4	2.3
Coarse Cereals	-5.1	-12.6	26.4	-19.3
All 13 Crops:	**11.9**	**-8.8**	**26.4**	**-6.3**

Note: The interaction term has not been reported in the Decomposition. The sum of the % changes, including the interaction term, add-up to the observed change in the real domestic price.
Source: Rosenblatt D., G. Pursell, A. Gupta, and B. Blarel, 1996: "Have Economy-Wide Reforms Helped Indian Agriculture?" World Bank, Washington.

real terms. Between 1990-91 and 1994-95, the average real US dollar price of a 13 commodities basket weighted by Indian production fell by an estimated 9 percent (Table 4.2). There was therefore less scope for domestic agricultural prices to increase in real terms.

In conclusion, the non-agricultural reforms, initiated during the 1980s and accelerated since July 1991, created a favorable environment for the agricultural sector by removing most of the anti-agricultural bias and realigning prices within agriculture by 1994-95. However, four major policy issues confront agriculture and threaten its ability to improve or even sustain this performance. *First*, in addition to the fiscal impact of public spending in agriculture, its composition is not supportive of a faster, more equitable and sustainable agricultural growth. *Second*, remaining external trade restrictions on agricultural goods imports and exports and on consumer goods imports may affect the profitability of agriculture. *Third*, the over-regulation of domestic trade and agro-processing industries is proving increasingly costly to the economy. *Fourth*, the rural financial system is not supportive of agriculture and other rural economic activities. Accordingly, the rest of this chapter discusses these challenges and suggests a strategy for reforms, which would yield substantial benefits for agriculture (including improvements in the terms of trade) and ultimately, for poverty reduction in India to which agriculture historically has made a substantial contribution. The central message of this chapter is that there is tremendous scope for unleashing the productive potential of agriculture to contribute more fully to overall faster and more equitable economic growth and this is an opportune time to reform.

PUBLIC EXPENDITURE: REMAINING ISSUES

Public spending in agriculture militates against growth and poverty reduction in three important ways. *First*, the level of spending is unsustainable from a macroeconomic perspective as discussed in Chapters 1 and 2. *Second*, the current composition of public

Table 4.3: India Spends Twice as Much on Agriculture as East Asian Countries (agriculture public expenditures expressed as a share of agricultural GDP, percentages)				
	India	Indonesia	Malaysia	Thailand
Average 1990-1993	29.1	6.9	10.1	12.9
Memo item: Ag annual GDP growth (1980-93)	3.0	3.2	3.5	3.8

Note: For Indonesia, figures only include central government expenditures. *Source*: Ministry of Finance, union budget documents. *Source*: Government Financial Yearbook, IMF; World Development Report, World Bank.

spending in agriculture is not growth enhancing, particularly in the poor states. *Third*, some public expenditures in agriculture are inefficient, partly because of ineffective delivery mechanisms and design, which entail significant fiscal, economic and environmental costs.

Enhancing the sustainability of public spending. India devotes considerable public resources (center and state) to agriculture which totaled Rs 685 billion (US$22 billion) in 1994-95, equivalent to 28 percent of agricultural GDP (8 percent of GDP). When measured as a share of agricultural GDP, India spends at least twice as much on

Figure 4.2: Subsidies Crowd Out Productivity -Enhancing Expenditures during the 1980s
Composition of Central and State Expenditures in Agriculture, Rs billion (1980-81 rupees)

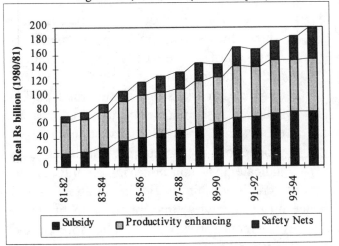

Source: Ministry of Finance, Union Budget documents.

Box 4.2: Budgeted Subsidies to Indian Agriculture

The Fertilizer Subsidy was designed to (i) stimulate greater and balanced use of fertilizers to increase agricultural production; (ii) support agricultural incomes by providing cheap inputs; (iii) improve regional equity; and (iv) achieve self-sufficiency in fertilizer production based on the utilization of indigenous resources. It is the difference between the retention price paid to manufacturing units and the consumer price of the fertilizer, less the distribution margin.

The Food Subsidy, transferred to Food Corporation of India (FCI), is the difference between FCI's cost of rice and wheat procurement and distribution, and the central issue price. The subsidy ensures: (i) a minimum support price for rice and wheat; (ii) food security through the maintenance of buffer stocks by FCI; (iii) adequate supply of foodgrains in all parts of the country through the Public Distribution System (PDS); and (iv) the protection of the vulnerable sections of the population from increases in prices of essential foodstuffs.

The Power Subsidy was designed to promote the adoption of private tubewells and thus promote increased agricultural production. The power subsidy is estimated as the difference between average cost of supplying electricity to all customers, and the tariff charged to agricultural customers. It is an unprecise estimate of the actual subsidy to agriculture. It under-estimates the power subsidy to agriculture since the cost of supplying electricity to agriculture is higher than for other sectors. At the same time, it over-estimates the actual budgetary costs of the power subsidy by the extent of the cross-subsidization of agricultural tariffs by industrial tariffs.

The Irrigation Subsidy is the difference between the operation and maintenance costs of the publicly operated irrigation infrastructure (surface and tubewells) and water charges recovered. Irrigation development has been a central pillar of the national agricultural development strategy. Government investment in irrigation was largely concentrated on canal irrigation development until the 1970s, but investment on groundwater development became increasingly important in the 1980s and 1990s.

The fertilizer and food subsidies are essentially centrally financed, whereas the power and irrigation subsidies are primarily state financed.

agriculture as some of the East Asian economies (Table 4.3). But this much higher level of spending devoted to agriculture in India does not translate into a significantly higher sectoral performance, suggesting that there is scope for significant improvements in the effectiveness and efficiency of these outlays.

Restructuring public expenditure on agriculture is an area of particular need and challenge. Agricultural public expenditures can be classified into three categories according to their economic objective: productivity growth-enhancing, subsidies, and safety net programs (Figure 4.2). Productivity growth-enhancing expenditure include all public spending on economic services in agriculture and its allied sub-sectors, and on new irrigation investments. Agricultural subsidies are the explicit provisions for fertilizer, food, credit, irrigation (the difference between operation and maintenance expenses and charges recovered) and power (the difference between average costs of supplying electricity and tariffs charged) in state budgets (Box 4.2). Safety net expenditures include spending on rural development and employment programs, and special area programs.

There is strong empirical evidence which shows that public investments in rural infrastructure (roads, canal irrigation, and electrification), rural services (regulated markets and commercial banks) and human capital (education and health) encourage private investment and production in agriculture. Studies also indicate that non-price factors (access to irrigation, proximity to delivery points, and access to credit and high yielding varieties) have a much larger influence on fertilizer use (and hence on productivity) than price or institutional (tenure, farm size) factors. Indeed, technology development (private and public, foreign and domestic) and dissemination, rural infrastructure, irrigation, and human capital are the major

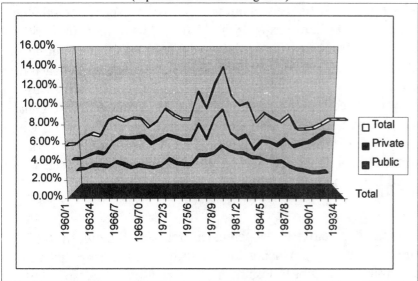

Figure 4.3: Capital Formation in Indian Agriculture is Declining
(expressed as a share of Ag GDP)

Source: Central Statistics Office.

determinants of (total factor) productivity growth in Indian agriculture; but that productivity growth has been on a declining trend since the mid-1980s.

It is therefore of much concern that total capital formation in agriculture as a share of agricultural GDP declined from a peak of 14 percent in 1979-80 to 8.5 percent in 1992-93 where it remained until 1994-95 (Figure 4.3). To a large extent, this fall reflects more efficient investment in the sector. In particular, more efficient private investment in tubewell irrigation has substituted for public investment in new irrigation schemes. In spite of this healthy development, available data indicate that private capital formation has been declining again in 1993-94, and possibly in 1994-95. If maintained, this renewed decline in private capital formation in agriculture would dampen the long-term prospects for agricultural growth and poverty reduction. The renewed decline in private capital formation is consistent with the limited improvements in agricultural terms of trade identified earlier, as well as the observed decline in the productivity enhancing expenditure by the public sector.

During the 1980s agricultural subsidies increased three times faster than expenditure which promote productivity growth and now dominate public spending (Figure 4.2). Since 1991, the annual rate of growth in agricultural subsidies more than halved but it remains as high as 3.6 percent per annum in real terms. Thus, by 1994-95, close to 40 percent of total spending on agriculture was absorbed by subsidies, and another 22 percent by safety net programs. Only 38 percent of total spending went to productivity enhancing expenditure, as opposed to more than 60 percent in 1981-82.

Irrigation related subsidies dominate total expenditure on subsidies. Power and irrigation subsidies account for more than half of the subsidy bill in agriculture, both of which are supported by the state governments (Figure 4.4). The Central Government achieved some success in containing its agricultural subsidies through the virtual elimination of the explicit credit subsidy by 1994-95, a modest reduction in the fertilizer subsidy from 0.9 percent in 1990-91 to 0.6

**Figure 4.4: Irrigation Related
Subsidies Dominate
Ag. Subsidies (1994-95)**

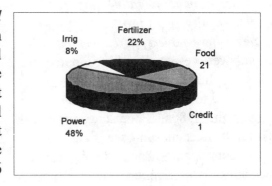

percent of GDP in 1995-96 and maintaining the food subsidy as a share of GDP at about 0.5 percent. The cost to the Central Government of its agricultural and rural debt relief schemes, announced in June 1990 fell from Rs 15 billion during 1990-93 to Rs 3.4 billion in 1994-95. However, continuing restrictions on interest rates for loans below Rs 200,000 are among the factors imposing a heavy toll on institutions that lend to agriculture. The fertilizer subsidy first increased by 12 percent in real terms between 1990-91 and 1992-93, and then declined by 30 percent in 1994-95. Urea prices were raised by 30 percent in August 1991 and by 20 percent in 1994. The subsidy on phosphatic and potassic fertilizers was eliminated in August 1992, while the prices of nitrogenous fertilizer prices were lowered by 10 percent. In September 1992, a flat subsidy of Rs 1000/ton was introduced for DAP and MOP fertilizers, which was raised to Rs 3000/ton for domestically produced DAP and to Rs 1500/ton for imported DAP and for MOP in July 1996.

The food subsidy bill increased by close to 40 percent in real terms between 1990-91 and 1995-96, but the share of the food subsidy financing food distribution and income transfer programs (PDS, RPDS, JRY) fell from 70 percent to less than 40 percent over the same period. This has created the perception that increasingly, the food subsidy is used to support producer prices rather than transfer incomes to the poor. In 1994-95, 60 percent of the food subsidy went to finance the buffer stock, sales on the open market, or exports. With the devaluation, the government had to raise rice and wheat procurement prices because of its dominant position on the domestic market. The need to contain the food subsidy prompted the government to raise issue prices in tandem with procurement prices--at least until 1994. The burgeoning food subsidy further prompted the government to free rice exports in 1994 and allow more wheat exports.

By contrast, states were much less successful in containing the subsidy on rural power which continued to expand very quickly--by 14 percent per annum in real terms between 1990-91 and 1994-95--to reach 1.1 percent of GDP in 1994-95. States were, however, more successful in containing the irrigation subsidy in real terms (1.2 percent per annum in real terms between 1990-91 and 1994-95). This occurred, however, at the expense of the quality and reliability of water delivery in the irrigation schemes, because non-wage expenditures for O&M were cut and cost recovery did not improve.

The composition of public expenditure in agriculture has a disproportionate negative impact on agricultural growth prospects in poor states where poverty is concentrated. States were responsible for 56 percent of agricultural subsidies in 1994-95, compared to an average of 40 percent during the 1980s. Poor states have a much weaker fiscal base than their rich counterparts, and so is their capacity to support agricultural

Table 4.4: Growth Prospects Suffer most among Poor States (key components of spending, 1990-91 to 1994-95)			
CapInv./GSDP: Social Sector Exp./GSDP:	Improved	Unchanged	Worsened
Improved	Maharashtra (+0.4; +0.1) Rajasthan (+0.3; +1.0)		Karnataka (-0.3; +0.4) Orissa (-1.9; +1.0)
No Change		Tamil Nadu (0; 0)	Gujarat (-0.8; -0.6)
Worsened		Andhra Pradesh (0.0; -0.3) West Bengal (0.0; -0.7)	Bihar (-0.8; -0.6) Uttar Pradesh (-0.2; -0.4)

Note: First figure in brackets refers to capital investments on power and irrigation; second figure refers to social spending.
Source: The Tenth Finance Commission and the Fiscal Challenge Facing Indian States; V.J. Ravishankar; World Bank, 1995.

subsidies in power and irrigation. In addition, the impact of the fiscal squeeze has fallen disproportionately on productivity enhancing expenditures--capital investments in irrigation and power, human capital investments--among the poorer states than among the richer ones (Table 4.4).

Some public expenditures in agriculture are inefficient partly because of ineffective government delivery mechanisms. Some public expenditure meant to support agriculture end-up in fact benefiting non-agricultural users. This is the case of the fertilizer subsidy, 50 percent of which accrued to the fertilizer industry during most of the 1980s and early 1990s as the retention price was well above import parity levels. In the case of the irrigation subsidy, most of actual expenses end-up financing the states' irrigation departments salary and wage payments to a bureaucracy with limited accountability for the operation and maintenance of government schemes. Equivalent considerations apply to the food subsidy which accrues to the Food Corporation of India. If diversion of rural power consumption to non-agricultural uses, or large-scale diversion from the PDS are included, the estimated leakages would be even higher.

The absence of targeting reduces the cost-effectiveness of agricultural input subsidies. As a result, the contribution of input subsidies in spreading the new technology and growth to the poorer states and farmers during the 1980s, was achieved at unnecessarily high and unsustainable fiscal costs. Moreover, there is evidence that richer states and irrigated areas, crops, and sometimes farmers, captured a disproportionately high share of the major input subsidy programs for fertilizer, power, and irrigation.

Agricultural subsidies contribute to costly resource misallocation and inefficiencies that often extend well beyond the agricultural sector. The fertilizer subsidy entails significant production inefficiencies at both the farm and fertilizer plant level. The (fertilizer) Price Retention Scheme provides no incentives for cost reduction and effectively rewards the inefficient fertilizer manufacturers. At the same time, the fertilizer subsidy causes serious nutrient imbalances in fertilizer application. Similarly, irrigation and rural power subsidies distort cropping patterns within India by promoting water-intensive crops like sugarcane in the relatively water-scarce areas (North-Eastern states of Punjab and Haryana, portions of Maharashtra, respectively), at the expense of the comparatively water-abundant regions of Eastern India. The power subsidy to agriculture, by contributing to significant financial losses and poor performance of SEBs, lowers the quality of delivery and results in the rationing of electricity to all customers.

Further, agricultural subsidies threaten environmental sustainability by mis-pricing inputs. In the case of surface and ground-water, mis-pricing promotes their over-exploitation, raising concerns about the long-term sustainability of agricultural production. Recent official studies have estimated the area affected by waterlogging, alkalinity and salinity as ranging from 9 percent of net irrigated areas (Ministry of Irrigation, Working Group on Waterlogging, Soil Salinity and Alkalinity, 1991) to 28 percent (Eighth Five-Year Plan). Inappropriate pricing of water, and high seepage losses from poor operations and maintenance of canal networks, are the major factors behind soil degradation and deteriorating water quality. The power subsidy to private tubewells in the form of flat rate electricity charges, coupled with inadequate regulatory and institutional mechanisms to control tubewell establishment and groundwater exploitation, also contribute to the over-exploitation of underground water resources, and other environmental problems such as salinity ingress.

PUBLIC EXPENDITURE REFORM

There is room to spend less but better in agriculture. Public expenditure in agriculture would need to be switched from non-targeted subsidies to growth-enhancing and targeted safety net programs. To protect the poor and reap the full economic benefits from fiscal adjustment in agriculture, some of the savings from the reduction in agricultural subsidies would need to be re-invested in agriculture and rural areas. Besides the obvious need to re-invest in the long term sources of agricultural growth, there are at least three other reasons for doing so.

First, the need to compensate the poor will increase as agricultural fiscal adjustment proceeds. Reducing subsidies in agriculture would have real (but possibly transitory) negative implications on rural incomes, poverty and growth. This result has been confirmed by the results of subsidy removal simulation exercises by several general equilibrium models of the Indian economy (Table 4.5). Therefore, compensatory, short term programs that target the poor would need to accompany the removal of input subsidies.

Table 4.5: Improved Composition of Expenditure Could Compensate for the Removal of Input Subsidies Results of Alternative Policy Simulations in a CGE Framework	GDP		Poverty	
	Ag.	Non-Ag.	Rural	Urban
Input subsidy removal, combined with:				
Tax relief	--	-	--	++
Tax relief, new irrigation investments earmarked (1 m. ha)	-	+	-	++
No tax relief, new irrigation investments earmarked (1 m. ha)	neg.	++	*	+
No tax relief, increased funding of safety net programs	neg.	+	++	+

Note: All results are compared to the base policy scenario of no subsidy removal in agriculture. + poverty effect indicates reduction of poverty. - indicates increase in poverty. * poverty effect indicates that the poorest rural income group gains marginally, while the second and third poorest rural income groups are losing. "Tax relief" means that the savings from the input subsidy removal are used to reduce the aggregate tax rate (i.e., both income and indirect taxes) such that the budget remains "in balance" (i.e., at the same level as before the intervention).
Source: Parikh, K.S., N.S.S. Narayana, M. Panda, & A.G. Kumar, 1995: Strategies for Agricultural Liberalization: Consequences for Growth, Welfare and Distribution, Indira Gandhi Institute of Development Research, Bombay.

Second, India's rapidly expanding demand for food will require more and better investment, not less. With incomes growing much faster, the domestic demand for food will accelerate further, and increasingly diversify into new commodities such as livestock, horticultural products, and processed food items. Reduction in poverty will boost future demand for food even further. Capturing such growth opportunities in agriculture will require that additional resources be invested in the long term sources of agricultural growth.

Third, investing in agricultural productivity growth is increasingly important for poverty reduction. Falling rice and wheat prices during the 1980s contributed significantly to the rise in the real rural wage (goods) and therefore to the reduction in poverty. A more open trade regime, fewer biases against agriculture, fast rising domestic and external demands for Indian agricultural products, make the prospects of falling agricultural prices in real terms quite remote. Hence, productivity growth will assume even greater importance in raising real rural wages.

Switching to growth-enhancing expenditure and targeted safety nets could compensate for the phased removal of input subsidies. Improving the composition of public expenditure in agriculture has the potential to avoid an agricultural recession, reduce poverty, while contributing to the overall fiscal adjustment effort. This is illustrated by the policy simulations conducted with the help of a computable general equilibrium (CGE) model of the Indian economy. This model traces the income and distribution effects of various compositions of public expenditure in agriculture. As indicated by Table 4.5, the policy simulations confirm that re-investing part of the savings from the removal of agricultural subsidies into a combination of growth-enhancing expenditure--approximated by increased public investment in irrigation-- and targeted safety net programs--approximated by increased funding of targeted food rations-- has the potential to accelerate rural growth, raise rural incomes, and simultaneously improve income distribution to the benefit of both the rural and urban poor.

Rehabilitation and modernization investment, combined with volumetric pricing and institutional changes would provide the basis for efficient water use, cost recovery, and improved service delivery in canal irrigation. Rehabilitation and modernization of minor, medium and large irrigation schemes would restore the reliability of water delivery without which farmers will be reluctant to pay for higher water charges. It will also permit the introduction of volumetric pricing of water and improved water management practices as recommended by the 1992 Report of the Committee on Pricing of Irrigation Water. Institutional reforms would provide the basis and necessary financial incentives for improved cost recovery as well as improved accountability in the delivery of water services to farmers. Tamil Nadu and Orissa recently initiated reforms that would lead to improved cost recovery, quality of service delivery to farmers, and systems turnover to beneficiaries. Karnataka, in its 1995 Agricultural Policy Resolution, is proposing to radically transform institutional incentives in the irrigation sector (Box 4.3).

The strategy to eliminate the power subsidy to agriculture should be based on two elements: (a) a gradual phasing over the medium term; and (b) a series of institutional innovations to improve the management of groundwater resources, and to facilitate access to groundwater irrigation by the poor and marginal farmers. A phasing of the subsidy removal is essential to give both farmers and the power industry time to adjust. In the short-run, raising rural tariffs to the recommended 50 paise/kwh with an automatic, annual adjustment to cover cost-increases would reduce the subsidy bill substantially. This would need to be complemented by policy reforms in the power industry that support the increased collection of tariffs, and the increased participation of the private sector in new, cost-effective power generation capacity and distribution networks. Recent reforms in Orissa's power industry provide such an example, and indicate that they are feasible.

Box 4.3: Institutional Reforms in Karnataka's Irrigation Sector

Karnataka was among the first state in the country to have prepared an Agriculture Policy Resolution in 1995. The resolution proposes, among other things, major institutional reform in the irrigation sector:

"...... Irrigation Department may be granted financial autonomy and converted into a corporation on the condition that it should recover at least operation and maintenance expenses from the direct beneficiaries. Also, water users' associations (WUAs) would be involved in the management and ownership of canal networks. Farmers would be made co-owners of these irrigation structures through issuing of "water equity shares". Farmers would get representation in the Management Board of Irrigation Corporation, where they can air their views more effectively. This would be the beginning of a process to convert the irrigation works from tops down to bottoms up. Canal waters would be sold to these WUAs in bulk quantities, leaving the individual-specific distribution of water, as also collection of dues thereof, to these WUAs on attractive commission basis."

[excerpt from Agriculture Policy Resolution, State Planning Board, Government of Karnataka, 1995]

The initial steps towards meeting some of these objectives were recently taken through the establishment of an autonomous public corporation for handling irrigation activities in the Upper Krishna basin. This corporation, called the *Karnataka Bhagya Jala Nigam Ltd.*, will have considerably greater autonomy in raising and deploying financial resources than the state irrigation department. It is also expected to have a close involvement with WUAs in water transactions. While it is still too early to judge the corporation's performance, initiatives of this nature are steps in the right direction to reform the irrigation sector.

Reforms in *rural power pricing* must accommodate environmental and equity considerations in an economy where water for half of the net irrigated area comes from groundwater sources. Raising power tariffs would provide the much needed price incentives for farmers to use water more efficiently and in a more sustainable fashion. However, there are limitations in using power tariffs alone in addressing environmental externalities and long term sustainability consequences of groundwater exploitation, and guiding individual decisions towards a socially optimal management of groundwater resources. *Legal and regulatory changes would be required* to clarify and delineate groundwater use rights, along with realistic enforcement mechanisms. At the same time, equitable access to groundwater resources and greater controls on groundwater exploitation are likely to become increasingly important with the elimination of the power subsidy. Promoting organizational innovations to foster the equitable and sustainable access to groundwater resources must accompany reforms of the rural power tariffs.

A fertilizer and kerosene program could target the poor to compensate for the elimination of the fertilizer subsidy. A feasible strategy to eliminate the fertilizer subsidy could be based on two elements: a gradual phasing over the medium term and a compensatory program targeting the poor segments of the farming population. A phasing of the subsidy removal is essential to give both farmers and the fertilizer industry time to adjust (prior to possible privatization of the publicly-owned industry). In the short-run, the subsidy bill could be reduced by introducing greater transparency on the costs of production and gradually adjusting retention prices to reduce the cost-plus-rate-of-return margin. Increases in the price of urea, and elimination of the ad-hoc subsidy on phosphate and potash would also reduce the subsidy burden in the short-run. In the medium-term, remaining quantitative restrictions and non-tariff barriers on fertilizer imports would need to be eliminated.

A fixed fertilizer allowance targeted to each poor farming household would compensate them for their income loss. A simple design could make such a targeted program implementable virtually overnight. For example, the program could be established through a fertilizer stamp program with beneficiaries identified in a participatory fashion by the Panchayati Raj Institutions (PRIs). A fixed allowance, time-bound program would achieve the income transfer objective, while at the same time avoid new price distortions by providing for an infra-marginal subsidy.

In addition to its positive impact on the efficiency of fertilizer use, eliminating the fertilizer subsidy would be expected to have positive consequences for agricultural labor use and the environment. The CGE simulations confirm that besides eliminating the current imbalance in nutrient application, the removal of the fertilizer subsidy will give farmers greater incentives to apply more manure which will have positive, environmental effects on soil management. Increased manure application will raise the demand for agricultural labor, in particular among women, pushing rural wages up.

Shifting the use of manure from cooking and lighting purposes to soil fertility management may raise pressure on already strained sources of fuelwood, in particular for the poor households who critically depend on the open access forestry resources. Targeting the subsidization of kerosene to poor rural households would complement the removal of the fertilizer subsidy. It would give the poorer households an alternative source of energy to the manure, and help minimize the pressure on already strained sources of fuelwood. However, since kerozene can be mixed with diesel for many uses, it is important to ensure that the subsidy does not create an incentive for the adulteration of kerozene with diesel.

Decentralization and institutional changes. Other measures also should be considered to improve the effectiveness and efficiency of public expenditure. Decentralization and beneficiary participation would help improve the cost effectiveness and sustainability of expenditures in rural infrastructure development. For instance, community participation and responsibility in program design and implementation would raise the cost effectiveness, social and environmental sustainability of the watershed programs. This is one of the conclusions of the 1995 Report of the Technical Committee on DPAP and DDP (1994) as well as the evaluations of the watershed programs.

Improvements in agricultural research and extension would provide a tremendous boost to productivity. Pay-offs from investments in technology have been and will remain extremely large in India. India has developed a dense and strong technical capacity for technology development and dissemination. That capacity has, however, eroded over time because of inadequate policy support and poor incentives. Increased commitment to agricultural research and dissemination would need to be complemented by institutional reforms for enhancing pay-offs from existing resources. Institutional reforms to strengthen the capacity and raise the accountability of extension services are badly needed also. There is significant scope for releasing the agricultural extension staff from involvement in commercial activities that would be more effectively performed by the private sector, farmers associations or cooperatives. Innovations and experimentation to raise the accountability and client-responsiveness of public extension services are also possible. This could include the financial and managerial decentralization of extension services to PRIs, the participatory and systematic interaction with NGOs and private sector institutions specialized in providing extension services, and the introduction of extension vouchers to farmers and rural communities.

FOREIGN TRADE DE-REGULATION

Prior to 1991, about 96 percent of internationally tradable agricultural production was protected by non-trade barriers (NTBs) against imports (Table 4.6). Exports of most commodities were also subject to quantitative restrictions (QRs), except long-established exports --tea, coffee, spices, jute, tobacco, castorseed, pepper, oilmeals--or those deemed to have an export potential--fruits and vegetables, and fish.

Table 4.6: Trade Reforms in Indian Agriculture				
Trade Status	**Exportables**		**Importables**	
	Imports	Exports	Imports	Exports
Prior to June 1991	NTBs for 96 percent of ag prod'n (rice, wheat, cotton)	QRs for most commodities (rice, wheat, cotton) Free for established exports (e.g., tea, coffee, oilseeds meals, spices, fish, fruit & vegetables)	NTBs for 96 percent of ag prod'n (coarse cereals, sugar, oilseeds, edible oils, dairy & livestock products, processed ag. products) Free for pulses, raw wool	QRs for most commodities
Significant Policy Changes	Cotton, 0 percent tariff (94)	Rice (94) Durum wheat & wheat flour (94)	Sugar, 0 percent tariff (94) Edible oils, 30 percent tariff (95), 20 percent tariff (96) Pulses, tariff reduced from 10 percent to 5 percent (95) SMP, 0 percent tariff (95) BO 30 percent tariff (95) Hides & skin Poultry, 10 percent tariff	rapeseeds & sunflower (95)
Status As of July 1996	NTBs for 77 percent of ag prod'n	QRs for most commodities, except rice (24 percent of ag. prod'n), established exports	NTBs for 77 percent of ag prod'n	QRs for most commodities, except rice (24 percent of ag. prod'n), established exports
Source: Pursell, G. and A. Sharma, 1996: "Indian Trade Policies Since the 1991/92 Reforms", World Bank, Washington D.C.				

The 1991-92 trade reforms initially relaxed QRs on a few minor commodities. Agricultural tariffs were reduced, but remained irrelevant since import licensing and other import controls were maintained. Gradual trade reforms culminated in 1994 with the full liberalization of a few but important commodities: rice exports, and imports of most edible oils (30 percent tariff), sugar and cotton (see Table 4.6). On the import side, these foreign trade reforms reduced the share of tradable agricultural production protected by NTBs from about 93 percent in May 1992 to about 77 percent in May 1995, if it is assumed that the liberalization of edible oils amounts to a liberalization of the corresponding oilseeds. There is no equivalent estimate on the export side. However, the abolition of rice alone is a significant step, since it accounts for about 16 percent of agricultural production. Further changes have been introduced in the 1996-97 budget. These include the tariff reduction from 30 to 20 percent for edible oils imports.

Three sets of reforms would improve price incentives to the agricultural sector. These are: (a) lower protection of the manufacturing sector; (b) extension of trade liberalization to additional crops; and (c) domestic de-regulation of agricultural markets and agro-processing.

Simulations using a CGE model developed for the purposes of this report suggest that lower protection of the manufacturing sector would improve price incentives to the agricultural sector and make farmers better off (see Annex II). This is because farmers would have access to cheaper inputs and consumers goods (Table 4.7).

Table 4.7: Evaluating Alternative Policies for Raising Relative Agriculture Prices Results of Alternative Policy Simulations in a CGE Framework	GDP		Poverty	
	Ag.	Non-Ag.	Rural	Urban
a. Agricultural trade liberalization	++	- -	+	- -
b. Manufacturing protection further reduced (20% tariffs for capital and intermediate goods; consumer good imports liberalized with 25% tariff)	+	++	+	+
c. a+b: agricultural and industrial trade liberalization	++	+	++	-
d. c with high world price scenario for rice and wheat	+++	0	+	- - -
e. d+fertilizer subsidy removed	++	0	++	- - -
f. Harmonization of relative protection between agriculture and industry (35% tariffs)	-	-	-	- -
Note: All results are compared to a base policy scenario of real devaluation, 30% tariffs for intermediates and 35% for capital goods, fertilizer subsidy bill constant in real terms. - poverty effect indicates worsening of poverty; + poverty effect indicates reduction of poverty. Source: Quizon, J., M. Panda, H. Binswanger, and B. Blarel forthcoming , World Bank, Washington.				

These improved incentives for agriculture would lead to faster sectoral growth (scenario b in Table 4.7). Real rural wages would rise as a result of improved relative agricultural prices, and faster agricultural GDP growth. In addition, the model indicates that lifting the ban on consumer goods imports would increase real incomes of all household groups in both rural and urban areas.

The CGE model was also used to explore the option of protecting agriculture by raising agricultural tariffs to parity levels with manufacturing goods. The results, however, indicate that such an harmonization policy would actually hurt all households, except for the top 50 percent of rural households. This result is not surprising. An harmonization policy, by raising food prices, would hurt the vast majority of consumers in India (scenario f in Table 4.7).

The World price environment is favorable to further agricultural trade liberalization. World agricultural prices, most notably rice and wheat, are currently high and likely to remain so for an additional couple of years. The combination of high world prices and high domestic stocks, provides India with a strategic opportunity to further liberalize trade and simultaneously reduce its input subsidies (scenario e in Table 4.7). CGE simulations suggest that, with currently high rice and wheat world prices, trade liberalization in agriculture, even if combined say with fertilizer subsidy removal, would boost agricultural growth. In terms of income distribution, the top 50 percent of rural households would gain the most by benefiting from higher export prices for rice, wheat, and other crops such as cotton, fruits and vegetables. Higher food prices would hurt the rural poor, although the higher agricultural growth and accompanying higher rural wages are expected to compensate for this increase. Urban households, in particular the bottom 50 percent, would suffer an income loss, however, since food prices increase and non-agricultural GDP stagnates.

The adverse impacts on the poor underscore the need for targeted, cost-effective alternatives to the PDS and other targeted safety net programs to protect the poor at least in a transitional period from the costs of subsidy removal in agriculture and further trade liberalization. Such a strategy would aim at alleviating the poor's chronic food insecurity by reducing the risks they face on both the food and labor markets. This strategy would require more funding of rural (and urban) employment guarantee programs while simultaneously improving their targeting. It would also involve developing cheaper and more effective alternatives to the Public Distribution System.

DOMESTIC TRADE DE-REGULATION

Domestic reforms since 1991-92 have included the *de facto* removal of price controls from wheat during harvest (in the surplus northwest region) through the lifting of informal controls on wheat movement by private trade in February 1993. And price and movement controls on sugar molasses were lifted by the Central Government in June 1993, although partially implemented by three states (Uttar Pradesh, Bihar, and Haryana). The discussion below of key commodities (Table 4.8) illustrates the far reaching agenda still to be tackled (Tables 4.9 and 4.10).

Table 4.8: Value of Output from Agriculture (percent of total agriculture output)					
	1985-86	1990-91	1991-92	1992-93	1993-94
Rice (paddy)	17.1	15.4	16.4	15.8	16.7
Wheat	9.2	8.7	9.2	8.8	8.9
Oilseeds	6.3	10.6	10.2	9.4	9.3
Sugar	5.2	5.5	5.0	5.2	5.6
Livestock	24.0	24.6	25.4	26.2	26.4

Source: CSO, National Accounts Statistics, 1996.

Table 4.9: Beyond Trade Policy, What are the Problems with Agricultural Markets?	Rice	Wheat	Sugar	Oilseeds	Cotton	Dairy & Poultry Feed
Inadequate infrastructure (transport, port, market)	✓✓✓	✓		✓✓	✓	
Processing margins	✓		✓✓✓	✓✓✓		✓✓
Marketing margins	✓	✓	✓✓✓	✓✓✓	✓✓	
Quality Management	✓✓✓			✓✓	✓✓✓	

Note: the number of ✓ indicates the intensity of the problem.

Table 4.10: What Causes the Problems with Agricultural Markets?	Rice	Wheat	Sugar	Oilseeds	Cotton	Dairy & Poultry Feed
GOI:						
FCI operations (levy procurement, pan seasonal & territorial prices, dominant player)	✓✓✓	✓✓✓				
Dual marketing system			✓✓✓			
Essential Commodities Act	✓✓✓	✓✓✓	✓✓✓	✓✓✓	✓✓✓	
Milk & Milk Products Order/Licensing			✓✓			✓✓✓
Selective Credit Controls (RBI)	✓✓✓	✓✓✓		✓✓✓	✓✓✓	
Small Scale Industry Reservation	✓			✓✓✓		✓✓✓
Sugarcane pricing/Ginning fees			✓✓		✓✓	
Forward Contracts (Regulation) Act		✓✓	✓✓	✓✓✓	✓✓✓	
Health safety legislations & enforcement				✓✓		
Intellectual property rights				✓✓	✓✓	
State Governments:						
Movement controls	✓✓		✓	✓✓✓	✓✓	
Regulated markets management	✓	✓		✓✓	✓✓	
Cane Cooperative Societies			✓✓			
Non-unitary & multi-point taxation			✓	✓	✓	

Note: The number of ✓ indicates the intensity of the problem.

Rice and Wheat. The liberalization of rice exports in October 1994 is a landmark policy change clearly beneficial to farmers. At the same time, it is also exposing the shortcomings of the current food policy. Specifically, food policies are increasingly costly to the exchequer, yet involve fewer income transfers to the poor; they do not support a more open trade regime; and are poorly equipped to deal with world price instability. Extensive government interventions in rice and wheat markets, pervasive controls and restrictions on private sector storage and movement, trade finance, milling activities explain the limited private investment in port and transport infrastructure, storage activities, and the inadequate attention to quality management on the domestic market. The price discounts currently faced by Indian exporters are significant--20 percent (about $60/mt) for common rice and about 15 percent ($26/mt) for wheat.

Domestic markets need to be allowed to operate more freely to support a more effective open trade policy. In the short-run, gradual improvements could be achieved by lifting the uncertainty about the open trade regime, phasing-out the rice levy system, eliminating pan-territorial and pan-seasonal pricing, and lifting commercial restrictions on trade, storage, movement, (rice) milling and trade finance. This would induce private investment in modern storage, port equipment and facilities, and improve quality management. The development of the warehousing system together with financial product innovations would further improve the efficiency and stability of private storage operations. It would also enable FCI to experiment with sub-contracting some of its storage and transport operations to the private sector, and to pilot alternative price stabilization mechanisms. An increasingly reliable, competitive and well-performing physical market for cereals would eventually enable the introduction of futures markets and commodity derivative instruments in wheat and, possibly for rice. Such instruments, in the long-run, could provide India with powerful and more cost effective alternatives to price risk management, food security, and producer support programs.

India, because of its large size, has the potential to influence the world price of rice. The extent to which India could rely on foreign trade as a cost-effective tool to complement domestic policies in meeting its food security and income support objectives needs to take this fact into account. The optimal policy choices would depend crucially on the price-depressing (large-country) effects of India's rice exports on the world market. Answers to that question would require detailed and careful analysis. Analytical work along these lines is now being conducted in India and should be helpful in guiding government's policy decisions in the future. Illustrative and preliminary simulations conducted for purposes of this CEM would suggest that, under optimal trade policy, domestic prices would have increased very little, while imparting greater stability on the world market.

India entered the export market for wheat and rice at an opportune time because of high world prices. India should continue to use this opportunity to break into the world market by developing its own markets and expertise, by improving its export quality, reliability of its services and supporting infrastructure. Current barriers to trade-- inadequate port infrastructure, poor quality exports--already act as an export tax, minimizing the need for further foreign trade intervention in rice as well as wheat in the short to medium-term (Box 4.4).

Better access by the poor to subsidized food and improved nutrition programs which are cost effective will be essential in protecting the (rural and urban) poor from higher food prices at minimum fiscal costs. At the same time, reforming the procurement side of the PDS for rice, wheat and sugar is central to the de-regulation of domestic trade and agro-processing for the rice, wheat and sugarcane crops. The PDS is not very effective in reaching the very poor. For instance, for every rupee spent in 1986-87, less than 22 paise reached the poorest 20 percent of poor households in all major states. Except in those instances where state-level initiatives are significant, such as in Kerala, Andhra Pradesh, Karnataka, income transfers to the poor via the PDS are negligible, and achieved at huge fiscal costs. Where state-level initiatives are significant, PDS transfers can reduce the severity of poverty, but this is also achieved at huge and sometimes non-sustainable fiscal costs, in large part because

---

Box 4.4: Deficiencies in Port and Port Services Impede Agricultural Exports

India's agricultural exports account for a mere one percent of world agricultural trade but commodities such as fruits and vegetables, cereals, floriculture and marine products appear to have significant export potential (see Chapter 6). Chapter 2 has already indicated that the country's major ports are over-crowded, poorly equipped and inefficiently laid out, and thus impede agricultural exports.

The greatest problem for exporters is the poor distribution and storage facilities (including those at the ports). This is leading to wastage of 30 percent of production annually. This wastage is substantial because India is the world's second largest grower of fruits and vegetables. At present, only 1 percent of production is commercially processed and only a few products are exported to markets in South Asia, the Middle East and Eastern Europe. However, the sector is recognized as potentially important for exports, with a target of US$650 million for the year 2000. Similar problems affect rice and wheat, and are linked to controls and restrictions on private sector marketing, trade finance, storage and milling activities which in turn have contributed to inadequate private investment *inter alia* in ports.

Marine exports have diversified in recent years from reliance on frozen shrimp and now encompass a variety of finfish and mollusks. Export growth has been rapid, rising from 20 percent of agricultural and allied exports in the early 1990s to 27 percent in 1994-95. Mechanization of the local fleet has contributed to this expansion. However, inefficiencies at the ports rob India of the full economic benefits of this trade because they have led many vessels to tranship catches at sea.

In addition to facilitating more efficient handling of cereals, fruit and vegetables and marine products, key investment in ports (as well as market, post-harvest, other transport infrastructure and quality management) would enable the oilseeds crushing industry to become more technically efficient and competitive internationally.

of the universal character of PDS distribution. The efficacy of the PDS in distributing food to the poor appears to have improved little since 1986-87. Regional mistargeting continues to plague the PDS and appears to be a direct reflection of the states' fiscal health and capacity to implement their own programs. In the richer states able to finance significant state-level initiatives such as Karnataka and Andhra Pradesh, available evidence indicates that non-food commodities (coarse cloth and kerosene) are at least as important as food commodities in transferring income to the poor, and are much better targeted presumably because of considerable self-targeting.

The revamped PDS, introduced in 1992, is targeted to those same poor and backward regions where the EAS is implemented, and represents a first attempt at geographical targeting. Results of the beneficiary assessments surveys carried out for this report (Chapter 1) would seem to indicate that the RPDS is not reaching the very poor either. Additionally, the government may wish to experiment with alternative transfer and targeting mechanisms such as food stamps through existing systems of health and nutrition programs (ICDS), and/or through PRIs.

Sugar. With the liberalization of sugar imports under zero percent tariff, the domestic sugar industry must now compete with imports. Historically, productivity growth in Indian sugar production and processing has lagged behind international levels. The dual marketing system--involving the compulsory delivery of about 35 percent of milled sugar output for the PDS at levy prices, and a "free" sugar market which absorbs the balance--is taxing domestic production relative to imports. It is also impeding productivity growth. Lack of competition between mills due to licensing restrictions, water subsidies particularly in Maharashtra, interventions such as cane societies in Uttar Pradesh, and government cane pricing further reduce the incentives for technological catch-up in the industry.

In the sugar industry alone, market oriented policies would permit technological catch-up by the industry, and would result in substantial economic and welfare gains. Recent and conservative estimates of the welfare gains from productivity improvements could reach as much as US$2 billion a year by 2005. With policy changes that encourage productivity growth, India could satisfy over 90 percent of its projected consumption growth over the next decade at world competitive prices and without tariff protection. Consumers would benefit from the increased availability at constant and stable prices; productivity growth would benefit sugarcane growers-- even with input subsidies removed--and avoid taking scarce resources away from other crops. Improved profitability in sugar processing would attract the needed private capital and alleviate the need for government subsidization. Government revenues and savings would increase which would amply cover the costs of a sugar subsidy program targeted to the poor.

Central to the technological catch-up by the sugar industry--from cane growers to sugar mills--is the phasing out of the dual marketing system, continued free trade, the elimination of licensing requirements, and reforming government interventions in cane pricing as indicated earlier. A government-supported subsidy program for sugar targeted to the poor would complement the phase-out of the dual marketing system. The phase-out of the dual marketing system would remove the taxation of domestic production relative to imports, and eliminate the main source of volatility in Indian sugar production, as well as uncertainty to the sugar mills. It would be key to releasing the growth potential of one of the largest sugar industries in the world.

Oilseed. Edible oils are now freely importable at 20 percent tariffs. By putting a cap on the price of edible oils, free imports greatly benefit Indian consumers who, until recently, had to pay two to three times world price levels. The need for high protection of oilseeds also has dissipated as a result of the devaluation, and the doubling in production which led to a 22 percent fall in oilseeds prices in real terms between 1990-91 and 1993-94. Imports of edible oils are creating competitive pressures for the domestic oilseed crushing industry to trim its marketing costs and crushing margins.

Recent analysis shows the oilseed crushing industry and trade performing poorly in processing and marketing. Four factors explain this poor performance: (i) India's crushing industry is small-scale, technically and economically inefficient, and is characterized by a dismally low capacity utilization rate (30 percent) by any international standard; (ii) the domestic market is not adequately integrated and crushing margin risks cannot be properly covered because there are storage and movement controls, small-scale industry reservations for the two most important oilseeds, restricted access to working capital, a ban on forward and futures markets, and a non-unitary and multi-point taxation regime; (iii) port and transport infrastructure is inadequate, raising the costs of exporting oilseed meals by as much as 50 percent; and (iv) incentives for quality and food health safety are very limited resulting in significant discounts on the world market for groundnut and rapeseed meals.

Shifting from successful import substitution to a modernization strategy is now needed to protect the incomes of the mostly rainfed, oilseed farmers, and sustain past production achievements. Lifting the regulatory barriers to modernization would enable the oilseed crushing industry to trim its large processing and marketing costs, and successfully compete with imports. During the modernization and restructuring process of the oilseed crushing industry, oilseed producers would need a price support mechanism. Free oilseed exports--already in place for rapeseed-mustardseed and sunflower--would provide such price support mechanism at no fiscal cost to the government.

De-regulation of domestic trade and agro-processing, key investment in port, market and post-market infrastructure, improved regulations and controls on food safety and intellectual property rights, would reduce considerably marketing and processing margins and raise export earnings from oilseeds and meals considerably. Expressed in terms of oilseed farmgate prices, efficiency gains could be as high as 20 percent.

Access to modern risk management instruments--technical efficiency, flexibility in sourcing raw material, forward and futures markets--would enable the crushing industry to manage its crushing margin risks, and take advantage of the 75 percent drop in oilseed production instability achieved over the last 15 years. Access to modern risk management tools is essential in an industry where crushing margin risks are an inescapable, structural feature. With the full exposure to foreign competition in oils and meals, they are now a necessity. In the absence of standard risk management techniques, farm prices will be forced down whenever processors feel a squeeze on their processing margins.

Cotton. With the liberalization of cotton imports at zero percent tariff, the poor quality management in cotton production, ginning and marketing will make it increasingly attractive for the textile mills, notably the export-oriented units, to import cotton of higher and more reliable quality rather than to rely on the domestic market. Until recently, cotton seed prices were also well above world prices, compensating cotton growers for the otherwise low cotton lint prices caused by the quantitative restrictions on cotton exports. Production shortfalls in 1994-95, caused by pests and diseases in the northern producing region, and increased domestic demand to feed the textile export boom have partly masked this phenomenon.

The domestic cotton industry's ability to compete in terms of both quality and price with imports is hampered by various government policies and regulations. Strict cotton export controls block incentives for improved quality management on the domestic market; the high protection of the yarn and textile industries from imports compounds the poor incentives for quality management in the cotton-textile industry. Restrictions on standard commercial practices--such as the movement and storage of cotton, trade finance, hedging and forward contracting, ginning fees, inadequate grading practices and facilities in regulated markets, and weaknesses in the seed industry--militate against improved marketing performance, transparency, competition and quality management. Pesticide subsidies, and weak cotton research and extension programs have also resulted in escalating pest and disease problems, which increasingly threaten both production volume as well as the quality of output. Experience in China, Mexico, and Thailand has shown that delayed action in addressing pest and disease problems could result in drastic production and economic losses.

The abolition of the Multi-Fibers Agreement (MFA) represents a tremendous opportunity for growth and employment for the Indian cotton-textile industry. The growth potential in cotton production, in the context of a more liberalized environment, will rest heavily on the degree to which the sector will be allowed to operate with minimum interference from government interventions in marketing and processing, and on key public interventions in raising yields, addressing pest and disease problems, and seed quality. Recent estimates indicate that, for the South Asia region as a whole, the textile industry is likely to more than double in size in just over 10 years. And the apparel industry will more than triple in size. India has begun the process of policy reform needed to take advantage of these emerging opportunities. The agreement by India to open-up imports of textile products is one such important step. It will provide India the negotiating leverage should the US or the EU contemplate negotiations on extending the MFA quotas. The availability of imported textiles and apparel should help make the domestic industry more price competitive and meet international quality standards. Recent policy changes in the man-made fibers industry will also facilitate inter-fiber substitution, and release the much needed cotton for the more lucrative export markets.

However, much more remains to be done to capture these emerging market opportunities. The historical subsidization of the textile industry by cotton growers is disappearing as a result of the free imports of edible oils, and cotton production problems.

Several policies stand in the way of making domestic cotton competitive in price and quality with imports. These include cotton and yarn export quotas; over-regulation of domestic trade, ginning and the formal sector textile industry, hank-yarn obligation; and high tariff barriers on imports of yarn, textile and apparel.

Concerns about the future of the handloom industry should be mitigated by the tremendous employment opportunities that would arise from a highly labor-intensive industry about to at least double in size; by the realization that market niches for handloom products do not require special protection; and by the presence of less distortive policy alternatives to protect the handloom industry. In the short-run, the textile industry, notably the yarn sector, should be given the flexibility to modernize and become more competitive, while simultaneously increasing the incentives for modernization through tariff reduction on textile imports, yarn export liberalization, and lower taxation of the man-made fibers industry. Domestic de-regulation in cotton marketing and ginning would permit the more efficient transmission of price and quality signals to cotton growers. Cotton export quotas should be gradually expanded, and be fully eliminated within a few years.

Livestock. The devaluation of the rupee and tariffication of dairy and poultry products is bringing domestic prices down to the benefit of consumers. Growth in the dairy sector (about 6 percent per annum) has been instrumental in alleviating poverty, since small and marginal farmers own a large proportion of dairy animals. Inefficiencies in the dairy and poultry feed industry, however, hinder the capacity of these sectors to satisfy the expected future increases in domestic demand and compete with imports. Analysis shows that in India the dairy industry's processing margins are high by international standards, causing low farmgate prices. In poultry, the unreliable supply and quality of feed has resulted in catastrophic losses in several states, such as the widespread slaughter of stock due to a feed shortfall in 1992.

In the dairy industry, two major policies contribute to the observed marketing and processing inefficiencies. *First*, the Milk and Milk Products Order (MMPO) 1992 limits entry and competition in the dairy industry, and helps maintain the inefficiencies caused by the earlier policy regime. *Second*, the continued state controls and subsidization of poorly performing dairy cooperatives, limit their incentives to improve efficiency. These policies, could block technological change, and thereby, hurt the industry.

Poultry production and breeding are generally efficient by international standards. Inefficiencies in poultry feed manufacturing limit, however, the capacity of the poultry industry to expand and remain competitive. Poultry feed is the largest cost component in poultry production. The small scale reservation of poultry feed manufacturing hinders feed manufacturers from taking advantage of economies of scale and technological innovation which would reduce production costs and enhance the quality of feed considerably. The development of the feed industry will, therefore, be a critical determinant of growth and competitiveness of the poultry industry.

In conclusion, substantial gains would result from domestic de-regulation of agriculture. The deregulation of domestic trade and agro-processing would significantly reduce marketing and processing margins, to the benefit of both farmers and consumers, making it a win-win proposition. It would bring additional incomes to the rural areas, raise farm profitability, and promote productivity growth in agriculture. De-regulation would actively complement and support the removal of agricultural subsidies. It would enable Indian farmers to compete with their foreign competitors, and to capture rapidly expanding domestic and foreign markets. Government would also benefit from a deregulation strategy which would strengthen food security objectives, improve price stability, promote rural growth--including in rainfed areas--and facilitate the pursuit of essential public concerns such as poverty alleviation and food safety concerns. In addition, the ratification of the Trade Related Aspects of Intellectual Property Rights (TRIPs) agreement will improve farmers' access to productivity enhancing technologies.

RURAL CREDIT REFORM

Reforms are needed to enable India's rural financial system to support agriculture and other rural economic activities. Estimates suggest that small farmers have little access to credit and long-term credit is highly concentrated among large farmers. Subsidized credit often is tied to particular investment, thus encouraging more capital-intensive/less labor-absorbing technologies. Credit arrangements typically are linked to specific crops and require borrowers to obtain their input supplies through the inefficient public delivery system. Guidelines set by the RBI dictate the amount of credit for individual investments in agro-processing (such as in sugar and oilseeds). Thus, the technologies in which investments are made often reflect how much credit is available (as per the RBI credit guidelines) rather than the appropriateness of the technologies. Selective credit controls, issued by the RBI, severely limit access to trade and storage credit for all major crops. They also prevent banks from offering more attractive financing terms when stocks are either hedged, or secured through warehouse receipts. Separately, the absence of credit for hedging limits the strategies for risk management.

These deficiencies vis-a-vis the agricultural sector, reflect three main generic weaknesses of the overall rural financial system, namely: (a) low autonomy of rural financial institutions emanating from state ownership, micro-regulation and measurement of performance based on the achievement of credit targets to the exclusion of self-sustainability; (b) the relatively high cost--both to lenders and to the borrowers--associated with the centrally planned credit and application of concessional on-lending rates that are below market-determined rates; and (c) the low eventual recovery rate on loans.

The Indian authorities began reforming the rural financial system in earnest in 1994. Steps taken to date include: (a) lowering target group lending (marginal and small farmers and rural artisans) from 100 percent to 40 percent in the case of regional rural banks; (b) allowing banks greater freedom to rationalize branches; (c) deregulating interest rates of rural cooperative banks; (d) allowing urban cooperative banks to lend to rural borrowers in contiguous areas; (e) relaxing "service area" restrictions to encourage competition and stimulate supply; and (f) applying of international prudential norms to RRBs. The RBI is also undertaking a program under which 49 RRBs are being re-capitalized and their management strengthened; another 68 RRBs were identified in December 1995 for inclusion in the program. Separately, the National

Bank for Agriculture and Rural Development (NABARD), the apex re-financing institution, has helped evolve Development Actions Plans (DAPs) for strengthening selected RRBs and cooperative banks and has entered into Memoranda of Understanding with state governments (as well as with specific cooperatives) on the operationalization of these DAPs. NABARD and banks, through NGOs, are also promoting self-help groups among the poor, which encourage savings and micro credit activities.

The Common Minimum Program indicated that the United Front Government planned to double the flow of credit to agriculture and agro-industries over the next five years. The recent full-year Budget (1996-97) provides for: (a) doubling the paid-up share capital of NABARD in 1996-97; (b) establishing state-level agricultural development financial institutions (DFIs) to promote investment in commercial or high technology agriculture and allied activities such as horticulture, floriculture and agro-processing, with NABARD and state governments providing the equity for these new DFIs; (c) setting up new private local area banks which will operate in two or three contiguous districts; and (d) recapitalizing and restructuring RRBs for which another installment of Rs 2 billion (US$57 million) was allocated.

A coherent strategy for increasing flows to agriculture and other rural economic activities must address issues of access to financial services by the rural population in general, as well as the financial sustainability of the RFIs. Measures are needed to encourage and facilitate an orderly re-orientation of India's rural financial system from the supply-led approach of concessional, targeted agriculture credit, to the systematic development of demand-oriented rural financial markets. Specific actions for consideration include: (a) redefining the role of the NABARD to increase its efficiency and self-sustainability in catalyzing flows to the sector through market based mechanism, and removing the conflict of interest inherent in its responsibilities as a supervisor and financier of the rural financial system; (b) deregulating the remaining lending rates; (b) relaxing credit guidelines/schemes and restrictions; (c) adopting regulatory changes to facilitate greater Regional Financial Institution (RFI) autonomy; (d) eliminating service area restrictions (while ensuring that districts remain adequately served); and (e) improving legal and other arrangements for loan recovery.

THE ENABLING FRAMEWORK FOR PRIVATE INVESTMENT IN INFRASTRUCTURE

INTRODUCTION

As highlighted in the last three Ministry of Finance's Economic Surveys, the new government Common Minimum Program (CMP), and indicated in Chapter 2, deficiencies in infrastructure and infrastructure services are a major impediment to achieving and sustaining higher economic growth in India. To address these problems, the economic program of 1991-96 ended decades of public sector monopolies in the provision of infrastructure. It assigned to the private sector a significant role in raising substantially the level of infrastructure investment and the efficiency of infrastructure services. The CMP envisages a similar role for the private sector as part of a broader effort to raise infrastructure investment from around four to six percent of GDP " ...in the next few years ...". For this to materialize, a re-examination of the enabling framework for private investment--that is the legal, administrative and regulatory framework--is needed.

Last year's CEM reviewed the generic legal issues affecting not only the development of the infrastructure sector, but also that of all sectors of the economy. It highlighted that India has a well developed legal system which provides for the comprehensive protection of property and contractual rights. This system was a key instrument through which the state regulated economic transactions when the Central Government pursued a planned approach to economic development. Several economic laws were established or modified during this period to provide a basis for state intervention and administrative discretion. Now, some of these legal instruments have become impediments, given the greater role assigned to the private sector. The instruments of particular concern are: (a) company law (a proposal was submitted to the last parliament but its consideration could not be completed during that parliamentary term; the new government in its 1996-97 budget reaffirmed its commitment to reform company law by February 1997); (b) labor laws; (c) tax laws; (d) land law (including collateral; tenancy; urban land ceiling; and construction); and (e) competition laws. These are all in urgent need of reform.

This chapter focuses on the progress and remaining challenges in developing the regulatory and administrative framework needed to accommodate this broader role for the private sector. On the regulatory and administrative front, suitable arrangements have been proposed in some cases and steps towards implementation are evident. But progress could be more penetrating, precipitous and prompt, not only in establishing new rules but also in generating new attitudes at operational levels to private sector involvement. This is especially true in power, ports and highways.

POWER

Private Investment in Generation

Few private investments have been brought to closure. India is facing an unprecedented power supply deficit that could severely undermine its development prospects. Since 1991, to attract private investment, the government has gradually evolved a fundamental transformation of the policies and institutions governing the power sector. And yet very little private investment has been brought to closure under the new national policy which was adopted five years ago precisely for this purpose. *The fundamental obstacle to private sector investment in the power sector is the weak financial position of the State Electricity Boards (SEBs)* which operate virtually all the country's distribution networks through which the power supplied by potential private investors would have to be sold. At this time, the SEBs are not financially viable clients for potential private power producers. The SEBs generally are prevented by their respective state government from charging commercially viable tariffs; they are not allowed to cut power from non-paying customers, and many of them are institutionally too weak to contain power theft in rural and urban areas. As a result, the SEBs' financial condition is one of the country's most serious structural constraints to the reduction of the public sector deficit. Other impediments to private investment include lack of clarity in the private power policy (though some of the issues have been addressed in the amendments), fuel supply risks emanating from government monopoly control over coal and railway transport, lack of legally enforceable fuel supply and transportation contracts, weak financial situation of the state governments to back-stop SEBs' obligations, and lack of clarity in Central Electricity Authority's review and approval process. Widespread debate on the array of complex issues arising out of private power policy and financing of IPP projects on a limited-recourse basis, has led to a better appreciation of the concerns of developers, investors, and lenders, by the SEBs and state government.

Meanwhile, the scope for private investment is enlarged. Over the last 12 months, the Ministry of Power (MOP) issued several new guidelines to complement the original policy of 1991, with a view to enlarging further the scope for private power generation. New guidelines released in October 1995 focused on private sector participation in the *renovation and modernization (R&M) of existing power plants.* Shortly thereafter, MOP issued a liquid fuel policy for power generation to facilitate the rapid installation of *diesel engine generating* (DG) units by the private sector. At the same time, MOP suggested that states facilitate the entry of *captive power units* into the system. This could be done by offering private investors an appropriate tariff for the purchase of surplus power by the grid and third party access for direct sale of power to the other industrial units. In another announcement in February 1996, also aimed at encouraging private investment, MOP advocated the use of *barge-mounted power plants* as a possible option for coastal states.

Captive generation cannot tackle a fundamental problem. Because progress in reforming SEBs is very limited, the government began over the last 12 months openly to encourage *captive plants* where the purchaser is likely to be (but need not always be) one or more industrial customers (with possible sales of surplus power to the utility). Generally, the technology selected for this kind of plants is based on liquid hydrocarbons as primary fuel, e.g., naphtha or fuel oil; plants are relatively small (i.e., a few megawatts); little investment in fuel handling is required at the plant site; and the construction period is normally very short (less than two years). Captive generation may be the best option available when connection to the grid is too costly for example in isolated and remote load centers. In other instances, it may at least be a short-term quick-fix option when the only alternative is no power at all.

In the long run, however, captive generation cannot be considered an effective solution to the acute power shortage on the scale presently afflicting India. Power supplied through captive plants is generally costlier than that generated through large conventional power generation (particularly for base-load generation). And transportation of liquid fuels over relatively long distances and in large volumes may pose serious environmental and safety hazards. In addition, fuel may not be available domestically in the volumes required, leading to imports which may further strain the limited port and transport infrastructure. Another issue is that captive plants supply industrial consumers directly and more generally, those who can best afford high electricity tariffs. In consequence, SEBs could start losing their "best" clients, incur increasing financial losses and face even more severe liquidity problems than before.

Any future structural, institutional, ownership or pricing reform may also become more difficult. For example, the financial viability of electricity distribution in an area with a large captive generation capacity might be more difficult to establish immediately as the margin of maneuver for cross-subsidization might be significantly reduced. The tariffs applicable to those consumers that have been traditionally subsidized--agricultural and domestic consumer--would have to increase more steeply than in the absence of captive generation. This would make it more difficult to involve the private sector in distribution and would correspondingly delay the much needed improvements in power supply.

To further enlarge the scope for private investment, the government proposed in November 1995 to facilitate the implementation by the private sector of *mega power projects.* These are defined as private power generation projects with capacity of 1,000 MW or more, which supply electricity to more than one state. The premise is that, given the regional concentration of coal resources in India and the enormous difficulties of transporting coal over long distances, it is more efficient to locate power generation closer to the source of fuel supply than to the load centers. Evidently, the promotion of such projects will need to be accompanied by a significant expansion and reinforcement of the transmission infrastructure, most probably under the auspices of the Power Grid Corporation of India (Powergrid).

Under the proposed framework, the Central Electricity Authority (CEA) would be responsible for identifying mega power projects. The National Thermal Power Corporation (NTPC) would carry out the feasibility studies and all related preparatory work (including site surveys, soil investigations, environmental assessments and socio-economic studies). Powergrid's responsibility would be to help with the bidding process--from the prequalification of bidders to the actual bidding process and evaluation--and facilitate the negotiation of power purchase agreements between the selected developer and the client states, and other related contracts.

So far, initial preparatory work on mega power projects has been driven by government alone. But the clients will be the states (SEBs, or their successors in reforming states), and their interest in mega power projects has not yet been fully ascertained. For the government's new initiative to succeed, the potential clients of each project will have to be identified at a very early stage--and their credit worthiness ascertained--to ensure that they are closely and actively involved. To win private sector confidence, it is crucial that this aspect of the program be given priority in the promotion by MOP and associated agencies of such mega projects. In fact, it would be advisable not to issue any solicitation document--be it for the prequalification of bidders or, a fortiori, for the invitation of detailed project proposals--until the client aspect of the projects has been considered with a reasonable degree of clarity, confidence and client commitment.

Another important factor that may determine the success or failure of the mega-project initiative is the degree to which greater flexibility will be provided to investors for developing coal mines. At present, even though private investment in the coal sector is permitted for captive consumption by power stations, the policy contains many restrictions that limit its scope considerably and may constrain the success of the mega project initiative. Other important issues will need to be addressed, such as the specific role of each government agency (particularly NTPC which can assume a larger role in development of such projects in view of its acknowledged expertise and Powergrid) in the development of mega projects; the availability of professional advice to guide government agencies and the client states in the preparation and negotiations of the complex contractual arrangements; and the need, in parallel, to expand significantly the infrastructure for transmission.

Competitive bidding is now mandatory for new projects. Following an announcement in January 1995, competitive bidding is now required by government for all private power projects and will be administered by the states (for their purchases) and by the center (for megaprojects for example). Guidelines have been issued by MOP for carrying out competitive bidding for private power projects. In addition, to avoid delays in the installation of small private power plants, the threshold for requiring CEA's techno-economic clearance of individual proposals was raised in December 1995 from 1 billion to 4 billion rupees for generating stations being developed through a process of competitive bidding. March 31, 1996 was the deadline set by MOP for obtaining CEA's "in-principle" clearance for the further processing of projects having been developed under the Memorandum of Understanding (MOU) route.

The government's decision to make competitive bidding its official policy is clearly a major step forward in the implementation of its private power development initiative. Given India's political system, the lack of competition to date has led to a public debate involving the SEBs and the state governments--accountable to the public and its elected representatives--on the terms and conditions (particularly the tariffs) under which private power proposals were approved, and whether these were the best projects available (as evidenced by a fair competition). This has led to reopening of a few project deals, significant delays in reaching financial closure, and the resulting negative effect it has had on investors' confidence.

Recent experience with MOU projects makes it all the more crucial to ensure that the government new policy on competitive bidding is implemented appropriately. The guidelines issued by MOP for screening the MOUs resulted in "in principle" clearance for about 99 projects in March 1996 (before the self imposed deadline for competitive bidding for all new projects). These guidelines have been further strengthened in July 1996 making it compulsory for the MOU holders to obtain final "techno-economic" clearance from CEA by March 1997.

To succeed where MOUs have failed, competitive bidding for private power will undoubtedly need to be conducted transparently, with adequate preparation, proper expertise, and careful planning. Power plant options must be evaluated based upon their value to the system as a whole. At times this will result in the selection of baseload units, while in other instances cycling capability may be the preferred choice. Competitive solicitations must be designed to obtain the best price and quality proposals for the preferred option.

The Notification process requires improvement. Although amendments to the Notification have made competitive bidding (based on price) possible, the process could be simplified. *First*, there continues to be a need for *two-part tariffs based upon availability*. The use of tariffs that reward plant load factor (PLF) rather than availability distort efficient system operations and are problematic for the financing of the cycling (non-baseload) units which the sector needs. If it is the intent of the Notification to provide payments for fixed charges and bonuses that are based solely upon availability, this should be clarified.

Second, the Notification could be clearer on such matters as how CEA will calculate ceiling prices, to determine if proposed deviations from the norms will be acceptable. For example, how will projected inflation rates (foreign and domestic) or projected exchange rates be handled? Will the ceiling prices and project prices be normalized and then compared, or will some other comparison be made? Levelized kWh prices, incorporating the projected effects of inflation and exchange rates, should be the mode of comparison. These are not trivial issues. The absence of a broadly acceptable methodology from CEA complicates the preparation of requests for proposals (RFPs) and associated documents, the proposer's development of bid prices, and the power purchaser's evaluation process.

Eventually, the Notification Should Be Phased Out. As competitive bidding proceeds, and the prices for various types of projects become known, the market will determine the appropriate ceiling price. Whatever protection is believed to be provided by calculated ceiling prices will be provided by the market, assuming that competitive bidding is carried out professionally by commercially viable purchasers.

Private Sector Participation in Distribution

Private sector experience, skills, and financing in electricity distribution are now seen as an essential ingredient for creating creditworthy, efficient utilities in India. The other ingredients include: (a) tariff reform, which includes both average tariff levels for the utility as a whole, the tariffs of each customer class, and two-part, availability-based power tariffs; (b) the incorporation of all public power sector entities under the Companies Act, at least as an interim step; and (c) the establishment of independent regulation, with an appropriate scope of responsibilities and authority. Such private sector participation in distribution can start to take place in two general ways: (a) the purchase of shares of (as well as lending to) public sector distribution companies; or (b) the operation of the distribution systems themselves, either under short-term operations' agreements or licenses. The sale of shares to the public will obviously require that the company operate commercially, and attain a sufficient degree of commercial success. Similarly, the ability of the public corporations to tap the private market for debt will also require commercial operation with returns commensurate with the risks.

For private sector participation in distribution to produce long-term benefits, it must be substantial in whichever form it takes. For example, where there is private sector operation, the private companies should become licensees, with the obligation to operate, maintain, and finance the required capital investments. While there may be acceptable alternative arrangements for an interim period (such as short-term operations agreements), private sector distribution licensing, subject to the authority of an independent regulator, will be a basic requirement.

Private sector participation in distribution should be accomplished within the framework of an overall sector reform plan. The main point is that problematic decisions made in isolation--such as cherry picking certain areas first--may make it both more difficult and expensive to implement a comprehensive, state-wide reform plan. It is better to analyze and then decide upon, for example, the number of disaggregated distribution areas to be created, the overall plan and sequence for offering areas to the private sector, the terms and conditions of the offering, and how these terms and conditions, including tariff setting, will be dealt with by the independent regulator.

Where the private sector is invited to operate the distribution system, whether as licensee or only for short-term operations' agreements, competitive bidding should be the preferred route. The solicitation should coincide with adequate preparation of the system, which will involve, inter alia, a significant and structured effort in data collection and load research. The solicitation should allow both domestic and foreign companies to seek to qualify and, if so, to offer proposals. Obviously, foreign companies must have Indian involvement--perhaps as members of a domestic/foreign consortium--since distribution operations will require significant customer contact. Similarly, of course, Indian companies may take the lead and bring in foreign expertise or capital as part of the team.

As the reforms proceed, and distribution is moved into private hands, *tariff differentials among the distribution areas will be inevitable.* Consumers in the same category in one distribution area will be charged differently from those in another. Each private sector company will be encouraged to utilize its skills and experience to operate and maintain the area under its control and to undertake the capital investments it believes are necessary. The result will be cost differentials among the areas which will have to be reflected in their respective tariffs. The determination of these tariffs, where there is significant reform underway, will lie with the independent regulator.

Reforms also are needed at the central level. With the implementation of a significant reform program underway in Orissa, the government now needs to be more pro-active in encouraging reform at both the state and central levels. Changes in the states will have implications for the roles of central sector agencies, particularly CEA. CEA should immediately withdraw from those functions that are not consistent with its role as regulator--that is, *inter alia*, from consulting, detailed design work during project techno-economic reviews, and from system operation (RLDCs and REBs)--so as not to review as a regulator the results of its own work. CEA's continuing involvement in national power system planning may be justified in the short to medium-term (in lieu of feasible alternatives), but it should be of an indicative, not prescriptive, nature. The burden of planning, project preparation, and so on, should be placed clearly on the utilities. MOP's recent decision to initiate work on power sector regulation, particularly its interface with state level regulation as it may emerge from state power sector reforms, is a welcome step in the right direction.

TRANSPORT

Introduction

Some progress has been made recently in facilitating private investment in mobile and fixed transport infrastructure. They have included the relaxation of some customs measures; an initiative by the Chief Ministers of seven northern states to identify and remove domestic barriers to the smooth flow of goods and services; and the completion of state government-sponsored techno-economic feasibility studies for ports which could serve as the basis for private investment.

Serious sector-wide concerns remain, however. They include: (a) the absence of a liability regime for the trucking industry; (b) the slow pace of meeting key requirements for efficient multimodal operations--such as redefining the liability of carriers under the Multimodal Transportation of Goods Act and further review of Customs requirements and procedures--which promise large economic benefits for India; (c) the slow pace at the center (in contrast to some state governments) in encouraging private investment in ports and port services; (d) limited efforts by Indian Railways to involve private enterprise, as an efficiency enhancing step, in maintaining its facilities, and manufacturing locomotives and other rolling stock; (e) inadequate staffing and funding at the National Highways Authority of India (NHAI), the body at the center which is mandated to manage the expansion of the highway sector, including the induction of private investment; and (f) the absence of independent regulatory bodies for ports and civil aviation.

Improving Competition and Efficiency

In trucking, the key issue continues to be the administrative barriers to efficiency. A recent initiative taken by the Chief Ministers of seven north Indian states--in setting up the Council for Cooperation and Regional Development--may in time lead to the dismantling of domestic barriers under their jurisdiction. Separately, extensive overhaul of vehicle insurance and carrier-liability legislation and policy is needed. In particular, several state level provisions have not been updated to match the nature of road technology and growth in commercial load-carrying capacities.

Bona fide Container Freight Station (CFS)/Inland Container Depot (ICD) operators, including private operators, are now permitted to transport containers between their facility and the gateway ports, by any mode under their custodianship. Thus the Container Corporation of India (CONCOR) is making extensive use of road services to avoid transit delays inherent in circuitous or shorter rail routes. This practice has now extended from one container depot in Indore to terminals in Hyderabad, Bangalore, Coimbatore and Ahmedabad. These developments, which also include relaxation of transit procedures, are promoting competition in road haulage and freight forwarders. *A critical constraint, however, is that the coverage of the trunk road system is limited and this makes it difficult for road haulers to organize efficient container transport at competitive prices.* In addition, many roads are in a state of disrepair partly because trucks exceed the axle-load limit by about 40 percent on average. Evidently, the rules regarding over-loading have to be enforced better.

Further liberalization of container movement by road beyond facilities and gateways is desirable. In India as in the rest of the world, shippers consider trucking to be more reliable than rail. Only four percent of Europe's total freight effort is carried by a combination of road and rail transport. In North America, only 10 percent of the inter-city freight market in excess of 500 miles is intermodal. Government regulations aimed at forcing shippers to use rail generally have been counter-productive. International experience indicates that the choice of mode should be left to the shipper.

Multimodal freight transport can be improved much more. The multimodal Transportation of Goods Act (1993) constitutes the legal framework for developing and promoting multimodal transport services in India. This legislation has shortcomings which have been pointed out by the International Chamber of Commerce (ICC) whose rules for the multimodal transport documentation are widely accepted for international trade-related service transactions. The principal shortcoming of the Indian multimodal transportation legislation relates to the liability regime which specifies responsibilities for cargo damage or loss. The ICC's review of the rules pointed out that some sections (13, 14, 15, and 16) impose absolute liability on the carrier beyond the scope of the Hague Visby Rules. At present, the draft amendments to improve the Act have been prepared by the Ministry of Surface Transport (MOST). They are now with the Ministry of Law for vetting before going to the parliament for approval and adoption.

During the last two years, private enterprises have been allowed to set up and operate ICDs and CFS facilities. As a result, the network of ICDs and CFSs is expanding rapidly and now comprises 36 facilities, with more under development. This has contributed to an increase in inland penetration of containers from 9.7 percent in 1990-91 to about 23 percent in 1995-96; it is expected to rise to 30-35 percent by the year 2000. Meanwhile, about 100 transport and freight forwarding companies have acquired the status of MTOs. Of these, 10 are foreign companies; four of which are shipping lines. These are welcome trends since the potential for full blown intermodal service, with all its benefits, is enormous.

Customs regulations have been relaxed considerably to facilitate easier and speedier movement of international cargo. Factory stuffing and stripping of International Standards Organization containers is gradually increasing. Approximately 40 to 45 percent of containers handled at inland container depots (ICDs) in Delhi and Bombay are now being house stuffed/de-stuffed. The procedural check of the goods by the Customs is now mostly confined to a random sample of 5-10 percent of the consignment, though the practice varies between various ICDs/CFSs. Still, the "green channel" facilities for export cargo introduced at some of the air cargo terminals could be extended to ICDs and CFSs. The Customs Service could increasingly make use of electronic data information (EDI) which permits advance information about all containers. This information, supplemented with database of past trends, would facilitate advance selection of containers for physical examination, thereby enabling faster clearance of containers from the terminals.

Some customs procedures are still not in tune with the requirements of containerized multimodal transport. For example, even when the goods are intended for an ICD/CFS, formal permission is required from Customs for moving such containerized goods out of the port of entry. Also, the shipping lines are required to file an elaborate import application with the port authorities to obtain "Charge Nil" endorsement despite the fact that they usually have a running account with these authorities. *It takes 18 signatures of various functionaries and a minimum of five days to complete this exercise, when this clearance could be given promptly based on the import manifest/sub-manifest, which in any case is required to be filed with the Customs.*

To further encourage seamless inter-modal transport of containers to and from quayside, *customs rules could permit remanifestation of containers from the port of entry to a CFS.* At present, the Customs Act only permits transshipment to a customs port notified under the Act. CFSs are not so notified and therefore, Customs does not permit such remanifestation to take place. Eliminating this restriction would enable seamless inter-modal transport of containers to and from quayside. Permission to use containers temporarily in domestic transport would also be helpful. It would save the empty positioning charges which have to be borne by the exporters and ICDs/CFSs would be less congested with a large number of empty containers.

Poor coordination between linehaul transport, provided by CONCOR through Indian Railways, and the port internal railways which are under the jurisdiction of the port authorities, must also be tackled. Central to this issue is the fact that government regulations for port management (derived, for instance, from the Major Port Trusts Act and the Sea Customs Act) have not been adjusted to enable seamless intermodal transport of containers to quayside from inland origins or from there to up-country destinations. As a result, CONCOR's ability to deliver containerized cargo at specified dates is impaired. Almost all container lines serving the Indian market operate on the basis of fixed-day-of-the-week arrivals and departures in the main local ports, and they have to make fixed time connections in the Persian Gulf, in Europe and in American ports. In general, it has been difficult for Indian shippers to meet the stringent requirements of their foreign trade partners in terms of timely and reliable delivery. Pervasive lack of information about the status and location of their cargo impedes the ability of exporters to organize merchandise distribution arrangements that satisfy clients. Some of these shortcomings will be overcome as CONCOR establishes electronic data interchanges to track shipments, but without changes in legal requirements, documentary procedures and transport modalities (including efficiency at the ports), progress will be limited.

In shipping, far-reaching changes in 1993 (in the Merchant Shipping Act) have encouraged private investment in Indian-owned vessels. Foreign interests can now set up companies that own and operate ships under the Indian flag. They can also acquire up to 51 percent of the shares of existing Indian carriers. Companies can procure ships (except oil tankers and off-shore supply vessels) without going through the previous protracted procedures for approval. Restrictions on registration and mortgage of ships have been removed. The procedure for scrapping of vessels has been simplified and control on repair of ships in foreign shipyards has been relaxed.

Shipping companies no longer have access to concessional finance from the government and the system of government guarantees for ship acquisition has been discontinued. However, these companies are now allowed to keep abroad a substantial proportion of revenue earnings, including proceeds from the sale of ships. They have also been allowed to raise external commercial borrowings for ship acquisitions. As a result, several shipping companies have been successful in tapping the foreign capital markets for their fund requirements. Cabotage laws have been relaxed in respect of lash barges and containers. The foreign shipping lines are now free to provide mainline/feeder container services at all the ports. The policy that permits acquisition of ships from Indian shipyards has been made transparent and costing is within competitive international prices.

The Indian shipping industry has responded positively to the reforms. The time taken for acquiring ships has been substantially reduced. The fleet is now better aligned to the needs of the trade and the comparative advantage. The shipping lines are increasingly deploying their bulk fleet in cross-trade, thereby improving their bottom line. The increased service competition has brought down the container rates for export cargo to UK and Europe. *Still, congestion at major ports--which may even be causing some ships to be turned away--is still a major constraint to realizing greater efficiency in shipping.*

Civil aviation has undergone dramatic changes. Since the repeal of the Air Corporation Act in 1994 and thereby the abolition of the state monopoly in the provision of domestic air services, private airlines have secured a market share of about 40 percent. There has been a significant increase in the overall capacity and the improvements in service quality have been substantial. The frequency of service on trunk routes has increased and a number of new destinations have been added to the air routes. While the international passenger segment has been operating in a competitive environment for several years, in 1995 several carriers increased capacity and flight frequency, and added new destinations to their schedules to capture the higher growth of international traffic. Similarly, the "open skies" policy for air cargo services has increased the availability of timely cargo capacity at competitive rates. The overall gains to the economy have been substantial, with cargo rates declining as much as 30 percent in the last two years.

To complement this dramatic liberalization of civil aviation, the technical and economic regulation of the sector should be separated. Currently, the government is the policy-maker for air transport through the concerned ministry, a regulator of the industry through DGCA and a majority equity holding in Air India and Indian Airlines. The appropriate role for the government would be policy-making to promote efficient, safe and affordable air services.

Facilitating Private Sector Investment in Fixed Transport Assets

Indian ports face acute capacity shortages and low productivity levels. The measures required to relieve these constraints include the creation of additional capacity at the existing ports, setting up of greenfield ports, and upgrading cargo-handling technology. There is ample scope for private sector to participate in all these areas. The international experience suggests that port productivity rises with commercialization and management contracting of entire cargo-handling activity. The government is planning to commission a Comprehensive Study on Strategic Planning of ports--Vision 2020 which will address all the above issues.

The Major Ports Trusts Act, 1963 empowers the Port Trusts to provide the full range of facilities and services, in respect of vessels. It enables the Trusts to authorize any person to perform such services. The Act also permits private parties to construct and provide, with their own funds, the full range of port facilities within the limits of the port or port approaches. However, it prevents the Board from leasing, farming, selling or alienating its power to levy rates under the Act, without the permission of the Government.

New cryogenic terminals and petroleum-handling facilities are now being financed entirely with private capital. Mumbai Port has successfully leased ship repair and dry dock facilities to the private sector along with berthing rights, at a premium. Jawahalal Nehru Port and dry-cargo berths at Vishakhapatnam Port have invited bids for extending container terms. In Gujarat, Pipapaw a minor port is being developed as an all-weather port to handle 10 million tones of cargo every year.

The major ports have identified a large portfolio of projects amounting to US $2 billion where private sector involvement is feasible. In addition, maritime state governments have identified such projects worth US$1 billion. However, techno-economic feasibility studies have to be conducted. *Only recently has some action been initiated by the major ports. The state governments have, however, done better in this regard.* The Government of Maharashtra has sponsored techno-economic feasibility studies for developing about 30 intermediate and minor ports in the state. Similarly, the Gujarat Maritime Board has initiated such studies for the development of new ports. The Government of Orissa is currently negotiating with a minerals and trading corporation for setting up a mega port with a capacity of about 50 million tones per year at Gopalpur to handle bulk cargo.

The Ministry of Surface Transport (MOST) recently issued guidelines to the Port Trusts for private sector participation. A significant feature is that it throws open all port-related activities to private enterprise. A noticeable drawback, however, is that the prior approval of the central government is required almost at every stage of processing the proposals. This stipulation leads to significant procedural delays, defeating the very objective. The delegation of powers, both financial and administrative, to port authorities would help to quicken the reform process and also ensure faster implementation of projects. To bring about such a change, a corporate form rather than a trust would be more suited for major ports. *Equally essential is establishing an independent regulatory body to take care of regulatory functions.* This would require appropriate legislative amendments.

In the Roads-Subsector, the legal framework for involving the private sector in the development and maintenance of national highways was created with the enactment of the National Highways (Amendment) Act, 1995. Its salient features are that: (a) the Central Government can enter into an agreement with any person to develop and maintain the whole or any part of a national highway; (b) the person is entitled to collect and retain fees fixed by the government, duly considering his investment and reasonable return; (c) the person will have powers to regulate and control traffic under Motor Vehicles Act, 1988; and (d) any encroachment or mischief on the portion of national highways will be a punishable offense. In addition, steps have been taken to encourage and expedite private investment in BOT projects (Box 5.1).

Some projects have advanced to substantive preparation. These include a bypass (20 km) near Mumbai and an expressway between Bangalore and Mysore (140 km), along with development of five self-contained urban nodal centers. While international experience indicates that major questions of financial viability and affordability limit the role that privately-financed BOT operations can play in road investment, there is, however, a niche for such private investments in large bridges, railway overbridges and urban bypasses that enjoy an effective monopoly position. Some states like Maharashtra, Madhya Pradesh, Gujarat have moved in this direction while the National Highway Authority of India (NHAI) and MOST have pursued this path at the central level.

Another niche for the private sector is in providing engineering services, and construction management and technology. This should be a priority area if India is to have good roads, capable of handling high volumes of traffic with higher axle loads. Speedy construction and quality output should form essential ingredients of highway projects.

At the Central Government level, NHAI which is now operational, is expected to manage the expansion of the highway sector, including the induction of private investment. In June 1995, NHAI invited private sector participation, for construction and operation of 10 identified expressways, through an open tender. A private entrepreneur would be awarded the contract to undertake detailed feasibility studies for 13,000 km of expressway at his own cost. The party that carried out the study was to be awarded 30 percent of route length of the project at the toll charges indicated in the best bid. A number of bids were received. However, award of contracts for feasibility studies has not yet been finalized. The slow progress is due to the NHAI's inadequate capacity to assess the results of the feasibility studies and its reluctance to accept external technical assistance.Furthermore, NHAI requires large capital funding to acquire the required strip of land for the expressway projects to be contracted out. It also needs adequately trained and experienced staff.

The Airports Authority of India (AAI) was established in April 1995 by merging the International Airports Authority and National Airports Authority, with a view to accelerating the integrated development, expansion and modernization of the operational, terminal, and cargo facilities in line with current international standards. This sets the stage for the commercialization and partial privatization of the major airports and the development of a landlord/coordinator role for the various airport authorities similar to that envisioned for the seaport authorities. Progress greatly depend on decentralization and local initiative.

The government is encouraging private sector participation in construction and operation of new airports using the BOT approach. Recently, agreements were concluded for the development of airports at Cochin and Bangalore and provision of additional facilities at Calicut airport. The salient features of these BOT projects are: involvement of state governments, establishment of separate corporate entities, extensive use of private professional services, and innovative methods of mobilizing funding. A tax paid by embarking international air passengers will be used to finance the facilities at Calicut. A similar method is expected to be adopted for development of airports in Rajasthan and Goa. These states have considerable potential for tourism.

Since 1994 the government has initiated steps towards private investment in fixed and mobile railway assets through the build-own-lease-transfer (BOLT) scheme. In the case of

BOLT projects, private consortia are allowed to build or procure a needed facility or an asset, such as an electrified line or rolling stock. The consortia own the asset for Indian Railways' use in exchange for an annual lease payment which ceases after a specified period of eight, ten or twelve years. At that time the facility reverts to ownership of Indian Railways. This mechanism has been used successfully in Germany to fund highway, rail and waterway projects associated with the reunification effort.

The first three BOLT projects covering conversion of 262 km of track to broad gauge were awarded to private parties recently. Bids have also been received for procurement of rolling stock and the leasing contracts are expected to be finalized shortly. There has also been a gradual shifting of the boundary in favor of the private sector in other areas. CONCOR, which was a wholly owned subsidiary of Indian Railways, has now divested 23 percent of its equity to the public. Its Board of Directors has been reconstituted to include non-official members who are expected to help CONCOR become a market-oriented entity sensitive to customer needs.

Indian railways would benefit from the involvement of private enterprise in the maintenance of its facilities. This would bring in the much-needed technological upgradation. Finally, the manufacture of locomotives and other rolling stock of Indian Railways can also be privatized. Such manufacture falls within the scope of the engineering industry which is now well-geared to undertake this job. An important step forward would be to corporatize and eventually privatize the industrial manufacturing units of Indian Railways. Several Indian Railways' workshops that manufacture rolling stock need to be modernized to enable them to manufacture products of contemporary technology. *The infusion of new technology, designs and modernization of manufacturing facilities could be realized by appropriate joint ventures with the private sector.*

TELECOMMUNICATIONS

Introduction

Despite impressive growth in basic telephone services of more than 17 percent per annum over the last four years, a large unmet demand persists (Box 5.2). The Telecoms Policy and guidelines of 1994 state *inter alia* that the private sector (including foreign ownership up to 49 percent of equity) will be the main provider of value added services and compete in basic services with the erstwhile monopoly provider, Department of Telecommunications (DOT). Since then, *strides have been made in extending the entry of private operators in all telecommunications services*:

- *Basic Telephone Services.* In January 1995, DOT issued tenders requesting bids for the provision of basic telephone services in 21 separate geographic regions ("circles") throughout India. As indicated earlier, one new entrant per region will be licensed on a non-exclusive basis as a local operator to provide basic telephone services in competition with DOT. Nine operators covering 13 of the 21 service areas have been selected and were provided in early June 1996 with drafts of the licenses and interconnection agreements for comment. The

---

Box 5.2: A Large Unmet Demand for Telecommunication Services Persists

In March 1996, the number of telephone lines in India was 11.98 million. The waiting list indicated an immediate unsatisfied demand of a further 2.27 million customers. In addition, about 75 percent of India's population lives outside urban areas. These areas are not adequately served with telephones. For instance, there are well over 100,000 villages without access to telephone services.

The Department of Telecommunications (DOT) has estimated that the total demand for telephone services by the end of the decade would be about 40 to 50 million. The investment needed to meet this demand would be about $38 billion dollars, well outside the government's financing capability. In addition, the supply constraints severely limit the provision of custom business services which are desperately needed.

There is scope also for improving the quality of the existing services. Over the last five years, call completion rates have improved significantly. But subscriber fault rates remain very high, averaging around two faults per line per year (about 10 times higher than international standards). Many telephone exchanges in outlying areas are out of order for long periods of time.

---

operators are required to begin service within twelve months of signing the license agreement.

- *Cellular Mobile.* The government has made significant progress in awarding licenses for cellular mobile services. There are two privately owned cellular operators in each of the four main cities. In addition, the government has selected and issued licenses to operators for 18 of the 20 remaining regions. These operators are required to begin service by December 1996.

- *Paging.* DOT has issued licenses to more than 20 different providers of paging services throughout India. In a first round of bidding, a maximum of four paging operators were selected for each of the 27 cities. In a second round, licenses were issued for the 18 territories outside the above cities. These operators have already started operations.

- *Value Added Services.* The new Telecoms Policy liberalized the provision of value added services except for packet switching and related data services for which DOT retains a monopoly. On application to DOT and the payment of specified fees, licenses may be granted for the provision of E-Mail, Voice Mail, VSAT 64Kbs closed user group systems, Videotex Service and Video Conferencing. Private investor interest in these services is beginning to emerge.

- *Regulation.* In July 1996, a bill for the creation of the Telecom Regulatory Authority of India (TRAI) was presented to the parliament. The proposed powers and responsibilities of the TRAI are appropriate and equip it with reasonable powers of autonomy and flexibility. The bill, which is awaiting Parliamentary approval, proposes that:

  - TRAI would be a statutory body comprising a Chairperson, and between two and four members;

  - the Chairperson shall have been a judge of the Supreme Court or Chief Justice of a High Court, and shall have a tenure of five years;

- TRAI shall have the authority to, *inter alia*, (i) ensure interconnectivity between service providers which is now provided by DOT and should be transferred to TRAI, (ii) ensure compliance of license conditions; (iii) regulate revenue sharing arrangements, (iv) levy fees; (v) facilitate competition and promote efficiency in the operation of telecom services; (vi) protect the interests of consumers, (vii) settle disputes between service providers; and (viii) ensure compliance of universal service obligations. One aspect requiring clarification is TRAI's responsibilities with regard to setting telecommunications tariffs.

Outstanding Issues

Operationalization of TRAI is critical. For TRAI to successfully carry out its functions, early action has to be taken to appoint the apex body, and have it appoint a team of highly qualified professionals. That team will need to be formed from a variety of disciplines including law, economics, telecom, business, and finance. Within a year or so, the telecom sector in India will be the most vibrant and liberal in the world except for the USA--but unlike the USA, in India all regulatory matters will rest (appropriately) with TRAI, the sole regulator. Based on other country experience, it will take TRAI a minimum of 18 to 24 months to be adequately equipped to resolve the vast array of issues to be laid before it.

Separation of policy and operations is appropriate. While regulatory functions will become the responsibility of TRAI, early action is needed to separate DOT's operational role from its policy functions so as to remove the conflict of interest and give operational staff sufficient independence in competing with the new entrants.

Tariff policy is required. Quick action by the expert body set up by the government to examine tariff policy would help DOT and new private sector in structuring their roll out plans and raising funds for capital development. Tariffs and revenue sharing are critical issues which impact directly on the profitability and roll over plans of all operators. The government needs to have a long term tariff policy which addresses existing imbalances in the tariff structure. These imbalances will become critical constraints as competition within the sector evolves. It would be appropriate for TRAI to advise the government on such a policy and assist in preparing an appropriate formula which rebalances tariffs in relation to the cost of service provision.

Other issues require attention. Other measures deserve urgent attention by the government to facilitate efficient growth of the sector. These include: (a) a complete revision of the existing telegraph Act and amendments to reflect current government policy and sector structure, and address modern issues such as convergence and multi-operator environments; and (b) permission for power companies, railways and others to share their long distance transmission networks with others.

Conclusion

Several lessons have emerged from India's experience with the involvement of the private sector in infrastructure. In particular: (a) processes for selection of developers need to be predictable and based on rules that are transparent; (b) projects proposed by government to the private sector need to be preceded by high quality preparatory work covering their technical, social and environmental aspects; (c) the existence of a transparent regulatory framework is critical for the efficient induction of private operators and for the commercial operation of the projects they undertake; and (d) guarantees, counterguarantees, escrow accounts and other financial arrangements are no substitute for an adequate policy and institutional framework providing the basis for predictable revenue streams and financially viable buyers.

6

EXTERNAL PROSPECTS AND
FINANCING REQUIREMENTS

INTRODUCTION

As discussed previously, the reform program has produced positive results. In particular, growth rose to 7 percent by 1995-96, outpacing the 5.9 percent average annual rate under the Eighth Plan. Growth is broad-based and more sustainable since it is led by exports and private investment and savings have increased. Nonetheless, lack of progress on fiscal adjustment poses a serious risk to macroeconomic stability while the remaining structural weaknesses are limiting improvements in productivity growth. The previous chapters have proposed an agenda of fiscal and structural reforms that could help address these issues. If implemented, it could help relieve the remaining policy and structural impediments to a private sector-led growth, and it would allow India to sustain and even gradually increase the current growth rates.

This chapter focuses on how supportive the external environment is likely to be, and India's potential export growth areas.

EXTERNAL ECONOMIC ENVIRONMENT AND IMPLICATIONS FOR INDIA

Overview. India faces a broadly favorable external environment over the coming decade, characterized by continued moderate world inflation, low real interest rates, stable economic growth and increasing trade openness and financial integration (Table 6.1). The Bank's GEP projects a strong world growth rate, averaging 3.5 percent per year for the 1996-05 period. Among industrial countries, which take about 60 percent of India's exports, real annual growth is projected at 2.9 percent over the coming decade. Growth in the EU, India's largest industrial country market, is expected to rebound in 1996-97. Recovery is expected to strengthen in Japan where the scope for expansion is considerable. India sells only 8 percent of its exports to Japan. Despite this favorable external environment, India will need to deepen its reform program to increase its world market share. Its export markets are expected to expand at 6 percent a year, a little below world trade growth (6.3 percent over 1996-2005) mainly because of India's low penetration in the fast growing Japanese and East Asian import markets. A shift in export orientation towards East Asia could boost India's export market growth to around 7 percent.

Policies implemented under the Uruguay Round should improve India's access to industrial country markets, notably for textiles and garments and for agriculture. *The benefits from phase-out of the MFA in particular will be substantial.* In agriculture, existing NTBs will be eliminated and replaced by tariffs and bound, tariffs on agriculture will be reduced on average by 36 percent over a six-year period for the developed countries. Overall, average tariffs on South Asian countries' exports to the OECD should fall by more than 2 percentage points to around 6 percent while those on exports to developing countries should fall 8.5 percentage points. Over and above the Uruguay Round, the continued trend towards trade liberalization on a unilateral or regional basis--for example the movement of APEC towards free trade--will generate steady pressure for further trade liberalization if India is not to fall further behind the trade policy standards being set in East Asia and other developing countries.

Table 6.1: External Environment for India, 1975-2005 (growth rate in percent)							
	1975-84	1985-90	1991-93	1994	1995	1996	1996-05
World GDP	2.8	3.2	1.1	3.0	2.7	3.0	3.5
OECD	2.5	3.3	1.2	2.9	2.4	2.4	2.8
Developing Countries	3.8	3.0	0.3	2.3	3.5	4.6	5.3
World Trade	3.7	5.5	4.1	9.4	8.8	7.0	6.3
OECD Imports	2.7	7.1	1.9	9.9	7.6	5.8	5.5
Developing Country Imports	4.3	2.1	7.1	8.1	10.0	9.2	8.2
India-Export Market Growth	6.2	5.9	2.4	9.9	8.8	6.9	6.0
Export Growth	3.2	8.6	10.7	16.6	15.0	15.3	10.0
Price Indicators (Nominal US$)							
G-5 MUV	5.3	6.6	2.1	3.6	4.5	3.4	2.5
Oil price - nominal	10.0	-3.6	-9.7	-5.7	8.2	-4.0	1.0
Non-fuel commodity prices	1.3	-0.8	-2.9	22.2	9.3	-7.4	0.8
India-Terms of Trade	0.5	1.5	5.8	2.2	-3.4	-0.6	0.4
Export Price	5.9	4.2	-1.6	5.2	3.1	0.4	2.5
Import Price	5.5	2.7	-6.9	3.0	6.7	1.0	2.1
Interest Rates							
6-month LIBOR, percent	10.7	8.1	4.5	5.1	6.0	5.4	6.1
6-month LIBOR, percent (Real)	2.8	4.0	1.0	2.4	3.3	2.3	3.3

Notes: MUV is Manufactures Unit Value Index, World Trade growth is the average growth rate of export and import volumes.
Source: Staff estimates.

Commodities Prices. After a sharp fall in 1996-97, commodity prices are expected to remain relatively constant over 1998-2005. This may have a relatively minor effect on India's terms of trade since India's exports are dominated by manufactures whose export prices are expected to increase in dollar terms at about the same rate as those of the industrial countries manufactures' exports (2.5 percent a year over the period). More significant, however, is the oil price, a major import item whose price is not expected to fall as it did in the 1980s and early 1990s, contributing to the 1.5 percent a year terms of trade gains India experienced in 1985-90 and an estimated 5-6 percent a year gain over 1991-93. In the absence of these windfall gains-- India's terms of trade are expected to be flat in the projection period. The external environment will therefore be both more supportive of continued reforms but more challenging in competitive terms. *Whether India can exploit it to achieve stronger export performance and hence accelerated growth will depend mostly on domestic policy developments.*

Outlook for Export Earnings. India's real annual export growth has almost doubled since the pre-reform period (8.6 percent real growth over 1985-90), reaching an average 10.7 percent over 1991-93, and 15.6 percent over 1994-96. Despite this impressive performance, India's penetration of world markets has not increased significantly (Figure 6.1). India's share in world exports fell from 0.5 percent at the start of the 1980s to 0.4 percent by mid-decade before rising to 0.6 percent by 1995. Over the same period, China's share rose from 0.9 percent to 3 percent while Korea's rose from 1 percent to 2.6 percent. *If India deepens its reforms, it has the potential to achieve the same success.* On present trends, India's real average export growth is expected to stabilize around 10 percent over 1996-2005. This conclusion is broadly supported by the evaluation of key export sectors below, results of which are summarized in Table 6.2, showing main current account revenue sources, and Table 6.3, showing key merchandise export components. Many of the key

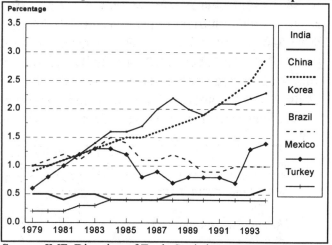

Figure 6.1: Export Market Share for India and Competitors

Source: IMF, Direction of Trade Statistics.

weaknesses in integration highlighted in Chapter 2--for example the remaining anti-export bias imparted by high trade protection or the loss of competitiveness due to poor infrastructure--are the main factors expected to slow export growth. The projections on this chapter are based on the assumption that fiscal imbalances and structural weaknesses will be addressed gradually. As a result, GDP growth is kept at a little over 6 percent per year and growth in real current account revenues is expected to stabilize at 8.3 percent a year in 1996-05 from its pre-reform rate of 5.5 percent.

Table 6.2: Sources and Growth of India's Foreign Exchange Earnings												
	Period Simple Average (US$ billions)				Shares of Current Account Revenue (percent)				Real Annual Average Growth Rate[a] (percent)			
	85-90	91-93	94-96	96-05	85-90	91-93	94-96	96-05	85-90	91-93	94-96	96-05
Merchandise Exports	13.3	19.9	32.1	66.1	65.9	68.0	66.5	73.1	8.6	10.7	15.6	10.0
Non-Factor Services	3.8	5.3	8.4	15.0	19.0	18.1	17.5	17.0	3.0	7.9	12.3	6.0
Travel	1.3	2.1	--	--	6.6	7.0	--	--	6.2	6.9	--	--
Transport	0.8	1.4	--	--	3.9	4.7	--	--	10.6	39.0	--	--
Other Services	1.7	1.9	--	--	8.5	6.4	--	--	-1.7	-5.3	--	--
Factor Income	0.5	0.6	1.2	1.1	2.5	2.1	2.5	1.3	-7.7	-1.3	107.6	2.3
Private Transfers	2.4	3.5	6.5	7.2	12.6	11.9	13.6	8.6	-3.7	20.1	22.3	-1.5
Current Account Revenue	19.9	29.3	48.3	89.4	100.0	100.0	100.0	100.0	5.5	10.2	15.9	8.3
Import of Goods & NFS	24.1	27.0	47.3	89.1					6.0	7.5	18.0	8.2
MEMO: US CPI									4.0	3.4	2.8	2.7
-- Not available.												
Note: Real 1990 US$ numbers are obtained by deflating with appropriate unit value indices for export of goods and imports. For other categories, US CPI deflator has been used.												
a. Least squares average growth rate for 85-90 and 96-05.												
Source: IMF Balance of Payments Statistics for historical series upto 1990, and then staff estimates.												

Within this total, real merchandise export growth is expected to improve only mildly to 10 percent from around 8.6 percent in the pre-reform years, supported by improvements in garment, textile and agricultural export growth. (Table 6.3). Non-factor service growth is expected to be buoyed by continued rapid growth in software exports of around 25 percent a expected to be buoyed by continued rapid growth in software exports of around 25 percent a year, but this will tend to be offset by a relatively slow growth rate for tourism, which will be constrained by poor supporting infrastructure among other factors. Workers' remittances surged in the early 1990s for contingent "one-off" factors but in the longer term, continued weak real oil prices are likely to curb remittances at their current level of around US$4.5 billion, resulting in a small erosion in real terms over the coming decade. Given India's still relatively high level of external debt to exports, the projections maintain the current account deficit at a prudent 2 percent of GDP or so, yielding sustainable real import growth of 8 percent a year.

Table 6.3: Performance of Key Export Sectors (percent current US$)					
	Average Growth			Share in Total Indian Exports	
	1974-84	1985-94	1996-05	1995	2005
Agriculture and allied	4.4	6.4	6.8	15.7	10.6
Textiles and garments	8.6	16.2	16.4	23.6	34.2
Gems and jewelry	6.0	15.4	15.0	16.6	25.2
Chemicals	16.2	23.4	12.0	9.2	8.4
Engineering goods (excl. auto parts)	1.5	14.4	11.8	11.4 [a]	7.9
Auto parts	-6.5	20.0	18.0	--	1.6
Leathers, total	8.0	2.8	2.5	5.4	1.0
Others	14.4	11.3	6.5	29.6	11.2
Total	8.1	12.7	12.4	100.0	100.0
-- Not available. a. 1995 estimate includes autoparts. Source: Staff estimates.					

Private and Official Capital Flows. Official concessional aid flows are unlikely to continue on past trends. However, such factors as moderate world real interest rates, continued liberalization in developing countries and portfolio diversification in industrial countries are likely to support further significant growth in private flows over the coming decade and India stands to attract a significant share of these private flows with the shift to private financing especially of infrastructure investment. While the massive inflows of portfolio capital to India has been part of the broader flow to emerging markets in the first half of the 1990s in general, there are clearly country-specific factors at play. These include the existence of well-known corporate names with established track records; ruled-based and reasonably well developed stock markets; familiar accounting and legal systems; and the potential for growth in a large domestic market.

The prospects for continued inflows are relatively favorable given continuity in macroeconomic and structural reforms and further capital market development. Sound macroeconomic policies are likely to be at even more of a premium than before as will appropriate administrative and legal framework for infrastructure investment. While there was a sharp pull back of private flows from most emerging markets in the immediate aftermath of the Mexico crisis, it was noticeable that flows recovered most quickly and substantially to those countries in East Asia and Latin America with the best performance in terms of export growth and sustainable current account deficits and equally important lower restrictions on FDI. As was discussed in Chapter 1, India's current FDI regime is as investor-friendly as that of China's or of other Asian comparators. However, comparative analysis of marginal effective tax rates on capital for FDI in manufacturing sector in India and China indicates that these marginal effective tax rates are much lower in China's Special Economic Zones and slightly less elsewhere in China than in India. Even when basic corporate tax holdings are taken into account, Indian marginal tax burden is still higher than China's because of the impact of high import duties and state-level sales tax on the cost of capital goods (McCarten, 1996). How fast India can achieve the levels of FDI inflows of successful integrators will depend, however, on how quickly it can move to improve weaknesses in its fundamentals. The government has set a target of US$10 billion per year which is not implausible if the appropriate policy framework is in place.

External Debt. The current account deficit is projected to increase to 2 percent of GDP by 2005, a prudent position. This would reduce India's external debt as a percent of GDP from the present 30 to 24 by the end of the decade, and 20 percent by the year 2005. As a share of current account receipts, the debt service ratio would decline from 24 percent at present to 13 percent by the end of the decade, and 11 percent by the year 2005.

PROSPECTS FOR HIGHER GROWTH AND EXPORTS

Accelerating growth would require a sustained and rapid growth of investment, savings and exports as the experience of the East Asian economies shows. As discussed in Chapter 2, the potential for increasing investment and exports significantly lies in India's ability to encourage more foreign investment across all sectors in the economy, correct fiscal imbalances and address key structural constraints. The experience of the East Asian economies also shows that foreign direct investment in labor-intensive export-oriented industries is the best instrument to raise growth, employment, and improve significantly the welfare of the population. This year's Government's Economic Survey has clearly emphasized the importance of higher levels of foreign direct investment both to accelerate growth and employment as well as reduce India's reliance on external debt to finance its investment needs. India can take the opportunity of a favorable external environment to deepen its macroeconomic and structural reform program. Assuming that significant progress is made in attracting foreign and domestic private investment to all areas of the economy and, in particular, infrastructure, India has the potential to accelerate its rate of economic growth from 7 percent in 1995-96 to 8 percent by the end of this decade and progressively reach 9 percent by 2005-06.

Under this growth scenario, the government is assumed to pursue its outward-oriented strategy more aggressively through significant reduction in the rate of protection, including the consumer goods industries. Remaining restrictions on domestic private sector and foreign investment would be removed. As a result, openness to trade is expected to increase from 26 percent of GDP in 1996 to 45 percent of GDP in 2005 (in China this ratio is 46 percent of GDP at present) and foreign investment (FDI and portfolio investment) is expected to be significant, rising from 1.5 percent of GDP in 1996 to 2.1 percent of GDP by 2005 (in China, this is 3.5 percent of GDP at present). The implementation of structural reforms discussed in the previous chapters, including the legal, administrative and regulatory framework for private sector investment in infrastructure is expected to bring in substantial foreign investments that might surpass these estimates as India is still considered a potentially strong emerging market for foreign inflows in the future. In this respect, in addition to FDI in infrastructure, four export areas stand out as those where FDI could help India achieve its target rate of sustainable 8-9 percent annual real growth by 2005, should the structural constraints, particularly the infrastructural bottlenecks be less binding. These are: garments and textile, diamonds, agricultural goods and software services exports.

Prospects for Selected Key Export Sectors

Garments, followed closely by textiles, are India's largest net foreign exchange earner. The competitiveness of the small and informal sector where the bulk of Indian garment exports are produced has attracted an influx of international clothing manufactures, including Levis, Benetton, Lacoste and Pierre Cardin. This structure is well suited to the fashion garment sector where cheap, temporary labor provides flexibility to produce small batches of garments tailored to precise customer specifications. The recent change in policy to allow large-scale units to enter the garment industry if they undertake an export obligation of 50 percent of their production will help the industry diversify its product mix. But limiting investment in fixed assets to Rs 30 million will keep out the large foreign investments that could help upgrade quality and improve technology.

The extent to which India can benefit from textile and garment trade liberalization depends on its current cost competitiveness, and on its ability to increase productivity and move up the value-added chain in the medium to long term. As indicated in Figure 2.2 of Chapter 2, India's actual total labor cost in the clothing industry is substantially higher than in many competitor countries after taking into account factors such as productivity, absenteeism, management and transport costs. India's cost per standard minute is higher than in Indonesia, Thailand, China, and even Korea, based on this measure.

Another constraint to more rapid garment export growth is India's concentration in cotton garments. This leads to a high degree of seasonality in demand and also keeps the value-addition lower than could be attained using synthetic fibers. Cotton garment exports amount to only about 15 percent of world clothing trade and demand growth is also slower than for man-made fiber blended garments. The price and quality of domestic synthetic fiber yarns and fabrics in India has not been internationally competitive. While imports were allowed through the licensing system, procedures were cumbersome and costly and a constraint on Indian exports of synthetic fiber garments. *Improving the internal efficiency of synthetic fiber producers and fully liberalizing imports of man-made fiber fabrics could strengthen the growth potential of the industry.* Given India's high quota growth rates during the phase-out of MFA, its competitive product niches and established links with retailers and importers in industrial countries, India's garment exports will remain buoyant but the potential for even higher growth will only be realized if there is a movement away from the current narrow focus on cotton fashion garments, higher productivity growth and movement up the value-added chain.

Diamonds. India's emergence as the world's largest exporter of polished small diamonds is attributable to the combination of low-cost skilled labor (which makes it possible to transform small roughs at an affordable price) and fiercely competitive family owned firms with an extensive presence in the world's major diamond centers. This is a traditional craft in India, which with adequate policies could grow faster. Its share of world small diamond sales (at

Figure 6.2: SITC 667 Pearls, Precious and Semi-Precious Stones
Percent Share of World Exports

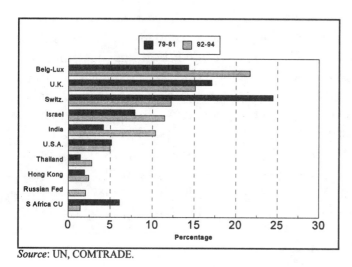

Source: UN, COMTRADE.

wholesale prices) grew from 2 percent in 1970 to 40 percent in 1994, while its share of the sector overall (SITC 667) rose from 4.5 percent to 10 percent over the period 1979-81 to 1992-94 (Figure 6.2).

Strengths and Weaknesses. In the near term India faces little competition in the small, low-quality end of the market. Other low-cost cutting centers such as Thailand, Malaysia, Indonesia, Sri Lanka and China are focusing on better quality, larger roughs. Manufacturing costs per carat are significantly higher in Thailand ($20/carat) but lower in China ($8/carat).

Diversification into polishing better quality, larger stones where the per carat yield is higher is one way to increase India's world market share. This end of the business requires modern machinery (currently present in only around 10 percent of the industry) and more control over the variety of roughs it can import and re-export. Recent changes to the export-import policy go some way to achieving this control. In this market segment, India will face more direct competition from such traditional cutting and polishing centers as Tel Aviv, Antwerp and New York, where salaries and productivity are significantly higher. Another way to increase market share is to integrate cutting and polishing operations with design and manufacture of gem studded jewelry. In addition to higher value added potential this is also a way for manufacturers to market their excess inventory of small stones. In recent years the growing number of jewelry production units in the Santacruz Export Processing Zone (SEPZ) has resulted in strong export growth. However, the poor image of Indian jewelry among industrial country retailers is a constraint. Overcoming this handicap will require improving design and the range of cuts it offers and proving it has the ability to deliver customized service to retailers.

Prospects. The demand for polished *small diamonds* is expected to be buoyant over the next decade. With respect to *larger stones*, India will increasingly put the traditional polishing centers at a competitive disadvantage as it upgrades its product quality and the range of cuts it can offer. Exports of *gem studded jewelry* are likely to increase in the coming years with the assistance of schemes such as the Indo-Argyle Diamond Council aimed at helping Indian firms develop sophisticated design skills and marketing capabilities. India's ability to diversify into this higher value-added sector will significantly bolster its export revenue prospects.

Agricultural Exports. India's agricultural exports account for a mere one percent of world agricultural trade, but a few commodities--cereals, fruits and vegetables and marine products--are thought to have significant export potential and have registered rapid growth in recent years. The policy reforms which have led to significant export of rice and wheat have been discussed in Chapter 4.

Fruit and Vegetables. Though India is the world's second largest grower of fruits and vegetables only one percent of production is commercially processed and only a few products are exported to a limited number of markets in South Asia, the Middle East and Eastern Europe. This sector is now recognized as potentially important for exports, with a target of US$650 million for the year 2000. *However, the greatest problems for exporters are poor distribution and storage facilities, leading to wastage of 30 percent of production annually.* Upgrading of infrastructure could be speeded by "tie-ups" with foreign companies. Since 1991, US$240 million of FDI in food processing has been approved (see also Box. 2.3). However, substantial modernization is required for India to realize its potential. The Eighth Plan earmarked soft loans for cold storage, packing houses, etc. but other impediments, such as high excise duties on cooling equipment (previously 110 percent and now 30-50 percent), continue to hamper upgrading and the quality (see Box 2.2). This is also an area that could considerably benefit from the liberalization of agriculture discussed in Chapter 4.

Floriculture. India also aims to play a larger role in the lucrative international cut flower market. Encouraged by substantial tax exemptions, new participants (including joint ventures with foreigners) are seeking to develop exports and over 50,000 hectares of land are now devoted to floriculture. Constraints include a need for improved greenhousing, irrigation and cooling systems, as is the introduction of higher quality flowers popular in many export markets. A number of recent initiatives are improving India's prospects, particularly tariff reforms cutting import duties on live trees, plants, flowers and bulbs from 55 percent to 10 percent, and exempting seeds and cuttings altogether. Speeding up the plant quarantine process to facilitate ease of import will also help.

Agricultural reforms could have a key impact in the long term on India's ability to exploit fully these export niches because they will free the private sector from existing constraint on building and operating essential infrastructure such as cold storage and access to credit to give just a few examples.

Prospects for Selected Key Service Exports

Software. India's software exports growth in current dollars averaged around 30 percent a year in 1986-93 and near 50 percent a year in the past two years. A shortage of software engineers in many industrial economies coupled with a trend towards outsourcing non-core operations have been the driving forces behind the growth of the software industry in developing countries, including in India. India's software exports were primarily concentrated (80-90 percent) on *contractual programming* at the clients' premises--low value added functions with low entry barriers in terms of capital, marketing skills and costs. These types of exports bring a degree of technology and skills transfer and build up credibility with potential clients. However, profitability is relatively low and leads to the loss of personnel who choose to stay abroad, an important factor contributing to the slow rate of assimilation and diffusion of information technology throughout India.

The share of *custom-made software* for off-shore clients has grown to around 35 percent of total software exports. The increased confidence in outsourcing information technology (IT) work to Indian software firms, has been substantially helped by the installation of dedicated satellite links which make it possible to overcome India's communication bottlenecks. This has also led to a new surge of foreign investment and joint ventures into India by multinational IT groups such as Oracle, Novell and Motorola. The export of application *software packages* is by far the most difficult segment of the international software market to penetrate, but it is the main driving force and accounts for the largest proportion of traded software. The capital, managerial and marketing skills required are higher than in other segments of the market, and correspondingly the level of profitability and skills transfer are greater as well. Additionally, the export of products may be less vulnerable to recession and easier to sell than services, but competition is intense and advantages based on low labor costs lose their relative importance.

Strengths and Weaknesses. India's main competitive advantage has been its low cost, skilled, English-speaking engineering force. Labor costs are an important component of programming--average earnings for a software engineer in the UK was £26,000; in India earnings were £1,000-2,000 a year. Similarly, many of the functions performed for off-shore clients--design, analysis, development and testing--can be completed for half the in-house costs in the UK based on a 100 person-year (200,000 hour) mainframe development project.

Small Domestic Markets. One important ingredient to building a viable software export market is a strong, discriminating domestic market which provides the platform for the development of increasingly sophisticated products. Because the hardware market was highly protected until recently, India has one of the lowest concentrations of computers in the world along with one of the poorest telephone networks. The steady reduction in import tariffs on computers, peripherals, software and components as part of the liberalization program has helped generate a surge in the demand for software and hardware in the last two years. While this growth is likely to be a positive factor for the industry's long-term performance, India starts from a very low base and is years behind other developing country exporters in terms of the sophistication of its domestic market. For instance in Chile, the government has pursued an open trade regime with respect to hardware imports for at least a decade. This led to the rapid diffusion of an information-based economy and provided Chile with a sophisticated market on which to test its products. It has consequently become a major software package supplier to the fast growing markets in Latin America

Prospects. With world sales exceeding US$100 billion annually, software constitutes the fastest growing segment of the information technology market. Though largely dominated by industrial country firms, opportunities for countries such as India to carve out niche segments will continue. The shift towards custom-made software for off-shore clients will help to sustain a competitive advantage in the future.

Travel and Tourism. Travel and tourism could also contribute significantly to growth in non-factor services' earnings in addition to promoting low skill employment, a significant contributor to poverty reduction since the poor's main asset is their low skill labor. For this sector to grow and achieve the above objective, a major constraint needs to be removed. This is the urban land ceiling legislation and other regulatory procedures, such as zoning restrictions which hamper the growth of the industry and act as barrier to entry of potential competitors. Travel and tourism was one of the fastest growing components in the current account between 1970 and 1980 when it peaked at US$1.5 billion. With further though slower growth after 1985 tourism now represents the sixth largest export earner, accounting for close to 6 percent of current account receipts. The underlying trend in tourist arrivals in 1980-93 was unimpressive, rising only 1.7 percent per annum compared to 4.6 percent in the world as a whole (Table 6.4). India's 1.5 million visitors pale in comparison with 19 million to China in 1993, although per capita spending of close to a thousand dollars in India is nearly four times the level in China. But growth of per tourist receipts in India in 1980-93 was flat compared with 3 to 14 percent in East Asia. With under 0.4 percent of the world's tourists and 1 percent of spending, India has barely tapped its potential.

Table 6.4: Foreign Tourism in India and Comparators								
	1993			Growth in			Per Tourist Receipts	
	Hotel Capacity (1990)	Tourist Arrivals (000)	Tourism Receipts ($ mill)	Hotel Capacity (84-90)	Tourist Arrivals (80-93)	Tourism Receipts	1993 (US$)	Growth (80-93)
India	49,068	1,492	1,487	5.9	1.7	2.0	997	0.3
Bangladesh	3,063	101	15	24.3	6.2	2.2	149	-3.8
Maldives	4,062	241	146	95.8	12.3	17.5	606	6.5
Nepal	4,000	254	157	3.9	3.8	10.0	618	6.0
Pakistan	35,500	333	111	5.8	1.2	-1.2	333	-2.3
Sri Lanka	10,636	391	208	1.7	0.5	3.8	531	3.4
China	293,827	18,982	4,683	25.0	13.9	17.8	247	3.5
Indonesia	167,592	3,403	3,988	4.5	15.4	23.9	1,172	7.3
Malaysia	61,005	6,504	1,876	5.4	9.1	16.2	288	6.6
Philippines	15,578	1,246	2,122	-1.0	1.8	15.7	1,703	13.6
Thailand	212,389	5,761	5,014	8.9	9.1	14.5	870	4.9
World	11,465,094	512,523	307,371	3.4	4.6	8.8	600	3.9
Source: World Tourism Organization (WTO), YEARBOOK various issues.								

EXTERNAL FINANCING REQUIREMENTS

As of March 1995, India's US$99 billion external debt is, in net present value terms, more than twice the value of the country's exports. Based on this, the World Bank debt tables classify India, together with Indonesia and Chile as "moderately indebted". Of the world's two major credit rating agencies, only one has rated India's sovereign foreign currency debt above investment grade. In response to this, the authorities have adopted a prudent approach to the management of the capital account. Since the 1990-91 crisis, they have placed considerable emphasis on achieving a strong balance of payments position with a lower indebtedness and debt service ratio.

Consistent with these objectives, and an indirect way of influencing the size of the current account deficit, the authorities have brought different degrees of liberalization to different types of capital inflows--depending on their contribution to the country's development, their potential volatility, interest cost, maturity profile, and risk sharing features. Thus, while there are virtually no restrictions on foreign direct investment, there are some on portfolio investment. In particular, although there are no limits on the total amount of investment by foreign institutional investors, there are restrictions related to the type of financial assets they can hold (for example, they cannot invest in government papers, nor can they hold more than 30 percent of their portfolio in debt papers) and to their equity holdings (they cannot hold equity positions which exceed 24 percent of a firm's total equity). Equivalent restrictions apply to Indian firms issuing equity or debt abroad. The rationale for these limitations is that while portfolio investment is attractive for the country because its servicing is not fixed and the foreign investors share the risks associated with fluctuations in domestic income and exchange rates, it does create long-term claims on the country's foreign exchange resources. Thus, its growth needs to remain in line with the growth in India's capacity to service it--that is in line with export growth. In the case of commercial borrowing, an indicative ceiling is set annually (US$5 billion in 1995-96) and, based on published guidelines and criteria, discretionary authority is used to direct borrowing to priority areas, and to limit short-term borrowing.

The authorities see full capital account liberalization as a medium-term objective, to be reached after a sustainable fiscal framework is firmly in place, and financial sector reforms are completed. They have wisely resisted the temptation to relax restrictions on external commercial borrowing over the past year as a means of relieving pressure on domestic interest rates. This would have not only diminished pressure for the urgently needed fiscal correction, but could have also stimulated a destabilizing consumption boom.

One consequence of this self-imposed discipline is that, for the foreseeable future, India will mostly need to rely on foreign direct investment and assistance from external development agencies to meet its substantial needs for infrastructure and human resource development. Therefore, this report continues to make a case for India's sustained access to long-term development assistance, including a substantial concessional component. With a modest current account deficit of 2 percent of GDP over the next few years, India would still require total gross financing of about US$8 billion in 1995-96, and an average of about US$13 billion in each of the following four years. Over the last two years, bilateral and multilateral participants in the India Development Forum have pledged about US$6.5 billion in official assistance as a recognition of India's strong commitment to reform and poverty reduction.

Portfolio Management. Over the last few years, the Government has taken several specific measures to improve the utilization of ODA: (a) advance release of funds are being made to state governments; (b) procedures for awarding contracts and procurement have been streamlined; and (c) a central Project Management Unit has been established in the Department of Economic Affairs, Ministry of Finance, for better portfolio management and project implementation. While these measures have accelerated aid disbursments, there remains scope for further improvements.

In conclusion, the Bank would advise the participants of the IDF to support India's ongoing fiscal adjustment and structural reforms through long-term official development assistance for high priority public investments in physical infrastructure and human capital development. With sustained improvements in the utilization of such aid commitments and gradual recourse to debt and non-debt commercial sources, India's remaining external financing needs would be met.

SELECTED REFERENCES

Aitken, Hanson and Harrison. 1994. "Spillovers, Foreign Investment, and Export Behavior." NBER Working Paper 4967. National Bureau of Economic Research, Cambridge, Mass.

Balasubramanyam, V.N., M. Salisu and David Sapsford. 1996. "Foreign Direct Investment and Growth in EP and IS Countries." The Economic Journal. 106 (January):92-105.

Barr and Lee. 1994. "Sources of Economic Growth". Carnegie-Rochester Conference Series on Public Policy (U.S.) 40:1-57.

Bhagwati, Jagdish. 1978. "Anatomy and Consequences of Exchange Control Regimes." Studies in International Economic Relations. Vol. 1 No. 10. National Bureau of Economic Research, Cambridge, Mass.

Bhagwati, Jagdish. 1993. "India in Transition". Oxford, Clarendon Press.

Blomstrom, Kokko and Zejan. 1992. "Host Country Competition and Technology Transfer by Multinationals." NBER Working Paper 4131. National Bureau of Economic Research, Cambridge, Mass.

Borensztein, Eduardo; De Gregorio, Jose and Lee, Jong-Wha. 1995. "How Does Foreign Direct Investment Affect Economic Growth?". NBER Working Paper No. 5057. National Bureau of Economic Research, Cambridge, Mass.

CMIE. Monthly review of the Indian Economy (various issues).

CMIE. Corporate Profitability (various issues).

Dinh, H.T. 1995. "Fiscal Solvency and Sustainability in Creditworthiness Analysis." mimeo. World Bank, Washington, D.C.

Galal, Ahmed et al. 1994 "Welfare Consequences of Selling Public Enterprises: An Empirical Analysis: A Summary." World Bank, Washington, D.C.

Government of India. The Economic Survey (various years) and 1995-96: An Update.

Guidotti, P. and Kumar, M. 1991. "Domestic Public Debt of Externally Indebted Countries." IMF Occasional Paper 80. Washington, D.C.

IMF. 1995. "India: Economic Reform & Growth". Washington, D.C.

Kokko and Blomstrom. 1995. "Policies to Encourage Inflows of Technology Through Foreign Multinationals." *World Development*. Vol. 23, No. 3:459-468.

Majumdar, Madhavi. 1996. "The MFA Phase-Out and EU Clothing Sourcing: Forecasts to 2005." Textile Outlook International. March 1996:31-61.

McCarten, William and Tsiopoulos, Thomas. 1996. "Investment Decisions and the Tax Competitiveness of Indian Industry: A Marginal Effective Tax Rate Analysis". Background paper for 1996 CEM. Washington, D.C.

Montek, Ahluwalia. 1995. "India's Economic Reforms in India: The Future of Economic Reform".

Rajaraman, Indira & Koshy, T. 1996. "A Minimum Alternative Asset-Based Corporate Tax for India". *Economic Polictical Weekly*, XXXI:29; 1941-1952.

Tanzi, V. and Fanizza, D. 1995. "Fiscal Deficits and Public Debt in Industrial Countries." IMF Working Paper 95/49. Washington, D.C.

World Bank. 1993. "The East Asian Miracle: Economic Growth and Public Policy." A World Bank Policy Research Report. Washington, D.C.

World Bank. 1996. "Global Economic Prospects and the Developing Countries". Washington, D.C.

METHODOLOGY AND KEY ASSUMPTIONS FOR ESTIMATING SAVINGS FROM PRIVATIZATION

The methodology used to simulate the gains from privatizing 50 percent of the equity of the central government in public enterprises closely follows that of Galal et al. (1994). The gains from privatization are calculated as the difference between the net present value (NPV) of the social value of the firm under the actual scenario (total or quasi-total public ownership) and the net present value of the private value of the firm under the counterfactual scenario (total private ownership). NPV is calculated by discounting the stream of benefits and costs over the firm's useful lifetime. Under the counterfactual scenario, the government forgoes dividends (or gets rid of PEs losses, if the latter are unprofitable and subsidies) but gains the net sale proceeds of the privatized firms. If, as expected, the privatized firms, will be performing better than under public ownership, then there is a stream of fiscal gains resulting from future higher tax revenues. In addition, the government may gain higher dividends from the remaining enterprises that are now subject to competition and hard budget constraint.

To establish the base case for the CPE sector under continued public ownership, we have made extensive use of the insights derived from the numerous analyses of the public enterprise performance by Indian (particularly O. Goswami) and World Bank researchers and the statistical information contained in the Public Enterprise Survey. A large number of reports and articles on the performance of the PE sector in India, and the evidence from other countries confirm that, like elsewhere, public enterprises' capacity to invest remains mainly constrained by their poor financial performance and remaining government interference and that productivity is low. To estimate the gains from divestiture and from a comprehensive reform strategy for public enterprise sector, we rely on the evidence obtained from productivity improvements and investment increases after privatization in other countries.

More specifically, we assume that if the government adopts a comprehensive strategy (privatization and commercialization of remaining PEs in the portfolio), privatization of 50 percent of the PE sector, for example, will increase productivity by 1.5 percent per year over the productivity obtained under continued public ownership. Furthermore, privatization will also increase annual investment above the level of investment under continued public ownership, so that after twelve years, the stock of fixed assets will be 50 percent larger than what it would have been had the firms remained fully public. The gains in productivity from privatization are assumed to be slightly lower (1.4 percent differential) when privatization takes place without any other reforms. Commercialization alone is assumed to improve productivity by 1 percent per annum and increase investment, to build after say twelve years, 20 percent more fixed assets than without any reform. Table 1.1 presents the results.

Table I.1: Increase in Public and Private Savings from Reforming CPEs						
	Annual increase in domestic savings (percent of GDP) [a]			Annual increase in domestic savings due to (percent of GDP)		
	Government	Private sector	TOTAL	Productivity improvement	More investment	Synergies	TOTAL
25% privatization w/ commercialization	0.7	0.6	1.2	0.5	0.6	0.1	1.2
25% privatization w/o commercialization	0.0	0.5	0.5	0.2	0.2	0.1	0.5
50% privatization w/ commercialization	0.4	1.0	1.4	0.6	0.7	0.2	1.4
50% privatization w/o commercialization	-0.1	0.9	0.8	0.3	0.4	0.1	0.8
Commercialization w/o privatization	0.9	0.0	0.9	0.5	0.4	0.1	0.9

a. Annual flows of additional savings.
Source: Staff estimates.

4.   Like with all simulations, the results depend critically on the parameters adopted. It is difficult to find agreed upon numbers on the impact of privatization. This is due in part to the fact that there has been little ex-post analysis of privatized firms. But, perhaps, more importantly, the gains from privatization crucially depend on the initial conditions of the PEs being privatized, and on how much room there is for improvement. To deal with these two problems, assumptions were deliberately on the conservative side and were supported by the evidence available from developing countries and from the Indian context.

Table I.2. presents a list of central public enterprises that could be candidates for privatization.

Table I.2: The Options for a Privatization Strategy of the Indian CPEs		
% of CPEs' portfolio divested	Time Span	Coverage
25	2 years	CPEs easy to privatize: All consumer goods, tourist services, fertilizers, plus some individual firms: SAIL, NTPC, HMT, BHEL and BEL. Independently of their individual performance, all selected firms are in booming and competitive sectors.
50	5 years	Ambitious privatization program, targets most sectors of the economy where PEs are active, even though it is reasonable to expect that within 5 years the actual privatizations that will take place will cover 50% only of the total portfolio for reasons to be explained below. In addition to the sectors included in the 25% option, this strategy covers mainly Power, Construction, Chemical and Pharmaceuticals, Engineering, Transportation Equipments and enterprises rendering services others than tourists, (transportation, financial, telecommunications, etc.). The only exceptions would be the activities reserved to the government such as radioactive minerals, oil extraction or unclear energy. Broad in scope, the timing of the implementation will vary according to the industry, the competitiveness of the markets, and the sale procedures involved in each transaction. 25% of the portfolio will be divested over two years by focusing on the competitive sectors and some large attractive enterprises, but the rest will take longer. Privatizing public utilities in non competitive activities, restructuring some industries like the oil sector to allow private participation (e.g. oil byproducts) will need more time because they will require regulatory reforms and other amendments to the current legal framework. Hence, after five years, the government could divest 50 percent of its portfolio after having put in place the regulatory framework.

A SUMMARY OF THE COMPUTABLE GENERAL EQUILIBRIUM MODEL

A Computable General Equilibrium (CGE) model of the Indian economy was built specifically for purposes of this Country Economic Memorandum.

Sectors: The Computable General Equilibrium (CGE) model determines quantities and prices for 13 commodity groups or sectors: four crops (rice, wheat, other cereals, other crops), livestock, two agro-processing sectors (edible oils and sugar), six non-agricultural sectors (fertilizer, consumer goods, intermediate goods, capital goods, infrastructure --including petroleum products-- and services --including construction). In addition, there are demand and supply balances for labor (separately for rural and urban areas) and foreign exchange.

Production: The domestic price clears the product markets. The crop supply and input demand equations follow the multi-market specification of Binswanger and Quizon (1986), whereby supply and demand functions are obtained from a profit function estimated using a flexible functional form. Non-crop outputs (livestock, edible oils, sugar, and all non-agricultural sectors) are determined by Constant Elasticity of Substitution (CES) type of production functions with capital and labor as primary inputs. Capital and labor inputs are extracted from the 1990-91 Social Accounting Matrix (SAM). An elasticity of substitution of 0.8 between labor and capital is assumed following Subramanian (1993). Capital is assumed to be sector-specific because of the short-run nature of the model. Demand for fertilizer, draught animal and labor in crop sectors are determined from the agricultural system. Other intermediate input demands in crop sectors (e.g., infrastructure) and all intermediate input demands in non-crop sectors are assumed to be fixed proportions of output under Leontieff technology; these fixed proportions are extracted from the 1990-91 SAM.

Labor Supply: The supply of labor is assumed to be responsive to the real wage, with a supply elasticity of 0.3. Both rural and urban labor markets clear to determine the rural and urban wage rates. Labor demand is determined by the production functions. At this stage, migration has not been taken into consideration because of the static nature of the model.

Income Groups: Households are divided into 8 income classes: 4 income quartiles in each of rural and urban areas. Factor incomes in agriculture and non-agriculture are distributed to each quartile on the basis of a mapping matrix based on income survey data of National Council of Applied Economic Research. Different household groups save different proportions of their income and only the urban top decile is assumed to pay income tax.

Consumer Demand: Consumption is modeled using the Linear Expenditure System (LES) with underlying Stone-Geary type of log-linear utility functions. The LES parameter estimates are available for the different quartile groups from a study by Radhakrishna and Ravi (1994) based on the National Sample Survey (NSS) data. Pulses, fruits and vegetables estimated demand functions are aggregated to match the category of other crops in the agricultural supply function. The estimated demand functions for milk and milk products, are aggregated with that of meat, fish and eggs to match with livestock category in the agricultural supply function. The demand for the non-food group is disaggregated into consumer goods, intermediate goods and capital goods using 1990-91 SAM consumption proportions.

Trade: International trade is modeled under the Armington assumption of imperfect substitution between domestic goods and imports/exports which has by now become a standard feature of trade focused CGE models. The Armington formulation defines a composite commodity which is a CES aggregation of the amount of commodity produced domestically and the level of imports. Consumer demand for domestically produced goods and for imports are derived demand, analogous to demand for factor inputs in a conventional production function. The ratio of imports to domestic demand is then obtained as a function of the corresponding price ratio using the first order conditions. Similarly, the decomposition of domestic output between domestic supplies and exports is treated as a choice problem for producers which depends on ratios of exports and domestic prices.

The nominal protection rates for agriculture and agro-processing sectors are obtained from Pursell, Gulati & Gupta (1996), and Gulati, Sharma and Kohli (1996). For manufactured products, nominal rates of protection are based on collection tariff rates.

Social Accounting Matrix: The model is based around a Social Accounting Matrix (SAM) developed for the year 1990-91, reflecting the situation prior to the reform measures undertaken since June 1991. The SAM provides a consistent data base taking into account intersectoral flows as well as income-expenditure balance of various agents in the economy --i.e., the producers of the 13 commodity groups, the 8 income classes, the government and the external sector. The production and income data in the SAM are based on National Account Statistics. The input-output table for 1989-90 and the Consumption Survey of National Sample Survey for 1987-88 (with updating of the parameters to tally with available 1990-91 totals) provide the other major disaggregated data base for the construction of the SAM.

Market Clearance and Closure: The overall domestic price acts as a numeraire; all other prices determined by the model are thus relative to the overall price. All sectoral domestic prices are determined by supply and demand equilibrium. The foreign exchange market has two alternative specifications. In some simulations, the exchange rate clears the market with foreign savings set at given level. In some other simulations, we examine the effect of devaluation by keeping the exchange rate exogenous and letting the foreign savings play the equilibrating role. The model follows the neoclassical closure where total capital formation (investment plus stock changes) is determined by total savings from three sources: private savings, government savings and foreign savings.

EXECUTIVE SUMMARIES OF BENEFICIARY ASSESSMENT SURVEYS[1]

Agricultural Reforms and the Rural Poor in Eastern Uttar Pradesh
Ravi Srivastava

The Impact of Agricultural Reforms on the Urban Poor: A Case Study of Eastern Uttar Pradesh
Nisha Srivastava

Agricultural Reforms and the Rural Poor in Bundelkhand
Madhavi Kuckreja

Impact of Agricultural Reforms on the Rural Poor: A Case Study of Tamil Nadu
M. Thangaraj

Economic Reforms and the Weaker Sections: Reflections from Maharashtra
Sarthi Acharya

The Impact of Agriculture Reforms on the Rural Poor in Punjab
S.S. Gill

---

[1] These executive summaries were prepared by the authors and were edited to a minimum to keep close to the authors' own assessments.

AGRICULTURAL REFORMS AND THE RURAL POOR IN EASTERN UTTAR PRADESH

Executive Summary

Introduction. This study was carried out in two districts of Eastern Uttar Pradesh - Allahabad and Gorakhpur. In each of the districts, two Development Blocks, and two villages in each of the Blocks, were selected for focus group and small sample interviews. Most of the individual respondents were landless labourers or marginal cultivators from scheduled castes and tribes or from backward castes and nearly a quarter were women. Fieldwork was carried out for about five weeks during February-March 1996.

The study focuses on the effect of agricultural reforms on the rural poor as producers, workers, or consumers. However, it was not always possible to exclude the impact of other reforms, or of changes unrelated to reforms.

Knowledge of reforms and changes in living standards. Very few among the respondents, including those with some education, had any knowledge of India's economic crisis in 1991. Fewer respondents had any idea of a directional change in economic policies since then. More than two-fifths of respondents said that they did not experience any change in their standards of livings in the last five years. Among those who experienced some decline, demographic reasons predominated. *But among respondents who experienced an improvement, the main reasons cited were an improvement in employment conditions, mainly as a result of out-migration, followed by improvement in agriculture.*

Impact on agriculture and agricultural producers. Input prices have risen sharply in the post-reform period. Items singled out by respondents include fertilizers, diesel, high yielding varieties (HYV) seeds, and irrigation charges. In some cases, fertilizer application, specially the application of phosphatic and potassic fertilizers and DAP which is a basal fertilizer mixture has gone down since 1990-91. Even where fertilizer applications have remained the same, or have risen, farmers complain that the (change in) application has not kept pace with increasing requirements because of high prices.

Output prices of several crops have also risen in the post-reform period, but most farmers say that they have to sell when prices are low and that, therefore, for them output prices have increased less than the increase in input prices. In any case most farmers in the region are subsistence farmers, consuming what they produce. The case is different with commercially oriented farmers who feel that profits have gone up in many cases despite increasing input costs.

About two-fifths of the cultivators interviewed reported an increase in paddy, potato, gram and peas yields, while one-fifth reported a decline. There are only some local changes in the cropping pattern, reflecting shifts to labour saving, input saving, or higher value crops. In some cases, reverse shifts have also taken place reflecting adverse market conditions. Depending on the area, the main constraints which farmers face are availability of irrigation, input prices and timely availability of inputs.

Employment and Wages. Most male wage workers in the study villages combine agricultural and non-agricultural labour, either locally, or in the nearby urban centres. In Gorakhpur, a large number of male labourers--nearly one-fourth in our sample migrate for employment to distant states--Punjab, Delhi, Maharashtra and Gujarat. Agricultural employment is meager. Female labourers are employed only for 2 to 3 months and have recourse to virtually no other wage employment. Male labourers get work for four to six months. Local non-agricultural employment is also only available to them for one to three months in a year. Not surprisingly, the younger members of the labour force seek work in the nearby as well as distant urban centres. It is difficult to establish whether migration has increased in post-reform years, but the households that we surveyed have a large number of very young people in the migration stream. While some distinct trends emerge over a longer time frame, most respondents do not recollect significant changes or fluctuations in agricultural or non-agricultural employment during the reform period.

Except in Shankargarh Block, general agricultural (cash) wages have increased by 50 to 65 percent since 1990-91. More importantly, harvest wages--which are in kind--have also increased in tandem in the Gorakhpur Blocks. Depending on how harvest and kind wages are valuated, total wages have risen by slightly less or more than the cash wage rates. Non-agricultural urban wages are higher than the rural wages and have also increased but the orders of magnitude could be smaller. The general picture is perhaps consistent with the labourers' perception: rural wages have increased nearly in line with the cost of living.

The latest regional consumer price indices for rural areas and agricultural labourers was not available to us at the time of writing, but we constructed an index using weights derived for 1990 and a typical food consumption basket for rural labour households in the sample, and rural retail prices. This shows an increase of sixty-eight percent between 1990 and 1995. Since agricultural labourers are partly insulated from the market (because of wages earned in kind), the actual increase in their food index would be less. *The impression at this stage is, therefore, sustained: real wages have remained virtually stagnant since 1990-91. This contrasts with the situation in the eighties when most studies show that real wages were rising in the region.*

Consumption pattern and changes in consumption. Poor households in the rural areas in Eastern U.P. "eat what they get". Deficit in food produced and earned is purchased from the market or taken as loan from employers. A typical meal of the labourer/marginal farmer consists of rice or wheat bread, taken with some vegetables (potatoes), or infrequently with cheaper pulses. On many days the poorer households would simply have rice or bread with salt or chutney. About 12 percent of households interviewed were seriously deficient in food consumption, having to occasionally go without food, or "going to sleep on a half-filled stomach". Often these were single parent or single earner households (both male and female) or households with disabled individuals, but in a few cases low employment/incomes were the cause of this deficiency. Many of the poorer respondents found it difficult to specify a few items whose consumption had been affected by the price rise since 1991. "Even salt has become so expensive", they said. But with local variations, food items whose consumption had been affected due to price increases were pulses, rice and oil. Pulse consumption has definitely declined, and the preferred pulse, Arhar or Toor (pigeon pea), has given way to cheaper pulses, mainly split peas and gram. Only in some cases, could the poorer households take recourse to animal proteins (pork, fish). On the other hand, the consumption of potatoes and vegetables had increased, both due to increased local production and market availability. Most respondents do not report changes (decline) in total cereal consumption over the period.

Safety Nets. The coverage of anti-poverty programs declined in the immediate post reform period. During 1995-96, the emphasis on weaker section's housing has increased but other asset-based income generating programs are below the 1990-91 level. Total employment generation has recovered to the pre-reform level during 1995-96. While there are some cases in which asset-based programs such as the Integrated Rural Development Program (IRDP) have succeeded in raising incomes in a sustainable way, there are several cases of failure and loan diversion. The subsidy element in the programs does not reach the beneficiaries, either wholly or in part. The evidence from both the individual and group interviews also suggests that the programs have provided less cover to certain groups among the poor.

From the group and individual interviews, we surmise that the employment programs have had a marginal impact on the generation of employment. The recent Employment Assurance Scheme (EAS) was in operation in three of the four Blocks surveyed by us. The days of employment generated was below stipulation and other norms such as grain payments, issue of employment cards and local hiring were not observed. In addition, employment is expected to have been generated though the Jawahar Rozgar Yojana (JRY). A small number of (mostly male) labourers were employed in public works executed under this and other schemes but the average days of employment was small.

The Revamped Public Distribution System (RPDS) is operational in one of the four study Blocks, and will soon be introduced in two others. PDS shops exist in each of the village panchayats visited but new ration cards have not yet been issued. A marginal improvement in the availability of sugar and kerosene was reported, but the monthly amounts per family are small--1 to 2 kg of sugar, and 2 litters of kerosene. Only one PDS shop (in the RPDS Block) lifts cereals--wheat and rice--but among those interviewed no one knew of the availability of cereals at this shop. Shop keepers say that there is no demand for cereals from the PDS in the rural areas, specially because the quality is poor, and the band of prices (PDS and open market) is very narrow. Indeed PDS prices are, for most times in the year, higher than open market prices, making the whole operation redundant. While this is correct, the argument does not hold in the RPDS Block where PDS prices are lower, even though there are seasonal variations in consumption, with the cheaper cereal being favored. The current failure of the RPDS in supplying cereals requires deeper analysis, especially since our observations are drawn from an area, where many poor households are entirely dependent on the open market for their grain requirements.

Education and Health. Both study districts are now part of an intensive effort to increase schooling facilities and literacy, and special programs such as the World Bank funded primary education project and the Total Literacy Campaign (TLC) are being implemented. In the study areas, some of the new schools are ready and have started functioning. The mid-day meal scheme is being implemented since 1995 in three of the four study Blocks in the form of a monthly incentive of 3 k.g. rice per child showing regular attendance. The implementation is uneven, but in most of the villages where this has been satisfactory, there has been a spurt in enrollments by 20-25 percent. However, a number of children are still not going to school. There are significant gender and social group disparities which require corrective measures and poor implementation of the program(s) can lead to a reversal of the situation.

Parents are quite sensitive to quality differentials in schooling. In general, upper caste, marginally well off, or even poor parents giving a high priority to education prefer to send their children to private schools. In one case, however, where the government school improved, its enrollments increased and children from private schools were enrolled there, even though the mid-day meal scheme was not operational in this area.

The public health system is in poor state in the study areas. People prefer to use private services, mostly of untrained doctors. Government doctors, they say, take fees and only prescribe medicines which have to be bought separately. In cases of hospitalisation, recourse is made to public hospitals. The cost of treatment is high, and respondents say that medicine prices have risen sharply in recent years. The cost of prolonged treatment has caused a severe downturn in the economic condition of some of the poorer respondents.

Impact of Recent Devolution. Following the 73rd Amendment, and legislative changes in Uttar Pradesh, elections to the first two levels of the three tier panchayat structure were held in U.P. in April 1995. The U. P. legislative changes have reserved seats at all levels for scheduled castes, backward castes, and women. In three of the panchayats we visited, the Pradhans were women. Three of the Pradhans were from the scheduled castes or tribes, two were from the backward castes, and three were from the general castes. It is difficult to say whether the changes had led to any greater empowerment of the weaker sections. The major problem is that no efforts have been made for improving the capacity of the local institutions to undertake the many responsibilities being thrust on them, nor is there, as yet, any systematic devolution of developmental functions.

Development Priorities. Respondents gave land, productive assets, employment, irrigation, lower input costs, flood control and better inputs (in decreasing order of importance) as their priorities for development. Few wanted assets through loans in the manner of the current schemes such as the IRDP.

THE IMPACT OF AGRICULTURAL REFORMS ON THE URBAN POOR: A CASE STUDY OF EASTERN UTTAR PRADESH

EXECUTIVE SUMMARY

Introduction. The present study is a survey of the impact of agricultural reforms on the urban poor and the occupational groups selected were such which could capture these impacts of the reform process. A heterogeneous sample was chosen: construction workers and rickshaw pullers to represent the first group, domestic workers to represent the second group and handloom and powerloom workers to represent the third. The survey was conducted in February-March 1996, in two districts of eastern Uttar Pradesh. The study of handloom and powerloom workers was done in Gorakhpur which has traditionally been the hub of handloom activity. The other occupational groups were surveyed in Allahabad.

The study used a variety of instruments. *First*, in-depth interviews based on semi-structured questionnaires were carried out with individual respondents. *Second*, informal and unstructured group interviews and discussions were held with the respondents at their work places, in their homes and localities. *Third*, a diverse group of people, including employers, contractors, master weavers, traders, corporation employees, PDS shop keepers were interviewed. *Finally*, we visited government offices to talk to the officials and for records of recent public intervention. The major limitations of the study arise from the small number of respondents and the problem of extricating reform-related changes from demographic and other changes. The conclusions are, therefore, at best tentative.

Awareness of Reforms. For the largely illiterate poor in urban areas, reforms are an unknown commodity. Apart from a small section of handloom and powerloom workers who were aware that export policies had become less restrictive, there was no awareness whatever of the reform process. It is possible that since many of the reforms had been put in place only in the last two years, the effects may not have worked their way through the economy and percolated down to the poor.

Employment, Wages and Earnings. Higher numbers of rural people are seeking work in the urban areas. Respondents cite various reasons for increased influx into the urban areas: low wages in the rural areas, declining employment as a consequence of mechanisation, non payment of wages on time by landlords, and changing labour practices. Among unskilled laborers, wages in Allahabad ranged between Rs 25-30 in 1990-91. In 1995-96, average wages ranged between Rs 35-45. The increase in wages is therefore of the order of 41.8 percent. In Gorakhpur, the secondary data collected by the Statistical Office shows an average wage increase of 27.4 percent between 1991-95.

Construction Workers: Our interviews with respondents among construction labourers and their employers suggests that the influx into the unskilled labour market has increased since

1990-91, and the competition for jobs has intensified. Demand for such work may not have picked up in proportion to the increasing supply of laborers. While private expenditure in the construction sector has remained brisk, public expenditure appears to be stagnating. Although male-female jobs in construction are equally arduous, there exists a loose demarcation between them. In recent years, wages of female workers were closer to those of male workers. Where women loose out is in their access to skilled work where wages are double. While most male workers graduate to become skilled masons after a few years on the job, women never do so.

Rickshaw Pullers: Evidence also suggests a sizable increase of new entrants in the rickshaw pulling profession. Mostly these are young workers, who faced with the uncertainty in the labour market take to rickshaw pulling. By all accounts, the job is extremely physically arduous and hence, not often a first choice. Number of days a rickshaw is plied may vary from 10-30 days a month but the average has increased from 160 days in a year earlier to 180 days now. Most pullers being migrants from the rural hinterland, the ebb and flow in their numbers is in consonance with the agricultural seasons.

The current earnings average to Rs 54 per day net of the rental charges of Rs 15; up from net earnings of Rs 35-40 per day about five years ago, an increase of 42 percent between 1990-91 and 1995-96. The privatisation of bus services and increase in three wheeler tempos had affected their business.

Domestic Workers: A poorly paid, highly insecure and pre-dominantly female job, domestic work provides easy entry and sustenance to poor, illiterate women in urban areas. Wages are a pittance; Rs 15 per day on an average, or less than half the wages of other occupational groups surveyed. Moreover, they have risen the least in the period from 1990-91, i.e., by 20-25 percent. Clearly, cash incomes do not appear to have kept pace with the rise in prices. In most domestic worker households, income from domestic work turns out to be less than one half the total income of the household. This is so despite the fact that women put in as many, or in most cases, more hours on the job than do the men in the household. Nevertheless, it is her income that keeps the family from starvation, as the male incomes are generally frittered away in one form of addiction or another.

The average income of the household worked out to Rs 1162 per month. The daily incomes of the males in the household were much higher than female incomes. This was so even when the males were solely engaged in some seasonal occupation and worked only for 8-9 months in the year. Women's incomes came to 38 percent of the total household earnings. Moreover, young girls in the family also accompany their mothers when they go out to work. This in effect pulls down the earnings per person from domestic work even lower. The work of young girls, in this profession is scarcely rewarded and truly invisible. Despite the pittance wages, despite the arduous work, the fact that the job affords women an income of their own is of immense importance to them.

Handloom and Powerloom Workers. Inevitably, in the process of reform there are some who gain and some who lose. The weavers of Gorakhpur are an example of the latter. Loosening of trade restrictions and crop failures in some years have led to phenomenal increases in the prices of yarn. Between 1989-96, prices of yarn have risen by 146 to 245 percent. The daily returns to weavers are estimated at Rs 30 to Rs 48 for wage workers and Rs 43 to Rs 84 for self-employed. Change in earnings are difficult to estimate, but given the dimensions of crisis in the industry, real earnings are unlikely to have increased and have, in all probability declined. Faced with the crisis of increasing yarn prices, weavers have adopted different strategies to cope: migration, switch to powerloom, diversification to new products, or simply 'roughing it out".

Thus, nominal daily earnings of all the occupational groups studied have risen to varying extents in the post-reform period. The estimated increase over five years, roughly corresponding to the post-reform period have been approximately in the range of 20 percent to 42 percent for the various occupational groups in the sample. Does this correspond to an increase in real earnings? At the time of writing, we did not have the regional Consumer price Indices for Agricultural Labourers (CPIAL) computed by the state Directorate of Economics and Statistics. But consumer prices are estimated to have risen by about 52 percent (Oct-Dec 1995 over Oct-Dec 1990). It would thus appear that real daily earnings of the surveyed groups in the study areas have fallen in the post-reform period.

The Allahabad study indicates that the increase in labour supply as a consequence of increased immigration from the countryside has a greater role to play in this compared to a slackening of demand, even though there is evidence of the latter in public sector construction activities.

Consumption. By any yardstick, the consumption and living standards of the poor continue to be abysmal. Most people felt that their consumption standards had remained the same during the period under review although the consumption of pulses, milk and potatoes had reportedly declined in some households. There were some substitution effects. Rise in prices of rice had meant that inferior quality rice was substituted for better quality rice, and cheaper seasonal vegetables were substituted for pulses; the latter implying that protein intake may have reduced. Among non-food items, consumption of clothes and medicines had been affected most adversely. In order to make ends meet, most respondents regularly take credit from employers and from shop-keepers. Owning consumer durables such as black and white TV sets had become a great attraction for the urban poor. Many of the households with somewhat more stable income profiles did actually own a TV set, even if it ran without an authorised electricity connection.

Safety Nets. The safety nets operational in the urban areas were weak and presented a fairly dismal picture despite the fact that these services were present in greater proximity to the urban poor. Respondents were generally aware of some of the new programs and schemes but none had availed of them. Very few had been beneficiaries of the older schemes. The PDS provides urban consumers with access to two commodities: kerosene and sugar. It does not provide any buffer against high foodgrain prices. The gap between open market and PDS prices of cereals has become inconsequential. As a result, the urban poor in the survey simply find it more expedient to purchase in the open market. By and large, the poor interviewed have not benefited from the government health infrastructure; private health care is excessively expensive, but still the preferred option. On the other hand, in education, government schools and anganwadis do fulfil a social function albeit less than satisfactorily.

Development Priorities. The development of infrastructure in urban areas would go a long way in mitigating hardships of the urban poor. Drinking water, sanitation and toilets, better roads, subsidised housing, access to welfare schemes for the genuinely needy and most importantly, more work opportunities, are some of universal demands. More specifically, each occupational group had its own priorities.

The measures rickshaw pullers felt would help them are: night shelters, setting up of handpumps and rickshaw stands at key places, accident insurance, ration cards, fixing of fares indexed to the cost of living, and a check on police excesses. The rural background of construction workers and pullers came through in their other demands: lowering the prices of fertilizers, grant of patta land and availability of work in or around their villages. The major problem of most workers was indebtedness.

The priorities of domestic workers are: a weekly day off, toilets in their localities, more jobs, ban on lotteries and on opening new liquor shops, shelter homes for battered women, and loans for house construction. Widows were aware of the widow pension scheme but despaired that they would be able to get it.

The priorities of handloom and powerloom workers were all related to their trade: better functioning of governmental institutions such as the Intensive Handloom Development Corporation, availability of raw materials, and loans.

Finally, the survey reveals a conspicuous absence of NGO intervention in Allahabad, and a very limited one in Gorakhpur.

AGRICULTURAL REFORMS AND THE RURAL POOR IN BUNDELKHAND

Main Findings of the Banda Case Study

Executive Summary

Awareness of Reforms. A majority of people in the interview sample had not heard of the New Economic Policy (NEP). Although they were aware of changes in input prices, and availability of new fertilizers and seeds, they did not connect this with changes in economic policy. None of the responses saw any linkages between NEP and changes in cropping patterns. The change in cropping patterns was attributed to the introduction of irrigation, dating back to the 1970s.

Impact of Agricultural Productivity. In summary, in the absence of land redistribution in Banda District and severe shortage of irrigation facilities and other infrastructure (roads, electricity, etc), all new agricultural policies are rendered meaningless, particularly for the small farmer.

Small and Marginal Farmers. In the case of small and marginal farmers, there was either negative or no impact of NEP on agricultural productivity and cropping patterns. Small farmers continue to cultivate small pockets of land, spend more on inputs, and generate little or no surplus grain to sell in the market. However, what little grain is sold does fetch a higher price. For a majority of the small farmers, the higher prices did not mean a greater net profitability. This is because the increased income is offset by greater expenditure on agriculture inputs (seeds, fertilizers, canal rates, pumping sets and tractor rental, diesel, electricity).

Large Farmers. In the case of larger farmers, there has been a change in cropping patterns, productivity, and profitability. However, the cropping pattern changes (introduction of wheat and sugar cane) are attributed to the introduction of irrigation over 15 years ago, not to NEP. What can be attributed to the last five years is the greater availability and dependability of new fertilizers and seeds. However, even this was seen as a mixed blessing because a majority of farmers interviewed (both small and large) reported that the amount of chemical fertilizers required virtually double every year. With the increase in fertilizer prices, this is eating into their profits,.

Overall, 6 out of 13 large farmers interviewed reported increased profitability due to higher prices of agricultural produce. Unlike small farmers, several large framers were able to buy mechanized agricultural implements, thereby saving on time and expense in the long term. Some large farmers also reported increased income from renting out this equipment.

Minor Forest Produce. The forest economy, a significant source of income for the Kol tribals in Banda, does not appear to have undergone any significant change in the last five years. Some people reported higher prices for some minor forest produce (mahua, tendu patta, chironjee). But this is an insecure source of income. Income from minor forest produce is critical for three months of the year (April, May, November). Collective rights are forked out by forest contractors, and prices are not determined in the open market, but by the state.

Impact of Employment and Wages. There was no significant change in the pattern of employment after 1991. Subsistence agriculture continues to be the mainstay of the economy. Many of those engaged in subsistence agriculture also work in the wage sector, as agricultural labourers. Work was not available the year round. Only half the respondents reported full employment the year round. Some work for ten months of the year, some for eight, and others for less than eight months (i.e. are unemployed for 2 months, 4 months or more). Those who remain unemployed for 2 or more are either landless or marginal farmers. The increased mechanization of farming was cited as one reason for the reduction of agricultural wage income in the last five years. There has been no industrial development in Banda since 1991 to absorb the large numbers of rural unemployed/underemployed. There is only a marginal increase since 1991 in seasonal migration to nearby towns and cities for employment.

Wages for agricultural work are low and discriminatory towards women. The respondents did, however, report an increase in absolute wages over the last five. The male/female differential remains unchanged. Another shift is the increasing cash payment for daily wage labourers, which earlier was in kind (grain). Wages for work on government rural development works continue to be more on paper and far less in practice. None of the respondents received the official rate of Rs.33 per day. The average government wage ranged from Rs.20 to Rs.30 per day.

Impact on Consumption. There has been a gradual shift in food consumption in the last ten years with the introduction of wheat and rice, in addition to coarse grain (line Jowar and Bajra). In the case of landless and marginal farmers, the shift appeared to be more recent (over the last 5-7 years). A small proportion also reported the introduction of vegetable consumption. This shift did not respond to any significant increase in real income, but to the greater availability of these food items. The last five years have also witnessed an increase in the consumption of consumer items like soap, hair oil, tooth powder, and (synthetic) clothes. Consumption of alcohol and expenditure on gambling (playing the lottery) were also visibly increasing. The fact that more landless and marginal farmers reported an increase in soap/oil/clothes consumption does not mean that the larger farmers are not consuming these items. It merely indicates that for the landless/marginal it is not an *increase* but *introduction* of these items. Many had not used soap until the last five to seven years. Similarly with synthetic clothes.

Does this mean that they have more disposable income now? The answer is a resounding NO. A majority of them were not assured of two square meals a day the year round. Some were in debt, and none were able to save. Obviously with the greater availability of consumer items and aggressive rural marketing, people's definition of "necessity" has undergone a significant change. A number of these consumables are now considered essential--even though what is treated as disposable income to buy these items is in fact only seasonal and subsistence earnings. During the agricultural season, the poor spend on these items, but during the lean season they often go to bed hungry. Similarly more poor households are consuming alcohol, and spending more on dowry and other marriage expenses even though they do not always have enough to eat and are frequently indebted. There was also increased expenditure on medical bills. More and more people in rural areas are seeking private doctors. This does not mean any improvement in their general health status. Most of the respondents were being manipulated into paying frees for unnecessary and sometime outrageous cures.

Impact of the Rural Safety Net. The "rural safety net" has had absolutely no impact in preserving let alone improving the minimum welfare levels of the rural poor. All the safety net programs covered by this case study were functioning poorly, if at all. These included JRY, IRDP, TRYSEM, India Awas and Nirbal Awas (housing schemes), and PDS. The sole exception was the Mahila Samakhya Program (MS), a central government sponsored program aimed at women's empowerment. JRY was marked by few employment days in the year, corruption (doctoring the books to show more wage payments than were actually made), and use of sub-contractors. In addition, no durable community assets were created through JRY. Many of the respondents had worked on building Khadanja (a gravel road), year after year - since the quality is so poor that it gets swept away with every rain.

None of the respondents had received IRDP loans. The housing schemes were marked by poor construction, and unjust beneficiary selection (i.e. well off people manipulating records, with the collusion of government officials, to show themselves as below poverty line). The exception to this was the housing project built by a local society, Vanangana. Here, as a result of participation by housing beneficiaries in the entire process from design to construction, there is 100 percent occupancy. It is the only government housing project in Manikpur block to have achieved this.

PDS supply was erratic and ineffective. It was also market by corruption of ration shop owners. The only positive change in the last five year in the study villages was that most people now possess ration cards. Part of the credit for this goes to MS program workers who have worked on helping the poor procure cards for the last several years.

Panchayati Raj can potentially play a watchdog role in ensuring proper implementation of government schemes, and beneficiary section. It has been totally ineffective. In fact the Pradhan was often cited as the chief conniver in denying the poor their due from safety net programs.

IMPACT OF AGRICULTURAL REFORMS ON THE RURAL POOR: A CASE STUDY OF TAMIL NADU

Executive Summary

This report examines the "Impact of Agriculture Reforms on the Rural Poor". The objective of the study is to analyze the impact of agriculture reforms on landless laborers and marginal small farmers. Both official and primary data were collected for this study. A survey was conducted in two districts viz. Thanjavur and Dharmapuri in Tamil Nadu and four village in each district were selected at random for in-depth analysis. Primary data were collected from 170 farmers (80 from Thanjavur and 90 from Dharmapuri) and 145 agricultural labourers (80 from Thanjavur and 65 from Dharmapuri), in February, 1996. We have also conducted 4 individual interviews and nine group interviews with farmers and agricultural labourers to verify the survey data.

Knowledge About the Economic Reforms. Most of the respondents were not aware of the economic reforms initiated since 1991. Out of 170 farmers and 145 agricultural labourers, only 24 (14 percent) farmers and 6 (4 percent) agricultural labourers were aware of the reform programs.

Major changes Since 1991

(a) *Prices*: All respondents in both districts have said that prices of essential commodities have gone up enormously during the reform period, including the prices of commodities sold under the Public Distribution System.

(b) *Credit*: In Thanjavur villages, out of 80 farmers, only 28 (35 percent) farmers; and in Dharmapuri villages out of 90 farmers, 27 (30 percent) said that the availability of credit facilities has improved. Credit facilities for agricultural labourers under IRDP have declined over the past five years. In Thanjavur and Dharmapuri districts, out of 80 and 65 agricultural labourers respectively, 56 and 22 said that credit facilities have declined.

(c) *Income*: In Thanjavur district, out 80 farmers 25 (31 percent) farmers, and in Dharmapuri district out of 90 farmers, 34 (48 percnet) felt that their income have declined. Lack of credit facilities and an increase in input prices were the main reasons for decrease in the income. The incomes of many agricultural labors have increased over the reform period in rural areas of Tamil Nadu. In Thanjavur district, out of 80 agricultural labourers 55 (69 percent) stated that their income has increased. While in Dharmapuri district out of 65 respondents, 49 (75 percent) stated that their income has increased. The main reason for the increase in income was due to increasing wage rates.

Benefit From Reforms. In Thanjavur district, 34 farmers and in Dharmapuri district, 24 farmers claim to have benefited from higher farm profits and low wage rates paid to agricultural labourers. Among those who have not benefited, 46 farmers belong to Thanjavur district and 66 belong to Dharmapuri district. The higher wage rate for agricultural labourers and input prices were cited as the main reasons for not benefiting from agricultural reforms.

Non-Farm Employment. Only two households out of 80 farmers' households in Thanjavur district, had members engaged in non-farm employment since 1991. In Dharmapuri district out of 90 farmers' household, 32 have non-farm employment. The main reason for higher non-farm employment in Dharmapuri district was the uncertainty of cultivation due to lack of irrigation water. Frequent crop failure and higher wages in urban areas encourage even farmers to migrate to urban areas. Agricultural laborers in rural areas historically do not work much in the non-farm sector. However this is changing in the Dharmapuri district. Out of 65 labourers households, 29 have stated that their family members have non-farm employment. In contrast, none from Thajavur district are working outside the agriculture sector.

Price Change in Key Crops. Both in Thanjavur and Dharmapuri districts, all farmers have stated that production costs have increased considerably over the last five years.

Safety Net Programs. A comparison of prices in the open market and in the fair price shops shows that the prices of commodities sold in the fair price shops, particularly rice, is only one-half the prices in the open market.

The government is implementing several development schemes in the rural areas. These programs include employment generation, agricultural extension work for higher agricultural output.

(a)   Who are using these schemes?

Both in Thanjavur and Dharmapuri districts, most of the respondents said that all works under the JRY programs were done by contractors. The contractors usually bring labourers from outside the village. None of the farmers from Thanjavur district have availed any employment opportunity under these schemes. Only 14 farmers in Dharmapuri have stated that they had employment, but for a few days only.

In one of the Thanjavur villages, a youth organization viz. Bharathidassan Narpani Mandram (Welfare Club) sub-contracted a JRY scheme to provide employment to local people. As a result, about one-third of the labourers in Thanjavur villages have availed employment in their village. While in Dharmapuri district, only 23 (35 percent) labourers were employed through these programs.

(b)   Are these schemes useful? Most of the respondents both in Thanjavur and Dharmapuri districts said that the schemes are useful in creating infrastructural facilities such as bus shelter, school buildings, community hall, etc.

(c)   In what way could these programs be improved?

In Thanjavur district, a high proportion of respondents stated that the schemes should be implemented by the village panchayat and some suggestions that the schemes should be given to local village people. The contracting of work relating to safety net programs by the members of the political parties should be stopped. This is against the JRY manual, 1994, which clearly states that anti-poverty programs should not be given to contractors. But in practice, most of the works were done by contractors both in Thanjavur and Dharmapuri districts.

ECONOMIC REFORMS AND THE WEAKER SECTIONS:
REFLECTIONS FROM MAHARASHTRA

Executive Summary

There has been intense debate on the impact of the reforms on the poor. Lack of adequate data on a large scale with sufficient disaggregation has however not permitted to arrive at firm conclusions. This paper reports the findings of a rapid rural survey (albeit on small scale) conducted in Maharashtra, to seek tentative results on the impact of reforms on both the rural and urban poor. The field work was done in January and February, 1996.

The methodology followed here consists of using a range of qualitative methods, including village meetings and focus group discussions with agricultural and non-agricultural laborers, small farmers, lorry drivers, semi-skilled factory workers, women workers, etc. (conventionally accepted to be the poor), in addition to limited individual interviews. The inquiry was conducted in the rural areas of four districts; Osmanabad (semi-arid, backward), Parbhani (cotton growing region), Pune (semi-arid but fast modernizing), and Thane (rain-fed, tribal); and in the informal sectors of Bombay city. A total of 17 villages and four low income settlements were visited for the investigation. The rural inquiry is much more detailed than that in Bombay. The findings from rural areas are reported under four broad sub-headings: earnings, production, opportunities, expenditure ratings and social conscription; and those of Bombay are separately reported.

Wages, Earnings and Work Availability. The rural economy of Maharashtra is mainly agrarian and semi-arid, and the majority of the poor are engaged in wage labor in addition to work on one's own land (if they possess any), and self provisioning. It is observed that the conditions of these groups have, by and large either stayed unchanged, or marginally improved. The two principal indicators, namely the number of days work available and wages, have both improved somewhat. In specific areas migration has risen since workers prefer to travel for seeking higher wages and working conditions, while in others it has fallen because they have found more employment locally in agriculture and/or in other activities. There are, of course, regional differences; with varied changes everywhere other than in those where the tribals have subsisted in isolation.

In Omanabad, the prevailing wage for unskilled manual work has been reported to be in the range Rs. 25-35 for male workers and Rs. 15-20 for females, depending on the location and type of work. Wages on large scale construction works (road, dams, other earth works) could reach up to Rs. 35-40 a day (male). In Parbhani wages are much the same as in Osmanabd, and here too there has been a marginal rise in areas near towns/main roads, though there is stagnation in the higherland over the period under reference. Wages in Pune are somewhat higher, but in Tahne, the tribals not only fetch lesser wages in absolute value, but wages were slightly lower in real terms too.

The laborers and small/marginal farmers work for about 60-70 days during June-September (almost wholly in agriculture), above 130-140 days during October-March (in mixed occupations) and about 30 days during April-June (mainly in non-agriculture). Work on one's land does not exceed 25-35 days per person since the plots are small and are often sharecropped out. Over the last 3-4 years, this 200-220 days of work in a year (all areas) has actually had a slightly higher than in previous year.

Cultivation Practices. The prices of most agricultural inputs have risen over the years, both due to reductions in subsidies and general inflation. Farmers are acutely aware of the costs and prices and tend to adjust to external changes. There has thus been a shift away from crops that fetch low profits or require higher costs, towards ones that maximize profits/minimize costs. Of course these shifts have occurred as a result of emerging opportunities such as enhanced irrigation facilities and marketing channels as well. The problem of input prices rise outstripping those of the outputs (at least when and where the farmers sell) has, however, been a constant cause of concern.

In Osmanabad many farmers have shifted their cropping patterns away from pulses and groundnut in favor of sunflower to save on fertilizer costs (prices rose by 75-80 percent), and resorted to limited mechanization for saving on labor costs (which rose by 50-60 percent). In Parbhani they have increasingly preferred to sow cotton despite numerous controls and imperfections in the market (including price controls) and pest attacks. In Pune district the trends are similar to those in Osmanabad, with the difference that tomatoes and vegetables are grown because there is a market for them in the large city of Pune. A general, reduction in area under sorghum and pulses has been observed because cash crops yield a higher profit. Farmers who have been able to access irrigation, either through the underground (private effort) or surfaces (public investment), are clear gainers. The sustainability of this trend is however under question since the under ground water table is drying up. Instead, surface irrigation is increasingly being used for high water intensive crops such as sugar cane, curtailing water to other crops and/or a wider geographic region. Unlike others, this region is not semi-arid; yet it is not able to irrigate its single (paddy) crop because most of its water is harnessed and transported to meet the requirements of the Bombay metropolitan region.

Consumption Practices. The staple food of people is sorghum. Its hybrid form is now universally being consumed by the poor, as the other varieties have become too expensive. The other cereals consumed are wheat and rice. The per capita consumption of cereals does not seem to have changed significantly. There has however been a general fall in the consumption of pulses and milk, and a rise in the intake of vegetables. The overall food consumption has not shown a visible rise, though limited non-food items seem to have found place in many houses. Younger people have began to opt for 'modern' goods such as tooth paste, soap, and the likes. The people interviewed have not reported an overall fall in consumption anywhere.

In Osmanabad people have begun to eat a little more meat than they did earlier "because they now have access to cash." This partly compensates for the proteins foregone due to cut back on pulses. In Parbhari, edible oil and meat consumption have fallen, in addition to pulses and milk. Though vegetable consumption has risen here, it is of interest to note that people's preferences have shifted towards non-food items rather than diversifying the food basket. The communities in Pune have reported much the same. In Thane, food consumption does not seem to have been affected because most people eat what they grow: market interface is minimal. The Public Distribution System (PDS) is mainly used for sourcing sugar in Parbhani, though in Osmanabad and Pune occasional consignments of wheat and edible oil also reach. In Thane there is no PDS. People everywhere reported that the PDS is inefficient, rigid in its operations (eg. customers have to take their full month's quota for which they seldom have ready cash,) and officials are corrupt.

The changing cropping pattern has so far not affected local food security since farmers grow some sorghum to meet their needs, many landless either sharecrop, thereby getting access to land and food, or gather some food during the harvesting operations. Most nevertheless buy food in off seasons, but have so far not been very adversely hit because the sorghum prices are still within their budget range.

Public Service and Social compensation. Most credit schemes are still operational but many loans are not sanctioned because people who have received loans (almost all eligible) earlier have not returned them. In general instances, the projects themselves were ill-conceived, and as a result, the money was wasted. Only in Pune it was observed that banks have begun to insist that villagers vet their projects by local NGOs or village institutions for ascertaining their financial viability. Osmanabad and Pune villages showed a higher prevalence of institutional loans than Parbhani. In the latter private money lending is widely prevalent. In Thane, institutional credit was totally absent.

The Employment Guarantee Scheme (EGS) is not uniformly present everywhere. In Osmanabad and Pune the EGS and its associated soil management programs are very popular, while in Parbhani such activities are relatively low (about half compared to the former on a per capita basis). In Thane they are riddled with corruption. Despite this regional disparity it is widely believed that a floor wage has been set in the state because of the EGS, except perhaps in the remote tribal belts.

Children's school attendance has risen over the last few years. Nutrition in pre-schools (ICDS) is provided in most places other than in Thane. Health services though have become more expensive. Earlier the Primary health Centers provided free diagnosis as well as some medicines, but now, medicines need to be purchased. Lastly, transport (bus) services have become expensive (about 50% rise over the last 5 odd years).

The Urban Informal Sector. Workers from four sectors, namely, small scale manufacturing, transport, construction and personal services, stated that job uncertainty and loss of jobs have risen and real wages have fallen over the last few years. The recent emergence of job sub-contracting and contract labor have helped cut costs for employees, but restricted the legal rights of workers. High costs of real-estate are forcing many small manufacturing units out of the city. Since workers are not always mobile, they lose their jobs.

Consumption levels have fallen in the recent times: pulses, vegetables, meat, fish and milk have all become dear and their intake reduced. Only in the case of domestic workers has consumption not been affected so much since it is not uncommon for employers to share some of their food with workers.

Health services have become expensive here too. Medicines are not typically available in public hospitals. The PDS is far from satisfactory; even though it stores more than in the villages, it suffers from all the problems stated in the rural context. Unlike in the rural sector, there are no institutional sources of credit, particularly for this category of workers. People tend to borrow exclusively from private sources at very high interest rates. Children mostly attend schools, but also take up part-time jobs to supplement family income.

Conclusions. Prices of many critical inputs and consumption items have risen, and certain activities have been adversely affected in the process of implementing the reforms program. In regions where opportunities have risen or successful adjustments have occurred, people have been able to ride over the problems, while in others, they have suffered. In the rural areas other than tribal, the safety nets and/or adjustment mechanisms have been functional. The reform process has scarcely reached the tribal areas and in the urban areas there are no safety nets. This inquiry suggests that the impact of the reforms process per--se has, across regions, been mixed, but has not been overtly anti-poor.

THE IMPACT OF AGRICULTURE REFORMS ON THE RURAL POOR IN PUNJAB

Executive Summary

Punjab is the most agriculturally advanced region in India. Modern farming methods are used, and the rural economy is highly commercialized. Commodity and labor markets are well developed, as are land lease and credit markets. Because of the high degree of commercialization, the impact of policy changes and reform measures are likely to be transmitted quickly through the rural economy. Development dynamism was rapid under the past policy framework, and the momentum has continued in the post-reform period. Because of this, it is difficult to distinguish between existing momentum and effects of the reforms.

Reform Measures Affecting Agriculture. Reform measures in agriculture are primarily reflected in changes in input prices. Fertilizer prices rose sharply--if we compare 1995 prices with 1991 prices, DAP increased by 172 percent, urea by 40 percent, and zinc sulfate by 25 percent. In addition, electricity charges rose by 242 percent over 1991 levels. Land rents are rising rapidly as well: in some areas, the increase is estimated to have been on the order of 70-80 percent in 1995 as compared to 1991. Water charges for canal irrigation more than doubled during the period. However, the increases in input prices were accompanied by rising wages for agriculture laborers. Agriculture in Punjab is becoming more mechanized over time (a past trend) and home-supplied animal power is being replaced by tractors, reapers, combines, etc.

All parts of the population are confronted with general increases in inflation. Particularly cited is the scarcity of essential drugs rural dispensaries and the collapse of the public education system in rural areas. Many people are forced to pay high prices for drugs and to send their children to costly private schools--further raising the basic cost of living.

Reforms have also brought numerous benefits: cultivators were compensated in terms of higher procurement prices for wheat, paddy, and sugarcane, as well as rising market prices for other crops. Unfortunately, this has pushed up the price of basic foodgrains for households who are net buyers. The withdrawal of the subsidy on foodgrains supplied through the PDS has negatively affected some segments of the population more than is reflected in the total rise in the price of food items. Net consumers have also been impacted by the relatively rapid increase in the prices of pulses, edible oil, butter oil, milk, vegetables, and clothes.

Coverage of the Case Studies. Patiala and Fatehgarh Sahib districts were selected for data collections for two reasons: **first**, they represent the dominant cropping pattern in the State -- wheat-paddy cropping. **Second**, the researchers had prior knowledge and contacts in the districts, which facilitated the work given the tight time constraints operating. Ten blocks within the district were selected for sampling--seven in Patiala and three in Fatehgarh Sahib. One village was then selected within each block. Information was collected in village-level town meetings and through individual interviews. A total of 197 persons were interviewed: 109 cultivators, 67 agriculture laborers, and 21 artisans. The vast majority of these were poor, although a few medium and large cultivators were also included in the sample, primarily for purposes of comparison.

Knowledge of Reform Measures. Although they had a vague feeling that something was being done by the government, a large number of both poor and nonpoor villagers were not aware of policy changes linked to the reform program as such. What they did know had been learned through state controlled media (television and radio) and through statements by political parties and groups. Most farmers were aware of changes in input prices. One group seemed particularly well-informed regarding reforms: the Bhartiya Kisan Union (BKU),

Impact on agriculture activities: changes in input use and cropping patterns. A large majority of cultivators did not report any major changes in input use since 1991. Despite the increase in fertilizer prices, only 10 percent reported using less of either DAP or urea, while 24 percent had actually used more fertilizer since 1991. Some also reported an increase in the use of insecticides, pesticides, and weedicides. Increased mechanization was also evident: as compared to pre-1991, some cultivators reported that they were now using oilseed threshing machines, combine harvesters, and a machine to convert wheat straw into fodder. With the exception of decreased use of fertilizers, all of the observed changes in input use are consistent with pre-reform secular trends.

Observed changes in cropping patterns are in part a function of the dynamism of a fast growing economy and in part due to reform changes. Many factors influence cropping patterns--relative price changes can impact on profitability as can changes in the conditions of production or markets. But changes in cropping patterns can involve greater risk as well as higher potential profitability, and cultivators with a poor resource base often lack initiative for change. Some 45 percent of farmers--most belonging to the group of small and marginal cultivators--did not introduce any changes. The remaining 55 percent who did change cropping patterns and mix include all large cultivators (more than 20 acres) and many of the medium-sized cultivators (5-20 acres). Those who did make changes had previously been growing a traditional pattern of wheat, paddy, and fodder, but started growing additional crops, including pulses, vegetables, mustard, potatoes, sunflower, sugarcane, and maize. In addition, some cultivators have introduced a new crop rotation that helps to control weeds and maintain soil fertility. Dairying is the major allied activity adopted by cultivators, followed by transport, sale of skilled and unskilled labor, custom hiring, bee-keeping, tailoring, etc.

Employment of Agriculture Laborers and Artisans. Three quarters of all laborers and artisans reported no change in the number of days they were employed. Of the remaining 25 percent, equal numbers reported an increase or decrease in days of employment. Note that many of the rural laborers migrate to nearby cities and towns to work in the slack agriculture season. The fact that they are working as intensively post-reform as pre-reform may be in part due to the fact that any decline in employment may simply mean less employment for migrant workers from Bihar and U.P. and steady employment for laborers from rural Punjab.

Wages and Earnings. The money wages paid to laborers appear in general to have increased in real terms over the reform period. Different groups of laborers have benefited differently, however. For example, contractual/regular agricultural laborers have experienced a consistent rise in real wages since 1991. In contrast, the wages of casual laborers, who tend to be among the poorest in rural areas, have actually deteriorated slightly over the reform period, although the sharpest drop was in the early years of the reforms. Similarly with artisans, who suffered a sharp decline in real wages between 1991-92 and 1992-93, and the gradual rise in ensuing years has not been sufficient to bring their wages back to 1991 levels. One must question whether the market forces that have come to play a greater role in the post-reform period have been favorable to the poorest sections in rural Punjab.

Changes in Levels and Patterns of Consumption. Respondents were asked two questions: whether they consumed more or less of certain commodities and whether certain commodities had appeared or disappeared from their consumption basket since the advent of reforms. Across the board, there was no significant drop in food grain consumption reported. Other changes did occur and these changes both in levels and patterns differed by group. For example, less than a half of all laborers and artisans said that their consumption patterns were unchanged. The remainder reported less consumption of certain items (i.e. vegetables, milk, clothing), severely reduced use of other items (i.e. liquor, butter oil, pulses) and replacement of some higher cost items with cheaper substitutes (i.e. milk was replaced by tea and sugar by gur). It is of concern that many of the items that contain either proteins or fats (for example, pulses and milk) were being consumed less frequently and in lesser amounts by the rural poor. Similarly, the majority of (poor) small and marginal farmers also reported declines in overall consumption levels and substitution of cheaper foodstuffs for more expensive commodities. In contrast, many of the larger farmers reported both more diversity in consumption patterns and higher levels of consumption. The net rise in consumption levels increased with the size of land holdings, and corresponded to overall household prosperity.

Public Safety Nets and the Rural Poor. The public safety net can provide a great deal of security to the rural poor, providing it functions effectively. Evidence suggests that safety net program are functioning very unevenly in rural Punjab. For example, while many of the poor in Punjab are using the PDS, they are only able to purchase sugar (when it is available) and kerosene. In order to establish eligibility for many of the targeted programs, the Punjab government has issued yellow cards to all qualifying poor households. However, a recent study showed that only one-third of the rural poor actually have these cards. This is in part due to the partisan attitudes of the villages sarpanches in issuing the cards and in part due to laxity of the state administration; it has not issued new cards since 1982.

A number of other schemes are in operation in rural Punjab: IRDP, the mid-day meals program in schools, JRY, Indira Awas Yogana, Mahila Mandel, Flood Relief, etc. But their coverage is very limited and they have not benefited the majority of the rural poor. The corruption of officials entrusted with the task of administering these programs has played havoc with existing programs. And, safety net program that are designed on the basis of all-India averages (for examples, that pay average minimum wages) are of little use in an advanced state like Punjab. The rural poor expect a larger and better role from Government in providing public safety nets.

STATISTICAL APPENDIX

CONTENTS

I. National Accounts

II. Balance of Payments - Current Accounts

III. Balance of Payments - Capital Accounts

IV. Public Finance

V, Money and Credit

VI. Agriculture, Industry, Transport, Energy and Prices

Table A1.1 (a)
National Accounts Summary
(Rs. billion at current prices)

	1985-86	1986-87	1987-88	1988-89	1989-90	1990-91	1991-92	1992-93	1993-94	1994-95
GDPfc	2337.99	2600.30	2948.51	3527.06	4086.62	4778.14	5527.68	6301.82	7231.03	8541.03
Agriculture	772.24	824.13	923.79	1140.73	1270.51	1480.01	1727.71	1930.45	2217.46	2659.14
Industry	658.14	737.46	838.29	1000.73	1196.93	1400.25	1540.74	1783.55	2005.25	2388.14
Mining	61.98	67.96	70.85	92.08	103.08	117.85	128.03	145.87	169.49	188.65
Manufacturing	417.75	461.66	528.65	628.63	770.76	891.60	963.05	1110.03	1234.77	1484.84
Construction	129.47	152.17	176.11	206.77	235.86	286.16	322.46	366.61	412.12	489.59
Electricity	48.94	55.67	62.68	73.25	87.23	104.64	127.20	161.04	188.87	225.06
Services	907.61	1038.71	1186.43	1385.60	1619.18	1897.88	2259.23	2587.82	3008.32	3493.75
Indirect Taxes	284.44	329.19	383.50	430.76	481.59	577.20	640.31	751.46	779.29	915.12
GDPmp	2622.43	2929.49	3332.01	3957.82	4568.21	5355.34	6167.99	7053.28	8010.32	9456.15
Resource Gap (M-X)	81.37	80.87	85.93	124.93	112.19	151.79	39.03	93.81	15.94	157.00
Imports (g+nfs)	237.67	255.25	296.23	388.59	465.46	565.11	610.00	776.69	923.40	1226.04
Exports (g+nfs)	156.30	174.37	210.31	263.66	353.28	413.32	570.97	682.88	907.46	1069.04
Total Expenditure	2703.80	3010.36	3417.94	4082.75	4680.40	5507.13	6207.02	7147.09	8026.26	9613.15
Consumption	2069.38	2331.37	2669.12	3118.64	3578.45	4155.57	4806.34	5451.61	6316.17	7423.95
General Gov't	291.74	346.25	408.43	473.31	542.03	617.79	694.59	785.96	896.78	1012.51
Private	1777.64	1985.12	2260.69	2645.33	3036.42	3537.78	4111.75	4665.65	5419.39	6411.44
Investment	634.42	678.99	748.82	964.11	1101.95	1351.56	1400.68	1695.48	1710.09	2189.20
Fixed Investment	542.55	620.52	721.94	856.69	1027.75	1240.04	1365.03	1587.38	1722.46	2130.64
Change in Stocks	91.87	58.47	26.88	107.42	74.20	111.52	35.65	108.10	-12.37	58.56
Domestic Savings	553.05	598.12	662.89	839.18	989.76	1199.77	1361.65	1601.67	1694.15	2032.21
Net Factor Income	-19.00	-26.16	-32.06	-38.12	-48.79	-67.35	-93.90	-99.07	-125.56	-122.61
Current Transfers	27.01	29.75	34.99	38.42	38.01	37.14	92.75	80.29	120.00	194.67
National Savings	561.05	601.71	665.82	839.48	978.98	1169.55	1360.50	1582.88	1688.60	2104.27
Foreign Savings	73.37	77.28	83.00	124.63	122.97	182.01	40.18	112.60	21.49	84.93
GDP per capita (Rs.)	3473.42	3799.60	4228.44	4916.55	5557.43	6383.00	7205.60	8088.62	9020.63	10460.34
Per capita private consumption	2354.49	2574.74	2868.89	3286.12	3693.94	4216.66	4803.45	5350.52	6102.91	7092.30
Average Exchange Rates:										
Rupees per US $	12.24	12.79	12.97	14.48	16.66	17.95	24.52	28.95	31.37	31.40
Rupees per SDR[a]	12.92	15.45	17.12	19.26	21.37	24.85	33.43	37.14	43.89	45.79
Memo Items:										
Priv. Consumption (CSO)	1777.58	1999.98	2240.61	2589.93	2900.72	3323.64	3851.50	4353.17	4936.02	5675.40
Population (mill)	755	771	788	805	822	839	856	872	888	904

a. Arrived at by crossing U.S. Dollar/ SDR rate with the RBI reference rate. *Source:* Economic Survey 1995-96.

Source: CSO, National Accounts Statistics 1996.

Table A1.1 (b)
National Accounts Summary
(Rs. billion at 1980-81 prices)

	1985-86	1986-87	1987-88	1988-89	1989-90	1990-91	1991-92	1992-93	1993-94	1994-95
GDPfc	1565.66	1632.71	1703.22	1884.61	2014.53	2122.53	2139.83	2248.87	2360.64	2510.10
Agriculture	542.18	532.81	534.79	622.14	632.63	656.53	641.18	680.17	702.31	736.88
Industry	432.25	463.82	493.67	538.66	593.98	637.00	628.67	654.72	682.51	739.02
Mining	26.23	29.78	30.80	35.42	38.01	42.07	43.62	44.12	45.93	47.91
Manufacturing	303.20	324.45	348.18	378.65	422.85	448.63	432.00	449.89	469.33	511.48
Construction	71.83	75.37	77.77	83.79	88.07	98.33	100.47	103.75	106.15	113.64
Electricity	30.99	34.22	36.92	40.80	45.05	47.97	52.58	56.96	61.10	65.99
Services	591.23	636.08	674.76	723.81	787.92	829.00	869.98	913.98	975.82	1034.20
Indirect Taxes	200.82	219.79	237.63	248.84	259.14	279.85	272.72	290.92	278.07	294.92
GDPmp	1766.48	1852.50	1940.85	2133.45	2273.67	2402.38	2412.55	2539.79	2638.71	2805.02
Terms of Trade Effect	17.17	24.54	14.73	23.52	22.83	8.96	7.43	12.00	11.75	17.59
Gross Domestic Income	1783.65	1877.04	1955.58	2156.97	2296.50	2411.34	2419.98	2551.79	2650.46	2822.61
Resource Gap (M-X)	62.39	62.06	55.84	71.72	53.45	61.45	12.43	27.40	4.29	38.09
Imports (g+nfs)	182.24	195.85	192.51	223.08	221.76	228.79	194.30	226.86	248.37	297.46
Capacity to import	119.85	133.80	136.67	151.36	168.31	167.34	181.87	199.46	244.09	259.37
[Exports (g+nfs)]	102.68	109.26	121.95	127.84	145.48	158.38	174.44	187.46	232.34	241.77
Total Expenditure	1846.04	1939.09	2011.42	2228.69	2349.95	2472.80	2432.42	2579.19	2654.74	2860.70
Consumption	1447.57	1537.38	1593.56	1732.92	1843.11	1903.95	1926.09	2010.49	2119.11	2219.12
General Gov't	189.24	208.49	226.60	238.68	252.15	260.59	259.25	267.77	284.14	292.62
Private	1258.33	1328.89	1366.96	1494.24	1590.96	1643.36	1666.84	1742.72	1834.97	1926.50
Investment	398.47	401.71	417.86	495.77	506.84	568.85	506.33	568.70	535.63	641.58
Fixed Investment	329.74	359.97	399.55	427.70	464.83	510.91	490.46	524.27	541.89	622.07
Change in Stocks	68.73	41.74	18.31	68.07	42.01	57.94	15.87	44.43	-6.26	19.51
Domestic Savings	336.08	339.65	362.02	424.05	453.39	507.40	493.90	541.30	531.34	603.49
Net Factor Income	-14.57	-20.07	-20.84	-21.89	-23.25	-27.27	-29.91	-28.94	-33.77	-29.75
Current Transfers	20.71	22.83	22.74	22.06	18.11	15.03	29.55	23.45	32.28	47.23
National Savings	342.21	342.41	363.92	424.23	448.25	495.16	493.53	535.81	529.85	620.97
Foreign Savings	56.26	59.30	53.94	71.54	58.59	73.69	12.80	32.89	5.78	20.61
GDP per capita (Rs.)	2339.71	2402.72	2463.01	2650.25	2766.02	2863.38	2818.40	2912.60	2971.52	3102.90
Per capita private consumption	1666.67	1723.60	1734.72	1856.19	1935.48	1958.71	1947.24	1998.53	2066.41	2131.09
Rupee Deflators (1980-81=100):										
GDPmp	148.5	158.1	171.7	185.5	200.9	222.9	255.7	277.7	303.6	337.1
Imports(g+nfs)	130.4	130.3	153.9	174.2	209.9	247.0	313.9	342.4	371.8	412.2
Exports(g+nfs)	152.2	159.6	172.5	206.2	242.8	261.0	327.3	364.3	390.6	442.2
Total Expenditure	146.5	155.2	169.9	183.2	199.2	222.7	255.2	277.1	302.3	336.0
Govt. Consumption	154.2	166.1	180.2	198.3	215.0	237.1	267.9	293.5	315.6	346.0
Priv. Consumption	141.3	149.4	165.4	177.0	190.9	215.3	246.7	267.7	295.3	332.8
Fixed Investment	164.5	172.4	180.7	200.3	221.1	242.7	278.3	302.8	317.9	342.5
Total Investment	159.2	169.0	179.2	194.5	217.4	237.6	276.6	298.1	319.3	341.2

-- Not available.

Source: CSO, National Accounts Statistics 1996.

Table A1.2 (a)
Gross Domestic Product at Factor Cost - By Industry of Origin
(Rs. billion at current prices)

	1985-86	1986-87	1987-88	1988-89	1989-90	1990-91	1991-92	1992-93	1993-94	1994-95
Agricultural Sector	772.24	824.13	923.79	1140.73	1270.51	1480.01	1727.71	1930.45	2217.46	2659.14
Agriculture	699.64	744.05	835.15	1041.03	1154.47	1351.62	1592.99	1779.10	2049.62	2451.39
Forestry & Logging	52.86	57.58	61.78	68.28	78.23	82.81	83.90	88.54	92.50	98.12
Fishing	19.74	22.50	26.86	31.42	37.81	45.58	50.82	62.81	75.34	109.63
Industry Sector	658.14	737.46	838.29	1000.73	1196.93	1400.25	1540.74	1783.55	2005.25	2388.14
Mining & Quarrying	61.98	67.96	70.85	92.08	103.08	117.85	128.03	145.87	169.49	188.65
Manufacturing	417.75	461.66	528.65	628.63	770.76	891.60	963.05	1110.03	1234.77	1484.84
Registered	258.06	282.54	322.07	390.50	483.69	555.53	608.43	688.12	765.09	902.62
Unregistered	159.69	179.12	206.58	238.13	287.07	336.07	354.62	421.91	469.68	582.22
Electricity,Gas &Water	48.94	55.67	62.68	73.25	87.23	104.64	127.20	161.04	188.87	225.06
Construction	129.47	152.17	176.11	206.77	235.86	286.16	322.46	366.61	412.12	489.59
Services Sector	907.61	1038.71	1186.43	1385.60	1619.18	1897.88	2259.23	2587.82	3008.32	3493.75
Transport, Storage & Com.	140.98	165.37	199.38	238.72	277.31	339.13	410.04	491.07	563.27	655.22
Railways	31.36	37.65	43.56	47.51	55.75	64.33	73.42	84.46	96.48	107.83
Other Transport	91.00	105.10	124.68	152.29	177.85	223.11	275.22	330.64	372.93	433.09
Storage	2.60	2.80	3.17	3.34	3.88	4.45	4.77	5.13	5.73	6.67
Communication	16.02	19.82	27.97	35.58	39.83	47.24	56.63	70.84	88.13	107.63
Trade, Hotels etc.	310.50	345.51	384.33	452.22	529.10	618.83	708.07	827.87	971.70	1146.00
Banking & Insurance	82.65	96.64	111.43	134.13	171.31	210.96	295.15	305.01	399.15	467.88
Real Estate etc.	116.17	126.45	136.13	148.43	164.46	178.06	195.41	214.07	234.89	261.65
Public Admin & Defence	125.11	149.33	179.48	208.58	241.33	271.09	314.41	362.50	400.05	453.09
Other Services	132.20	155.41	175.68	203.52	235.67	279.81	336.15	387.30	439.26	509.91
GDP at Factor Cost	2337.99	2600.30	2948.51	3527.06	4086.62	4778.14	5527.68	6301.82	7231.03	8541.03

Source: CSO, National Accounts Statistics 1996.

Table A1.2 (b)
Gross Domestic Product at Factor Cost - By Industry of Origin
(Rs. billion at 1980-81 prices)

	1985-86	1986-87	1987-88	1988-89	1989-90	1990-91	1991-92	1992-93	1993-94	1994-95
Agricultural Sector	542.18	532.81	534.79	622.14	632.63	656.53	641.18	680.17	702.31	736.88
Agriculture	498.55	489.95	492.58	579.40	585.68	609.91	593.98	633.35	654.93	688.51
Forestry & Logging	31.81	30.90	29.86	29.40	31.95	31.05	30.83	29.50	28.87	29.02
Fishing	11.82	11.96	12.35	13.34	15.00	15.57	16.37	17.32	18.51	19.35
Industry Sector	432.25	463.82	493.67	538.66	593.98	637.00	628.67	654.72	682.51	739.02
Mining & Quarrying	26.23	29.78	30.80	35.42	38.01	42.07	43.62	44.12	45.93	47.91
Manufacturing	303.20	324.45	348.18	378.65	422.85	448.63	432.00	449.89	469.33	511.48
Registered	184.53	195.21	209.02	231.26	263.36	276.57	270.24	278.41	290.52	314.09
Unregistered	118.67	129.24	139.16	147.39	159.49	172.06	161.76	171.48	178.81	197.39
Electricity,Gas &Water	30.99	34.22	36.92	40.80	45.05	47.97	52.58	56.96	61.10	65.99
Construction	71.83	75.37	77.77	83.79	88.07	98.33	100.47	103.75	106.15	113.64
Services Sector	591.23	636.08	674.76	723.81	787.92	829.00	869.98	913.98	975.82	1034.20
Transport, Storage & Com.	79.51	84.83	92.27	98.04	106.63	111.64	117.85	124.32	131.38	142.31
Railways	14.04	15.14	15.76	15.60	16.23	16.77	17.78	17.58	17.46	17.69
Other Transport	53.09	56.51	62.61	67.92	75.01	78.53	82.75	87.72	92.95	100.59
Storage	1.63	1.70	1.69	1.64	1.70	1.77	1.75	1.77	1.83	1.88
Communication	10.75	11.48	12.21	12.88	13.69	14.57	15.57	17.25	19.14	22.15
Trade, Hotels etc.	196.49	208.52	218.01	233.85	252.31	265.80	268.27	286.52	310.26	334.81
Banking & Insurance	58.28	66.92	73.99	86.23	102.69	111.69	131.07	134.67	151.86	158.89
Real Estate etc.	88.80	92.24	94.72	97.93	101.34	105.31	108.65	112.23	116.00	120.48
Public Admin & Defence	80.16	88.07	97.04	103.42	112.14	113.28	115.70	121.70	124.99	128.75
Other Services	87.99	95.50	98.73	104.34	112.81	121.28	128.44	134.54	141.33	148.96
GDP at Factor Cost	1565.66	1632.71	1703.22	1884.61	2014.53	2122.53	2139.83	2248.87	2360.64	2510.10

Source: CSO, National Accounts Statistics 1996.

Table A1.2 (c)
Implicit Price Deflators for GDP at Factor Cost
(1980-81=100)

	1985-86	1986-87	1987-88	1988-89	1989-90	1990-91	1991-92	1992-93	1993-94	1994-95
Agricultural Sector	142.43	154.68	172.74	183.36	200.83	225.43	269.46	283.82	315.74	360.86
Agriculture	140.33	151.86	169.55	179.67	197.12	221.61	268.19	280.90	312.95	356.04
Forestry & Logging	166.17	186.34	206.90	232.24	244.85	266.70	272.14	300.14	320.40	338.11
Fishing	167.01	188.13	217.49	235.53	252.07	292.74	310.45	362.64	407.02	566.56
Industry Sector	152.26	159.00	169.81	185.78	201.51	219.82	245.08	272.41	293.81	323.15
Mining & Quarrying	236.29	228.21	230.03	259.97	271.19	280.13	293.51	330.62	369.02	393.76
Manufacturing	137.78	142.29	151.83	166.02	182.28	198.74	222.93	246.73	263.09	290.30
Registered	139.85	144.74	154.09	168.86	183.66	200.86	225.14	247.16	263.35	287.38
Unregistered	134.57	138.59	148.45	161.56	179.99	195.32	219.23	246.04	262.67	294.96
Electricity,Gas &Water	157.92	162.68	169.77	179.53	193.63	218.14	241.92	282.72	309.12	341.05
Construction	180.25	201.90	226.45	246.77	267.81	291.02	320.95	353.36	388.24	430.83
Services Sector	153.51	163.30	175.83	191.43	205.50	228.94	259.69	283.14	308.29	337.82
Transport, Storage & Com.	177.31	194.94	216.08	243.49	260.07	303.77	347.93	395.00	428.73	460.42
Railways	223.36	248.68	276.40	304.55	343.50	383.60	412.94	480.43	552.58	609.55
Other Transport	171.41	185.98	199.14	224.22	237.10	284.11	332.59	376.93	401.22	430.55
Storage	159.51	164.71	187.57	203.66	228.24	251.41	272.57	289.83	313.11	354.79
Communication	149.02	172.65	229.07	276.24	290.94	324.23	363.71	410.67	460.45	485.91
Trade, Hotels etc.	158.02	165.70	176.29	193.38	209.70	232.82	263.94	288.94	313.19	342.28
Banking & Insurance	141.82	144.41	150.60	155.55	166.82	188.88	225.19	226.49	262.84	294.47
Real Estate etc.	130.82	137.09	143.72	151.57	162.29	169.08	179.85	190.74	202.49	217.17
Public Admin & Defence	156.08	169.56	184.95	201.68	215.20	239.31	271.75	297.86	320.07	351.91
Other Services	150.24	162.73	177.94	195.05	208.91	230.71	261.72	287.87	310.80	342.31
GDP at Factor Cost	149.33	159.26	173.11	187.15	202.86	225.12	258.32	280.22	306.32	340.27

Source: Derived from Tables 1.2(a) and 1.2(b).

Table A1.3
Gross Savings and Investment
(Rs. billion)

	1985-86	1986-87	1987-88	1988-89	1989-90	1990-91	1991-92	1992-93	1993-94	1994
				(At current prices)						
GROSS NATIONAL SAVINGS	561.05	601.71	665.82	839.48	978.98	1169.55	1360.50	1582.88	1688.60	2104.
Households	423.30	469.57	535.69	675.28	788.25	965.79	1046.72	1276.27	1368.22	1584.
Private corporate sector	53.18	52.12	57.90	83.19	116.50	149.40	194.90	198.41	276.66	359.
Public sector	84.57	80.02	72.23	81.01	74.23	54.36	118.88	108.20	43.72	159.
Foreign Savings	73.37	77.28	83.00	124.63	122.97	182.01	40.18	112.60	21.49	84.
GROSS DOMESTIC INVESTMENT	634.42	678.99	748.82	964.11	1101.95	1351.56	1400.68	1695.48	1710.09	2189.
Change in stocks	91.87	58.47	26.88	107.42	74.20	111.52	35.65	108.10	-12.37	58.
GROSS FIXED CAPITAL FORMATION	542.55	620.52	721.94	856.69	1027.75	1240.04	1365.03	1587.38	1722.46	2130.
By Type of Asset:										
Construction	274.53	305.73	347.87	414.45	478.92	583.63	669.32	755.07	821.15	970.2
Machinery & Equipment	268.02	314.79	374.07	442.24	548.83	656.41	695.71	832.31	901.31	1160.3
By Sector:										
Public sector	275.01	332.54	345.71	398.66	438.62	501.76	587.37	601.00	672.01	818.2
Private sector	267.54	287.98	376.23	458.03	589.13	738.28	777.66	986.38	1050.45	1312.3
GDPmp at current prices	2622.43	2929.49	3332.01	3957.82	4568.21	5355.34	6167.99	7053.28	8010.32	9456.1
				(At 1980-81 prices)						
GROSS DOMESTIC INVESTMENT	398.47	401.71	417.86	495.77	506.84	568.85	506.33	568.70	535.63	641.5
Change in Stocks	68.73	41.74	18.31	68.07	42.01	57.94	15.87	44.43	-6.26	19.5
GROSS FIXED CAPITAL FORMATION	329.74	359.97	399.55	427.70	464.83	510.91	490.46	524.27	541.89	622.0
By Type of Asset:										
Construction	139.60	145.90	150.45	164.23	170.69	187.57	191.91	197.14	196.46	213.7
Machinery & Equipment	190.14	214.07	249.10	263.47	294.14	323.34	298.55	327.13	345.43	408.3
By Sector:										
Public sector	170.80	192.31	186.60	195.39	196.51	206.01	210.12	194.98	207.65	236.6
Private sector	158.94	167.66	212.95	232.31	268.32	304.90	280.34	329.29	334.24	385.3

Source: CSO, National Accounts Statistics 1996.

Table A1.4
Disposable Income and Its Uses
(Rs. billion at current prices)

	1985-86	1986-87	1987-88	1988-89	1989-90	1990-91	1991-92	1992-93	1993-94	1994-95
GDPmp	2622.4	2929.5	3332.0	3957.8	4568.2	5355.3	6168.0	7053.3	8010.3	9456.2
Net Factor Income from abroad	-19.0	-26.2	-32.1	-38.1	-48.8	-67.4	-93.9	-99.1	-125.6	-122.6
Other current transfers	27.0	29.8	35.0	38.4	38.0	37.1	92.8	80.3	120.0	194.7
Disposable income	2630.4	2933.1	3334.9	3958.1	4557.4	5325.1	6166.8	7034.5	8004.8	9528.2
Private disposable income	2254.1	2506.8	2854.3	3403.8	3941.2	4653.0	5353.4	6140.3	7064.3	8355.8
Public disposable income	376.3	426.3	480.7	554.3	616.3	672.2	813.5	894.2	940.5	1172.4
Gross National Savings	561.1	601.7	665.8	839.5	979.0	1169.6	1360.5	1582.9	1688.6	2104.3
Private savings	476.5	521.7	593.6	758.5	904.7	1115.2	1241.6	1474.7	1644.9	1944.4
Public savings	84.6	80.0	72.2	81.0	74.2	54.4	118.9	108.2	43.7	159.9
Final Consumption	2069.4	2331.4	2669.1	3118.6	3578.4	4155.6	4806.3	5451.6	6316.2	7423.9
Private Consumption	1777.6	1985.1	2260.7	2645.3	3036.4	3537.8	4111.8	4665.7	5419.4	6411.4
Public Consumption	291.7	346.3	408.4	473.3	542.0	617.8	694.6	786.0	896.8	1012.5

Source : CSO, National Accounts Statistics 1996; World Bank Staff estimates.

Table A1.5 (a)
Gross Domestic Investment by Industry of Origin
(Rs. billion at current prices)

	1985-86	1986-87	1987-88	1988-89	1989-90	1990-91	1991-92	1992-93	1993-94	1994-9
Agricultural Sector	82.7	77.3	91.8	99.8	111.1	128.5	147.8	181.2	202.1	230.
Agriculture	70.2	70.5	83.9	90.6	100.3	115.9	133.9	166.2	184.8	209.
Forestry & Logging	2.0	2.4	2.6	3.0	3.8	4.6	4.4	4.5	4.8	5.
Fishing	10.5	4.5	5.4	6.3	7.1	8.1	9.4	10.5	12.5	15.
Industry Sector	265.6	265.6	329.2	470.8	454.0	543.4	572.8	765.2	674.6	926.
Mining & Quarrying	40.3	44.6	42.2	47.9	63.0	66.3	63.4	65.9	64.3	153.
Manufacturing	142.0	115.4	170.9	298.6	248.6	311.0	303.0	484.5	370.2	510.
Registered	101.3	69.3	118.7	238.1	171.5	223.8	223.1	378.0	259.8	355.8
Unregistered	40.7	46.1	52.2	60.5	77.2	87.1	80.0	106.6	110.4	154.7
Electricity,Gas &Water	70.6	95.1	103.8	113.0	123.4	144.1	189.0	189.8	213.8	233.0
Construction	12.6	10.4	12.4	11.3	18.9	22.1	17.5	24.9	26.2	29.0
Services Sector	263.4	317.7	274.1	315.0	405.8	511.1	562.9	594.2	759.6	854.7
Transport, Storage & Com.	60.4	78.8	80.6	106.4	128.2	143.3	161.6	197.5	238.4	261.2
Railways	16.7	22.9	21.5	26.4	26.4	30.8	33.2	49.2	55.8	59.6
Other Transport	34.1	44.6	44.0	57.9	73.6	83.3	95.8	97.8	124.4	128.9
Storage	0.6	0.7	0.8	0.8	0.9	0.7	0.5	0.5	0.6	0.6
Communication	9.1	10.6	14.3	21.4	27.3	28.6	32.1	50.0	57.5	72.1
Trade, Hotels etc.	73.5	78.2	17.1	3.0	56.0	87.9	75.1	30.1	95.5	110.0
Banking & Insurance	5.5	8.7	14.8	21.1	23.6	30.9	49.8	47.3	68.2	70.5
Real Estate etc.	68.8	80.9	90.1	101.6	118.1	147.4	168.2	194.1	218.1	245.8
Public Admin & Defence	48.0	55.0	55.1	62.2	55.8	75.1	82.3	95.2	108.4	128.5
Other Services	7.3	16.2	16.5	20.8	24.2	26.5	26.0	30.1	31.2	38.7
Gross Domestic Investment	611.7	660.6	695.2	885.6	971.0	1183.0	1283.5	1540.5	1636.3	2011.1
Memo Items										
Gross Domestic Investment [a]	581.7	611.6	764.6	969.7	1138.2	1448.5	1440.2	1631.8	1733.3	2384.1
Errors & Omissions	-52.8	-67.4	15.7	5.6	36.2	96.9	39.6	-63.7	23.2	194.9
Gross Domestic Investment (unadjusted) [b]	634.4	679.0	748.8	964.1	1102.0	1351.6	1400.7	1695.5	1710.1	2189.2

a. Refers to CSO's savings-based estimate of investment.
b. Refers to Gross Capital Formation unadjusted for errors and omissions, which is CSO's direct estimate of investment based on physical flows.

Source : CSO, National Accounts Statistics 1996.

Table A1.5 (b)
Gross Domestic Investment by Industry of Origin
(Rs. billion at 1980-81 prices)

	1985-86	1986-87	1987-88	1988-89	1989-90	1990-91	1991-92	1992-93	1993-94	1994-95
Agricultural Sector	46.5	43.6	47.8	47.3	47.9	50.8	52.1	58.7	61.2	64.3
Agriculture	43.3	40.1	44.1	43.5	43.5	45.9	47.3	53.7	55.9	58.6
Forestry & Logging	1.2	1.2	1.2	1.3	1.5	1.7	1.4	1.2	1.2	1.2
Fishing	2.0	2.2	2.4	2.6	2.9	3.1	3.4	3.8	4.1	4.5
Industry Sector	174.3	158.6	192.2	258.8	220.2	242.3	218.5	276.6	223.8	288.4
Mining & Quarrying	26.5	27.2	24.3	25.5	29.9	28.4	23.8	22.2	19.6	48.2
Manufacturing	94.1	67.4	101.6	170.1	122.6	141.9	118.2	180.8	124.8	161.0
Registered	69.2	41.5	74.4	141.0	88.3	106.4	91.1	145.8	91.2	116.2
Unregistered	24.9	25.9	27.2	29.1	34.4	35.6	27.2	34.9	33.5	44.8
Electricity,Gas &Water	45.7	57.3	58.6	56.6	57.7	61.5	69.3	64.3	69.9	69.5
Construction	8.0	6.6	7.7	6.7	10.0	10.4	7.1	9.3	9.6	9.7
Services Sector	165.8	181.9	136.8	141.5	174.5	205.8	196.6	186.0	231.5	239.5
Transport, Storage & Com.	38.8	48.4	45.7	53.8	58.8	60.4	59.9	67.6	79.1	80.8
Railways	9.2	12.4	10.0	11.1	9.8	10.6	10.0	14.4	15.7	15.5
Other Transport	23.6	29.6	27.4	31.9	36.5	37.9	38.6	37.0	45.6	44.2
Storage	0.3	0.4	0.3	0.3	0.4	0.3	0.1	0.1	0.2	0.1
Communication	5.7	6.1	7.9	10.5	12.1	11.7	11.2	16.1	17.6	21.0
Trade, Hotels etc.	53.6	54.1	10.0	-0.5	28.7	43.2	31.4	9.2	34.1	35.7
Banking & Insurance	3.4	5.2	8.8	11.3	11.4	13.7	19.4	16.9	23.4	22.1
Real Estate etc.	34.4	35.9	36.6	38.6	42.3	49.7	50.0	54.1	55.7	57.7
Public Admin & Defence	28.2	29.8	27.4	28.7	23.1	28.4	27.1	28.9	30.2	32.7
Other Services	7.5	8.5	8.4	9.6	10.2	10.3	8.7	9.3	9.1	10.4
Gross Domestic Investment	386.5	384.1	376.8	447.6	442.6	498.9	467.2	521.4	516.5	592.1
Memo Items										
Gross Domestic Investment [a]	366.4	362.6	426.6	498.6	523.2	608.8	520.5	547.7	543.6	698.5
Errors & Omissions	-32.1	-39.1	8.7	2.8	16.4	39.9	14.2	-21.0	8.0	56.9
Gross Domestic Investment (unadjusted) [b]	398.5	401.7	417.9	495.8	506.8	568.9	506.3	568.7	535.6	641.6

a. Refers to CSO's savings-based estimate of investment.
b. Refers to Gross Capital Formation unadjusted for errors and omissions, which is CSO's direct estimate of investment based on physical flows.

Source: CSO, National Accounts Statistics 1996.

Table A1.5 (c)
Investment Deflators by Industry of Use
(1980-81=100)

	1985-86	1986-87	1987-88	1988-89	1989-90	1990-91	1991-92	1992-93	1993-94	1994
Agricultural Sector	177.9	177.6	192.2	210.9	231.9	253.2	283.5	308.6	330.3	35!
Agriculture	162.2	175.6	190.1	208.5	230.3	252.3	283.1	309.4	330.8	35&
Forestry & Logging	166.9	190.3	206.5	234.1	252.3	271.4	316.4	362.1	391.0	42(
Fishing	524.5	205.9	223.3	239.8	246.0	256.4	274.9	279.7	304.4	34(
Industry Sector	152.4	167.5	171.3	181.9	206.2	224.3	262.2	276.6	301.4	321
Mining & Quarrying	151.9	163.8	173.3	188.0	210.7	233.0	266.2	296.2	328.2	319
Manufacturing	150.9	171.2	168.2	175.6	202.7	219.1	256.4	268.1	296.8	317
Registered	146.4	167.1	159.5	168.9	194.3	210.5	245.0	259.2	284.8	306
Unregistered	163.4	177.9	192.1	207.9	224.4	244.9	294.5	305.1	329.3	345
Electricity, Gas & Water	154.7	166.0	177.3	199.7	213.9	234.2	272.6	295.1	305.9	335
Construction	157.9	157.5	160.8	169.5	190.2	212.8	244.8	267.8	273.3	299
Services Sector	158.9	174.6	200.4	222.7	232.6	248.3	286.3	319.4	328.2	356
Transport, Storage & Com.	155.9	162.6	176.3	197.8	218.2	237.2	269.6	292.2	301.5	323
Railways	181.9	184.5	214.3	237.4	269.1	291.8	332.7	342.6	355.3	383
Other Transport	144.5	150.8	160.3	181.4	201.8	219.8	248.0	264.2	273.0	291
Storage	190.3	200.0	229.4	253.3	251.4	255.6	353.8	384.6	381.3	430
Communication	159.5	173.4	181.2	204.2	225.7	243.9	287.0	310.6	326.6	343
Trade, Hotels etc.	137.1	144.6	171.1	-592.0	194.9	203.4	239.2	327.6	280.3	308.
Banking & Insurance	160.2	165.8	168.3	186.2	206.7	225.1	256.1	279.3	291.7	318.
Real Estate etc.	200.2	225.3	246.3	263.3	279.4	296.2	336.4	359.0	391.3	425.
Public Admin & Defence	170.3	184.4	200.7	216.9	241.3	264.6	303.5	328.8	359.2	393
Other Services	97.3	191.4	198.1	216.6	236.7	256.7	297.9	323.1	343.6	373.
Gross Domestic Investment	158.2	172.0	184.5	197.9	219.4	237.1	274.7	295.5	316.8	339.
Memo Items										
Gross Domestic Investment [a]	158.7	168.7	179.2	194.5	217.5	237.9	276.7	298.0	318.9	341.
Gross Domestic Investment (unadjusted) [b]	159.2	169.0	179.2	194.5	217.4	237.6	276.6	298.1	319.3	341.

a. Refers to CSO's savings-based estimate of investment.

b. Refers to Gross Capital Formation unadjusted for errors and omissions, which is CSO's direct estimate of investment based on physical flows.

Source : CSO, National Accounts Statistics 1996.

Table A1.6 (a)
Gross Domestic Investment in Public Sector
(Rs. billion at current prices)

	1985-86	1986-87	1987-88	1988-89	1989-90	1990-91	1991-92	1992-93	1993-94
Agricultural Sector	28.17	28.95	33.03	34.42	33.54	36.28	36.53	41.75	50.05
Agriculture	26.21	26.67	30.57	31.62	29.89	31.93	32.30	37.50	45.56
Forestry & Logging	1.93	2.23	2.42	2.78	3.62	4.33	4.20	4.23	4.47
Fishing	0.03	0.05	0.04	0.02	0.03	0.02	0.03	0.02	0.02
Industry Sector	166.28	188.05	192.84	204.32	235.48	277.65	324.88	309.12	292.68
Mining & Quarrying	38.89	42.09	40.96	47.59	62.46	65.04	61.92	63.76	62.99
Manufacturing	57.43	55.87	50.73	51.72	54.66	71.45	85.08	82.95	49.41
Electricity,Gas &Water	67.23	89.57	98.81	105.62	117.55	137.69	174.10	158.41	174.99
Construction	2.73	0.52	2.34	-0.61	0.81	3.47	3.78	4.00	5.29
Services Sector	99.72	124.42	104.72	154.91	186.64	207.58	203.96	276.22	344.76
Transport, Storage & Com.	34.28	50.78	46.40	61.50	75.92	79.58	92.16	123.75	157.55
Railways	16.70	22.88	21.52	26.37	26.43	30.78	33.17	49.20	55.81
Other Transport	8.10	16.78	10.12	13.48	21.86	19.73	26.67	24.39	43.95
Storage	0.42	0.56	0.46	0.27	0.36	0.46	0.20	0.18	0.30
Communication	9.06	10.56	14.30	21.38	27.27	28.61	32.12	49.98	57.49
Trade, Hotels etc.	1.20	-2.06	-22.61	-2.98	17.48	14.54	-16.67	12.73	32.27
Banking & Insurance	3.16	4.92	9.49	14.82	16.99	17.98	23.59	18.04	19.28
Real Estate etc.	5.08	6.51	6.70	7.57	7.32	6.16	8.66	10.19	11.25
Public Admin & Defence	48.03	55.01	55.08	62.24	55.78	75.13	82.27	95.16	108.36
Other Services	7.97	9.26	9.66	11.76	13.15	14.19	13.95	16.35	16.05
Gross Domestic Investment	294.17	341.42	330.59	393.65	455.66	521.51	565.37	627.09	687.49

Source : CSO, National Accounts Statistics 1996.

Table A1.6 (b)
Gross Domestic Investment in Public Sector
(Rs. billion at 1980-81 prices)

	1985-86	1986-87	1987-88	1988-89	1989-90	1990-91	1991-92	1992-93	1993-94
Agricultural Sector	16.37	15.44	15.76	14.82	13.01	13.13	11.43	11.82	13.17
Agriculture	15.20	14.25	14.58	13.62	11.56	11.53	10.13	10.55	11.99
Forestry & Logging	1.15	1.16	1.16	1.19	1.43	1.59	1.29	1.27	1.17
Fishing	0.02	0.03	0.02	0.01	0.02	0.01	0.01	0.00	0.01
Industry Sector	110.27	114.65	110.85	105.93	111.40	120.36	120.84	101.13	101.57
Mining & Quarrying	25.62	25.67	23.59	24.76	29.63	27.85	22.19	20.63	22.79
Manufacturing	39.65	34.68	30.36	28.60	26.49	32.49	34.18	24.82	22.05
Electricity,Gas &Water	43.35	53.85	55.59	52.65	54.81	58.56	63.35	54.58	55.69
Construction	1.65	0.45	1.31	-0.08	0.47	1.46	1.12	1.10	1.04
Services Sector	58.40	69.02	50.73	72.20	81.98	82.39	77.85	82.03	92.91
Transport, Storage & Com.	20.43	29.77	24.34	28.90	32.74	31.14	33.46	38.44	47.86
Railways	9.18	12.40	10.04	11.11	9.82	10.55	10.31	13.90	13.83
Other Transport	5.35	10.99	6.21	7.22	10.69	8.68	10.66	8.64	15.99
Storage	0.22	0.29	0.20	0.10	0.15	0.18	0.10	0.09	0.11
Communication	5.68	6.09	7.89	10.47	12.08	11.73	12.39	15.81	17.93
Trade, Hotels etc.	0.62	-1.65	-14.53	-1.94	9.56	7.19	0.51	0.48	0.55
Banking & Insurance	1.95	3.02	5.71	8.05	8.26	8.03	9.31	6.61	6.69
Real Estate etc.	2.56	2.99	2.82	2.98	2.69	2.12	2.64	2.87	2.94
Public Admin & Defence	28.21	29.83	27.44	28.70	23.12	28.39	27.20	28.66	30.07
Other Services	4.63	5.06	4.95	5.51	5.61	5.52	4.73	4.97	4.80
Gross Domestic Investment	185.04	199.11	177.34	192.95	206.39	215.88	210.12	194.98	207.65

Source : CSO, National Accounts Statistics 1996.

Table A2.1
Balance of Payments[a]
(US$ million at current prices)

	1985-86	1986-87	1987-88	1988-89	1989-90	1990-91	1991-92	1992-93	1993-94	1994-95
Exports of Goods and Non-Factor Services	12773	13637	16217	18213	21201	23028	23287	23585	28925	34141
Merchandise (fob)	9463	10420	12646	14257	16955	18477	18266	18869	22700	26857
Non-factor Services	3310	3217	3571	3956	4246	4551	5021	4716	6225	7284
Imports of Goods and Non-Factor Services	19422	19962	22843	26843	27934	31485	24879	26825	29433	39450
Merchandise (cif)	17298	17740	19816	23618	24411	27914	21064	23237	23985	31672
Non-factor Services	2124	2222	3027	3225	3523	3571	3815	3588	5448	7778
Trade Balance	-7835	-7320	-7170	-9361	-7456	-9437	-2798	-4368	-1285	-4815
Nonfactor Services Balance	1186	995	544	731	723	980	1206	1128 .	777	-494
Resource Balance	-6649	-6325	-6626	-8630	-6733	-8457	-1592	-3240	-508	-5309
Net Factor Income	-1553	-2046	-2472	-2633	-2928	-3753	-3826	-3422	-4002	-3905
Factor Service Receipts	547	501	446	397	936	1123	758	733	272	1264
Factor Service Payments[b]	2100	2547	2918	3030	3864	4876	4584	4155	4274	5169
Net Current Transfers	2207	2327	2698	2654	2281	2069	3783	2773	3825	6200
Transfer Receipts	2219	2339	2724	2670	2297	2083	3798	2784	3850	6220
Transfer Payments	12	12	26	16	16	14	15	11	25	20
Current Account Balance	-5995	-6044	-6400	-8609	-7380	-10141	-1635	-3889	-685	-3014
Foreign Investment	160	208	181	287	350	165	158	587	4110	4895
Direct Foreign Investment	160	208	181	287	350	165	150	341	620	1314
Portfolio Investment	0	0	0	0	0	0	8	246	3490	3581
Official Grant Aid	359	403	410	406	500	462	461	363	370	390
Net Medium & Long-Term Capital[c]	2120	2490	3417	3846	3074	2653	4319	1636	1716	278
Gross Disbursements	5009	6605	7304	8123	7332	6586	7178	6587	6824	5938
Principal Repayments	1310	2290	1895	1949	1963	2397	2569	2949	4169	4814
Other LT Inflows (NRI)	1579	1825	1992	2328	2295	1536	290	2001	940	847
Capital Flows NEI	2588	1837	1144	1520	1320	2525	-982	-961	2086	3462
Net Short-Term Capital	686	588	727	685	1143	1043	-1474	-730	-2714	1463
Others[d]	474	-102	-731	141	167	-1193	-1240	-878	-745	-1050
Capital flows n.e.i.[e]	1428	1351	1148	694	10	2675	1732	647	5545	3049
Overall Balance	812	720	744	-222	158	-2799	2611	-263	8537	6858
Net IMF Credit	-264	-648	-1082	-1210	-1008	1028	773	1290	190	-1174
Change in Reserves (Excl. Gold) (- = increase)	-548	-72	338	1432	850	1771	-3384	-1027	-8727	-5684
Memorandum Items:										
End of Year Gross Reserves (Excl. Gold)	6657	6729	6391	4959	4109	2338	5722	6749	15476	21160
Reserves in Months of Imports	4.6	4.6	3.9	2.5	2.0	1.0	3.3	3.5	7.7	8.0
Current Account Deficit / GDP	2.8%	2.6%	2.5%	3.1%	2.7%	3.4%	0.6%	1.6%	0.3%	1.0%
Debt Service Ratio[f]	22.7%	32.0%	29.4%	28.0%	27.6%	30.1%	26.9%	27.0%	25.6%	25.3%

a. BOP based on revised treatment of non-custom imports as adopted by GOI from 1990-91 onwards.
b. Includes interest on military debt to FSU and returns on foreign investments.
c. Excluding non-resident deposits, shown below under Other LT Inflows (NRI).
d. Corresponds to bilateral balance or servicing of the Russia debt from 1990-91 onwards.
e. Residual item including reserve valuation changes, rupee trade imbalance, etc.
f. As proportion of gross current receipts.

Source: Government of India; Reserve Bank of India; Ministry of Commerce; Ministry of Finance, Economic Survey, various issues; World Bank Staff estimates.

Table A2.2 (a)
Merchandise Exports
(US$ million at current prices)

	1985-86	1986-87	1987-88	1988-89	1989-90	1990-91	1991-92	1992-93	1993-94	1994-95
Primary Exports	3152	3279	3287	3254	3853	4354	4189	3935	5002	5242
Fish	334	421	411	435	412	535	588	602	813.5	1127
Rice	160	154	261	229	256	257	308	337	410.3	384
Cashews	184	256	243	191	221	249	276	259	334.1	397
Coffee	217	232	202	203	208	140	135	130	174.1	335
Tea	511	451	463	421	550	596	494	337	337.6	311
Spices	227	218	260	190	170	133	161	136	181.4	195
Iron Ore	473	428	427	465	557	584	585	381	438	413
Other Primary	1046	1118	1020	1121	1478	1859	1641	1753	2313	2080
Manufactured Exports	5639	6457	8797	10693	12715	13781	13773	14607	17233	21088
Chemicals	407	456	618	890	1288	1176	1591	1378	1813.2	2434
Leather Manufactures	629	721	964	1051	1170	1448	1276	1278	1299.6	1611
Textiles	860	994	1407	1312	1598	2266	2164	2153	2536.4	3297
Garments	872	1041	1403	1452	1936	2235	2211	2394	2585.9	3282
Gems & Jewellery	1228	1622	2015	3033	3179	2923	2753	3073	3995.2	4501
Engineering Goods	779	886	1141	1558	1967	2157	2246	2458	3023.3	3486
Petroleum Products	417	321	500	349	418	522	417	476	398	440
Other Manufactures [a]	447	416	750	1049	1159	1053	1115	1398	1582	2039
TOTAL EXPORTS (Commerce) [b]	8791	9736	12085	13948	16569	18136	17962	18542	22235	26330
Statistical Discrepancy	672	684	561	310	387	341	304	327	465	527
TOTAL EXPORTS (B.O.P.)	9463	10420	12646	14257	16955	18477	18266	18869	22700	26857

a. Including unclassified exports.
b. Net of crude petroleum exports.

Source: Ministry of Commerce (D.G.C.I.S); Reserve Bank of India; Ministry of Finance, Economic Survey, various issues; World Bank Staff estimates.

Table A2.2 (b)
Merchandise Exports
(US$ million at 1980-81 prices)

	1985-86	1986-87	1987-88	1988-89	1989-90	1990-91	1991-92	1992-93	1993-94	1994-95
Primary Exports	3078	3184	3099	3220	3986	4499	4368	4530	5619	5276
Fish	325	357	354	386	424	480	571	571	424	778
Rice	96	97	152	137	165	197	265	227	300	348
Cashews	204	236	229	202	266	305	288	344	404	441
Coffee	295	231	317	291	437	339	343	445	437	453
Tea	471	418	479	451	487	463	503	390	487	353
Spices	153	138	114	122	115	110	115	104	115	137
Iron Ore	497	468	461	541	578	530	490	344	578	428
Other Primary	1037	1239	994	1090	1513	2075	1793	2106	2874	2339
Manufactured Exports	5875	6698	8414	9184	10418	11303	12678	14142	17009	18413
Chemicals	377	463	542	847	1182	1585	2157	1333	1724	2269
Leather Manufactures	781	770	899	958	962	980	957	1071	1151	1413
Textiles	669	757	1074	915	1123	1329	1873	2513	2267	2869
Garments	837	917	1142	1137	1485	1641	1759	1823	1807	2177
Gems & Jewellery	1021	1419	1602	2082	1909	1573	1646	2082	2641	2983
Engineering Goods	952	978	1391	1728	2221	2470	2514	3229	5018	4457
Petroleum Products	535	645	986	694	784	917	980	1242	1336	1074
Other Manufactures [a]	704	749	777	823	752	808	793	850	2401	2245
TOTAL EXPORTS (Commerce) [b]	8954	9883	11513	12403	14404	15802	17046	18673	22628	23689
Statistical Discrepancy	684	695	535	275	336	298	289	329	473	474
TOTAL EXPORTS (B.O.P.)	9638	10577	12048	12679	14740	16100	17335	19001	23101	24163

a. Including unclassified exports.
b. Net of crude petroleum exports.

Source: Ministry of Commerce (D.G.C.I.S); Reserve Bank of India; Ministry of Finance, Economic Survey, various issues;
World Bank Staff estimates.

Table A2.2 (c)
Export Unit Value Indices
(US$ terms: 1980-81 = 100)

	1985-86	1986-87	1987-88	1988-89	1989-90	1990-91	1991-92	1992-93	1993-94	1994-95
Primary Exports	102.4	103.0	106.1	101.1	96.7	96.8	95.9	86.9	89.0	99.4
Fish	102.9	118.1	116.1	112.7	97.2	111.5	103.1	105.5	191.7	144.7
Rice	167.3	159.0	172.1	167.4	155.6	130.5	116.3	148.7	136.8	110.4
Cashews	90.2	108.6	106.3	94.5	82.9	81.7	95.8	75.1	82.7	90.1
Coffee	73.4	100.4	63.7	69.7	47.7	41.4	39.5	29.2	39.9	74.1
Tea	108.6	107.9	96.7	93.3	113.0	128.8	98.2	86.6	69.3	87.9
Spices	148.1	158.2	228.0	155.2	147.3	121.3	139.3	130.4	157.2	142.8
Iron Ore	95.1	91.4	92.7	85.9	96.4	110.2	119.4	110.9	75.8	96.5
Other Primary	100.8	90.3	102.6	102.9	97.7	89.6	91.5	83.2	80.5	88.9
Manufactured Exports	96.0	96.4	104.6	116.4	122.1	121.9	108.6	103.3	101.3	114.5
Chemicals	107.9	98.4	113.9	105.0	108.9	74.2	73.8	103.4	105.2	107.3
Leather Manufactures	80.6	93.6	107.2	109.8	121.7	147.9	133.4	119.3	112.9	114.0
Textiles	128.7	131.4	131.0	143.4	142.3	170.5	115.5	85.7	111.9	114.9
Garments	104.2	113.5	122.9	127.7	130.4	136.2	125.7	131.3	143.1	150.8
Gems & Jewellery	120.3	114.3	125.7	145.7	166.5	185.8	167.3	147.6	151.3	150.9
Engineering Goods	81.8	90.6	82.0	90.1	88.6	87.3	89.4	76.1	60.3	78.2
Petroleum Products	77.9	49.8	50.8	50.3	53.4	57.0	42.5	38.3	29.8	40.9
Other Manufactures [a]	63.5	55.6	96.4	127.4	154.0	130.3	140.5	164.5	65.9	90.8
TOTAL EXPORTS (Commerce) [b]	98.2	98.5	105.0	112.4	115.0	114.8	105.4	99.3	98.3	111.2
Statistical Discrepancy	98.2	98.5	105.0	112.4	115.0	114.8	105.4	99.3	98.3	111.2
TOTAL EXPORTS (B.O.P.)	98.2	98.5	105.0	112.4	115.0	114.8	105.4	99.3	98.3	111.2

a. Including unclassified exports.
b. Net of crude petroleum exports.

Source: Ministry of Commerce (D.G.C.I.S); Reserve Bank of India; Ministry of Finance, Economic Survey, various issues; World Bank Staff estimates.

Table A2.3 (a)
Merchandise Imports
(US$ million at current prices)

	1985-86	1986-87	1987-88	1988-89	1989-90	1990-91	1991-92	1992-93	1993-94	1994-95
Food	1321	1068	1292	1203	714	690	424	702	550	1464
Foodgrains	90	37	25	437	227	102	70	334	93	29
Edible Oils	600	479	709	503	127	182	101	58	53	199
Others	631	552	557	263	361	407	253	311	404	1236
Other Consumer Goods	452	594	600	700	800	851	634	782	680	790
P.O.L	4054	2187	3148	2938	3766	6028	5364	5919	5753	5928
Crude Petroleum [a]	3013	1672	2395	1891	2455	3423	3194	3711	3468	3428
Petroleum Products	1041	515	753	1047	1311	2605	2170	2208	2285	2500
Capital Goods [b]	3503	5073	5064	4803	5304	5833	4233	3743	5312	6366
Intermediate: PRIMARY	2156	2474	2997	3800	4488	4653	3801	4553	4533	4296
Fertilizer Raw Material	313	218	243	301	329	348	309	279	194	288
Gems	899	1170	1538	1984	2546	2082	1957	2442	2634	1630
Other	944	1087	1217	1515	1613	2223	1534	1832	1705	2378
Intermediate: MANUFACTURES	4471	4316	4054	6053	6147	6018	5673	6183	6479	9810
Fertilizer Manufactures	860	387	132	341	737	636	645	699	632	764
Iron & Steel	1140	1134	982	1341	1383	1177	799	779	795	2438
Non-Ferrous Metals	443	324	444	544	752	614	341	395	479	941
Others	2028	2470	2496	3827	3275	3591	3888	4311	4574	5668
TOTAL IMPORTS (Commerce) [a]	15957	15712	17156	19497	21219	24073	20128	21882	23307	28654
Statistical Discrepancy	1341	2028	2660	4121	3192	3841	936	1355	678	3018
TOTAL IMPORTS [a]	17298	17740	19816	23618	24411	27914	21064	23237	23985	31672

a. Net of crude oil exports.
b. 1987-88 onwards Capital Goods includes Project Goods.

Source: Ministry of Commerce (D.G.C.I.S); Reserve Bank of India; Ministry of Finance, <u>Economic Survey</u>, various issues;
World Bank Staff estimates.

Table A2.3 (b)
Merchandise Imports
(US$ million at 1980-81 prices)

	1985-86	1986-87	1987-88	1988-89	1989-90	1990-91	1991-92	1992-93	1993-94	1994-95
Food	1454	1527	1710	1968	865	807	445	1014	615	1365
Foodgrains	113	56	35	1021	310	126	77	662	165	33
Edible Oils	564	770	980	539	160	259	111	51	56	171
Others	777	701	695	409	395	422	256	302	394	1162
Other Consumer Goods	471	567	513	555	643	647	472	558	486	545
P.O.L	5240	5053	5944	6734	7272	8287	9409	11391	12067	11784
Crude Petroleum [a]	3956	4041	4630	4651	5089	5405	6264	7637	8047	7141
Petroleum Products	1285	1012	1314	2083	2183	2882	3145	3755	4020	4642
Capital Goods [b]	3875	4703	4203	3702	4142	4311	2610	2594	3692	4269
Intermediate: PRIMARY	2461	3038	2419	2841	3363	3314	2646	3071	3099	2821
Fertilizer Raw Material	140	197	161	178	157	174	151	147	121	169
Gems	977	1127	1262	1511	1965	1521	1400	1673	1810	1080
Other	1344	1714	996	1151	1242	1619	1095	1251	1168	1572
Intermediate: MANUFACTURES	5468	4644	3529	4728	5057	4797	4335	4817	4958	6871
Fertilizer Manufactures	1163	813	320	472	876	808	830	1117	989	770
Iron & Steel	1319	1110	874	1275	1162	936	622	581	594	1759
Non-Ferrous Metals	642	481	540	553	775	599	325	361	440	833
Others	2344	2240	1795	2428	2244	2454	2557	2758	2935	3510
TOTAL IMPORTS (Commerce) [a]	18970	19531	18318	20528	21342	22163	19916	23446	24918	27655
Statistical Discrepancy	1594	2521	2840	4339	3210	3536	926	1452	725	2913
TOTAL IMPORTS [a]	20564	22052	21158	24867	24552	25699	20842	24898	25643	30568

a. Net of crude oil exports.
b. 1987-88 onwards Capital Goods includes Project Goods.

Source: Ministry of Commerce (D.G.C.I.S); Reserve Bank of India; Ministry of Finance, Economic Survey, various issues;
World Bank Staff estimates.

Table A2.3 (c)
Import Unit Value Indices
(US$ Terms: 1980-81 = 100)

	1985-86	1986-87	1987-88	1988-89	1989-90	1990-91	1991-92	1992-93	1993-94	1994-95
Food	90.8	70.0	75.5	61.1	82.6	85.5	95.3	69.2	89.4	107.2
Foodgrains	79.6	66.1	72.0	42.8	73.1	80.6	91.4	50.4	56.1	89.4
Edible Oils	106.4	62.2	72.4	93.4	79.3	70.1	90.4	114.0	94.5	116.5
Others	81.1	78.8	80.2	64.5	91.4	96.4	98.6	102.9	102.6	106.4
Other Consumer Goods	95.9	104.8	117.1	126.1	124.5	131.5	134.3	140.2	139.8	144.9
P.O.L	77.4	43.3	53.0	43.6	51.8	72.7	57.0	52.0	47.7	50.3
Crude Petroleum	76.2	41.4	51.7	40.7	48.2	63.3	51.0	48.6	43.1	48.0
Petroleum Products	81.0	50.9	57.3	50.3	60.1	90.4	69.0	58.8	56.8	53.8
Capital Goods	90.4	107.9	120.5	129.7	128.1	135.3	162.2	144.3	143.9	149.1
Intermediate: PRIMARY	87.6	81.5	123.9	133.8	133.4	140.4	143.6	148.3	146.3	152.3
Fertilizer Raw Material	223.6	110.5	150.7	168.7	209.6	200.0	204.7	190.1	160.9	170.5
Gems	92.0	103.8	121.9	131.3	129.6	136.9	139.8	146.0	145.6	150.9
Other	70.2	63.4	122.2	131.6	129.9	137.3	140.2	146.4	146.0	151.3
Intermediate: MANUFACTURES	81.8	92.9	114.9	128.0	121.6	125.4	130.9	128.3	130.7	142.8
Fertilizer Manufactures	73.9	47.6	41.3	72.3	84.2	78.7	77.7	62.5	63.9	99.2
Iron & Steel	86.4	102.1	112.3	105.2	119.0	125.7	128.4	134.1	133.7	138.6
Non-Ferrous Metals	69.0	67.5	82.3	98.3	97.0	102.5	104.7	109.3	109.0	113.0
Others	86.5	110.3	139.1	157.6	145.9	146.3	152.1	156.3	155.8	161.5
TOTAL IMPORTS (Commerce)	84.1	80.4	93.7	95.0	99.4	108.6	101.1	93.3	93.5	103.6
Statistical Discrepancy	84.1	80.4	93.7	95.0	99.4	108.6	101.1	93.3	93.5	103.6
TOTAL IMPORTS	84.1	80.4	93.7	95.0	99.4	108.6	101.1	93.3	93.5	103.6

Source: Ministry of Commerce (D.G.C.I.S); Reserve Bank of India; Ministry of Finance, Economic Survey, various issues;
World Bank Staff estimates.

Table A2.4
Invisibles on Current Account
(US$ million)

	1985-86	1986-87	1987-88	1988-89	1989-90	1990-91	1991-92	1992-93	1993-94	1994-95
GROSS RECEIPTS	6076	6057	6741	7023	7479	7757	9577	8233	10347	14768
Non-Factor Services of which:	3310	3217	3571	3956	4246	4551	5021	4716	6225	7284
Transport	494	538	680	898	907	983	939	982	2327	1460
Travel	972	1256	1431	1419	1433	1456	1977	2098	2075	2325
Others	1844	1423	1460	1639	1906	2112	2105	1636	1823	3499
Factor Income	547	501	446	397	936	1123	758	733	272	1264
Current Transfers [a]	2219	2339	2724	2670	2297	2083	3798	2784	3850	6220
GROSS PAYMENTS	4236	4781	5971	6271	7403	8461	8414	7754	9747	12967
Non-Factor Services of which:	2124	2222	3027	3225	3523	3571	3815	3588	5448	7778
Transport [b]	667	585	870	1027	1115	1093	1289	1485	2250	3016
Travel	336	290	376	405	403	392	465	385	750	1205
Others	1121	1347	1781	1793	2005	2086	2061	1718	2448	3557
Factor Income	2100	2547	2918	3030	3864	4876	4584	4155	4274	5169
Current Transfers	12	12	26	16	16	14	15	11	25	20
NET RECEIPTS	1840	1277	770	752	76	-704	1163	479	600	1801
Non-Factor Services of which:	1186	995	544	731	723	980	1206	1128	777	-494
Transport	-173	-47	-190	-129	-208	-110	-350	-503	77	-1556
Travel	636	966	1055	1014	1030	1064	1512	1713	1325	1120
Others	723	76	-321	-154	-99	26	44	-82	-625	-58
Factor Income	-1553	-2046	-2472	-2633	-2928	-3753	-3826	-3422	-4002	-3905
Current Transfers	2207	2327	2698	2654	2281	2069	3783	2773	3825	6200

a. Excluding foreign grants, and including the Bhopal settlement in 1988-89.
b. Excluding freight included in c.i.f value of merchandise imports.

Source: Ministry of Commerce (D.G.C.I.S); Reserve Bank of India; Ministry of Finance, <u>Economic Survey</u>, various issues;
World Bank Staff estimates.

Table A2.5
Decomposition of Recent Export Growth
(US$ million at current prices - annual averages)

	1983-84 88-89	1989-90 94-95	Increase	Contribution to Growth (percent)
Manufactured Exports	7039	15533	8494	87.3
Consumption goods	4592	9527	4935	50.7
Leather	730	1347	617	6.3
Gems (gross)	1699	3404	1705	17.5
Garments	1052	2441	1389	14.3
Textiles	1111	2336	1225	12.6
Investment goods [a]	992	2556	1565	16.1
Intermediate goods	1456	3449	1994	20.5
Chemicals	515	1613	1098	11.3
Petroleum Prod.	358	445	87	0.9
Others [b]	582	1391	809	8.3
Primary Exports	3195	4429	1235	12.7
Fish	379	680	300	3.1
Rice	176	326	150	1.5
Cashews	195	289	94	1.0
Coffee	201	187	-14	-0.1
Tea	499	438	-61	-0.6
Spices	197	163	-34	-0.4
Iron Ore	428	493	65	0.7
Other Primary	1119	1854	735	7.6
TOTAL EXPORTS (Customs) [c]	10234	19962	9728	100.0
Discrepancy	707	392	-315	
TOTAL EXPORTS (BOP) [c]	10941	20354	9413	
Memo:				
Gems (Net) [d]	445	1189	744	

a. Refers to engineering goods.
b. Including unclassified exports.
c. Total exports, f.o.b., net of crude oil.
d. Exports less imports of gems and jewellery.

Source: Ministry of Commerce, (D.G.C.I.S.); Reserve Bank of India.

Table A3.1(a)
External Debt Summary: Debt Outstanding and Disbursed
(US$ million at current prices)

	1983-84	1984-85	1985-86	1986-87	1987-88	1988-89	1989-90	1990-91	1991-92	1992-93	1993-94	19
A. Public & Publicly Guar. LT	22769	24355	30284	37175	44379	48040	62775	69328	71875	77479	81668	8
1. Official Creditors	18983	19236	22729	26396	30394	31221	43659	48429	49512	54018	56422	6
a. Multilateral	9801	10462	12400	14268	16588	18060	19665	21768	23964	26130	27826	3
aa. of which IBRD	1779	1688	2396	3475	4661	5590	6614	7685	8459	9067	9870	1
ab. of which IDA	7820	8545	9750	10529	11615	12019	12521	13312	14203	15339	15978	1
b. Bilateral [a]	9182	8774	10329	12129	13806	13161	23994	26661	25548	27888	28596	3
2. Private Creditors	3786	5119	7555	10779	13985	16819	19116	20899	22363	23461	25245	2
a. Commercial Banks	3228	3933	5728	7986	10934	13332	15076	16666	16576	17464	18901	1
b. Suppliers Credits	96	466	629	805	715	632	539	434	430	588	756	
c. Bonds (including IDB)	30	259	657	1117	1317	1876	2577	2948	4436	4351	4157	
d. Other Private	432	461	541	871	1019	979	924	851	921	1057	1431	
B. Private Non-Guaranteed LT	1185	1341	1497	1388	1652	1473	1551	1488	1545	1205	1770	
C. Total LT DOD (A+B)	23954	25696	31781	38563	46031	49513	64326	70816	73420	78684	83438	8
D. Use of IMF Credit	4713	4456	4832	4768	4023	2573	1566	2623	3451	4799	5040	
E. Short-Term Debt	3338	3672	4358	4946	5673	6358	7501	8544	7070	6340	3626	
F. Total External Debt (C+D+E)	32004	33825	40971	48277	55727	58444	73393	81982	83941	89822	92104	9
Memo item:												
Total NRI Deposits	2809	3265	4915	6595	8616	10482	12368	13953	12926	14523	14498	1

a. Data have been revised from March 1990 to include military debt to the former Soviet Union amounting to about $10.0 billion as of March 1990,

$11.6 billion as of March 1991, $9.2 billion as of March 1992, $9.7 billion as of March 1993, $9.2 billion as of March 1994, and $8.8 billion as of March 1995.

Source: World Bank, DRS data.

Table A3.1(b)
External Debt Summary: Disbursements
(US$ million at current prices)

	1983-84	1984-85	1985-86	1986-87	1987-88	1988-89	1989-90	1990-91	1991-92	1992-93	1993-94	1994-95
Public & Publicly Guar. LT	3329	3825	4506	6280	6956	7948	7092	6372	6869	6333	5764	5561
Official Creditors	1934	1836	2079	2265	3627	3642	3574	3570	4368	3645	3666	3426
Multilateral	1366	1144	1403	1314	2269	2625	2105	2210	2758	2424	2084	2230
aa. IBRD	471	291	328	641	1295	1716	1445	1219	1231	852	1216	741
of which fast-disbursing	0	0	0	0	0	0	0	0	150	100	300	0
ab. IDA	874	823	1047	656	917	755	566	762	953	1186	669	966
of which fast-disbursing	0	0	0	0	0	0	0	0	155	350	0	260
Bilateral	568	693	675	951	1358	1017	1469	1360	1610	1221	1582	1197
Private Creditors	1395	1989	2427	4015	3329	4306	3518	2802	2501	2688	2098	2134
Commercial banks	1244	1258	1857	3057	3030	3416	2645	2198	612	2200	1391	1358
Suppliers Credits	41	405	193	283	5	16	3	8	77	237	249	590
Bonds (including IDB)	21	232	330	359	116	679	773	586	1644	0	0	0
Other Private	89	94	47	316	178	195	97	10	169	251	458	187
Private Non-Guaranteed LT	407	450	503	325	348	175	240	214	309	254	1060	377
Total LT Disbursements (A+B)	3736	4275	5009	6605	7304	8123	7332	6586	7178	6587	6824	5938
IMF	1376	201	0	0	0	0	0	1754	1233	1623	323	0
Net Short-Term Capital	941	334	686	588	727	685	1143	1043	-1474	-730	-2714	1463
Total Disbursements (C+D+E)	6053	4810	5695	7193	8031	8808	8475	9383	6936	7480	4433	7401

Source: World Bank, DRS data.

Table A3.1(c)
External Debt Summary: Principal Repayments
(US$ million at current prices)

	1983-84	1984-85	1985-86	1986-87	1987-88	1988-89	1989-90	1990-91	1991-92	1992-93	1993-94	199
A. Public & Publicly Guar. LT	825	786	947	1810	1606	1669	1641	2079	2302	2643	3674	4
1. Official Creditors	602	549	656	851	1121	991	1115	1223	1467	1658	2372	2
a. Multilateral	122	131	161	242	509	397	467	609	703	838	1000	1
aa. of which IBRD	87	87	104	174	430	303	352	472	527	634	758	
ab. of which IDA	33	41	53	61	69	81	98	114	141	155	174	
b. Bilateral	480	418	494	609	613	594	648	614	763	820	1372	1
2. Private Creditors	223	237	291	959	485	678	526	856	836	986	1301	1
a. Commercial Banks	154	178	200	773	284	409	278	331	391	545	723	1
b. Suppliers Credits	38	30	47	120	98	96	98	113	82	100	120	
d. Bonds (including IDB)	2	0	0	0	6	14	27	282	244	211	343	
e. Other Private	29	29	44	66	97	159	123	130	119	130	116	
B. Private Non-Guaranteed LT	261	305	363	480	289	280	322	318	273	306	495	
C. Total LT Repayments (A+B)	1086	1091	1310	2290	1895	1949	1963	2397	2575	2949	4169	4
D. IMF Repayments	70	134	264	648	1082	1210	1008	726	460	334	133	1
E. Total LT Repayments (C+D)	1156	1225	1574	2938	2977	3159	2971	3123	3035	3283	4302	59

Note: Historical amortization payments of the Debt Reporting System differ from numbers of the GOI. These discrepancies are currently under review.

Source: World Bank, DRS data.

Table A3.1(d)
External Debt Summary: Net Flows
(US$ million at current prices)

	1983-84	1984-85	1985-86	1986-87	1987-88	1988-89	1989-90	1990-91	1991-92	1992-93	1993-94	1994-95
ublic & Publicly Guar. LT	2504	3039	3559	4470	5350	6279	5451	4293	4567	3690	2091	1182
fficial Creditors	1332	1287	1423	1414	2506	2652	2459	2347	2901	1987	1294	976
Multilateral	1244	1012	1242	1072	1761	2228	1639	1602	2054	1586	1084	1128
aa. of which IBRD	384	203	224	467	865	1414	1094	747	703	219	458	-86
ab. of which IDA	841	782	994	595	848	675	468	648	812	1030	495	772
Bilateral	88	275	181	342	745	423	820	746	847	400	210	-152
rivate Creditors	1172	1752	2136	3056	2844	3628	2992	1946	1666	1703	797	206
Commercial Banks	1090	1080	1657	2284	2746	3007	2367	1867	221	1655	668	227
Suppliers Credits	3	375	146	163	-93	-80	-95	-105	-5	137	130	402
Bonds (including IDB)	19	232	330	359	110	665	746	304	1400	-211	-343	-386
Other Private	60	65	3	250	81	36	-26	-119	49	122	342	-37
rivate Non-Guaranteed LT	146	145	140	-155	59	-105	-82	-104	36	-53	565	-58
otal LT Repayments (A+B)	2650	3184	3699	4315	5409	6174	5369	4189	4602	3637	2656	1125
et IMF Credit	1306	67	-264	-648	-1082	-1210	-1008	1028	773	1290	190	-1174
et Short Debt Flows	941	334	686	588	727	685	1143	1043	-1474	-730	-2714	1463
otal Net Flows (C+D+E)	4897	3585	4121	4255	5054	5649	5504	6260	3901	4197	132	1413
o item:												
NRI Net Flows	938	814	1579	1825	1992	2328	2295	1536	290	2001	940	847

ce: Derived from Tables 3.1(b) and 3.1(c).

Table A3.1(e)
External Debt Summary: Interest Payments
(US$ million at current prices)

	1983-84	1984-85	1985-86	1986-87	1987-88	1988-89	1989-90	1990-91	1991-92	1992-93	1993-94	1994
A. Public & Publicly Guar. LT	786	833	1120	1505	1845	2003	2870	3603	3322	3247	3373	37
1. Official Creditors	432	443	558	694	812	941	1352	1492	1513	1629	1701	18
a. Multilateral	218	239	282	388	479	581	640	738	799	899	943	10
aa. of which IBRD	158	169	209	296	378	474	529	615	647	709	721	7
ab. of which IDA	58	68	71	91	98	98	90	97	101	109	114	1
b. Bilateral	214	204	276	306	332	360	712	754	714	730	757	8
2. Private Creditors	354	390	562	811	1033	1062	1518	2111	1809	1618	1672	19
a. Commercial Banks	305	340	449	634	806	816	1240	1790	1476	1258	1193	13
b. Suppliers Credits	8	8	48	64	67	61	53	43	31	30	37	
c. Bonds (including IDB)	3	3	17	55	85	111	150	207	223	258	365	3
d. Other Private	38	39	48	58	75	74	75	70	79	71	78	
B. Private Non-Guaranteed LT	130	138	154	158	147	127	140	135	126	123	138	
C. Total LT Interest (A+B)	916	971	1274	1663	1992	2130	3010	3738	3448	3370	3511	38
D. IMF Service Charges	277	374	360	317	297	233	184	134	203	271	271	2
E. Interest Paid on ST Debt	261	389	326	356	429	437	570	899	826	399	367	4
F. Total Interest Paid (C+D+E)	1454	1734	1960	2336	2718	2800	3764	4771	4478	4040	4150	45
Memo item:												
Total NRI Interest Payments	243	291	400	524	715	609	1076	1282	1036	918	905	10

Note: Historical interest payments of the Debt Reporting System differ from numbers of the GOI. These discrepancies are currently under review.

Table A3.2
External Reserves
(US$ million)

	Foreign Exchange	SDRs	Reserve Position in the Fund	Reserves excluding Gold	Gold[a]	Reserves including Gold	Use of IMF Credit	Net Reserves
1980-81	5850	603	405	6858	370	7228	327	6901
1981-82	3582	473	405	4460	335	4795	964	3831
1982-83	4281	291	393	4965	324	5289	2876	2413
1983-84	5099	230	518	5847	320	6167	4150	2017
1984-85	5482	145	483	6110	325	6435	3932	2503
1985-86	5972	131	554	6657	416	7073	4290	2783
1986-87	5924	179	626	6729	470	7199	4291	2908
1987-88	5618	97	676	6391	507	6898	3653	3246
1988-89	4226	103	630	4959	473	5432	2364	3067
1989-90	3368	107	634	4109	487	4596	1493	3102
1990-91	2236	102	--	2338	504	2842	2623	219
1991-92	5631	90	1	5722	542	6264	3451	2812
1992-93	6434	18	297	6749	557	7306	4798	2508
1993-94	15068	108	300	15476	583	16059	5040	11019
1994-95	20809	19	332	21160	695	21855	4312	17543
1995-96	17044	82	311	17436	654	18090	2374	15715
End of the Month								
1993								
March	6434	18	297	6749	557	7306	4798	2508
June	6553	187	298	7038	560	7598	5102	2495
September	7629	61	302	7992	569	8561	5109	3452
December	9807	100	292	10199	551	10750	4924	5826
1994								
March	15068	108	300	15476	583	16059	5040	11019
June	16372	45	308	16725	598	17323	4002	13321
September	18856	3	312	19171	606	19777	4055	15722
December	19386	2	310	19698	603	20301	4034	16267
1995								
March	20809	19	332	21160	695	21855	4312	17543
June	19601	95	334	20030	702	20732	3933	16799
September	19064	49	320	19433	674	20107	3377	16729
December	17467	139	316	17922	665	18587	2923	15664
1996								
March	17044	82	311	17436	654	18090	2374	15715
June	17526	128	307	17961	646	18607	2079	16527

Note: IMF Credit refers to Use of IMF credit within the General Resources Account (GRA) excluding Trust Fund,
    Structural Adjustment Facility (SAF), and Enhanced Structural Adjustment Facility (ESAF) loans.

a. Valued at 35 SDR's per fine troy ounce.

Source: IMF, International Financial Statistics, various issues.

Table A4.1
Central Government Finances Summary
(Rs billion at current prices)

	1990-91	1991-92	1992-93	1993-94	1994-95	1995-96 B.E.	1995-96 R.E.	1996-97 B.E.
Revenue[a]	549.5	690.7	760.9	754.1	966.9	1077.9	1105.5	1353.5
Tax Revenue	429.8	500.7	540.4	534.5	674.5	743.7	810.9	973.1
Customs	206.4	222.6	237.8	221.9	267.9	295.0	353.5	444.4
Union Excise[b]	141.0	160.2	163.7	172.2	210.6	231.3	230.2	250.7
Income Tax[b]	12.5	16.3	18.3	13.5	34.7	37.7	38.1	48.2
Corporate Tax	53.4	78.5	89.0	100.6	138.2	155.0	162.5	196.0
Other	16.5	23.2	31.7	26.3	23.1	24.8	26.5	33.8
Non-Tax Revenue	119.8	190.0	220.5	219.6	292.4	334.1	294.6	380.4
Interest Receipts	87.3	109.3	124.9	150.6	158.0	184.2	183.7	213.9
Asset Sales	0.0	30.4	19.6	-0.5	56.1	70.0	3.6	50.0
Other	32.5	50.3	76.0	69.4	78.3	79.9	107.3	116.4
Expenditure[c]	995.9	1053.9	1162.6	1356.6	1543.9	1654.2	1745.6	1976.1
Non-Plan Expenditure	769.3	804.5	859.6	981.9	1133.6	1236.5	1332.9	1499.7
Interest Payments	215.0	266.0	310.4	367.0	440.5	520.0	520.0	600.0
Defense	154.3	163.5	175.8	218.5	232.5	255.0	268.8	278.0
Subsidies	121.6	122.5	120.4	128.6	129.8	124.0	137.3	163.2
Other Non-Plan Expenditure	278.5	252.6	253.0	267.9	330.8	337.5	406.7	458.6
Plan Expenditure	283.7	309.6	366.6	436.6	473.8	485.0	486.8	546.9
Less: Recovery of Loans	57.1	60.2	63.6	61.9	63.5	67.3	74.1	70.5
Gross Fiscal Deficit	446.3	363.3	401.7	602.6	577.0	576.3	640.1	622.7
Financed by:								
Reserve Bank of India (net)[d]	164.3	59.0	32.7	13.5	21.8	50.0	198.6	65.8
Marketable Securities (net)[e]	49.1	117.7	165.2	295.5	110.0	270.9	146.8	255.0
Other Domestic Borrowing (n	201.2	132.4	150.6	242.9	393.8	210.9	275.1	277.3
External Borrowing (net)	31.8	54.2	53.2	50.7	51.5	44.6	19.7	24.6
Memo:								
GDPmp	5355.3	6168.0	7053.3	8010.3	9456.2	10478.9	10978.0	12603.0
Fiscal Deficit / GDP	8.3%	5.9%	5.7%	7.5%	6.1%	5.5%	5.8%	4.9%
Revenue / GDP	10.3%	11.2%	10.8%	9.4%	10.2%	10.3%	10.1%	10.7%
Expenditure / GDP	18.6%	17.1%	16.5%	16.9%	16.3%	15.8%	15.9%	15.7%

Note: BE = Budget estimates; RE = Revised estimates.

a. Including sale of public assets (disinvestment).
b. Net of states' share.
c. Net of loan recoveries.
d. Monetized deficit (equal to net RBI credit to Central Government).
e. T-Bills and dated securities, excluding those issued to RBI.

Source: Ministry of Finance, Union budget documents.

Table A4.2
Tax Revenue: Center and States
(Rs. billion at current prices)

	1987-88	1988-89	1989-90	1990-91	1991-92	1992-93	1993-94	1994-95	1995-96 B.E.	1995-96 R.E.	1996-97 B.E.
evenue receipts	370.37	435.91	499.96	549.54	660.30	741.28	754.53	910.83	1007.87	1101.91	1303.45
ax revenue	280.15	337.51	383.49	429.78	500.69	540.44	534.49	674.54	743.74	810.88	973.10
Non-tax revenue	90.22	98.40	116.47	119.76	159.61	200.84	220.04	236.29	264.13	291.03	330.35
interest from state governments	31.58	37.70	44.24	51.74	65.22	77.54	95.53	111.83	133.48	131.31	151.13
evenue expenditure (A+B+C+D)	461.75	541.06	642.07	735.15	823.08	927.02	1081.69	1221.11	1363.29	1435.22	1618.20
A. Developmental	114.25	140.36	184.15	196.01	198.17	208.60	243.68	301.50	325.06	367.47	414.27
1. Social services	19.35	22.43	24.99	27.53	30.57	34.30	40.97	47.43	53.57	75.57	93.36
2. Economic services	94.90	117.93	159.17	168.48	167.60	174.30	202.71	254.07	271.49	291.90	320.91
B. Non-developmental	244.59	287.69	335.47	391.00	450.34	521.58	613.17	708.20	810.79	837.47	958.55
Defence services	88.60	95.58	101.94	108.74	114.42	121.09	149.77	164.26	181.46	188.35	188.55
Interest payments	112.36	142.61	177.57	214.71	265.63	310.35	366.95	440.49	520.00	520.00	600.00
C. Grants-in-aid and contributions	93.49	102.08	109.36	134.39	159.53	180.54	211.11	204.83	220.47	222.61	237.43
Grants to state governments	91.36	100.15	107.44	132.02	157.00	178.30	213.77	200.47	215.44	216.82	231.31
D. Revenue expenditure of UTs	9.43	10.92	13.09	13.75	15.05	16.30	13.73	6.59	6.97	7.66	7.95
et current balance	-91.38	-105.15	-142.11	-185.61	-162.78	-185.74	-327.16	-310.28	-355.42	-333.31	-314.75
apital expenditure (A+B+C+D-E)	179.07	204.08	237.18	260.88	200.63	215.99	275.41	266.75	220.93	306.80	307.91
A. Developmental	56.67	60.03	70.95	69.23	58.26	73.82	55.60	73.96	59.59	43.06	47.24
1. Social services	2.80	3.51	3.21	2.47	2.39	2.59	3.32	7.26	5.49	5.57	6.41
2. Economic services	53.86	56.52	67.74	66.77	55.87	71.23	52.28	66.70	54.09	37.48	40.83
B. Non-developmental	33.39	40.76	45.27	49.56	52.32	58.88	73.92	72.51	83.88	90.34	100.87
Defence services	31.08	37.83	42.22	45.52	49.05	54.73	68.67	68.19	73.54	80.44	89.44
C. Capital expenditure of UTs	2.88	1.76	1.87	2.68	3.42	3.50	2.78	2.44	2.52	2.37	2.41
D. Loans and advances (net)	86.13	101.53	119.09	139.40	117.01	99.41	142.63	173.91	144.94	174.60	207.40
to States & UTs	58.51	67.30	79.55	98.69	94.18	86.97	100.72	143.13	115.27	142.67	170.76
to Others	27.62	34.23	39.55	40.71	22.83	12.44	41.92	30.78	29.67	31.93	36.64
E. Disinvestment of equity in PSEs	0.00	0.00	0.00	0.00	30.38	19.61	-0.48	56.07	70.00	3.57	50.01
ross fiscal deficit (GOI Defn.)	270.45	309.22	379.30	446.50	363.41	401.74	602.57	577.04	576.35	640.11	622.66
inance by instruments											
Market loans	58.62	84.18	74.04	80.01	75.10	36.76	289.28	203.26	227.00	275.00	254.98
mall savings	39.11	58.35	85.75	91.04	66.40	57.17	91.00	165.78	80.00	135.00	140.00
rovident funds	52.74	71.12	90.86	89.37	79.56	87.55	93.58	102.65	109.64	107.13	117.98
xternal loans	28.93	24.60	25.95	31.81	54.21	53.19	50.74	51.46	44.56	19.69	24.61
reasury bills	56.52	62.44	109.11	117.69	68.87	117.73	119.82	-2.68	49.99	64.77	65.78
ther	34.53	8.53	-6.41	36.58	19.27	49.33	-41.85	56.57	65.15	38.51	19.31

Note: BE = Budget estimates; RE = Revised estimates.

Source: Ministry of Finance, Union budget documents; Department of Expenditure, Finance Accounts.

Table A4.3
Tax Revenue: Center and States
(Rs. billion at current prices)

	1987-88	1988-89	1989-90	1990-91	1991-92	1992-93	1993-94	1994-95 R.E.	1995-96 B.E.[a]
Revenue receipts	448.00	507.09	589.08	673.19	813.59	911.04	1056.11	1212.67	1331.77
Tax revenue	289.20	330.70	392.27	448.80	529.53	603.90	686.66	792.60	901.31
Direct tax	19.85	24.13	30.06	33.75	39.59	42.28	49.73	64.17	69.31
Indirect tax	173.37	199.88	229.89	269.70	317.98	356.40	414.51	480.00	538.12
State share in central taxes	95.98	106.69	132.32	145.35	171.97	205.22	222.42	248.43	293.88
Non-tax revenue	158.80	176.38	196.81	224.39	284.06	307.14	369.45	420.07	430.46
Grants from centre	91.36	100.15	107.44	132.02	157.00	178.30	213.77	202.63	215.44
Revenue expenditure [A+B+C]	451.54	522.96	602.53	717.73	861.86	962.05	1093.76	1310.14	1469.05
A. Developmental (1+2)	318.20	362.37	407.81	488.55	585.05	634.65	708.38	802.39	876.85
1. Social services	177.06	205.74	240.17	279.62	310.92	345.65	389.61	456.15	519.96
2. Economic services	141.14	156.63	167.64	208.92	274.13	288.99	318.78	346.24	356.89
B. Non-developmental	128.44	155.06	188.69	221.34	266.66	315.06	373.67	493.91	577.56
Interest payments	52.68	64.11	76.68	92.21	109.44	138.65	165.45	202.51	233.97
To centre	31.58	37.70	44.24	51.74	65.22	77.54	95.53	113.80	133.48
To others	21.10	26.41	32.44	40.47	44.23	61.11	69.92	88.71	100.49
C. Other expenditure[b]	4.91	5.53	6.03	7.84	10.16	12.35	11.71	13.84	14.64
Net current balance	-3.55	-15.87	-13.45	-44.54	-48.27	-51.01	-37.65	-97.47	-137.28
Capital expenditure [A+B+C]	101.31	98.66	117.52	134.78	132.49	157.77	167.84	214.27	237.73
A. Developmental (1+2)	64.29	68.53	77.28	89.61	98.61	103.44	120.51	157.34	155.68
1. Social services	10.74	11.28	11.71	12.57	16.47	16.64	18.31	24.93	28.70
2. Economic services	53.55	57.25	65.57	77.03	82.14	86.80	102.21	132.41	126.97
B. Non-developmental	2.26	2.25	2.36	2.63	2.34	3.10	3.99	4.80	8.20
C. Loans and advances (net)	34.77	27.88	37.88	42.55	31.54	51.22	43.33	52.13	73.85
Gross fiscal deficit	104.85	114.53	130.96	179.32	180.77	208.78	205.48	311.74	375.02
Finance by instrument:									
Market loans	18.01	22.46	25.95	25.60	33.10	38.50	42.28	51.23	65.19
Loans from centre (Net)	58.31	67.07	79.30	98.39	93.75	86.60	99.01	137.48	110.02
Small savings & Provident fund	16.28	20.01	23.07	30.69	29.09	36.22	43.30	43.96	45.44
Others	12.26	4.98	2.65	24.63	24.82	47.45	20.89	79.07	154.38

Note: BE = Budget estimates; RE = Revised estimates.

a. Figure for 1994-95 includes Union Territory of Delhi.

b. Other expenditure include compensation and assignments to local bodies and panchayat raj institutions and reserve with the finance department.

Source: Ministry of Finance, Union budget documents; Reserve Bank of India, RBI bulletins on state finances.

Table A4.4
Tax Revenue: Center and States
(Rs. billion at current prices)

	1987-88	1988-89	1989-90	1990-91	1991-92	1992-93	1993-94	1994-95 R.E.[a]	1995-96 B.E.[b]
Revenue receipts	695.43	805.15	937.36	1038.97	1251.67	1396.48	1501.35	1809.01	1990.72
Tax revenue	569.35	668.21	775.76	878.58	1030.22	1144.34	1221.15	1467.11	1645.05
Non tax revenue	126.08	136.94	161.60	160.39	221.45	252.13	280.20	341.90	345.67
Revenue expenditure [A+B+C+D]	790.35	926.17	1092.92	1269.12	1462.72	1633.23	1866.16	2218.95	2483.42
A. Developmental	432.44	502.73	591.96	684.56	783.22	843.24	952.06	1103.89	1201.91
1. Social services	196.40	228.17	265.15	307.16	341.49	379.95	430.58	503.58	573.53
2. Economic services	236.04	274.55	326.80	377.40	441.72	463.29	521.48	600.31	628.38
B. Non-developmental	341.45	405.05	479.92	560.60	651.78	759.10	891.30	1090.28	1254.87
C. Revenue disbursements of UTs	9.43	10.92	13.09	13.75	15.05	16.30	13.73	6.59	6.97
D. Other expenditure[c]	7.04	7.46	7.95	10.21	12.68	14.59	9.06	18.20	19.67
Net current balance	-94.93	-121.02	-155.56	-230.15	-211.05	-236.75	-364.81	-409.94	-492.70
Capital expenditure [A+B+C+D-E	221.87	235.44	275.15	296.97	238.95	286.80	342.53	337.90	343.40
A. Developmental (1+2)	120.95	128.56	148.23	158.84	156.87	177.26	176.11	231.30	215.26
1. Social services	13.54	14.79	14.92	15.04	18.86	19.23	21.63	32.19	34.20
2. Economic services	107.41	113.76	133.31	143.80	138.00	158.03	154.49	199.11	181.07
B. Non-Developmental	35.65	43.01	47.63	52.19	54.67	61.98	77.90	77.32	92.09
C. Loans and advances (net)	62.38	62.11	77.42	83.26	54.37	63.67	85.25	82.92	103.53
D. Capital disbursements of UTs	2.88	1.76	1.87	2.68	3.42	3.50	2.78	2.44	2.52
E. Disinvestment of equities in PS	0.00	0.00	0.00	0.00	30.38	19.61	-0.48	56.07	70.00
Gross fiscal deficit	316.79	356.45	430.71	527.12	450.00	523.55	707.34	747.84	836.10
Finance by Instrument:									
Market Loans	76.63	106.64	99.99	105.61	108.20	75.26	331.56	254.49	292.19
Small Savings	39.11	58.35	85.75	91.04	66.40	57.17	91.00	165.78	80.00
Provident Funds	69.02	91.13	113.93	120.06	108.65	123.77	136.88	146.61	155.08
External Loans	28.93	24.60	25.95	31.81	54.21	53.19	50.74	51.46	44.56
Treasury Bills	56.52	62.44	109.11	117.69	68.87	117.73	119.82	-2.68	49.99
Other	46.58	13.29	-4.02	60.90	43.66	96.43	-22.67	132.18	214.28

Note: BE = Budget estimates; RE = Revised estimates.

a. Actuals for the center and revised estimates for the states.

c. Other expenditure include compensation and assignments to local bodies and panchayat raj institutions and reserve with the finance department.

Source: Ministry of Finance, Union budget documents; Reserve Bank of India, RBI bulletins on state finances; Dept. of Expenditure, Finance Accounts.

Table A4.5
Tax Revenue: Center and States
(Rs. billion at current prices)

	1987-88	1988-89	1989-90	1990-91	1991-92	1992-93	1993-94	1994-95 R.E.[a]	1995-96 B.E.	1995-96 R.E.	1996-97 B.E.
Central Government											
A. Gross tax revenue	376.66	444.74	516.36	575.76	673.61	746.37	757.44	922.94	1037.62	1103.54	1321.45
Corporation tax	34.33	44.07	47.29	53.35	78.53	88.99	100.60	138.22	155.00	162.50	196.00
Taxes on income	31.92	42.41	50.04	53.71	67.31	78.88	91.15	120.25	135.00	151.00	178.43
Customs	137.02	158.05	180.36	206.44	222.57	237.76	221.93	267.89	295.00	353.52	444.35
Union Excise Duties	164.26	188.41	224.06	245.14	281.10	308.32	316.97	373.47	427.80	410.00	468.84
Other	9.13	11.80	14.61	17.12	24.10	32.42	26.79	23.11	24.82	26.52	33.83
B. States Share of Tax Revenue	95.98	106.69	132.32	145.35	171.97	205.22	222.42	248.40	293.88	292.66	348.35
Income Tax	25.89	27.49	39.22	41.21	51.04	60.57	77.69	85.57	97.34	112.88	130.24
Estate Duty	0.06	0.01	0.00	0.00	0.00	0.00	0.00	0.00	0.00	0.00	0.00
Union Excise Duties	70.03	79.19	93.10	104.14	120.93	144.65	144.73	162.83	196.54	179.78	218.11
C. Assignments of UT taxes to local bodies	0.53	0.54	0.55	0.63	0.95	0.71	0.53	0.00	0.00	0.00	0.00
Tax Revenue (net) [A-B-C]	280.15	337.51	383.49	429.78	500.69	540.44	534.49	674.54	743.74	810.88	973.10
State Government											
States own Tax Revenue	193.22	224.01	259.95	303.45	357.56	398.68	464.24	544.17	607.43		
Direct Tax	19.85	24.13	30.06	33.75	39.59	42.28	49.73	64.17	69.31		
Taxes on income	2.70	3.12	4.53	6.34	6.45	6.02	6.50	7.20	7.80		
Land revenue	4.48	5.94	6.90	6.07	6.36	6.17	7.32	10.06	10.36		
Stamps and registration fees	12.54	14.86	18.45	21.12	26.54	29.78	35.55	46.50	50.59		
Other	0.13	0.21	0.19	0.22	0.24	0.31	0.36	0.41	0.57		
Indirect Tax	173.37	199.88	229.89	269.70	317.98	356.40	414.51	480.00	538.12		
Sales Tax	111.85	131.22	150.60	176.67	210.64	233.49	276.38	301.00	347.96		
State excise	28.67	30.81	38.64	47.95	54.39	62.65	71.06	76.30	80.85		
Taxes on Vehicles	11.75	12.90	14.15	15.66	18.37	21.94	25.83	28.24	31.22		
Other	21.09	24.96	26.49	29.41	34.58	38.32	41.25	74.47	78.08		
State's Share of Central Taxes	95.98	106.69	132.32	145.35	171.97	205.22	222.42	248.43	293.88		
Tax revenue retained by states	289.20	330.70	392.27	448.80	529.53	603.90	686.66	792.60	901.31		

Note: BE = Budget estimates; RE = Revised estimates.

a. Actuals for the center and revised estimates for the states.

Source: Ministry of Finance, Union budget documents; Reserve Bank of India, RBI bulletins on state finances.

Table A4.6
Tax Revenue: Center and States
(Rs. billion at current prices)

	1987-88	1988-89	1989-90	1990-91	1991-92	1992-93	1993-94	1994-95 R.E.[a]	1995-96 B.E.	1995-96 R.E.	1996-97 B.E.
Central Government											
Non-tax revenue	90.22	98.40	116.47	119.76	159.61	200.84	220.04	236.29	264.13	291.03	330.35
Interest receipts	57.55	69.81	84.66	87.30	109.33	124.87	150.62	157.97	184.20	183.69	213.93
from state governments	31.58	37.70	44.24	51.74	65.22	77.54	95.53	111.83	133.48	131.31	151.13
Dividends and profits	6.05	4.75	7.16	7.74	10.58	24.93	24.48	27.16	29.46	32.29	40.51
Other general services	3.37	3.95	4.05	5.06	5.72	10.14	10.46	11.87	11.01	14.83	13.53
Social services	0.60	0.80	0.57	0.65	0.90	0.79	1.01	0.95	1.44	1.36	1.40
Economic services	12.73	8.93	5.45	8.60	21.46	17.86	13.26	18.60	19.08	38.76	46.73
Grants-in-aid and contributio	4.92	6.00	7.54	5.86	9.47	9.19	9.93	10.38	11.54	12.07	8.09
Other	5.00	4.16	7.04	4.55	2.15	13.06	10.28	9.36	7.40	8.03	6.16
State Government											
States own Non-tax revenue	67.44	76.24	89.37	92.37	127.06	128.84	155.69	217.44	215.02		
Interest receipts	19.47	23.87	26.34	24.03	53.20	39.38	47.25	52.17	52.12		
General services	7.54	9.51	11.40	19.13	17.28	18.44	29.47	81.35	75.01		
Social services	5.04	5.73	6.76	5.86	7.74	8.48	9.12	9.76	10.58		
Economic services	35.12	36.64	44.59	43.01	48.39	61.48	69.21	73.52	76.63		
Forestry and wild life	10.67	10.08	11.96	11.37	12.71	12.72	14.94	15.40	16.05		
Industries	9.11	12.08	14.31	12.23	15.37	23.17	25.09	28.33	30.41		
Other	15.33	14.48	18.32	19.41	20.31	25.59	29.19	29.79	30.18		
Other	0.28	0.49	0.28	0.34	0.45	1.06	0.63	0.64	0.67		
Grants from centre	91.36	100.15	107.44	132.02	157.00	178.30	213.77	202.63	215.44		
Non-tax revenue retained by st	158.80	176.38	196.81	224.39	284.06	307.14	369.45	420.07	430.46		

Note: BE = Budget estimates; RE = Revised estimates.

a. Actuals for the center and revised estimates for the states.

Source: Ministry of Finance, Union budget documents; Reserve Bank of India, RBI bulletins on state finances.

Table A4.7
Tax Revenue: Center and States
(Rs. billion at current prices)

	1987-88	1988-89	1989-90	1990-91	1991-92	1992-93	1993-94	1994-95	1995-96 B.E.	1995-96 R.E.	1996-97 B.E.
Revenue expenditure (A+B+C+D)	461.75	541.06	642.07	735.15	823.08	927.02	1081.69	1221.11	1363.29	1435.22	1618.20
A. Developmental	114.25	140.36	184.15	196.01	198.17	208.60	243.68	301.50	325.06	367.47	414.27
1. Social services	19.35	22.43	24.99	27.53	30.57	34.30	40.97	47.43	53.57	75.57	93.36
Education, Sports, Art and Cultur	10.13	11.12	11.41	12.74	13.72	14.97	18.37	22.30	22.19	32.59	39.86
Health and Family welfare	2.67	3.11	3.48	3.97	4.50	5.59	6.47	7.82	8.96	8.91	10.55
Information and Broadcasting	2.10	2.36	3.23	3.60	4.43	4.61	4.15	5.08	4.76	5.09	5.35
Water supply and Sanitation	0.13	0.51	0.78	0.93	0.64	0.63	0.84	0.84	3.98	3.63	3.63
Labour and labour welfare	1.64	2.43	2.64	2.78	3.00	3.29	5.11	4.14	5.07	5.73	5.88
Social security and welfare	1.92	1.96	2.36	2.25	2.81	3.44	3.71	4.47	5.43	10.32	14.43
Other	0.76	0.94	1.09	1.27	1.47	1.77	2.33	2.77	3.18	9.31	13.65
2. Economic services	94.90	117.93	159.17	168.48	167.60	174.30	202.71	254.07	271.49	291.90	320.91
Agriculture and allied services	5.55	7.45	7.75	22.92	19.25	21.26	18.73	33.86	35.35	39.26	53.75
Fertilizer Subsidy	21.64	32.01	45.42	43.89	51.85	61.36	51.94	52.41	59.00	67.35	83.72
Food Subsidy	20.00	22.00	24.76	24.50	28.50	28.00	55.37	51.00	52.50	55.00	58.84
Export Subsidy	9.62	13.86	20.14	27.42	17.58	8.18	6.65	6.58	3.15	3.15	4.60
Irrigation and Flood Control	0.76	0.85	0.81	0.89	1.20	1.07	1.68	1.35	1.77	1.59	2.20
Rural Development	3.13	3.61	3.70	3.77	3.57	4.06	16.25	41.56	57.00	53.61	48.42
Special Areas Programmes	0.06	0.05	0.07	0.12	0.19	0.17	0.20	7.92	8.10	7.98	8.11
Energy	3.94	5.59	6.90	7.49	5.37	2.67	5.48	3.97	5.62	5.10	5.61
Industry and Minerals	13.57	12.20	17.96	12.26	12.03	17.98	17.93	12.88	19.00	20.19	26.84
Transport and Communications	6.06	6.79	15.62	8.05	9.19	9.68	14.45	17.80	15.69	18.19	19.94
Science, Technology and Enviro	7.57	9.34	10.40	11.27	12.87	13.68	15.86	17.20	18.76	19.22	21.24
General Economic Services	2.99	4.18	5.62	5.90	6.00	6.20	-1.84	7.53	-4.45	1.27	-12.37
B. Non-developmental	244.59	287.69	335.47	391.00	450.34	521.58	613.17	708.20	810.79	837.47	958.55
Defence services	88.60	95.58	101.94	108.74	114.42	121.09	149.77	164.26	181.46	188.35	188.55
Interest payments	112.36	142.61	177.57	214.71	265.63	310.35	366.95	440.49	520.00	520.00	600.00
on Internal Debt	55.14	69.13	82.73	96.22	109.09	129.89	154.83	193.91	232.83	222.67	267.30
on External Debt	9.77	12.42	14.94	17.78	25.69	34.51	37.92	41.10	43.09	48.99	52.74
on Small Savings, PFs. etc.	44.90	58.01	75.73	96.37	124.20	138.83	168.42	198.91	237.35	239.45	270.75
Other	2.56	3.06	4.17	4.34	6.66	7.12	5.78	6.57	6.73	8.89	9.21
Administrative Services	15.32	17.91	20.71	25.24	27.98	37.83	38.27	42.14	44.46	49.30	95.52
Fiscal Services	10.94	11.00	12.78	12.12	17.69	20.48	21.37	23.55	24.75	27.12	26.70
Pensions and misc. services	17.37	20.60	22.46	30.19	24.63	31.84	36.80	37.76	40.13	52.70	47.78
C. Grants-in-aid and contributions	93.49	102.08	109.36	134.39	159.53	180.54	211.11	204.83	220.47	222.61	237.43
Grants to State Governments	91.36	100.15	107.44	132.02	157.00	178.30	213.77	200.47	215.44	216.82	231.31
a. Non Plan	19.80	24.11	23.69	42.19	86.45	27.41	32.39	92.54	61.07	60.50	64.13
b. State Plan Schemes	34.43	35.59	35.38	38.78	70.55	82.80	102.39	107.93	84.03	88.35	95.63
c. Central and Centrally sponsored schemes	37.14	40.46	48.37	51.05	54.93	66.34	78.99	68.25	70.34	67.98	71.54
Grants to UTs. and Others	2.13	1.93	1.92	2.37	2.53	2.24	-2.65	4.36	5.03	5.79	6.12
D. Revenue Disbursments of UTs (	9.43	10.92	13.09	13.75	15.05	16.30	13.73	6.59	6.97	7.66	7.95

Memo Items:

	1987-88	1988-89	1989-90	1990-91	1991-92	1992-93	1993-94	1994-95	1995-96 B.E.	1995-96 R.E.	1996-97 B.E.
Total Subsidies	59.80	77.32	104.74	121.58	122.53	120.43	128.64	129.82	124.01	137.26	163.20
Major Subsidies	51.26	67.87	90.32	95.81	97.93	94.15	107.64	115.30	109.65	125.50	147.16
Other Subsidies	8.54	9.45	14.42	25.77	24.60	26.28	21.00	14.52	14.36	11.76	16.04
(annual averages at constant 1980-81 prices - Rs. billion)											
Rural Employment Programme	14.10	12.44	21.00	20.00	18.17	25.46	39.06	46.75	54.32	47.71	38.35
RLEGP	6.66	7.84	0.02	0.00	0.00	0.00	0.00	0.00	0.00	0.00	0.00
NREP	7.45	4.60	0.02	0.00	0.00	0.00	0.00	0.00	0.00	0.00	0.00
Jawahar Rojgar Yojana	0.00	0.00	20.96	20.00	18.17	25.26	33.06	35.35	38.62	29.55	18.65

Note: BE = Budget estimates; RE = Revised estimates.

Source: Ministry of Finance, Union budget documents; Department of Expenditure, Finance Accounts.

Table A4.8
Tax Revenue: Center and States
(Rs. billion at current prices)

	1987-88	1988-89	1989-90	1990-91	1991-92	1992-93	1993-94	1994-95 R.E.	1995-96 B.E.[a]
Revenue expenditure (A+B+C)	451.54	522.96	602.53	717.73	861.86	962.05	1093.76	1310.14	1469.05
A. Developmental (1+2)	318.20	362.37	407.81	488.55	585.05	634.65	708.38	802.39	876.85
1. Social services	177.06	205.74	240.17	279.62	310.92	345.65	389.61	456.15	519.96
Education, Sports, Art and Culture	90.10	109.43	135.71	155.28	170.77	192.61	215.94	254.50	281.69
Health and Family Welfare.	30.53	34.77	39.64	45.86	50.54	56.62	66.69	74.72	79.97
Water supply and Sanitation	13.22	13.94	14.77	16.38	18.45	20.95	24.24	27.23	29.15
Welfare of SC, ST and BCs	11.84	13.18	14.69	17.90	20.71	23.01	25.70	30.83	34.85
Social security and welfare	8.23	9.70	11.07	13.62	14.77	16.63	18.65	24.28	26.49
Other	23.13	24.72	24.29	30.59	35.68	35.83	38.38	44.58	67.81
2. Economic services	141.14	156.63	167.64	208.92	274.13	288.99	318.78	346.24	356.89
Agriculture and Allied Services	38.98	42.65	48.29	62.67	69.81	84.34	88.93	88.26	99.15
Crop Husbandry	9.59	11.06	12.65	16.97	20.82	29.37	29.12	27.74	27.58
Food Storage and Warehousing	1.20	1.23	1.56	1.88	2.38	4.16	3.81	4.37	8.36
Forestry and Wild Life	8.69	9.46	10.28	11.75	13.42	14.90	15.74	17.74	19.81
Other	19.50	20.90	23.80	32.06	33.19	35.91	40.25	38.42	43.40
Rural Development	32.20	36.54	28.27	46.75	52.87	63.62	72.77	79.00	83.78
Special Areas Programmes	2.35	3.09	3.54	3.57	4.11	3.96	4.88	5.42	6.15
Irrigation and Flood Control	27.75	33.19	33.94	34.56	41.40	48.68	54.28	62.60	64.71
Energy	9.14	7.74	10.92	9.89	50.30	26.15	31.68	33.35	24.08
Industry and Minerals	7.33	8.69	12.17	11.65	12.71	13.56	14.18	17.61	19.75
Transport and Communications	16.01	17.35	19.22	23.36	27.59	31.28	35.12	37.55	39.67
Science, Technology and Environ	0.24	0.23	0.26	0.29	0.36	0.39	0.53	0.71	0.81
General Economic Services	7.14	7.15	11.02	16.18	14.98	17.01	16.40	21.74	18.79
B. Non-Developmental	128.44	155.06	188.69	221.34	266.66	315.06	373.67	493.91	577.56
Interest Payments	52.68	64.11	76.68	92.21	109.44	138.65	165.45	202.51	233.97
On loans from the centre	31.58	37.70	44.24	51.74	65.22	77.54	95.53	113.80	133.48
On the Internal Debt	8.95	10.42	13.41	15.68	21.70	24.67	27.77	38.85	46.91
On Small Savings, PFs.	7.63	10.58	12.70	17.03	21.17	24.73	30.87	36.54	41.29
Other	4.51	5.41	6.34	7.76	1.36	11.71	11.28	13.31	12.29
Administrative Services	44.18	50.31	59.74	70.18	78.10	93.44	104.73	118.10	160.34
Pensions and Miscellaneous Servic	17.58	23.92	29.31	35.93	44.79	52.72	69.99	127.43	135.57
Other	13.99	16.72	22.96	23.01	34.33	30.24	33.51	45.87	47.68
C. Other expenditure[b]	4.91	5.53	6.03	7.84	10.16	12.35	11.71	13.84	14.64

Note: BE = Budget estimates; RE = Revised estimates.

a. Figure for 1994-95 includes Union Territory of Delhi.

b. Other expenditure include compensation and assignments to local bodies and panchayat raj institutions and reserve with the finance department.

Source: Reserve Bank of India, RBI bulletins on state finances.

Table A4.9
Tax Revenue: Center and States
(Rs. billion at current prices)

	1987-88	1988-89	1989-90	1990-91	1991-92	1992-93	1993-94	1994-95	1995-96 B.E.	1995-96 R.E.	1996-97 B.E.
Central Government											
Capital expenditure [A+B+C+D-	179.07	204.08	237.18	260.88	200.63	215.99	275.41	266.75	220.93	306.80	307.91
A. Developmental (1+2)	56.67	60.03	70.95	69.23	58.26	73.82	55.60	73.96	59.59	43.06	47.24
1. Social services	2.80	3.51	3.21	2.47	2.39	2.59	3.32	7.26	5.49	5.57	6.41
Education, Sports, Art etc.	0.05	0.13	0.08	0.06	0.04	0.05	0.06	2.25	0.12	0.14	0.11
Health and Family welfare	0.19	0.15	0.20	0.00	0.20	0.07	0.03	0.69	0.14	0.13	0.41
Housing	0.75	0.99	0.98	1.11	1.26	1.78	1.87	1.86	2.07	2.37	2.82
Information and Broadcasti	1.74	1.71	1.78	1.06	0.35	0.07	0.24	0.25	0.58	0.51	0.57
Other	0.08	0.52	0.18	0.24	0.53	0.62	1.12	2.23	2.58	2.42	2.52
2. Economic services	53.86	56.52	67.74	66.77	55.87	71.23	52.28	66.70	54.09	37.48	40.83
Agriculture and allied	0.54	0.55	0.45	0.45	0.49	0.47	0.48	2.83	4.48	3.76	3.45
Energy	18.46	19.05	26.07	27.09	19.91	16.21	17.69	22.68	13.22	11.60	9.86
Industry and Minerals	14.07	13.10	11.52	7.71	6.70	8.82	9.87	8.04	8.06	6.57	5.48
Transport & Communicatio	18.40	21.51	26.15	26.45	24.72	33.81	19.45	22.14	21.77	21.14	25.34
General Economic Services	0.65	0.00	1.26	2.52	2.57	9.07	1.58	6.86	2.37	-10.19	-8.21
Other	1.75	2.31	2.28	2.56	1.48	2.85	3.21	4.14	4.19	4.62	4.91
B. Non-developmental	33.39	40.76	45.27	49.56	52.32	58.88	73.92	72.51	83.88	90.34	100.87
Defence Services	31.08	37.83	42.22	45.52	49.05	54.73	68.67	68.19	73.54	80.44	89.44
Other	2.32	2.93	3.05	4.04	3.27	4.14	5.24	4.32	10.34	9.90	11.43
C. Capital Expenditure of UTs	2.88	1.76	1.87	2.68	3.42	3.50	2.78	2.44	2.52	2.37	2.41
D. Loans and Advances(Net)	86.13	101.53	119.09	139.40	117.01	99.41	142.63	173.91	144.94	174.60	207.40
To State Governments & UTs	58.51	67.30	79.55	98.69	94.18	86.97	100.72	143.13	115.27	142.67	170.76
To Others	27.62	34.23	39.55	40.71	22.83	12.44	41.92	30.78	29.67	31.93	36.64
E. Disinvestment of equity in P	0.00	0.00	0.00	0.00	30.38	19.61	-0.48	56.07	70.00	3.57	50.01
State Government											
Capital expenditure [A+B+C]	101.31	98.66	117.52	134.78	132.49	157.77	192.57	214.27	237.73		
A. Developmental (1+2)	64.29	68.53	77.28	89.61	98.61	103.44	117.86	157.34	155.68		
1. Social Services	10.74	11.28	11.71	12.57	16.47	16.64	19.80	24.93	28.70		
Education, Sports, Art etc.	1.29	1.68	2.64	2.84	2.78	3.02	3.23	4.04	4.70		
Health and Family welfare	1.88	2.04	1.84	2.37	2.76	2.63	3.31	3.65	4.33		
Water supply and Sanitation	4.00	4.04	3.37	3.54	4.99	5.49	7.01	9.25	9.77		
Other	1.45	1.63	1.87	2.00	3.86	3.62	4.18	5.29	6.43		
2. Economic Services	53.55	57.25	65.57	77.03	82.14	86.80	98.06	132.41	126.97		
Agriculture and allied	2.17	2.69	5.91	6.11	8.32	7.85	8.87	10.47	10.07		
Irrigation and Flood control	29.66	32.66	32.91	36.56	38.52	42.93	46.46	53.61	61.87		
Transport	9.43	10.27	11.59	13.42	13.92	15.90	19.98	25.86	26.95		
Other	12.28	11.63	15.16	20.94	21.38	20.13	22.75	42.46	28.08		
B. Non-developmental	2.26	2.25	2.36	2.63	2.34	3.10	4.02	4.80	8.20		
C. Loans and advances(Net)	34.77	27.88	37.88	42.55	31.54	51.22	70.70	52.13	73.85		

Note: BE = Budget estimates; RE = Revised estimates.

Source: Ministry of Finance, Union budget documents; Reserve Bank of India, RBI bulletins on state finances.

Table A4.10
Tax Revenue: Center and States
(Rs. billion at current prices)

	1987-88	1988-89	1989-90	1990-91	1991-92	1992-93	1993-94	1994-95	1995-96 B.E.	1995-96 R.E.	1996-97 B.E.
States' share in central taxes	95.98	106.69	132.32	145.35	171.97	205.22	222.42	248.40	293.88	292.66	348.35
Union excise duties	70.03	79.19	93.10	104.14	120.93	144.65	144.73	162.83	196.54	179.78	218.11
Income tax	25.89	27.49	39.22	41.21	51.04	60.57	77.69	85.57	97.34	112.88	130.24
Estate duty	0.06	0.01	0.00	0.00	0.00	0.00	0.00	0.00	0.00	0.00	0.00
Grants to States	91.36	100.15	107.44	132.02	157.00	178.30	213.77	200.47	215.44	216.82	231.31
Non-plan grants	19.80	24.11	23.69	42.19	86.45	27.41	32.39	92.54	61.07	60.50	64.13
State plan schemes	34.43	35.59	35.38	38.78	70.55	82.80	102.39	107.93	84.03	88.35	95.63
Central and Centrally sponsored schemes	37.14	40.46	48.37	51.05	54.93	66.34	78.99	68.25	70.34	67.98	71.54
Loans to States & UTs	86.98	99.15	109.16	135.66	123.30	121.41	139.85	188.04	162.81	196.17	224.36
Loan Repayments by States and	28.47	31.85	29.62	36.97	29.12	34.44	39.13	44.91	47.54	53.50	53.60
Interest Payments by States	31.58	37.70	44.24	51.74	65.22	77.54	95.53	111.83	133.48	131.31	151.13
NET TRANSFER (Centre to Stat	214.28	236.43	275.07	324.32	357.93	392.94	441.37	480.17	491.10	520.84	599.28

Note: BE = Budget estimates; RE = Revised estimates.

Source: Ministry of Finance, Union budget documents; Reserve Bank of India, RBI bulletins on state finances; Dept. of Expenditure, Finance Accounts.

Table A4.11
Tax Revenue: Center and States
(Rs. billion at current prices)

	1987-88	1988-89	1989-90	1990-91	1991-92	1992-93	1993-94	1994-95	1995-96 B.E.	1995-96 R.E.	1996-97 B.E.
A. Major Subsidies	51.26	67.87	90.32	95.81	97.93	94.15	107.64	115.30	109.65	125.50	147.16
1. Food	20.00	22.00	24.76	24.50	28.50	28.00	55.37	51.00	52.50	55.00	58.84
2. Indegenious Fertilizers	20.50	30.00	37.71	37.30	35.00	48.00	38.00	40.75	37.50	43.00	45.00
3. Imported Fertilizers	1.14	2.01	7.71	6.59	13.00	9.96	7.62	11.66	16.50	19.35	16.48
4. Other Fertilizer Subsidy	0.00	0.00	0.00	0.00	3.85	3.40	6.32	0.00	0.00	0.00	0.00
5. Export Promotion and Market Development.	9.62	13.86	20.14	27.42	17.58	8.18	6.65	6.58	3.15	3.15	4.60
6. Sale of decontrolled fertilis with concession to farmers	0.00	0.00	0.00	0.00	0.00	0.00	0.00	5.31	5.00	5.00	22.24
B. Debt relief to farmers	0.00	0.00	0.00	15.02	14.25	15.00	5.00	3.41	0.00	0.00	0.00
C. Other Subsidies	8.54	9.45	14.42	10.75	10.35	11.28	16.00	11.11	9.36	11.76	16.04
5. Railways	1.74	2.07	2.33	2.83	3.12	3.41	4.05	4.23	4.11	4.18	4.69
6. Mill-made cloth	0.23	0.27	0.10	0.10	0.15	0.15	0.00	0.10	0.01	0.01	0.01
7. Handloom Cloth	1.24	1.46	1.81	1.85	1.87	1.94	1.90	1.59	1.57	1.47	1.39
8. Import/Export of Sugar, Edible Oils etc.	0.05	0.40	0.00	..	0.00	0.00	0.00	0.00	0.00	0.00	0.00
9. Interest Subsidies	3.93	4.06	8.81	3.79	3.16	1.12	1.13	0.76	0.34	0.34	4.34
10. Other Subsidies	1.35	1.19	1.37	2.18	2.05	1.26	2.44	4.43	3.33	4.76	4.81
TOTAL - Subsidies	59.80	77.32	104.74	121.58	122.53	120.43	128.64	129.82	124.01	137.26	163.20

-- Not available.

Note: BE = Budget estimates; RE = Revised estimates.

Source: Minstry of Finance, Union Budget Documents.

Table A4.12
Tax Revenue: Center and States
(Rs. billion at current prices)

	1980-81	1981-82	1982-83	1983-84	1984-85	1985-86	1986-87	1987-88	1988-89	1989-90	1990-91	1991-92	1992-93	1993-94[b]
1. To Reserve Bank of India	152.78	184.86	218.53	258.02	318.58	380.47	451.38	516.97	582.00	720.13	867.58	922.66	965.23	967.83
a. Treasury bills	118.44	99.55	159.05	146.47	189.85	242.49	185.61	70.91	123.18	235.73	49.80	61.59	167.17	238.38
b. CG Securities	38.58	51.26	63.34	77.91	98.19	104.23	82.26	88.43	110.89	141.02	174.50	171.47	86.43	33.11
c. Special securities	5.85	41.10	42.10	45.70	46.50	51.87	198.67	371.77	369.87	368.81	671.01	720.47	720.47	720.47
d. Other liabilities	-2.92	-4.19	-7.52	-10.52	-9.84	-16.64	-6.95	-6.12	-11.69	-25.43	-27.73	-30.87	-8.84	-24.13
e. Cash balances and Dpts.	7.17	2.86	38.44	1.54	6.12	1.48	8.21	8.02	10.25	--	--	--	--	--
2.To commercial banks	73.64	78.79	98.59	106.70	118.26	151.90	202.10	241.46	287.66	333.85	388.13	460.46	531.12	795.85
a. Treasury bills	5.21	1.51	11.55	9.38	2.98	0.46	0.16	0.14	0.03	0.06	0.10	0.11	3.06	0.72
b. CG Securities	68.43	77.28	87.04	97.32	115.28	151.44	201.94	241.32	287.63	333.79	388.03	460.35	528.06	795.13
To Banking system	226.42	263.65	317.12	364.72	436.84	532.37	653.48	758.43	869.66	1053.98	1255.71	1383.12	1496.35	1763.68
3.To Private Sector	258.09	294.93	394.78	433.12	531.20	660.94	808.99	964.95	1170.59	1344.52	1574.62	1794.02	2100.19	2542.56
a. Small savings	79.76	93.75	110.98	135.07	171.57	214.49	247.25	283.58	338.33	417.91	501.00	557.55	601.27	672.85
b. Others	178.33	201.18	283.80	298.05	359.63	446.45	561.74	681.37	832.26	926.61	1073.62	1236.47	1498.92	1869.71
4. External Debt	112.98	123.28	136.82	151.20	166.37	181.53	202.99	232.23	257.46	283.43	315.25	369.48	422.69	473.45
5. Total outstanding debt	597.49	681.86	848.72	949.04	1134.41	1374.84	1665.46	1955.61	2297.71	2681.93	3145.58	3546.62	4019.24	4779.68

-- Not available.

a. End of year stocks.

b. Provisional.

Source : RBI, Report on Currency and Finance, various issues; Ministry of Finance, Union Budget & Indian Economic Statistics
(Public Finance); Ministry of Finance, Economic Survey, various issues; World Bank Staff estimates.

Table A4.13
Tax Revenue: Center and States
(Rs. billion at current prices)

	1980-81	1981-82	1982-83	1983-84	1984-85	1985-86	1986-87	1987-88	1988-89	1989-90	1990-91	1991-92	1992-93	1993-9
1. To Reserve Bank of India	11.65	19.54	9.70	10.08	24.92	6.31	11.47	9.90	14.14	16.70	20.90	17.50	19.26	25.
a. Gross	12.11	19.66	9.84	10.93	25.76	10.65	14.58	10.09	14.29	--	--	--	--	-
b. Cash balances and Dpts.	0.46	0.12	0.14	0.85	0.84	4.34	3.11	0.19	0.15	--	--	--	--	-
2.To commercial banks	19.11	23.14	25.75	31.62	41.66	44.53	55.25	75.37	89.92	100.83	125.32	182.01	245.28	252.2
a. SG Securities	16.81	19.59	23.17	29.12	38.38	47.74	56.18	69.47	85.02	103.49	122.90	150.12	171.82	195.0
b. Others	2.30	3.55	2.58	2.50	3.28	-3.21	-0.93	5.90	4.90	-2.66	2.42	31.89	73.46	57.1
To Banking System (1)+(2)	30.76	42.68	35.45	41.70	66.58	50.84	66.72	85.27	104.06	117.53	146.22	199.51	264.54	277.4
3.To Private Sector	45.00	47.00	59.38	70.26	68.84	108.06	106.36	119.05	150.40	189.33	219.89	234.90	236.46	326.8
a. Provident Fund	24.63	29.27	36.30	44.27	48.46	58.17	66.99	83.27	103.29	126.35	157.04	186.14	222.36	278.2
b. Others	20.37	17.73	23.08	25.99	20.38	49.89	39.37	35.78	47.11	62.98	62.85	48.76	14.10	48.6
4.To Central Govt. (a-b-c)	164.01	187.61	230.40	271.90	308.52	352.23	421.58	483.69	542.06	623.41	719.56	809.63	903.29	996.
a. Loans from Center	170.71	190.80	235.58	274.56	312.26	369.84	437.02	495.34	562.22	623.41	741.17	834.90	924.12	1019.4
b. States' holding of Trs.Bil	4.35	1.09	2.97	0.17	1.43	15.20	12.68	8.88	17.38	15.18	18.80	24.95	20.83	22.9
c. States' holding of CG Se	2.35	2.10	2.21	2.49	2.31	2.41	2.76	2.77	2.78	2.80	2.81	0.32	0.00	0.0
5. Total outstanding debt	239.77	277.29	325.23	383.86	443.94	511.13	594.66	688.01	796.53	930.27	1085.67	1244.04	1404.29	1600.7

-- Not available.

a. End of year stocks.
b. Provisional.

Source : RBI, Report on Currency and Finance, various issues; Ministry of Finance, Union Budget & Indian Economic Statistics
(Public Finance); Ministry of Finance, Economic Survey, various issues; World Bank Staff estimates.

Table A4.14
Tax Revenue: Center and States
(Rs. billion at current prices)

	1980-81	1985-86	1986-87	1987-88	1988-89	1989-90	1990-91	1991-92	1992-93	1993-94[b]
1. To Reserve Bank of India	164.43	386.78	462.85	526.87	596.14	736.83	888.48	940.16	984.49	993.00
a. Centre	152.78	380.47	451.38	516.97	582.00	720.13	867.58	922.66	965.23	967.83
b. State	11.65	6.31	11.47	9.90	14.14	16.70	20.90	17.50	19.26	25.17
2.To commercial banks	92.75	196.43	257.35	316.83	377.58	434.68	513.45	642.47	776.40	1048.09
a. Centre	73.64	151.90	202.10	241.46	287.66	333.85	388.13	460.46	531.12	795.85
b. State	19.11	44.53	55.25	75.37	89.92	100.83	125.32	182.01	245.28	252.25
To Banking System (1)+(2)	257.18	583.21	720.20	843.70	973.72	1171.51	1401.93	1582.63	1760.89	2041.09
3.To Private Sector	296.39	751.39	899.91	1072.35	1300.84	1515.87	1772.90	2003.65	2315.84	2846.45
a. Small savings	79.76	214.49	247.25	283.58	338.33	417.91	501.00	557.55	601.28	672.85
b. Others	216.63	536.90	652.66	788.77	962.51	1097.96	1271.90	1446.10	1714.56	2173.60
4. External Debt	112.98	181.53	202.99	232.23	257.46	283.43	315.25	369.48	422.69	473.45
5. Total outstanding debt	666.55	1516.13	1823.10	2148.28	2532.02	2970.81	3490.08	3955.76	4499.41	5360.98
Loans to States from Centre	170.71	369.84	437.02	495.34	562.22	641.39	741.17	834.90	924.12	1019.45

-- Not available.

a. End of year stocks.
b. Provisional.

Source: RBI, Report on Currency and Finance, various issues; Ministry of Finance, Union Budget & Indian Economic Statistics (Public Finance); Ministry of Finance, Economic Survey, various issues; World Bank Staff estimates.

Table 4.15(a)
Tax Revenue: Center and States
(Rs billion)

	Sixth Plan (80-81 - 84-85)		Seventh Plan (85-86 - 89-90)		Annual Plans		Eighth Plan			
					90-91	91-92	92-93 - 96-97)	92-93	93-94	1994-95
	Proj.	Actuals	Proj.	Actuals	Actuals	Actuals	Projected	Actuals	Actuals	Revised
A Agriculture & Allied Programs	119.15	152.02	222.34	315.10	85.44	90.59	636.43	105.91	126.60	154.13
Agriculture	56.95	66.24	105.24	127.93	33.96	38.51	224.67	42.16	42.64	56.78
Rural Development	53.64	69.97	89.06	152.46	41.21	41.42	344.25	50.91	70.33	82.70
Special Area Program	14.80	15.81	28.04	34.70	10.27	10.67	67.50	12.84	13.64	14.66
B Irrigation & Flood Control	121.60	109.31	169.79	165.91	38.37	42.32	325.25	47.05	53.71	54.10
Minor Irrigation	18.10	18.48	28.05	31.92	8.35	8.44	59.77	9.95	10.48	10.79
Major Irrigation	84.48	74.93	115.56	110.20	25.01	28.24	224.15	30.47	35.71	35.97
Flood Control	10.45	8.11	9.47	9.45	2.08	2.64	16.23	3.30	3.66	2.97
Command Area Development	8.56	7.79	16.71	14.33	2.93	3.00	25.10	3.33	3.85	4.37
C Industry and Minerals	150.18	169.50	221.08	290.99	82.40	65.64	469.22	74.44	84.81	107.90
Village & Small Scale	17.81	19.45	27.53	32.49	9.07	9.41	63.34	9.95	11.52	14.59
Large & Medium Industries	132.37	150.05	193.55	258.50	73.33	56.23	405.88	64.49	73.29	93.30
D Energy	265.35	307.51	551.29	618.20	179.98	197.34	1155.61	202.90	269.09	290.26
Power	192.65	182.98	342.74	378.95	113.34	145.18	795.89	121.57	147.73	156.72
Petroleum	43.00	84.82	129.35	161.31	41.30	33.40	240.00	56.98	95.89	105.09
Coal	28.70	38.08	74.01	71.22	23.92	17.10	105.07	22.77	22.93	25.40
E Transport	124.12	142.07	229.71	297.70	86.96	93.14	559.26	106.63	119.77	152.12
Railways	51.00	65.87	123.34	165.50	49.16	53.93	272.02	61.62	59.01	68.89
Roads & Road Transport	46.35	50.82	71.90	84.59	21.32	24.82	169.52	28.48	32.49	39.84
Ports & Shipping[a]	14.86	12.13	23.13	26.07	10.97	8.45	76.14	7.28	15.95	19.27
Civil Aviation	8.59	9.57	7.58	18.99	4.92	5.47	40.83	8.82	11.46	23.41
F Communication & Broadcastin	31.34	34.69	61.14	98.93	33.54	36.14	289.66	51.51	62.02	74.98
G Science & Technology	8.65	10.11	24.63	30.23	7.87	8.62	90.42	9.30	11.53	14.74
H Social Services	140.35	159.15	295.78	332.61	87.90	102.99	751.55	113.23	140.16	182.23
Education	25.24	29.78	63.83	76.85	20.63	23.75	196.00	26.19	31.47	42.82
Health & Family Welfare	28.31	34.12	64.49	68.09	17.46	19.48	140.76	22.22	26.13	31.39
Housing & Urban Developme	24.88	28.38	42.30	48.36	12.53	13.52	105.50	14.42	21.47	24.31
Water Supply & Sanitation	39.22	39.97	65.22	70.92	18.45	22.46	167.11	22.84	27.20	34.35
Other Social Services	22.70	26.90	59.94	68.38	18.84	23.77	142.19	27.55	33.89	49.35
I Others	8.02	16.50	24.24	57.94	12.72	10.74	63.60	17.56	13.11	31.59
J TOTAL	975.0	1100.9	1800.0	2207.6	615.18	647.51	4341.00	728.52	880.81	1062.04

Note: The Plan totals are at base year prices for projections and at current prices for actuals.

a. Covers major and minor ports, shipping, lighthouses and inland water.

Source: Planning Commission.

Table 4.15(b)
Projected and Actual Plan Outlays by Sectors
(annual averages at constant 1980-81 prices - Rs. billion)

	Sixth Plan (80-81 - 84-85)		Seventh Plan (85-86 - 89-90)		Annual Plans		Eighth Plan			
					90-91	91-92	92-93 - 96-97)	92-93	93-94	1994-95
	Proj.	Actuals	Proj.	Actuals	Actuals	Actuals	Projected	Actuals	Actuals	Revised
A Agriculture & Allied Programs	26.8	24.8	30.3	33.7	36.0	32.7	46.0	35.5	39.7	45.2
Agriculture	12.8	10.8	14.3	13.7	14.3	13.9	16.2	14.1	13.4	16.6
Rural Development	12.1	11.4	12.1	16.3	17.3	15.0	24.9	17.1	22.0	24.2
Special Area Program	3.3	2.6	3.8	3.7	4.3	3.9	4.9	4.3	4.3	4.3
B Irrigation & Flood Control	27.3	17.8	23.1	17.7	16.2	15.3	23.5	15.8	16.8	15.9
Minor Irrigation	4.1	3.0	3.8	3.4	3.5	3.1	4.3	3.3	3.3	3.2
Major Irrigation	19.0	12.2	15.8	11.8	10.5	10.2	16.2	10.2	11.2	10.5
Flood Control	2.3	1.3	1.3	1.0	0.9	1.0	1.2	1.1	1.1	0.9
Command Area Development	1.9	1.3	2.3	1.5	1.2	1.1	1.8	1.1	1.2	1.3
C Industry and Minerals	33.7	27.6	30.1	31.1	34.7	23.7	33.9	25.0	26.6	31.6
Village & Small Scale	4.0	3.2	3.8	3.5	3.8	3.4	4.6	3.3	3.6	4.3
Large & Medium Industries	29.7	24.4	26.4	27.6	30.9	20.3	29.3	21.6	23.0	27.3
D Energy	59.6	50.1	75.2	66.0	75.8	71.3	83.5	68.1	84.3	85.1
Power	43.3	29.8	46.7	40.5	47.7	52.5	57.5	40.8	46.3	45.9
Petroleum	9.7	13.8	17.6	17.2	17.4	12.1	17.4	19.1	30.0	30.8
Coal	6.4	6.2	10.1	7.6	10.1	6.2	7.6	7.6	7.2	7.4
E Transport	27.9	23.1	31.3	31.8	36.6	33.7	40.4	35.8	37.5	44.6
Railways	11.5	10.7	16.8	17.7	20.7	19.5	19.7	20.7	18.5	20.2
Roads & Road Transport	10.4	8.3	9.8	9.0	9.0	9.0	12.3	9.6	10.2	11.7
Ports & Shipping[a]	3.3	2.0	3.2	2.8	4.6	3.1	5.5	2.4	5.0	5.6
Civil Aviation	1.9	1.6	1.0	2.0	2.1	2.0	3.0	3.0	3.6	6.9
F Communication & Broadcastin	7.0	5.6	8.3	10.6	14.1	13.1	20.9	17.3	19.4	22.0
G Science & Technology	1.9	1.6	3.4	3.2	3.3	3.1	6.5	3.1	3.6	4.3
H Social Services	31.5	25.9	40.3	35.5	37.0	37.2	54.3	38.0	43.9	53.4
Education	5.7	4.9	8.7	8.2	8.7	8.6	14.2	8.8	9.9	12.5
Health & Family Welfare	6.4	5.6	8.8	7.3	7.3	7.0	10.2	7.5	8.2	9.2
Housing & Urban Developme	5.6	4.6	5.8	5.2	5.3	4.9	7.6	4.8	6.7	7.1
Water Supply & Sanitation	8.8	6.5	8.9	7.6	7.8	8.1	12.1	7.7	8.5	10.1
Other Social Services	5.1	4.4	8.2	7.3	7.9	8.6	10.3	9.2	10.6	14.5
I Others	1.8	2.7	3.3	6.2	5.4	3.9	4.6	5.9	4.1	9.3
J TOTAL	219.1	179.3	245.4	235.9	258.9	234.1	313.8	244.4	275.9	311.2
Memo Item: Investment Deflator	89.0	122.8	146.7	187.2	237.6	276.6	276.6	298.1	319.3	341.2

Note: See note to Table 4.15(a).

a. Covers major and minor ports, shipping, lighthouses and inland water.

Source: Planning Commission.

Table A4.15(c)
Projected and Actual Plan Outlays by Sectors
(percentage distribution and achievement rates)[a]

	Sixth Plan (80-81 - 84-85)		Seventh Plan (85-86 - 89-90)		Annual Plans		Eighth Plan (92-93 - 96-97)			
					90-91	91-92		92-93	93-94	94-95
	% share[b]	Achieve-ment[c]	% share[b]	Achieve-ment[c]	Achieve-ment[c]	Achieve-ment[c]	% share[b]	Achieve-ment[c]	Achieve-ment[c]	Achieve-ment[c]
A Agriculture & Allied Programs	12.2	13.8	12.4	14.3	13.9	14.0	14.7	14.5	14.4	14.5
Agriculture	5.8	6.0	5.8	5.8	5.5	5.9	5.2	5.8	4.8	5.3
Rural Development	5.5	6.4	4.9	6.9	6.7	6.4	7.9	7.0	8.0	7.8
Special Area Program	1.5	1.4	1.6	1.6	1.7	1.6	1.6	1.8	1.5	1.4
B Irrigation & Flood Control	12.5	9.9	9.4	7.5	6.2	6.5	7.5	6.5	6.1	5.1
Minor Irrigation	1.9	1.7	1.6	1.4	1.4	1.3	1.4	1.4	1.2	1.0
Major Irrigation	8.7	6.8	6.4	5.0	4.1	4.4	5.2	4.2	4.1	3.4
Flood Control	1.1	0.7	0.5	0.4	0.3	0.4	0.4	0.5	0.4	0.3
Command Area Development	0.9	0.7	0.9	0.6	0.5	0.5	0.6	0.5	0.4	0.4
C Industry and Minerals	15.4	15.4	12.3	13.2	13.4	10.1	10.8	10.2	9.6	10.2
Village & Small Scale	1.8	1.8	1.5	1.5	1.5	1.5	1.5	1.4	1.3	1.4
Large & Medium Industries	13.6	13.6	10.8	11.7	11.9	8.7	9.3	8.9	8.3	8.8
D Energy	27.2	27.9	30.6	28.0	29.3	30.5	26.6	27.9	30.6	27.3
Power	19.8	16.6	19.0	17.2	18.4	22.4	18.3	16.7	16.8	14.8
Petroleum	4.4	7.7	7.2	7.3	6.7	5.2	5.5	7.8	10.9	9.9
Coal	2.9	3.5	4.1	3.2	3.9	2.6	2.4	3.1	2.6	2.4
E Transport	12.7	12.9	12.8	13.5	14.1	14.4	12.9	14.6	13.6	14.3
Railways	5.2	6.0	6.9	7.5	8.0	8.3	6.3	8.5	6.7	6.5
Roads & Road Transport	4.8	4.6	4.0	3.8	3.5	3.8	3.9	3.9	3.7	3.8
Ports & Shipping[d]	1.5	1.1	1.3	1.2	1.8	1.3	1.8	1.0	1.8	1.8
Civil Aviation	0.9	0.9	0.4	0.9	0.8	0.8	0.9	1.2	1.3	2.2
F Communication & Broadcastin	3.2	3.2	3.4	4.5	5.5	5.6	6.7	7.1	7.0	7.1
G Science & Technology	0.9	0.9	1.4	1.4	1.3	1.3	2.1	1.3	1.3	1.4
H Social Services	14.4	14.5	16.4	15.1	14.3	15.9	17.3	15.5	15.9	17.2
Education	2.6	2.7	3.5	3.5	3.4	3.7	4.5	3.6	3.6	4.0
Health & Family Welfare	2.9	3.1	3.6	3.1	2.8	3.0	3.2	3.1	3.0	3.0
Housing & Urban Developme	2.6	2.6	2.4	2.2	2.0	2.1	2.4	2.0	2.4	2.3
Water Supply & Sanitation	4.0	3.6	3.6	3.2	3.0	3.5	3.8	3.1	3.1	3.2
Other Social Services	2.3	2.4	3.3	3.1	3.1	3.7	3.3	3.8	3.8	4.6
I Others	0.8	1.5	1.3	2.6	2.1	1.7	1.5	2.4	1.5	3.0
J TOTAL	100.0	100.0	100.0	100.0	100.0	100.0	100.0	100.0	100.0	100.0

a. Derived from Table 4.15(a).
b. Percentage share in total plan outlay.
c. Actual outlay as a percentage of target outlay for the Plan.
d. Covers major and minor ports, shipping, lighthouses and inland water.

Source: Planning Commission.

Table A5.1
Money Supply and Sources of Change, 1985-86 - 1995-96
(Rs. billion)

	1985-86	1986-87	1987-88	1988-89	1989-90	1990-91	1991-92	1992-93	1993-94	1994-95	1995-96[a]
BROAD MONEY SUPPLY (M3)	1193.99	1416.42	1642.79	2002.41	2309.48	2658.28	3170.49	3668.25	4344.07	5308.02	6004.98
Narrow Money Supply (M1)	440.99	515.22	585.59	711.01	810.58	928.92	1144.06	1240.66	1507.78	1914.72	2131.82
Currency with Public	250.59	283.82	335.59	380.71	463.00	530.48	610.98	682.73	823.01	1007.89	1182.53
Deposit Money (total)	187.50	228.30	246.00	323.40	341.60	391.70	524.23	544.80	659.52	873.03	949.29
Time Deposits with Banks	753.00	901.20	1057.20	1291.40	1498.90	1729.36	2026.43	2427.59	2836.29	3393.30	3873.14
SOURCES OF CHANGE											
Net Bank Domestic Credit	1411.24	1667.61	1918.57	2300.36	2688.57	3119.62	3462.56	3963.73	4416.92	5120.71	6013.08
To Government	583.21	720.20	843.70	973.73	1171.53	1401.93	1582.63	1762.38	2039.18	2224.16	2626.69
From Reserve Bank of India (RBI)	386.78	462.85	526.87	596.15	736.83	888.48	940.16	984.49	993.00	1014.78	1269.61
From Other Banks	196.43	257.35	316.83	377.58	434.70	513.45	642.47	777.89	1046.18	1209.38	1357.08
To Commercial Sector	828.03	947.41	1074.87	1326.63	1517.04	1717.69	1879.93	2201.35	2377.74	2896.55	3386.39
From Reserve Bank of India	30.52	33.94	37.90	55.24	63.49	63.42	72.60	62.20	64.45	65.93	68.54
From Other Banks	797.51	913.47	1036.97	1271.39	1453.55	1654.27	1807.33	2139.15	2313.29	2830.62	3317.85
Net Foreign Exchange Assets of Banking Sector	38.72	48.15	56.72	68.00	66.51	105.81	212.26	244.43	526.26	759.24	754.10
Government's Currency Liabilities to the Public	9.40	11.92	13.80	14.75	15.55	16.21	17.04	18.24	19.90	23.79	22.90
Net Non-Monetary Liabilities	265.37	311.26	346.30	380.70	461.15	583.36	521.37	558.15	619.01	595.72	785.11
of Reserve Bank of India	107.07	134.44	142.25	169.36	175.36	270.22	274.15	282.46	260.37	293.61	378.19
of Other Banks	158.30	176.82	204.05	211.34	285.79	313.14	247.22	275.69	358.64	302.11	406.92
Broad Money Supply (M3)	1193.99	1416.42	1642.79	2002.41	2309.48	2658.28	3170.49	3668.25	4344.07	5308.02	6004.98
GDP at market prices	2622.43	2929.49	3332.01	3957.82	4568.21	5355.34	6167.99	7053.28	8010.32	9456.15	10918.5

Note: 1995-96 figures are as of March 31 on the basis of the closure of government accounts.

a. The data for 1994-95 are not strictly comparable with those of the previous years, as M3 data for 1994-95 include scheduled commercial banks' data for 27 fortnights while for the previous years they include 26 fortnights.

Source: Ministry of Finance, Economic Survey, various issues; Reserve Bank of India, RBI Bulletin (Weekly Statistical Supplement).

Table A5.2

Base Money Supply and Sources of Change, 1985-86 - 1995-96

(Rs. billion)

	1985-86	1986-87	1987-88	1988-89	1989-90	1990-91	1991-92	1992-93	1993-94	1994-95	1995
TOTAL BASE MONEY SUPPLY	381.66	448.08	534.90	629.59	775.91	877.79	995.05	1107.79	1386.71	1692.79	1943
Currency with Public	250.59	283.82	335.59	380.71	463.00	530.48	610.98	682.73	823.01	1007.89	1182
Other Deposits with RBI	2.89	3.09	3.97	6.94	5.98	6.74	8.85	13.13	25.25	33.80	34
Cash with Banks	14.65	15.31	15.63	19.72	19.86	22.34	26.40	30.53	30.94	38.92	41
Bank Deposits with RBI	113.53	145.86	179.71	222.22	287.07	318.23	348.82	381.40	507.51	612.18	685
SOURCES OF CHANGE											
RBI Claims	441.92	524.39	609.18	722.18	875.03	1051.97	1063.78	1145.54	1112.96	1215.41	1557
On Government (net)	386.78	462.85	526.87	596.15	736.83	888.48	940.16	984.49	993.00	1014.78	1269
On Banks	24.62	27.60	44.41	70.79	74.71	100.07	51.02	98.85	55.51	134.70	219
On Commercial Sector	30.52	33.94	37.90	55.24	63.49	63.42	72.60	62.20	64.45	65.93	68.
Net Foreign Exchange Assets of RBI	37.41	46.21	54.17	62.02	60.69	79.83	188.38	226.47	514.22	747.20	740
Government's Currency Liabilities to the Public	9.40	11.92	13.80	14.75	15.55	16.21	17.04	18.24	19.90	23.79	22.
Net Non-Monetary Liabilities of Reserve Bank of India	107.07	134.44	142.25	169.36	175.36	270.22	274.15	282.46	260.37	293.61	378.
Total Base Money Supply	381.66	448.08	534.90	629.59	775.91	877.79	995.05	1107.79	1386.71	1692.79	1943.
GDP at market prices	2622.43	2929.49	3332.01	3957.82	4568.21	5355.34	6167.99	7053.28	8010.32	9456.15	10918

Note: 1995-96 figures are as of March 31 on the basis of the closure of government accounts.

a. The data for 1994-95 are not strictly comparable with those of the previous years, as M3 data for 1994-95 include scheduled commercial banks' data for 27 fortnights while for the previous years they include 26 fortnights.

Source: Ministry of Finance, Economic Survey, various issues; Reserve Bank of India, RBI Bulletin (Weekly Statistical Supplement).

Table A5.3
Selected Monetary Policy Instruments

Year & Month	Bank Rate	Minimum Cash Reserve[a] Ratio	Statutory Liquidity[b] Ratio
1981 July 31	10	6.5	34.0
August 21	10	7.0	34.0
September 25	10	7.0	34.5
October 30	10	7.0	35.0
November 27	10	7.3	35.0
December 25	10	7.5	35.0
1982 January 29	10	7.8	35.0
April 10	10	7.3	35.0
June 11	10	7.0	35.0
1983 May 28	10	7.5	35.0
July 30	10	8.0	35.0
August 27	10	8.5	35.0
November 12	10	Incremental CRR of 10% over November 11, 1983	35.0
1984 February 4	10	9.0	35.0
July 28	10	9.0	35.5
September 1	10	9.0	36.0
October 30	10	9.0	36.0
1985 June 8	10	9.0	36.5
July 6	10	9.0	37.0
1987 February 28	10	9.5	37.0
April 25	10	9.5	37.5
October 24	10	10.0	37.5
1988 January 2	10	10.0	38.0
July 2	10	10.5	38.0
July 30	10	11.0	38.0
1989 July 1	10	15.0	38.0
1990 September 22	10	15.0	38.5
1991 July 4	11	15.0	38.5
October 9	12	15.0	38.5
1992 April 1	12	15.0	30.0
1993 April 17	12	14.5	30.0
May 15	12	14.0	30.0
September 17	12	14.0	25.0
1994 June 11	12	14.5	25.0
July 9	12	14.8	25.0
August 6	12	15.0	25.0
1995 November 11	12	14.5	25.0
December 9	12	14.0	25.0
1996 April 27	12	13.5	25.0
May 11	12	13.0	25.0
July 6	12	12.0	25.0

Note: Dates given are those on which the announced measures take effect.

a. Minimum cash reserves to be deposited with the RBI as % of net demand and time liabilities (NDTL).

b. The ratio of liquid assets, exclusive of those under (a), to aggregate demand and time liabilities upto March 28, 1985 and net demand and time liabilities with effect from March 29, 1985.

Sources: Reserve Bank of India, Report of the Committee to Review the Working of the Monetary System, 1985; Reserve Bank of India, Annual Report, various issues.

Table A5.4
Structure of Short-term and Long-term Interest Rates
(percent per annum)

	1980-81	1985-86	1990-91	1991-92	1992-93	1993-94	199
A. SHORT-TERM RATES							
Reserve Bank Rate	9.0	10.0	10.0	12.0	12.0	12.0	
Treasury Bills:							
91-day [a]	4.6	4.6	4.6	4.6	8.8-10.7	7.1-11.1	7.2-
182-day			10.0-10.1	8.8-10.1	7.8-8.4		
364-day					9.9-10.3	10.0-11.4	9.4-
Call Money Rate (Bombay)	7.1	10.0	15.9	19.6	14.4	7.0	
Commercial Bank Rates:							
Maximum Deposit Rate [b]	10.0	11.0	11.0	13.0	11.0	10.0	
Minimum Lending Rate	13.5		16.0	19.0	17.0	14.0	
B. LONG-TERM RATES							
I.D.B.I. Prime Lending Rate	14.0	14.0	14.0-15.0	18.0-20.0	17.0-19.0	14.5-17.5	
Company Deposit Rates: [c]							
Private Sector Companies [d]							
(i) 1 year	9.0-13.5	10.0-15.0	10.5-14.0	10.5-15.0	12.0-15.0	12.0-14.0	13.0-
(ii) 2 years	10.0-14.5	12.0-15.0	12.0-14.0	12.0-15.0	13.0-15.0	13.0-14.0	14.0-
(iii) 3 years	13.0-15.5	13.0-15.0	13.5-14.0	14.0-15.0	15.0	14.0	14.0-
Public Sector Companies							
(i) 1 year	11.0	11.5-12.0	10.5-12.0	10.5-15.0	13.0	12.0-15.0	12.0-
(ii) 2 years	12.0	12.0-13.0	11.5-13.0	11.5-15.0	14.0	13.0-15.0	13.0-
(iii) 3 years	13.5	13.5-14.5	13.0-14.0	13.0-15.0	15.0	14.0-15.0	14.0-
Average Yield - Ordinary Shares	5.9	3.2	2.6	2.1	1.7	2.2	
Redemption Yield - Government of India Securities							
(i) Short-term (1-5 years)	4.7-6.0	5.4-9.8	7.0-21.7	8.4-26.3	9.1-23.8	11.9-12.9	9.8-
(ii) Medium-term (5-15 years)	5.8-6.8	6.5-9.5	9.4-12.7	9.5-13.4	9.5-14.8	12.7-13.3	11.3-
(iii) Long-term (above 15 years)	6.4-7.5	8.4-11.5	10.9-12.0	9.9-12.4	8.8-12.5	12.9-13.4	11.8-

Note: 1994-95 is preliminary.

a. Effective 8 January, 1993, a new auction system for 91-day Treasury Bills was introduced.

b. Effective 22 April, 1992, a single 'maximum deposit rate' has been for deposits of various maturities.
   Earlier different rates were prescribed for different deposit maturities.

c. Deposits accepted from the public.

d. Well-established private sector companies.

Source: Reserve Bank of India, <u>Report on Currency and Finance</u>, various issues.

Table A5.5
Sectoral Deployment of Gross Bank Credit
(Rs billion - change during year)

	1985-86	1986-87	1987-88	1988-89	1989-90	1990-91	1991-92	1992-93	1993-94	1994-95	April-August 1994-95	April-August 1995-96
Gross Bank Credit	72.57	73.56	76.91	154.68	169.43	153.48	79.86	211.34	97.18	407.46	18.13	-9.67
Public Food Procurement Credit	-1.30	-4.31	-29.14	-14.21	12.37	25.00	1.64	20.73	41.64	13.68	6.23	18.45
Gross Non-Food Credit	73.87	77.87	106.05	168.89	157.06	128.48	78.22	190.61	55.54	393.78	11.90	-28.12
Priority Sectors	31.57	34.84	40.20	51.49	61.64	25.32	25.10	44.07	40.48	102.61	9.41	-1.00
Agriculture	13.98	15.12	14.39	19.41	25.76	2.24	14.07	18.06	12.45	27.72	0.49	0.08
Small Scale Industries	12.04	12.92	17.12	23.15	24.08	16.38	9.69	18.76	25.91	49.95	2.28	-2.39
Other Priority Sectors	5.55	6.80	8.69	8.93	11.80	6.70	1.34	7.25	2.12	24.94	6.64	1.31
Industry (Medium & Large)	24.83	29.34	37.97	70.32	60.87	62.46	25.82	115.46	-7.71	174.76	-4.69	-7.11
Wholesale Trade (other than food procurement)	4.17	0.14	5.18	11.69	7.05	4.38	2.44	8.15	3.61	24.19	0.68	-0.30
Other Sectors	13.30	13.55	22.70	35.39	27.60	36.32	24.86	22.93	19.16	92.22	6.50	-19.71
Export Credit (included in Gross Non-Food Credit)	0.74	7.37	7.71	22.24	21.04	9.41	11.08	50.62	17.30	82.96	18.81	-12.90
Priority Sector advances as percent of net bank credit [a]	40.80	42.20	44.10	43.20	42.40	39.20	38.70	35.10	35.30	33.20	35.40	33.20

In the last month of each period, advances include Participation Certificates.

Source: Ministry of Finance, Economic Survey, various issues.

Table A6.1
Production of Major Crops

	1980-81	1983-84	1984-85	1985-86	1986-87	1987-88	1988-89	1989-90	1990-91	1991-92	1992-93	1993-94	19
Total Foodgrains	129.6	152.4	145.5	150.4	143.4	140.4	169.9	171.0	176.4	168.4	179.5	184.3	
Kharif	77.6	89.2	84.5	85.2	80.2	74.6	95.6	101.0	99.4	91.6	101.5	100.4	
Rabi	51.9	63.1	61.0	65.2	63.2	65.8	74.3	70.0	77.0	76.8	78.0	83.9	
Total Cereals	119.0	139.5	133.6	137.1	131.7	129.4	156.1	158.2	162.1	156.4	166.6	170.9	
Kharif	73.9	83.9	79.8	80.7	76.0	70.2	90.0	95.5	94.0	87.2	95.8	95.0	
Rabi	45.1	55.6	53.8	56.4	55.7	59.2	66.1	62.7	68.1	69.2	70.8	75.9	
Rice	53.6	60.1	58.3	63.8	60.6	56.9	70.5	73.6	74.3	74.7	72.9	80.3	
Kharif	50.1	55.0	53.8	59.4	53.6	49.0	63.4	65.9	66.3	66.4	65.3	70.7	
Rabi	3.5	5.0	4.6	4.4	7.0	7.8	7.1	7.7	8.0	8.3	7.6	9.6	
Wheat	36.3	45.5	44.1	47.1	44.3	46.2	54.1	49.8	55.1	55.7	57.2	59.8	
Barley (Jowar)	10.4	11.9	11.4	10.2	9.2	12.2	10.2	12.9	11.7	8.1	12.8	11.4	
Kharif	7.5	8.7	7.8	7.3	6.5	8.6	7.1	9.2	8.3	5.7	9.4	7.3	
Rabi	2.9	3.3	3.6	2.9	2.7	3.6	3.1	3.7	3.4	2.4	3.4	4.1	
Maize	7.0	7.9	8.4	6.6	7.6	5.7	8.2	9.7	9.0	8.1	10.0	9.6	
Bajra	5.3	7.7	6.0	3.7	4.5	3.3	7.8	6.6	6.9	4.7	8.9	5.0	
Total Pulses	10.6	12.9	12.0	13.4	11.7	11.0	13.8	12.8	14.3	12.0	12.8	13.3	
Kharif	3.8	5.4	4.8	4.6	4.2	4.4	5.6	5.5	5.4	4.4	5.6	5.4	
Rabi	6.8	7.5	7.2	8.8	7.5	6.6	8.2	7.3	8.9	7.6	7.2	7.9	
Gram	4.3	4.8	4.6	5.8	4.5	3.6	5.1	4.2	5.4	4.1	4.4	5.0	
Tur	2.0	2.6	2.6	2.4	2.3	2.3	2.7	2.7	2.4	2.1	2.3	2.7	
Total Oilseeeds [a]	9.4	12.7	12.9	10.8	11.3	12.6	18.0	16.9	18.6	18.6	20.1	21.5	
Kharif	5.0	7.2	7.0	6.0	6.4	6.4	10.5	9.6	9.8	9.3	12.0	12.3	
Rabi	4.4	5.5	5.9	4.8	4.9	6.2	7.5	7.3	8.8	9.3	8.1	9.2	
Groundnut	5.0	7.1	6.4	5.1	5.9	5.8	9.7	8.1	7.5	7.1	8.6	7.8	
Kharif	3.7	5.3	4.7	3.7	4.4	4.2	7.5	6.1	5.1	5.0	6.7	5.7	
Rabi	1.3	1.8	1.7	1.4	1.4	1.7	2.2	2.0	2.4	2.1	1.9	2.1	
Rapeseed & Mustard	2.3	2.6	3.1	2.7	2.6	3.4	4.4	4.1	5.2	5.9	4.8	5.3	
Sugarcane	154.2	174.1	170.3	170.7	186.1	196.7	203.0	225.6	241.0	254.0	228.0	229.7	
Cotton	7.0	6.4	8.5	8.7	6.9	6.4	8.7	11.4	9.8	9.7	11.4	10.7	
Jute & Mesta	8.2	7.7	7.8	12.6	8.6	6.8	7.9	8.3	9.2	10.3	8.6	8.4	
Jute	6.5	6.3	6.5	10.9	7.3	5.8	6.7	7.1	7.9	8.9	7.5	7.3	
Mesta	1.7	1.4	1.3	1.8	1.3	1.0	1.2	1.2	1.3	1.4	1.1	1.1	
Potato	9.7	12.1	12.6	10.4	12.7	14.1	14.9	14.8	15.2	16.4	15.2	17.6	

-- Not available.

Notes: Units of measurement of all commodities is million tonnes, except in the case of cotton, jute and mesta where production is in terms of millions of bale
Figures for 1994-95 are provisional.

a. Includes groundnuts, rapeseeds and mustard, sesame, linseed, castorseed, nigerseed, safflower, sunflower and soybean.

Source: Ministry of Finance, Economic Survey, various issues.

Table A6.2
Irrigated Area Under Different Crops
(million hectares)

	1980-81	1982-83	1983-84	1984-85	1985-86	1986-87	1987-88	1988-89	1989-90	1990-91	1991-92	1992-93
Foodgrains	37.6	38.4	40.2	40.1	40.4	41.8	40.5	43.9	44.3	44.5	45.5	46.3
al Cereals	35.8	36.6	38.5	38.4	38.3	39.5	38.4	41.8	41.9	41.9	43.0	43.8
ce	16.4	16.0	17.4	17.7	17.7	18.1	17.0	19.1	19.4	19.2	19.9	19.6
war	0.8	0.6	0.6	0.7	0.7	0.8	0.8	0.8	0.9	0.9	0.8	0.8
jra	0.6	0.6	0.6	0.6	0.6	0.7	0.8	0.6	0.7	0.6	0.7	0.6
aize	1.2	1.2	1.0	1.0	1.1	1.3	1.2	1.2	1.2	1.2	1.3	1.3
heat	15.6	17.0	17.9	17.5	17.3	17.7	17.8	19.1	18.8	19.4	19.5	20.7
rley	0.9	0.7	0.7	0.6	0.7	0.6	0.6	0.6	0.5	0.5	0.6	0.6
Pulses	2.0	1.8	1.7	1.8	2.1	2.3	2.0	2.2	2.3	2.6	2.4	2.4
r Crops												
eeds [a]	2.3	2.6	3.1	3.5	3.4	3.4	4.3	5.0	5.2	5.6	6.6	6.4
ton	2.1	2.3	2.3	1.9	2.3	2.2	2.1	2.4	2.6	2.5	2.6	2.7
arcane	2.4	2.8	2.6	2.6	2.6	2.8	3.0	3.0	3.1	3.3	3.6	3.6

ilseeds include groundnuts, rapeseed and mustard, linseed, sesame, and others.

ce: Ministry of Finance, Economic Survey, various issues.

Table A6.3
Yield Per Hectare of Major Crops
(kgs. per hectare)

	1980-81	1983-84	1984-85	1985-86	1986-87	1987-88	1988-89	1989-90	1990-91	1991-92	1992-93	1993-94	1994-95
Total Foodgrains	1023	1102	1149	1175	1128	1173	1331	1349	1380	1382	1457	1501	1547
Kharif	933	1060	1041	1042	985	996	1166	1241	1231	1174	1302	1324	1341
Rabi	1195	1343	1341	1410	1382	1468	1628	1544	1635	1751	1725	1787	1864
Total Cereals	1142	1296	1285	1323	1266	1315	1493	1530	1571	1574	1654	1701	1763
Kharif	1015	1148	1129	1140	1074	1082	1270	1366	1357	1305	1440	1465	1488
Rabi	1434	1608	1617	1718	1673	1763	1964	1875	2010	2126	2068	2132	2280
Rice	1336	1457	1417	1552	1471	1465	1689	1745	1740	1751	1744	1888	1921
Kharif	1303	1413	1374	1514	1393	1368	1627	1677	1670	1676	1676	1807	1840
Rabi	2071	2205	2274	2329	2563	2640	2548	2678	2671	2720	2720	2816	2837
Wheat	1630	1844	1870	2046	1916	2002	2244	2121	2281	2394	2327	2380	2553
Barley (Jowar)	660	726	715	633	576	762	697	869	814	655	982	898	783
Kharif	737	851	820	761	665	892	789	1053	969	757	1230	1065	970
Rabi	520	522	563	447	437	568	550	604	582	496	632	704	570
Maize	1159	1352	1456	1146	1282	1029	1395	1632	1518	1376	1676	1602	1493
Bajra	458	652	519	344	401	378	646	610	658	465	836	521	707
Total Pulses	473	548	526	547	505	515	598	549	578	533	573	598	609
Kharif	361	483	453	412	392	435	504	480	471	393	495	492	459
Rabi	571	605	589	658	604	587	686	616	672	672	654	701	736
Gram	657	663	661	742	649	629	753	652	712	739	684	783	855
Tur	689	801	819	767	722	685	779	763	673	588	652	762	651
Total Oilseeds [a]	532	679	684	570	605	629	824	742	771	719	797	799	848
Kharif	492	655	633	516	554	559	805	691	698	604	804	759	810
Rabi	588	713	758	651	687	720	851	822	872	886	786	860	900
Groundnut	736	940	898	719	841	855	1132	930	904	818	1049	941	1042
Kharif	629	835	779	602	733	737	1066	824	751	687	969	813	948
Rabi	1444	1484	1518	1549	1540	1425	1442	1532	1611	1501	1473	1624	1495
Rapeseed & Mustard	560	674	771	674	700	748	906	831	904	895	776	847	944
Sugarcane	57844	55974	57673	60000	60000	60000	61000	65000	65000	66000	64000	67000	68000
Cotton	152	141	196	197	169	168	202	252	225	216	257	249	260
Jute & Mesta	1130	1323	1242	1524	1454	1274	1540	1646	1634	1662	1658	1713	1803
Jute	1245	1417	1411	1710	1647	1496	1748	1879	1833	1837	1857	1907	1983
Mesta	828	869	764	910	865	680	909	956	988	1019	955	1008	1100
Potato	13256	15206	14806	12000	15000	16000	16000	16000	16000	16000	15000	--	--

-- Not available.

Note: Figures for 1994-95 are provisional.

a. Includes groundnuts, rapeseeds and mustard, sesame, linseed, castorseed, nigerseed, safflower, sunflower and soybean.

Source: Ministry of Finance, Economic Survey, various issues.

Table A6.4
Net Availability, Procurement and Public Distribution of Foodgrains [a]
(million tonnes)

	1980-81	1985-86	1986-87	1987-88	1988-89	1989-90	1990-91	1991-92	1992-93	1993-94	1994-95
Production	113.4	131.6	125.5	122.8	148.7	149.7	154.3	147.3	157.0	161.2	167.2
Imports	0.7	-0.5	-0.2	3.8	1.2	1.3	-0.1	-0.4	2.6	0.5	--
ange in Government Stocks	-0.2	-1.6	-9.5	-4.6	2.6	6.2	-4.4	-1.5	10.3	7.5	-0.6
Availability	114.3	133.8	134.8	130.8	147.2	144.8	158.6	148.4	149.3	154.2	167.8
curement	13.0	19.7	15.7	14.1	18.9	24.0	19.6	17.9	28.1	26.0	22.5
lic Distribution	13.0	17.3	18.7	18.6	16.4	16.0	20.8	18.8	16.4	14.0	15.3

ot available.

roduction figures relate to agricultural year. Figures for procurement and public distribution relate to calendar years.

rce: Ministry of Finance, Economic Survey, various issues.

Table A6.5
New Index of Industrial Production
(1980-81=100)

					Index						1993-94 over 1992-93	1994-9 ove 1993-9
	Weight	1986-87	1987-88	1988-89	1989-90	1990-91	1991-92	1992-93	1993-94	1994-95		
General Index	100.00	155.1	166.4	180.9	196.4	212.6	213.9	218.9	232.0	251.9	6.0	8.
Mining and Quarrying	11.46	177.9	184.6	199.1	211.6	221.2	222.5	223.7	231.5	245.8	3.5	6.
Electricity Generated	11.43	168.1	181.0	198.2	219.7	236.8	257.0	269.9	290.0	314.6	7.5	8.
Manufacturing Index	77.11	149.7	161.5	175.6	190.7	207.8	206.2	210.7	223.5	243.6	6.1	9.
Food products	5.33	133.2	139.0	148.5	150.9	169.8	178.0	175.3	160.0	181.7	-8.7	13.
Beverages, tobacco, etc.	1.57	98.5	84.9	92.1	103.0	104.8	107.3	113.7	137.8	134.4	21.2	-2.
Cotton textiles	12.31	112.5	111.2	107.8	112.3	126.6	139.0	150.1	160.5	155.8	6.9	-2.
Jute textiles	2.00	101.1	91.0	101.9	97.4	101.6	90.8	87.0	103.2	92.4	18.7	-10.
Textile products	0.82	87.1	91.7	134.2	151.7	103.2	97.2	75.8	73.4	78.4	-3.2	6.
Wood & wood products	0.45	246.1	161.7	171.7	176.0	197.2	185.0	190.5	199.3	203.0	4.6	1.
Paper & paper products	3.23	163.2	166.3	171.3	181.5	198.0	203.0	210.9	224.8	257.5	6.6	14.
Leather & leather products	0.49	177.7	185.5	177.4	188.3	194.3	181.3	187.7	204.3	211.1	8.8	3.
Rubber, plastic & petroleum prod.	4.00	149.6	155.1	168.3	173.5	174.0	172.0	174.6	176.4	181.9	1.0	3.
Chemical & chemical products	12.51	175.5	200.9	233.4	247.6	254.1	261.2	276.9	297.9	327.7	7.6	10.
Non-metallic mineral products	3.00	160.3	158.1	184.6	189.9	193.1	205.2	208.9	218.5	233.7	4.6	7.
Basic metal & alloy products	9.80	126.8	135.6	144.9	143.7	158.8	167.8	168.4	224.2	199.2	33.1	-11.
Metal products	2.29	124.5	129.6	133.5	142.6	143.1	133.1	124.6	126.5	149.5	1.5	18.
Machinery & machine tools	6.24	141.8	139.2	161.2	171.9	186.9	183.3	181.1	189.2	207.6	4.4	9.
Electrical machinery	5.78	254.7	335.2	346.0	459.2	563.6	493.7	483.6	460.1	609.2	-4.9	32.
Transport equipment	6.39	144.9	151.9	171.3	181.1	192.5	191.1	200.6	211.2	239.1	5.3	13.
Miscellaneous products	0.90	235.4	272.1	306.3	333.2	321.8	269.9	281.3	267.0	267.8	-5.1	0.

Note: Figures for 1994-95 are provisional.

Source: Ministry of Finance, Economic Survey, various issues.

Table A6.6
Production, Imports and Consumption of Fertilizers
(000' nutrient tons)

(Apr-Mar)	Nitrogenous [a]			Phosphatic [b]			Potassic		Total		
	Production	Imports	Consumption	Production	Imports	Consumption	Imports	Consumption	Production	Imports	Consumption
1980-81	2163.9	1510.2	3678.1	841.5	452.1	1213.6	796.8	623.9	3005.4	2759.1	5515.6
1981-82	3143.3	1055.1	4068.7	950.0	343.2	1322.9	643.8	676.2	4093.3	2042.1	6067.8
1982-83	3429.7	424.6	4242.5	983.7	63.4	1432.7	643.7	726.3	4413.4	1131.7	6401.5
1983-84	3491.5	656.1	5204.4	1064.1	142.6	1730.3	556.4	775.4	4555.6	1355.1	7710.1
1984-85	3917.3	2008.6	5486.1	1317.9	745.2	1886.4	871.0	838.5	5235.2	3624.8	8211.0
1985-86	4328.0	1680.0	5661.0	1428.0	816.0	2005.0	903.0	808.0	5756.0	3399.0	8474.0
1986-87	5410.0	1103.0	5716.0	1660.0	255.0	2079.0	952.0	850.0	7070.0	2310.0	8645.0
1987-88	5466.0	175.0	5717.0	1665.0	0.0	2187.0	809.0	880.0	7131.0	984.0	8784.0
1988-89	6712.0	219.0	7251.0	2252.0	407.0	2721.0	982.0	1068.0	8964.0	1608.0	11040.0
1989-90	6747.0	523.0	7386.0	1796.0	1311.0	3014.0	1280.0	1168.0	8543.0	3114.0	11568.0
1990-91	6993.0	414.0	7997.0	2052.0	1016.0	3221.0	1328.0	1328.0	9045.0	2758.0	12546.0
1991-92	7301.0	566.0	8046.0	2562.0	967.0	3321.0	1236.0	1361.0	9863.0	2769.0	12728.0
1992-93	7430.0	1160.0	8426.0	2306.0	746.0	2842.0	1082.0	884.0	9736.0	2988.0	12152.0
1993-94	7231.0	1564.0	8789.0	1816.0	722.0	2669.0	880.0	908.0	9047.0	3166.0	12366.0
1994-95 [c]	7945.0	1476.0 [d]	9507.0	2493.0	380 [d]	2932.0	1109.0 [d]	1125.0	10438.0	2965.0 [d]	13564.0
1995-96 [c]	8633.0	--	10754.0	2667.0	--	3560.0	--	1351.0	11300.0	13564.0	15665.0

Not available.

Excludes nitrogen meant for non-agricultural purposes.
Excludes data in respect of bonemeal and rockphosphate.
Anticipated.
Incorporates import of Urea in nutrient terms, the only controlled fertiliser imported on Government account.

Source: The Fertilizer Association of India, Fertilizer Statistics, various issues; Ministry of Finance, Economic Survey, various issues.

Table A6.7
Indian Railways: Freight and Passenger Traffic

| | Revenue Earning Freight Traffic | | | Passenger Traffic | | | | | | |
| | | | | Non-Suburban | | | Suburban [a] | | |
Year	Originating tonnage (mln.tons)	Net tons-kilometers (million)	Average lead (kilometers)	Passenger originating (million)	Passenger-kilometers (million)	Average lead (kilometers)	Passenger originating (million)	Passenger-kilometers (million)	Average lead (kilometers)
1980-81	195.9	147652	754	1613	167472	103.9	2000	41086	20.5
1981-82	221.2	164253	743	1640	176822	107.8	2064	43965	21.3
1982-83	228.8	167781	733	1626	181142	111.4	2029	45789	22.6
1983-84	230.1	168849	734	1491	180808	121.3	1834	42127	23.0
1984-85	236.4	172632	730	1449	182318	125.8	1884	44264	23.5
1985-86	258.5	196600	760	1549	195175	126.0	1884	45439	24.1
1986-87	277.8	214100	771	1610	208057	129.0	1970	48411	24.6
1987-88	290.2	222528	767	1637	217632	133.0	2171	51859	23.9
1988-89	302.1	222374	736	1495	211819	141.6	2022	52023	25.7
1989-90	310.0	229602	741	1544	226045	76.9	2129	54933	25.8
1990-91	318.4	235785	741	1599	236066	147.6	2281	59724	26.2
1991-92	338.0	250238	740	1637	251174	153.4	2436	63543	26.1
1992-93	350.1	252388	721	1467	239655	163.3	2298	60547	26.4
1993-94	358.7	252411	704	1406	233200	165.9	2318	63147	27.2
1994-95	373.0	259810	697	1451	243798	168.0	2359	63275	26.8
1995-96	398.0	278766	700	1509	253549	168.0	2454	65806	26.8

Note: Figures for 1994-95 and 1995-96 are revised estimates and budget estimates respectively.

a. Passengers booked between stations within the suburban areas of Bombay; from 1988/89 onwards suburban passenger traffic include
   Metro Railway, Calcutta.

Source: Ministry of Railways, Railway Budget.

Table A6.8
Petroleum Summary
Commodity Balance of Petroleum and Petroleum Products
(million tonnes)

	1980-81	1981-82	1982-83	1983-84	1984-85	1985-86	1986-87	1987-88	1988-89	1989-90	1990-91	1991-92	1992-93	1993-94	1994-95 [a]
CRUDE PETROLEUM															
Refinery Throughput	25.8	30.2	33.2	35.3	35.6	42.9	45.7	47.7	48.8	51.9	51.8	51.4	53.5	54.3	56.3
Domestic Production	10.5	16.2	21.1	26.0	29.0	30.2	30.5	30.4	32.0	34.1	33.0	30.4	27.0	27.0	32.2
(a) On-shore	5.5	8.2	8.2	8.6	8.9	9.4	9.9	10.2	10.9	12.4	11.8	11.4	11.2	11.6	12.0
(b) Off-shore	5.0	8.0	12.9	17.4	20.1	20.8	20.6	20.2	21.1	21.7	21.2	19.0	15.8	15.4	20.2
Imports	16.2	15.3	16.9	16.0	13.7	15.1	15.5	18.0	17.8	19.5	20.7	24.0	29.2	30.8	27.3
Exports	--	0.8	4.5	5.5	6.5	0.5	--	--	--	--	--	--	--	--	--
Net Imports (3-4)	16.2	14.5	12.4	10.5	7.2	14.6	15.5	18.0	17.8	19.5	20.7	24.0	29.2	30.8	27.3
PRODUCTS															
Domestic Consumption [b]	30.9	32.5	34.7	35.8	38.5	40.8	43.4	46.4	50.1	54.1	55.0	57.0	58.9	60.8	65.5
of which:															
(a) Naphtha	2.3	3.0	3.0	2.8	3.1	3.1	3.2	2.9	3.4	3.4	3.4	3.5	3.4	3.2	3.4
(b) Kerosene	4.2	4.7	5.2	5.5	6.0	6.2	6.6	7.2	7.7	8.2	8.4	8.4	8.5	8.7	9.0
(c) High Speed Diesel	10.3	10.8	12.0	12.6	13.7	14.9	16.0	17.7	18.8	20.7	21.1	22.7	24.3	25.9	28.3
(d) Fuel oils	7.5	7.2	7.3	7.6	7.9	7.9	7.9	8.1	8.5	8.8	9.0	9.2	9.3	9.2	9.9
Domestic Production	24.1	28.2	31.1	32.9	33.2	39.9	42.8	44.7	45.7	48.7	48.6	48.3	50.4	51.1	52.9
(a) Naphtha	2.1	3.0	3.0	3.6	3.5	5.0	5.6	5.5	5.4	5.2	4.9	4.5	4.6	4.7	5.7
(b) Kerosene	2.4	2.9	3.4	3.5	3.4	4.0	4.9	5.1	5.2	5.7	5.5	5.3	5.2	5.3	5.3
(c) High Speed Diesel	7.4	9.0	9.8	10.9	11.1	14.6	15.5	16.3	16.7	17.7	17.2	17.4	18.3	18.8	19.6
(d) Fuel oils	6.1	6.9	8.0	8.0	7.9	8.0	8.0	8.5	8.9	9.0	9.4	9.6	10.4	10.3	9.8
Imports	7.3	4.9	5.0	4.3	6.1	3.9	3.1	3.9	6.5	6.6	8.7	9.4	11.3	12.1	14.0
Exports [c]	--	0.1	0.8	1.5	0.9	2.0	2.5	3.4	2.3	2.6	2.6	2.9	3.7	4.0	3.3
Net Imports	7.3	4.8	4.2	2.8	5.2	1.9	0.6	0.5	4.2	4.0	6.1	6.5	7.6	8.1	10.7

Not available.

Provisional.
Excludes refinery fuel consumption.
Excludes supplies of POL products to Nepal.

Source: Ministry of Finance, Economic Survey, various issues.

Table A6.9
Generation and Consumption of Electricity
(in '000 GWH)

	1980-81	1985-86	1986-87	1987-88	1988-89	1989-90	1990-91	1991-92	1992-93	1993-94 [a]
A. GENERATION OF ELECTRICITY BY SOURCE AND REGION										
1. Thermal [b]										
Northern	13.69	25.73	29.80	37.74	41.24	48.82	52.13	60.44	66.17	71.48
Western	25.37	48.94	54.58	61.80	63.39	73.08	76.95	84.33	88.50	96.27
Southern	9.22	20.45	24.10	28.07	30.53	34.03	35.76	40.39	44.31	51.06
Eastern	12.53	18.37	19.31	20.77	21.40	21.55	20.39	22.40	24.56	28.44
North-Eastern	0.50	0.87	1.06	1.24	1.15	1.22	1.31	1.19	1.23	1.08
All-India	61.30	114.35	128.85	149.61	157.71	178.70	186.55	208.75	224.77	248.33
2. Hydro										
Northern	15.08	19.49	22.02	20.86	23.57	25.01	27.16	27.21	25.45	24.33
Western	7.81	6.18	6.15	5.06	7.54	6.87	8.31	8.16	7.27	8.72
Southern	20.28	21.15	21.08	17.35	21.64	24.54	29.17	29.63	30.70	30.72
Eastern	2.96	3.17	3.67	3.19	3.76	4.11	5.34	5.87	4.52	4.46
North-Eastern	0.41	1.03	0.92	0.97	1.36	1.58	1.66	1.89	1.93	2.20
All-India	46.54	51.02	53.84	47.44	57.87	62.12	71.64	72.76	69.87	70.43
3. Nuclear										
Northern	1.23	1.28	1.32	1.39	1.87	1.73	2.16	1.66	2.77	1.53
Western	1.77	1.96	2.00	1.61	1.90	1.55	1.90	1.71	1.97	2.48
Southern	-	1.74	1.70	2.04	2.05	1.35	2.07	2.16	1.98	1.39
All-India	3.00	4.98	5.02	5.04	5.82	4.63	6.14	5.53	6.72	5.40
4. Utilities- All India (1 + 2 + 3)	110.84	170.35	187.71	202.09	221.40	245.44	264.33	287.03	301.36	324.16
5. Self-Generation in Industry and Railways	8.42	13.04	13.57	16.89	19.91	23.23	25.11	28.60	31.35	32.10
6. Total- All India (4 + 5)	119.26	183.39	201.28	218.98	241.31	268.66	289.44	315.63	332.71	356.26
B. CONSUMPTION OF ELECTRICITY BY SECTORS										
1. Mining & Manufacturing [c]	55.35	78.30	81.98	82.97	92.05	100.40	105.38	110.62	116.17	121.28
2. Transport	2.31	3.08	3.23	3.62	3.77	4.07	4.11	4.52	5.07	5.54
3. Domestic	9.25	17.26	19.32	22.12	24.77	29.58	31.98	35.85	39.72	43.14
4. Agriculture	14.49	23.42	29.44	35.27	38.88	44.06	50.32	58.56	63.33	70.69
5. Others	8.30	12.26	13.66	15.42	17.02	17.01	19.74	21.42	22.38	24.25
6. Total	89.70	134.32	147.64	159.40	176.49	195.12	211.53	230.97	246.67	264.90

a. Data for 1993-94 are provisional.

b. Includes steam, diesel, wind and gas.

c. Includes industrial power from utilities plus net generation in the non-utilities.

Source: Central Electricity Authority, Power Data Bank & Information Directorate.

Table A6.10
New Index Numbers of Wholesale Prices - by Years
(Base 1981-82=100)

	Weights	82-83	86-87	87-88	88-89	89-90	90-91	91-92	92-93	93-94	94-95	95-96	percent change[a]
TOTAL FOOD ARTICLES	17.386	111.1	147.8	161.1	177.1	179.3	200.6	241.1	271.0	284.4	313.8	334.6	6.6
Food Grains	7.917	109.1	129.4	141.3	161.8	165.4	179.2	216.4	242.4	260.8	293.0	313.7	7.1
Other Food	9.469	112.8	163.2	177.7	189.9	190.9	218.5	261.8	294.9	304.2	331.1	352.1	6.3
INDUSTRIAL RAW MAT.	14.909	101.6	124.4	142.8	140.3	145.3	166.6	192.3	192.2	211.8	247.1	267.6	8.3
Non-Food Articles	10.081	100.8	134.1	163.0	160.2	166.0	194.2	229.2	228.7	249.1	297.0	322.8	8.7
Minerals	4.828	103.3	104.2	100.5	98.6	102.2	109.0	113.5	116.1	133.9	142.9	152.4	6.7
FUEL, POWER & LUB.	10.663	106.5	138.6	143.3	151.2	156.6	175.8	199.0	227.1	262.4	280.4	284.4	1.4
MANUF. PRODUCTS	57.042	103.5	129.2	138.5	151.5	168.6	182.8	203.4	225.6	243.2	268.8	292.4	8.8
Food Products	10.143	97.4	129.1	140.5	147.8	165.4	181.7	206.3	223.8	246.7	269.9	279.3	3.5
Beverage & Tobacco	2.149	100.2	133.0	155.0	180.7	207.7	242.1	265.7	293.7	306.6	341.2	372.5	9.2
Textiles	11.545	104.8	116.0	126.6	139.6	158.2	171.2	188.0	201.3	219.9	255.4	293.1	14.8
Chemicals and Chemical Products	7.355	103.5	124.6	131.9	135.8	140.1	147.9	168.4	192.6	207.8	231.5	247.9	7.1
Basic metals and Products	7.632	104.5	141.3	149.7	176.4	205.6	219.9	234.8	256.6	276.6	298.7	326.3	9.3
Machinery and Machine Tools	6.268	102.8	127.3	132.3	150.8	166.2	180.2	208.3	230.6	237.9	260.7	281.9	8.1
Transport Eqpt.	2.705	103.6	129.6	135.5	148.9	166.2	181.3	202.5	218.1	223.9	238.2	253.2	6.3
ALL COMMODITIES	100.0	104.9	132.7	143.6	154.3	165.7	182.7	207.8	228.7	247.8	274.7	294.8	7.3

Note: This WPI series based 1981-82 was introduced as of July 1989. Data for 1995-96 are provisional.

a. Refers to percent change in fiscal year 1995-96 over 1994-95.

Sources: Ministry of Industry, Office of the Economic Adviser; Centre for Monitoring Indian Economy.

Table A6.11
Contribution of Selected Commodities to
Increase in WPI in Calendar Year 1994[a]

	1994	1995	1995 over 1994 Percent Change	percent contribution to change in WPI
Agriculture	296.9	327.2	9.2	34.7
Food	304.5	330.0	7.7	18.5
Cereals	275.6	297.6	7.4	6.3
Pulses	355.9	389.7	8.7	1.5
Others	319.4	346.4	7.8	10.7
Non-Food	283.9	322.4	11.9	16.2
Minerals	141.1	150.3	7.1	1.9
Fuel and Power	278.3	284.1	2.3	2.6
Coal	359.4	367.8	2.5	0.4
Mineral oils	234.0	235.0	0.4	0.3
Electricity	348.0	363.2	5.1	1.7
Manufactured Products	261.7	288.1	11.1	62.9
Food products	263.7	278.4	6.1	6.2
Sugar	244.7	223.0	-11.0	-3.7
Edible oils	269.0	301.9	13.0	3.4
Other food products	281.3	324.3	15.4	6.5
Textiles	246.4	285.4	18.3	18.8
Cement	225.4	263.1	18.1	1.4
Iron and Steel	266.1	285.9	8.0	2.0
Capital goods	--	--	--	--
Others	332.4	364.3	10.4	34.4
ALL COMMODITIES of which	267.4	291.3	9.9	100.0
Agriculture-based	288.0	314.0	10.1	40.9
Non-Agricultural	255.0	277.6	9.8	59.1

-- Not available.

a. Weighted share of each commodity in total absolute change in Wholesale Price.

Source: Ministry of Industry, Office of the Economic Adviser.

Table A 6.12
Consumer Price Index Numbers for Industrial Workers, Urban Non-Manual
Employees and Agricultural Laborers

Year (April-March)	Industrial Workers		Urban Non-Manual Employees (1984-85=100)	Agricultural Laborers [a] General Index (1960-61=100)
	Food Index (1982=100)	General Index (1982=100)		
1985-86	128	126	107	546
1986-87	141	137	115	572
1987-88	154	149	126	629
1988-89	169	163	136	708
1989-90	177	173	145	746
1990-91	199	193	161	803
1991-92	230	219	183	958
1992-93	254	240	202	1076
1993-94	272	258	216	1114
1994-95	297	279	232	1204
Average of weeks				
1992				
March	241	229	192	1046
June	251	236	197	1068
September	258	243	204	1112
December	256	243	205	1067
1993				
March	252	243	205	1053
June	262	250	210	1057
September	275	259	217	1113
December	281	264	221	1166
1994				
March	281	267	222	1175
June	294	277	230	1189
September	309	288	238	1251
December	311	289	240	1297
1995				
March	311	293	244	1300
June	331	306	254	1337
September	345	317	261	1413
December	--	317	--	--
1996				
March	--	319	--	--
Percentage Change in Index over the corresponding month of previous year				
1993				
March	4.6	6.1	6.8	0.7
June	4.4	5.9	6.6	-1.0
September	6.6	6.6	6.4	0.1
December	9.8	8.6	7.8	9.3
1994				
March	11.5	9.9	8.3	11.6
June	12.2	10.8	9.5	12.5
September	12.4	11.2	9.7	12.4
December	10.7	9.5	8.6	11.2
1995				
March	10.7	9.7	9.9	10.6
June	12.6	10.5	10.4	12.4
September	11.7	10.1	9.7	12.9
December	--	9.7	--	--
1996				
March	--	8.9	--	--

-- Not available.

a. Indices relate to Agricultural Years (July-June).

Source: Ministry of Labor, Labor Bureau, Simla; Central Statistical Organization; Ministry of Finance,
Economic Survey, various issues; CMIE, Monthly Review of the Indian Economy.

Table A 6.13
Evolution of the Wholesale Price Index, 1991-96
(index and twelve months point-to-point increase)

	Weight	June 1991		June 1993		June 1994		June 1995		June 1996	
		Index	percent	Index	percent	Index	percent	Index	percent	Index	percent
WPI	100.00	100.0	11.2	120.9	7.0	135.1	11.8	146.3	8.3	154.3	5.4
Primary Articles	32.30	100.0	8.3	116.7	3.7	133.8	14.6	144.2	7.8	155.4	7.8
Food	17.39	100.0	0.6	121.6	2.0	136.7	12.4	145.5	6.4	160.1	10.1
Food grains	7.92	100.0	18.6	124.9	-1.6	146.1	17.0	159.8	9.4	173.9	8.9
Non-Food	10.08	100.0	10.1	107.5	3.8	131.2	22.0	145.3	10.7	151.8	4.4
Minerals	4.83	100.0	6.4	122.2	18.2	126.4	3.5	133.5	5.6	139.9	4.8
Fuel, Power, Lubricants	10.66	100.0	9.2	133.7	18.3	146.7	9.8	150.2	2.4	155.7	3.7
Manufactured Products	57.04	100.0	9.4	120.8	6.9	133.7	10.6	146.8	9.8	153.1	4.3
Food products	10.14	100.0	12.0	121.9	10.2	134.3	10.2	139.0	3.5	141.1	1.6
Textiles	11.55	100.0	5.1	116.3	6.5	137.2	18.0	160.1	16.7	167.9	4.9
Chemicals	7.36	100.0	6.5	129.1	11.3	141.1	9.2	154.9	9.8	163.4	5.5
Metal and Metal Products	7.63	100.0	8.7	116.0	4.7	126.8	9.3	139.6	10.2	145.7	4.3
Machinery	6.27	100.0	9.5	119.2	3.9	128.0	7.4	141.3	10.3	146.7	3.8
Memo Items											
Administered Prices:	15.93	100.0		131.7		143.9		147.1		151.5	
Petroleum crude & natural gas	4.27	100.0		123.4		127.1		130.3		130.3	
Petroleum products	6.67	100.0		129.9		138.5		138.3		139.6	
Coal	1.26	100.0		146.9		154.1		158.1		158.4	
Electricity	2.74	100.0		134.3		160.4		169.3		185.5	
Urea	0.99	100.0		127.9		148.4		155.3		155.2	
Decontrolled Prices:											
Iron and steel	2.44	100.0		116.6		128.3		139.1		142.4	
Phosphatic fertilizers	0.18	100.0		307.7		302.7		306.0		317.5	
Super phosphate	0.06	100.0		295.3		282.2		290.9		320.9	
Ammonium phosphate	0.12	100.0		315.4		315.4		315.4		315.4	
Lubricating oil	0.45	100.0		160.3		171.0		168.7		184.8	

Note: The last column indicates each item contribution to the WPI increase, that is the index item percentage change in June 1996 times the weight of the item in the WPI.

Source: Ministry of Finance, Economic Survey, various issues; CMIE, Monthly Review of the Indian Economy, various issues.

Distributors of World Bank Publications

Prices and credit terms vary from country to country. Consult your local distributor before placing an order.

ALBANIA
Adrion Ltd.
Perlat Rexhepi Str.
Pall. 9, Shk. 1, Ap. 4
Tirana
Tel: (42) 274 19; 221 72
Fax: (42) 274 19

ARGENTINA
Oficina del Libro Internacional
Av. Cordoba 1877
1120 Buenos Aires
Tel: (1) 815-8156
Fax: (1) 815-8354

AUSTRALIA, FIJI, PAPUA NEW GUINEA, SOLOMON ISLANDS, VANUATU, AND WESTERN SAMOA
D.A. Information Services
648 Whitehorse Road
Mitcham 3132
Victoria
Tel: (61) 3 9210 7777
Fax: (61) 3 9210 7788
http://www.dadirect.com.au

AUSTRIA
Gerold and Co.
Graben 31
A-1011 Wien
Tel: (1) 533-50-14-0
Fax: (1) 512-47-31-29
http://www.gerold.co.at/online
E-mail: buch@gerold.telecom.at

BANGLADESH
Micro Industries Development
  Assistance Society (MIDAS)
House 5, Road 16
Dhanmondi R/Area
Dhaka 1209
Tel: (2) 326427
Fax: (2) 811188

BELGIUM
Jean De Lannoy
Av. du Roi 202
1060 Brussels
Tel: (2) 538-5169
Fax: (2) 538-0841

BRAZIL
Publicacões Tecnicas
Internacionais Ltda.
Rua Peixoto Gomide, 209
01409 Sao Paulo, SP.
Tel: (11) 259-6644
Fax: (11) 258-6990

CANADA
Renouf Publishing Co. Ltd.
1294 Algoma Road
Ottawa, Ontario K1B 3W8
Tel: 613-741-4333
Fax: 613-741-5439
http://fox.nstn.ca/~renouf
E-mail: renouf@fox.nstn.ca

CHINA
China Financial & Economic
Publishing House
8, Da Fo Si Dong Jie
Beijing
Tel: (1) 333-8257
Fax: (1) 401-7365

COLOMBIA
Infoenlace Ltda.
Apartado Aereo 34270
Bogotá D.E.
Tel: (1) 285-2798
Fax: (1) 285-2798

COTE D'IVOIRE
Centre d'Edition et de Diffusion
  Africaines (CEDA)
04 B.P. 541
Abidjan 04 Plateau
Tel: 225-24-6510
Fax: 225-25-0567

CYPRUS
Center of Applied Research
Cyprus College
6, Diogenes Street, Engomi
P.O. Box 2006
Nicosia
Tel: 244-1730
Fax: 246-2051

CZECH REPUBLIC
National Information Center
prodejna, Konviktska 5
CS – 113 57 Prague 1
Tel: (2) 2422-9433
Fax: (2) 2422-1484
http://www.nis.cz/

DENMARK
SamfundsLitteratur
Rosenoerns Allé 11
DK-1970 Frederiksberg C
Tel: (31)-351942
Fax: (31)-357822

EGYPT, ARAB REPUBLIC OF
Al Ahram
Al Galaa Street
Cairo
Tel: (2) 578-6083
Fax: (2) 578-6833

The Middle East Observer
41, Sherif Street
Cairo
Tel: (2) 393-9732
Fax: (2) 393-9732

FINLAND
Akateeminen Kirjakauppa
P.O. Box 23
FIN-00371 Helsinki
Tel: (0) 12141
Fax: (0) 121-4441
URL: http://booknet.cultnet.fi/aka/

FRANCE
World Bank Publications
66, avenue d'Iéna
75116 Paris
Tel: (1) 40-69-30-56/57
Fax: (1) 40-69-30-68

GERMANY
UNO-Verlag
Poppelsdorfer Allee 55
53115 Bonn
Tel: (228) 212940
Fax: (228) 217492

GREECE
Papasotiriou S.A.
35, Stournara Str.
106 82 Athens
Tel: (1) 364-1826
Fax: (1) 364-8254

HONG KONG, MACAO
Asia 2000 Ltd.
Sales & Circulation Department
Seabird House, unit 1101-02
22-28 Wyndham Street, Central
Hong Kong
Tel: 852 2530-1409
Fax: 852 2526-1107
http://www.sales@asia2000.com.hk

HUNGARY
Foundation for Market Economy
Dombovari Ut 17-19
H-1117 Budapest
Tel: 36 1 204 2951 or
36 1 204 2948
Fax: 36 1 204 2953

INDIA
Allied Publishers Ltd.
751 Mount Road
Madras - 600 002
Tel: (44) 852-3938
Fax: (44) 852-0649

INDONESIA
Pt. Indira Limited
Jalan Borobudur 20
P.O. Box 181
Jakarta 10320
Tel: (21) 390-4290
Fax: (21) 421-4289

IRAN
Kowkab Publishers
P.O. Box 19575-511
Tehran
Tel: (21) 258-3723
Fax: 98 (21) 258-3723

Ketab Sara Co. Publishers
Khaled Eslamboli Ave.,
6th Street
Kusheh Delafrooz No. 8
Tehran
Tel: 8717819 or 8716104
Fax: 8862479
E-mail: ketab-sara@neda.net.ir

IRELAND
Government Supplies Agency
Oifig an tSoláthair
4-5 Harcourt Road
Dublin 2
Tel: (1) 461-3111
Fax: (1) 475-2670

ISRAEL
Yozmot Literature Ltd.
P.O. Box 56055
Tel Aviv 61560
Tel: (3) 5285-397
Fax: (3) 5285-397

R.O.Y. International
PO Box 13056
Tel Aviv 61130
Tel: (3) 5461423
Fax: (3) 5461442

Palestinian Authority/Middle East
Index Information Services
P.O.B. 19502 Jerusalem
Tel: (2) 271219

ITALY
Licosa Commissionaria Sansoni
SPA
Via Duca Di Calabria, 1/1
Casella Postale 552
50125 Firenze
Tel: (55) 645-415
Fax: (55) 641-257

JAMAICA
Ian Randle Publishers Ltd.
206 Old Hope Road
Kingston 6
Tel: 809-927-2085
Fax: 809-977-0243

JAPAN
Eastern Book Service
Hongo 3-Chome,
  Bunkyo-ku 113
Tokyo
Tel: (03) 3818-0861
Fax: (03) 3818-0864
http://www.bekkoame.or.jp/~svt-ebs

KENYA
Africa Book Service (E.A.) Ltd.
Quaran House, Mfangano Street
P.O. Box 45245
Nairobi
Tel: (2) 23641
Fax: (2) 330272

KOREA, REPUBLIC OF
Daejon Trading Co. Ltd.
P.O. Box 34
Yeoeida, Seoul
Tel: (2) 785-1631/4
Fax: (2) 784-0315

MALAYSIA
University of Malaya Cooperative
Bookshop, Limited
P.O. Box 1127
Jalan Pantai Baru
59700 Kuala Lumpur
Tel: (3) 756-5000
Fax: (3) 755-4424

MEXICO
INFOTEC
Apartado Postal 22-860
14060 Tlalpan,
Mexico D.F.
Tel: (5) 606-0011
Fax: (5) 624-2822

NETHERLANDS
De Lindeboom/InOr-Publikaties
P.O. Box 202
7480 AE Haaksbergen
Tel: (53) 574-0004
Fax: (53) 572-9296

NEW ZEALAND
EBSCO NZ Ltd.
Private Mail Bag 99914
New Market
Auckland
Tel: (9) 524-8119
Fax: (9) 524-8067

NIGERIA
University Press Limited
Three Crowns Building Jericho
Private Mail Bag 5095
Ibadan
Tel: (22) 41-1356
Fax: (22) 41-2056

NORWAY
Narvesen Information Center
Book Department
P.O. Box 6125 Etterstad
N-0602 Oslo 6
Tel: (22) 57-3300
Fax: (22) 68-1901

PAKISTAN
Mirza Book Agency
65, Shahrah-e-Quaid-e-Azam
P.O. Box No. 729
Lahore 54000
Tel: (42) 7353601
Fax: (42) 7585283

Oxford University Press
5 Bangalore Town
Sharae Faisal
PO Box 13033
Karachi-75350
Tel: (21) 446307
Fax: (21) 454-7640
E-mail: oup@oup.hi.erum.com.pk

PERU
Editorial Desarrollo SA
Apartado 3824
Lima 1
Tel: (14) 285380
Fax: (14) 286628

PHILIPPINES
International Booksource Center
Inc.
Suite 720, Cityland 10
Condominium Tower 2
H.V dela Costa, corner
Valero St.
Makati, Metro Manila
Tel: (2) 817-9676
Fax: (2) 817-1741

POLAND
International Publishing Service
Ul. Piekna 31/37
00-577 Warzawa
Tel: (2) 628-6089
Fax: (2) 621-7255

PORTUGAL
Livraria Portugal
Rua Do Carmo 70-74
1200 Lisbon
Tel: (1) 347-4982
Fax: (1) 347-0264

ROMANIA
Compani De Librarii Bucuresti
S.A.
Str. Lipscani no. 26, sector 3
Bucharest
Tel: (1) 613 9645
Fax: (1) 312 4000

RUSSIAN FEDERATION
Isdatelstvo <Ves Mir>
9a, Kolpachniy Pereulok
Moscow 101831
Tel: (95) 917 87 49
Fax: (95) 917 92 59

SAUDI ARABIA, QATAR
Jarir Book Store
P.O. Box 3196
Riyadh 11471
Tel: (1) 477-3140
Fax: (1) 477-2940

**SINGAPORE, TAIWAN,
MYANMAR, BRUNEI**
Asahgate Publishing Asia
Pacific Pte. Ltd.
41 Kallang Pudding Road #04-03
Golden Wheel Building
Singapore 349316
Tel: (65) 741-5166
Fax: (65) 742-9356

SLOVAK REPUBLIC
Slovart G.T.G. Ltd.
Krupinska 4
PO Box 152
852 99 Bratislava 5
Tel: (7) 839472
Fax: (7) 839485

SOUTH AFRICA, BOTSWANA
For single titles:
Oxford University Press
Southern Africa
P.O. Box 1141
Cape Town 8000
Tel: (21) 45-7266
Fax: (21) 45-7265

For subscription orders:
International Subscription Service
P.O. Box 41095
Craighall
Johannesburg 2024
Tel: (11) 880-1448
Fax: (11) 880-6248

SPAIN
Mundi-Prensa Libros, S.A.
Castello 37
28001 Madrid
Tel: (1) 431-3399
Fax: (1) 575-3998
http://www.tsai.es/mprensa

Mundi-Prensa Barcelona
Consell de Cent, 391
08009 Barcelona
Tel: (3) 488-3009
Fax: (3) 487-7659

SRI LANKA, THE MALDIVES
Lake House Bookshop
P.O. Box 244
100, Sir Chittampalam A.
Gardiner Mawatha
Colombo 2
Tel: (1) 32105
Fax: (1) 432104

SWEDEN
Fritzes Customer Service
Regeringsgaton 12
S-106 47 Stockholm
Tel: (8) 690 90 90
Fax: (8) 21 47 77

Wennergren-Williams AB
P. O. Box 1305
S-171 25 Solna
Tel: (8) 705-97-50
Fax: (8) 27-00-71

SWITZERLAND
Librairie Payot
Service Institutionnel
Côtes-de-Montbenon 30
1002 Lausanne
Tel: (021)-341-3229
Fax: (021)-341-3235

Van Diermen Editions Techniques
Ch. de Lacuez 41
CH1807 Blonay
Tel: (021) 943 2673
Fax: (021) 943 3605

TANZANIA
Oxford University Press
Maktaba Street
PO Box 5299
Dar es Salaam
Tel: (51) 29209
Fax: (51) 46822

THAILAND
Central Books Distribution
306 Silom Road
Bangkok
Tel: (2) 235-5400
Fax: (2) 237-8321

TRINIDAD & TOBAGO, JAMAICA
Systematics Studies Unit
#9 Watts Street
Curepe
Trinidad, West Indies
Tel: 809-662-5654
Fax: 809-662-5654

UGANDA
Gustro Ltd.
Madhvani Building
PO Box 9997
Plot 16/4 Jinja Rd.
Kampala
Tel/Fax: (41) 254763

UNITED KINGDOM
Microinfo Ltd.
P.O. Box 3
Alton, Hampshire GU34 2PG
England
Tel: (1420) 86848
Fax: (1420) 89889

ZAMBIA
University Bookshop
Great East Road Campus
P.O. Box 32379
Lusaka
Tel: (1) 213221 Ext. 482

ZIMBABWE
Longman Zimbabwe (Pte.)Ltd.
Tourle Road, Ardbennie
P.O. Box ST125
Southerton
Harare
Tel: (4) 6216617
Fax: (4) 621670